DJing

FOR

DUMMIES®

2ND EDITION

DJing

FOR

DUMMIES®

2ND EDITION

by John Steventon

WILEY

A John Wiley and Sons, Ltd, Publication

DJing For Dummies®, 2nd Edition

Published by
John Wiley & Sons, Ltd
The Atrium, Southern Gate, Chichester, West Sussex
PO19 8SQ
England

Email (for orders and customer service enquires): cs-books@wiley.co.uk

Visit our Home Page on www.wiley.com

Wiley also publishes its books in a variety of electronic formats. Some content that appears in print may not be available in electronic books.

British Library Cataloguing in Publication Data: A catalogue record for this book is available from the British Library.

ISBN: 978-0-470-66372-1

ISBN: 978-0-470-97074-4 (ebk), ISBN 978-0-470-66404-9 (ebk), ISBN 978-0-470-66405-6 (ebk)

Printed and bound in Great Britain by TJ International, Padstow, Cornwall.

10 9 8 7 6 5 4

WILEY

About the Author

John Steventon, also known as Recess, was transformed from clubber to wannabe DJ by BBC Radio 1's 1996 'Ibiza Essential Mix'. Fascinated by what he heard, he bought a second-hand pair of turntables, his best friend's record collection, and started to follow the dream of becoming his newest hero, Sasha.

With no other resource available when he first started DJing, John would take notes, writing articles to refer to if ever he felt like he needed help. Joining the Internet revolution meant 15 megabytes of free Web space, and as he'd already written these notes about learning how to DJ, John thought it would be good to share that information with the rest of the world wide web. He created the 'Recess' persona, and expanded the site as his knowledge grew. Originally a small, basic Web site, www.recess.co.uk has grown over the years both in size and reputation, to become one of the foremost online resources for learning how to DJ – the place where newbie DJs turn to.

Having developed a career as a TV editor at the same time, now heading up post-production at a TV production company, he has scaled down the time spent DJing in clubs, but Recess is always online to help the new DJ over-come those first few hurdles, and offer advice to those who need that extra bit of reassurance.

John is 31, plays way too much squash and poker, is married to Julie, and they both live together with their daughter, cats and a smile on the outskirts of Glasgow, Scotland.

Dedication

This book is dedicated to my Dad, Richard Steventon, who I'm sure would have got a kick out of seeing his son write a book.

To Julie: my best friend, my wife, my smile; without whom I'd be half a person. You are my lobster. And for this second edition, a new addition; to Jaime Steventon, I still can't believe we made a person. I can't wait to know you.

Author's Acknowledgements

My list of acknowledgments is surprisingly long, but these are the people without whom this book would not have been inspired, created, or nearly as long as it ended up!

Thanks to Graham Joyce, who sold me his record collection and started me on this journey, who got me my first break in a roundabout way, and took me to the place that I eventually met my wonderful wife. My sister, Pamela Tucker, who claims if it wasn't for her, I wouldn't have made friends with Graham and is therefore responsible for everything good in my life! My mum, Mary Steventon for being my Mum and for helping with the text accuracy in this book (even if she had NO idea what it all meant). My uncle, David Steventon, for sowing the seed that maybe people would find my writing interesting; my lovely in-laws, Jim (sorry, '*Sir*'), Margaret (the lasagne queen), and Vicki Fleming for entertaining Julie while I spent months writing this book; Carol Wilson for making sure I wasn't signing away the rest of my life; and Lucky, Ziggy, and Ozzy for being my writing companions.

Ian, Jason, Nichol, Al, Gus, Jonny, Dave, Gary, Tony, Iain, and the other poker people for letting me blow off steam until 7 in the morning trying to take their money. All the staff and DJs at what used to be Café Cini in Glasgow where I got my break as a DJ. Paul Crabb for inspiration and distraction (I know, I still can't believe I wrote a book before you!) and Flora Munro for work deflection and a hell of a cup of coffee.

This book wouldn't have had half the info in it if it wasn't for the following people helping me out and kindly granting me permission to reuse images of their gear: David Cross at Ableton, Adam Peck at Gemini, Stephanie Lambley for Vestax images, Sarah Lombard at Stanton, Tara Callahan at Roland, Mike Lohman at Shure, Sarah O'Brien at PPLUK, Carole Love at Pioneer, Grover Knight at Numark, David Haughton at Allen & Heath, Wilfrid at Ortofon, Justin Nelson at NGWave, Ryan Sherr at PCDJ, Laura Johnston at Panasonic, Jeroen Backx at Freefloat, all at Etymotic, NoiseBrakers, Sony, and Denon, Mark Davis from Harmonic-mixing.com, Yakov V at Mixedinkey.com for his help with the Harmonic Mixing info, everybody on all DJing Internet forums for letting me bug them for the past eight months, all the visitors to my Recess Web site, and everyone else who has touched this book in any way – I can't mention every-one, but thank you all.

And finally, from Wiley, Rachael Chilvers, whose support, understanding, and encouragement made it a pleasure to write this book, so that it never felt like *work* and never became something I didn't want to do (and also for laughing at my poor jokes and stories).

Phew . . . let's hope I never win an Oscar!!

Thanks for reading this book. Good luck, keep the beats tight.

Publisher's Acknowledgements

We're proud of this book; please send us your comments through our Dummies online registration form located at www.dummies.com/register/.

Some of the people who helped bring this book to market include the following:

Commissioning, Editorial and Media Development

Publisher: David Palmer

Commissioning Editor: Nicole Hermitage

Assistant Editor: Ben Kemble

Production Manager: Daniel Mersey

Project Editor: Rachael Chilvers

Content Editor: Jo Theedom

Proofreader: Charlie Wilson

Cover Photo: © Sergei Bachlakov

Cartoons: Rich Tennant, www.the5thwave.com

Composition Services

Project Coordinator: Lynsey Stanford

Layout and Graphics: Ashley Chamberlain, Melanee Habig, Joyce Haughey

Proofreader: Laura Albert

Indexer: Ty Koontz

Contents at a Glance

Table of Contents

· ·

Introduction

People come to DJing from different places and for different reasons, but you can split them up into those who love the music, those who want to make money and those who think that DJing is cool and want to be famous. You may fall into one or all three of these categories, but the most important one is loving the music.

If you're a good DJ and get lucky you could become rich and famous, but when starting off if you don't love the music you may become bored and impatient with the time and practise you need to invest in your skills, and quit. Even if you do manage to get good at DJing, if you don't love playing and listening to the music night after night, working in clubs will start to feel too much like work. DJing isn't work; it's getting paid to do something you love.

When I started DJing I already loved the music, but the first time I experienced the true skill of a DJ working a crowd (Sasha, Ibiza 1996) I fell in love with DJing, and knew I wanted to be one. The mechanics of it didn't occur to me until I first stood in front of two turntables and a mixer; all I wanted to do was play other people's music and have control over a crowd.

About This Book

This book is based on my website www.recess.co.uk that, since 1996, has given new DJs all over the world the start they needed to become great DJs.

Because beatmatching is a complicated and important skill for DJs who want to play electronic dance music (house, trance, progressive, drum and bass, breakbeat and so on) it has its own chapter (14), and I mention it frequently. However, the book also contains the mixing skills and musical structure knowledge that enable you to mix rock, indie and pop music, or to DJ at weddings or other parties, so no one's left out. I use a very simple technique for starting off as a DJ, which begins with the basics of starting tunes and matching beats and then covers the skill of creating transitions between tunes, important for any kind of DJ to master, whether you're a rock, wedding, pop or dance DJ. You can find many other ways to develop your skills, but because these other approaches skip the basics, and involve a lot of trial and error and confusion, I've had much more success coaching DJs with this method than with any other.

You can find the equipment sections and how to use the variety of function options available to you in Parts I and II, and these are relevant to all DJs. Part III covers mixing skills like beatmatching, scratching, musical structure and mix transitions. Please don't assume that because different skills are associated with certain genres that party DJs should rip out the beatmatching and scratching information or that club DJs should skip anything that mentions party DJing. Knowledge is skill, and the more skilful you are as a DJ, the better you'll become, and the more work you'll get.

Conventions Used in This Book

DJs often describe musical terms like *beat structure* using phrases that, to the uninitiated, can sound like gibberish. So if a boffin uses ten words to describe something, I try to put it across in a reader-friendly way.

I call the music you DJ with *tunes* or *tracks*. I've steered away from calling each track a song, because songs can imply vocals, and not all music you play as a DJ will have vocals.

A friend of mine read Michael Crichton's *Jurassic Park* and decided that instead of reading the various different dinosaur names, she'd read each one as *dinosaur*. I've done the same thing with CD/turntables/MP3 players and software in this book, describing them as *decks* unless I'm writing in specifics. I figured you'd get bored of lines such as 'Go to your turntable/CD player/PC/iPod and start the tune. Then go to the other turntable/CD player/PC/iPod and put on a different tune'. Repetition isn't a good thing. I repeat, repetition isn't a good thing.

On a practical note:

- ✔ *Italic* emphasises and highlights new words or terms that I define.

- ✔ **Boldfaced** text indicates the action part of numbered steps.

- ✔ Monofont text displays web addresses.

- ✔ I alternate between male and female pronouns to be fair to both genders!

Foolish Assumptions

I assume that you find lines like the last one in the previous section amusing. Don't worry; I know I'm not funny, so I don't try too often. I won't distract you from the subject at hand, but every now and then something takes over and I try to be funny and entertaining. I apologise for that now, but after all, an entertaining, humorous approach is what the *For Dummies* series of books is famous for.

Apart from that, this book assumes that you want to be a DJ, that you want to put in the time it takes to get good at it, you love the music and you won't get fed up when it takes longer than ten minutes to become the next Tiësto, Zane Lowe, DJ Qbert or award-winning wedding DJ. I also assume that you don't have vast experience of music theory.

How This Book Is Organised

All *For Dummies* books are put together in a reader-friendly, modular way. You can look at the table of contents, pick a subject, flick to that page and find the information you need.

The book still has a structure as a whole, like any other book. It starts at the beginning, with choices on what equipment to use, moves onto the process of developing DJ skills and ends playing live to a crowd of a thousand people. This structure means that you can read it from cover to cover like any book, with you as the good-looking hero or heroine!

Part I: Stepping Up to the Decks

Part I describes the core pieces of equipment that you need in order to be a DJ and the best ways to build your collection of tunes. I also dedicate a chapter to the art of shopping, with advice on shopping in the high street and going online to research and buy your tunes and equipment.

Part II: Stocking Up Your DJ Toolbox

From a format choice of CD or vinyl or digital DJing, to how the controls on the mixer work, Part II is all about using, choosing, connecting and setting up your equipment for DJ use. I wouldn't dare to presume to tell you exactly what to buy, but I do offer advice on what may be most suitable for you and your budget.

Part III: The Mix

The nitty-gritty of DJing. From creating transitions between tunes, starting them at the correct points, beatmatching and the complicated moves demanded by the scratch artist, Part III deals with all the information you need to develop your skills as a DJ. This information is important, so spend lots of time with this part, because these chapters describe key techniques that mould and shape you as a DJ.

Part IV: Getting Noticed and Playing Live

After developing your DJ skills, the next step is to get work and show people just how good you are. Part IV gives lots of information on how to sell yourself, how to create a great sounding (and looking) demo and what to do when you get work. DJing isn't simply a case of standing in the DJ booth expecting everyone to love everything you play!

Part V: The Part of Tens

These chapters squeeze in the last tips, tricks and common sense reminders that ease the way toward you becoming a successful, professional DJ.

Icons Used in This Book

Every now and then, a little *For Dummies* symbol pops up in the margin of the book. It's there to let you know when something's extra useful, essential for you to remember, may be dangerous to your equipment or technique, or if what follows is technical gobbledegook.

This one's easy: it highlights something you should burn into your memory to help your progress and keep you on the right path on your journey to becoming a great DJ.

Tips are little bits of info that you may not need, but they can help speed up your development, make you sound better and generally make your life easier as a DJ.

When you're starting out as a DJ, you may need to navigate your way through a number of tricky situations. A few of them end with broken records/needles and CDs, a crashed computer or a damaged reputation as a DJ. Heed the advice when you see this icon, and proceed with caution.

They're unavoidable; words put together by someone else in a small room that mean absolutely nothing. Where possible, I try to translate technical DJing terms into plain English for you.

Where to Go from Here

Go to the kitchen, make yourself a sandwich, pour a nice cold glass of water or hot pot of coffee, put on some music you love and jump into Chapter 1 – or whichever chapter takes your fancy! If you want to know about beatmatching, go to Chapter 14; if you want to know how to connect your equipment, go to Chapter 13.

When you feel inspired, put down the book and try out some of the techniques you've read about. If you want to spend 20 minutes mixing between tunes so you can hear the music, but don't want to concentrate on your skills, do it! Your love of the music and DJing is just as important as the mechanics of how you do it, if not more.

You can also jump online and check out the video and audio clips that support this book at www.recess.co.uk. The site that I've used to develop DJs from all over the world is now a resource for this book, just for you. You can drop me a line there, and ask me anything you want to know.

Part I
Stepping Up to the Decks

The 5th Wave   By Rich Tennant

"No, I don't want my CDs browned or toasted — I want them _burned_."

In this part . . .

Knowing what equipment you need, and where to get the music you want to play when you start your DJing journey can be a bit of a mystifying minefield. These opening chapters take you through the essentials you need to start DJing, and explore the shopping options open to you.

Chapter 1

Catching DJ Fever

. . . .

In This Chapter

▶ Having what it takes to be a DJ

▶ Mixing mechanics and creativity

▶ Reaching the journey's end – the dance floor

. . . .

*T*he journey you take as a DJ – from the very first tune you play when you enter the DJ world to the last tune of your first set in front of a club filled with people – is an exciting, creative and fulfilling one, but you need a lot of patience and practice to get there.

DJ gadgets, iPod apps and console games like *DJ Hero* are introducing and inspiring new waves of people to become DJs daily. Hundreds of DJs over the world are on a quest to entertain and play great music. Everyone needs an advantage when they compete with hundreds of like-minded people. Your advantage is knowledge. I can help you with that.

Discovering DJing Foundations

DJing is first and foremost about music. The clothes, the cars, the money and the fame are all very nice, and nothing to complain about, but playing the right music and how a crowd reacts is what makes and moulds a DJ. As the DJ, you're in control of everybody's night. As such, you need to be professional, skilful and knowledgeable about what the crowd wants to hear, and ready to take charge of how much of a good time they're having.

What kind of DJ you become lies in how you choose, use and respect your DJ tools and skills. Become a student of DJing as well as someone who loves music and performing to a crowd, and your foundations will be rock solid.

Equipping yourself

When you first begin your DJing journey, you can equip yourself with two things: knowledge and hardware.

You can split knowledge into two: what you're about to learn, and what you already know. In time, you can pick up and develop mixing skills like beat-matching, scratching, creating beautiful transitions and choosing music that plays well together.

A sense of rhythm, a musical ear for what tunes play well over each other and the ability to spot what makes a tune great are all things that you'll have developed from the day you were born. Out of those three things, a sense of rhythm can be the best secret weapon you bring when first finding out how to DJ. I've played the drums since I was ten, which gave me a very strong sense of rhythm and a sixth sense for beat and song structure.

Don't worry if you don't know your beats from your bars, or your bass drums from your snare drums; I explain all in Chapters 14 and 15. You need to dedicate some considerable time to developing a feel for the music and training your brain to get into the groove, but with time and concentration, you won't get left behind. The same goes for developing a musical ear, and recognising what tunes have the potential to be great. With experience, dedication, determination and yes, more time, you can develop all the musical knowledge you need to become a great DJ.

The hardware you use as a DJ can define you just as much as the music you play. The basic equipment components you need are:

- **Input devices to play the music:** You can choose from CD players, MP3 players, a computer with DJing software or DJ turntables that play records.

- **A mixer:** This box of tricks lets you change the music from one tune to the other. Different mixers have better control over how you can treat the sound as you mix from tune to tune.

- **A pair of headphones:** Headphones are essential for listening to the next record while one is already playing.

- **Amplification:** You have to be heard, and depending on the music you play, you have to be LOUD!

- **Records/CDs/MP3s:** What's a DJ without something to play?

Providing that your wallet is big enough, making the choice between CD and vinyl is no longer a quandary. The functions on a turntable are equally matched by those on a CD player, and digital DJing (see Chapter 9) means you can use your turntables to play MP3s on computer software, so you're not even limited by the availability of music that's released (or not released)

on vinyl. So the decision comes down to aesthetics, money and what kind of person you are. You may love the retro feel of vinyl and enjoy hunting for records in shops, or you may like the modern look of CD players or the versatility of computer DJing and prefer the availability of MP3s and CDs – it's your choice.

Making friends with your wallet

DJing costs money. Whether you shop online or go to the high street, the first thing to do is look at your finances. If you've been saving up money for long enough, you may have a healthy budget to spend on your equipment. Just remember, the expense doesn't stop there. New tunes are released every day and you'll be bursting to play the newest, greatest tunes. You may start to think of buying other items in terms of how many tunes you could get instead. I remember saying once, 'Fifty pounds for a shirt? That's ten records!'

You don't get the personal touch, but shopping online can be cheaper for equipment and music. And if you can't afford new DJ equipment right now use demo software on a computer to develop your skills, and then spend money on DJ equipment or controllers for the software when you can. Flip through to Chapters 3 and 9 for more information.

Knowing your music

Throughout the years I've been helping people to become DJs, one of the most surprising questions I've been asked is, 'I want to be a DJ. Can you tell me what music I should spin?' This question seems ridiculous to me. Picking the genre (or genres) of your music is really important, because you need to love and feel passionate about playing this music for the rest of your DJ career. (Head to Chapters 4 and 5 for more on genre and music formats.)

After you've found your musical elixir, start to listen to as much of it as you can. Buy records and CDs, listen to the radio, search the Internet for information on this genre and discover as much as you can. This groundwork is of help when choosing tunes you want to play and when looking for artists' remixes, and is an aid to developing your mixing style. Doing a tiny bit of research before you leap into DJing goes a long way towards helping you understand the facets and building blocks of the music you love. Become a student of trance, a scholar of jungle, a raconteur of rock and a professor of pop – just make sure that you start treating your music as a tool, and be sure to use that tool like a real craftsman.

Researching and discovering

You know the music you want to play, you've decided on the format that's right for you, you've been saving up for a while; now you need to wade through the vast range of equipment that's available and be sure that you're buying the best DJ setup for the job at hand.

With technology advancing faster than I can write this book, you can easily get lost in the features that are available to you on CD decks, turntables, mixers and software releases. Take as much time as you can to decide on what you want to buy. Go online and do some research and ask others in DJ forums for their thoughts on the equipment you're thinking about buying. Make sure that you're buying something that does what you want it to do, and that any extra features aren't bumping up the price for something you'll never use.

Here's a brief guide to what to look for when buying equipment:

✔ Turntables designed for DJ use need a strong motor, a pitch control to adjust the speed the record plays at and a good needle. They also need to have sturdy enough construction to handle the vibrations and abuse that DJing dishes out. A home hi-fi turntable won't do, I'm afraid. Check out Chapter 6 for more.

✔ Mixers ideally have 3-band EQs (equalisers) for each input channel, a cross-fader, headphone cue controls and a good display to show you the level (volume) at which the music is sent out of the mixer so you don't blow any speakers accidentally. Chapter 10 goes into more detail on this and other functions on the mixer.

✔ CD decks need to be sturdy enough that they won't skip every time the bass drum booms over the speakers. Jog wheels, easy-to-navigate time and track displays, and a pitch bend along with the pitch control are all important core features of a CD turntable. Chapter 8 is dedicated to everything CD-related.

✔ You can use computers that use DJ software in various ways. From mouse clicks and keyboard strokes and dedicated hardware to simply using your existing turntables/CD decks and a mixer to control music on the computer, I explain all the choices in Chapter 9.

✔ Headphones need to be comfortable, sound clear when played at high volume and cut out a lot of external noise from the dance floor so that you don't have to play them too loud. Your ears are very important, so try not to have your headphones at maximum all the time. Chapter 11 is the place to go for guidance on headphones and protecting your ears.

✔ Volume and sound control are the watchwords for amplification. You don't need a huge amplifier and bass-bins for your bedroom, but similarly, a home hi-fi isn't going to be much use in a town hall. Chapter 12 helps you find the right balance.

Connecting your equipment

After you have all the pieces of your DJ setup, your final task is to put together the jigsaw. Knowing how to connect your equipment isn't just important, it's totally vital. If you don't know what connects to what, and what the ins and outs of your setup are, you can't troubleshoot when things go wrong. And things do go wrong, at the worst of times.

Eventually, you'll be showing off your DJ skills and someone may ask you to play at a party with your equipment; equipment that you connected up a year ago, with the help of your 4-year-old brother. Think of the soldier who has to assemble a gun from parts to functional in minutes; that's how comfortable you need to be when connecting together the parts of your DJ setup – except you only need to kill 'em on the dance floor. (Chapter 13 tells you all you need to know about connections.)

DJing Takes Patience and Practice

No matter what kind of DJ you are – rock, dance, party, indie, drum and bass or any of the hundreds of other genres out there – it's all about picking the right tunes to play for the people in front of you, and the transition as you mix between them.

Picking the right tunes comes with knowledge, experience and the ability to read how the people are reacting on the dance floor (check out Chapters 20 and 21 for more on this), but you can discover, develop and refine the mechanics of how to get from tune to tune through practise and dedication.

Beatmatching (adjusting the speed that two tunes play at so that their bass drum beats constantly play at the same time) is the mechanical aspect that's regarded as the core foundation of the house/trance DJ. Given enough time, patience and practice, anyone can learn the basics I describe in Chapter 14.

Many genres of music aren't so tied into the skill of beatmatching because the speeds of the various tunes mixed together vary so much it's almost impossible to do. But this doesn't mean there's no skill in rock, pop or party DJing – the music you play is a lot more important than the transition, but you still need to avoid a cacophony of noise as you mix between tunes.

After the core skills of creating the right kinds of transitions, what sets a good DJ apart from an okay DJ is his or her creativity. You need another set of building blocks to help develop this creativity. How you stack up these blocks plays a big part in determining how skilled a DJ you become:

✔ Good sound control is the first building block of your skill and creativity. You need a good ear to gauge whether one tune is too loud during a mix, or if you have too much bass playing to the dance floor. This skill is something that develops, and you can hone it through experience, but a DJ with a good ear for sound quality is already halfway there. Chapter 16 covers sound control to create a great-sounding mix, and Chapters 19 and 21 have information about controlling the overall sound of your mix when playing live or when making demo mixes.

✔ A knowledge of the structure of a tune is the second essential building block in your quest to becoming a creative DJ. Knowing how many bars and phrases make up larger sections of tunes is important for creating exciting mixes. In time, DJs develop a sixth sense about how a tune has been made, and what happens in it, so they don't have to rely on pieces of paper and notes to aid them with their mixes. Chapter 15 takes you through this structure step by step.

✔ Although scratching is considered more of a stand-alone skill, you can harness this technique to add a burst of excitement and unpredictability to the mix. This is the third building block to creative DJing. Instead of letting a CD or record play at normal speed, you stop it with your hand and play a short section (called a sample) backwards and forwards to create a unique sound.

This also helps with the mechanics of using your equipment when DJing. People are taught to be scared of touching their records, or don't have the gentle touch needed to work with vinyl or a CD controller properly. Scratching soon sorts all that out, leaving no room for excuses. Your dexterity working with your tunes increases tenfold by the time you've developed even the most basic of scratch moves as described in Chapter 17.

It's all about style

Style is the true creative avenue, because it's all down to the music. The order you play your tunes in, changing keys, mixing harmonically, switching genre, increasing the tempo and creating a roller-coaster ride of power and energy are the reasons why one DJ is better than the other.

Working as a DJ

The hardest bit about performance is actually getting the chance to perform. Hundreds of people fight over every job in the entertainment industry and you need to come out on top if you want to succeed.

You need to set yourself apart from the competition and make sure that you have the skills to sell yourself. Convince club owners and promoters that you're going to be an asset to their club, and then perform on the night. Here's what you need to do:

✔ Demo mixes are your window to the world. They're the first way to let people know what you're like as a DJ. Whether it's your friends, your boss or someone in the industry, a demo is an exhibition of your DJ skills. Only release your best work, and don't make excuses if it's not good enough. Chapter 19 has the information you need about demos.

✔ Market yourself well. Use all the avenues I describe in Chapter 20 to get even the most basic start in a club or pub or party night.

After you've secured any kind of work, your development from beginner to DJ is only halfway through. You've spent time creating a good mix in the bedroom, but now, no matter whether you're playing Cream in Liverpool or the Jones's wedding in a town hall, you need to pull off a successful night.

Your technique may be a little weak, but if you're playing the right tunes, that can be forgiven. (That's not an excuse to skip the basics, though!) The idea is to create a set that tries to elicit emotional and physical reactions from the crowd; in other words, they dance all night and smile all night.

Consider the following (all of which I cover in more detail in Chapters 20 and 21):

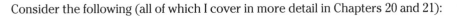

✔ Like anything new, preparation is the key to a successful night. Leave yourself with no surprises, do as much investigation as possible, research the unknown, settle any money matters and make sure that you and the management (or wedding party) are on the same musical playing field, so that all you have to worry about on the night is entertaining the crowd.

✔ Reading the crowd is the most important skill you can develop and you may take weeks, months, even years to master the technique properly. The tells you pick up from the body language on the dance floor rival any poker player's. You look at the dance floor and instantly react to how people dance, and what their expressions are, and then compensate for a down-turn in their enjoyment or build upon it to make it a night to remember.

✔ Because you're the main focal point of the night, you also have to be a people person. You're the representative of the club, and so need to act accordingly. One wrong word to the wrong person, one wrong tune played at the wrong time or even something as simple as appearing as if you're not enjoying yourself can rub off on the dance floor, and your job as an entertainer is on thin ice.

Above all, always remember – from the bedroom to a bar, from a town hall wedding to the main set at a huge night club in Ibiza, or playing a warm-up DJ set before a huge rock band takes the stage – you're here because you want to be a DJ. You love the music, you want to put in the time, you want to entertain people and you want to be recognised for it.

Chapter 2

Starting Up with the Bare Bones

. . . .

. . . .

*Y*ou have lots of options when it comes to choosing and buying your first set of DJ equipment. The amount of money you have to spend is one factor. Any decision about using vinyl, CDs or MP3s to mix with obviously has a huge impact on what you buy, and the music and mixing style you want to adopt also plays a big part in your first DJ setup.

Consider this chapter as a shopping list of equipment you need to be a DJ. Later chapters help guide you towards the best equipment to use, and the most suitable equipment for your budget.

Making a List, Checking It Twice

As with any craft, you need to ensure that you get the right set of tools for the job. Any DJ setup consists of the following basic elements, each of which I describe later in this chapter:

✔ **Input devices:** Turntables, CD decks, MP3 players and computers are the common DJ input devices. In the case of turntables and CDs, you usually need two of them.

✔ **A mixer:** You use this to change the music that plays through the speakers from one input device to the other.

✔ **Headphones:** These plug into the mixer so you can hear the next tune you want to play without anyone else hearing it through the speakers.

✔ **Amplifier:** Without an amplifier (and speakers), the people on the dance floor won't hear any of the great music you've chosen to play.

✔ **Something to put it all on:** You could sit on the floor cross-legged, with everything laid out on the carpet, but it's probably easier to build, buy or borrow some furniture.

Add to that a few metres of cabling, some understanding neighbours and a bunch of CDs, MP3s or records, and your DJ journey can begin.

Considering Input Devices

As a DJ you can choose from a wide range of input devices. Because even the most basic of DJ skills involves mixing from one tune to another without a pause in the music, this often means you need two of them:

✔ **Turntables:** These play records, usually vinyl. If you're only using turntables to DJ with, you'll need two.

✔ **CD decks:** These come either as individual players, or two CD players built into one box. Some only play CDs, others also play MP3 files burnt to CD (see the later section 'Musing on MP3s and PCs', and Chapters 4 and 8 for more).

✔ **DJ software on a computer:** This usually has at least two windows with a player in each for controlling music stored on a hard drive.

✔ **MP3 players and MP3 gadgets:** iPods and the Tonium Pacemaker spring to mind, for example. Sometimes you only need one of these, depending on the mixer you use and what the DJ gadget is.

✔ **Whatever else comes along in the future:** Who knows, you may soon be able to think of music and it'll play out of your fingers . . .

Although what to use is technically your choice, depending on the genre of music you want to play, your decision may already have been made for you. Check out Chapter 5 for more on format decisions.

If you have loads of CDs and loads of records and want to mix between formats, it may seem like a good idea to just have one CD deck and one turntable and mix between them. However, this may lead to a lot of confusion, and force your hand in many mix situations. You'll have to mix from vinyl to CD, to vinyl to CD, and so on. You'll never be able to mix one CD to another, or one record to another. If you think you'll primarily be a vinyl DJ, you could gamble and buy one CD deck to go with your two turntables in the hope that you'll never want to mix from CD to CD, but that's still a risk. If you're planning on just using CDs, you may want to have a turntable that you can incorporate into your DJ setup, or use to transfer your vinyl tunes onto CD.

Thinking about turntables

Turntables are the workhorse of the DJ industry. They've been around in one form or another since the dawn of recorded music, and have played records in clubs and been a vital part of dance music since its conception. A record is a circular piece of hard but flexible vinyl with a single spiral groove cut into each side that starts on the outer edge and eventually ends up near the centre of the record. This groove contains millions of tiny bumps and variations that contain the music information.

To turn these bumps back into music, the needle (also called a *stylus*, with a diamond tip) sits inside this groove. You place the record on a rotating disc (called a *deckplatter*) so that the needle travels from any particular starting point in the groove and gradually works its way towards the centre. The bumps and variations in the groove cause the needle to vibrate and these vibrations are converted to an electrical signal, which (in a DJ setup) is sent to a mixer that converts this signal into music.

You must use the correct kind of turntable. The one that comes with your parents' hi-fi is unlikely to be suitable for DJing (unless of course your dad is Fatboy Slim). Record players on home hi-fis are meant for playing records in one direction, at a normal speed, and aren't built to deal with knocks and vibrations like a DJ turntable must.

The bare minimum requirements for a DJ's turntable are:

- ✔ A variable pitch control to adjust the speed of the record (typically through a range of 8 to 12 per cent faster or slower than normal). Advanced turntables give the option of up to 100 per cent pitch change, but if this is your first turntable, that isn't a vital option right now.

- ✔ A removable headshell to use different kinds of DJ-suitable needles and cartridges (see Chapter 7 for more information).

- ✔ A smooth surface to the deckplatter so it will turn under the *slipmat* (a circular piece of felt that sits between the record and the deckplatter; see Chapter 7 for more).

- ✔ Enough motor power to keep the turntable spinning under the slipmat if you hold the record stopped with your hand.

Because of their build quality and strength, the Technics 1200 and 1210 series of turntables have become the industry standard in the DJ booth, although the top-range Vestax turntables have made a considerable dent in Technics' former monopoly. However, even second-hand Technics and Vestax decks are expensive pieces of kit, so fortunately for the DJ on a budget, DJ turntables by other manufacturers emulate this classic design, such as the Gemini TT02 shown in Figure 2-1.

The advantages of this familiar design are the layout of controls and the position and size of the pitch control. The long pitch control running down the right-hand side of the turntable enables the DJ to be a lot more precise when setting the playing speed for the record. Some of the really cheap turntables on the market have very small pitch sliders or knobs, making it harder to change the pitch by the minute amounts sometimes necessary.

Although the manufacturers have added features, rounded corners and improved upon designs, this basic design in Figure 2-1 is one you come across most often when choosing a DJ turntable – all around the world. (Chapter 6 has a lot more detail about turntables and their various features including different styles of turntable motor, and how the torque (power) of the motor can help or hinder your mixing capabilities.)

Figure 2-1:
The Gemini
TT02
turntable.

Deciding on CD decks

Once upon a time you could only play a CD at normal speed, and you had to place your CD players on cotton wool to prevent vibrations making the CD skip. As for starting a CD at the right time, from the right place? *Hit and hope* was a common mantra when CDs first came out.

Fortunately for everyone, the design and technology of CD decks for DJ use has improved immensely over the years.

As with turntables (see the preceding section), when choosing your CD decks try to avoid standard domestic CD players that you use with a hi-fi or portable, personal CD players. Even if you're a rock, indie or party DJ who isn't planning to beatmatch, where you need to change the speed of the music using a pitch control (see Chapter 14 for more on beatmatching), DJ CD decks are a lot easier to control and can take a lot more abuse and vibration than a typical home CD player.

CD decks designed for DJs should include the following vital functions:

- ✔ Pitch control (the same as with turntables, having a range of at least 8 per cent faster or slower than normal).

- ✔ A set of controls that lets you easily find the song or part of the song you want to play. These controls are either buttons that skip through the CD, or a jog wheel, which turns clockwise and anti-clockwise to skip through the CD with more precision.

- ✔ A time display that you don't have to squint at to read (especially in the dark!).

Optional basic controls that I strongly suggest include:

- ✔ Pitch bend (to temporarily speed up or slow down the CD without using the pitch control).

- ✔ An anti-skip function built into the CD player (which prevents the CD from skipping from all the bass vibrations in a loud environment).

- ✔ Ability to play CD-RW discs (rewritable CDs that you can write to and erase a number of times) and MP3 discs (see the next section).

The pitch bend feature isn't necessarily vital on beginners' CD decks, but without it, you'll face a lot of difficulty if you're beatmatching. And without anti-skip, you have to be careful not to bump your decks or set the bass in the music too high because the CD will most likely skip. There's sometimes a familiar, 'retro cool' sound when a record jumps, but when a CD skips, you want to hit the decks with a hammer!

Even though most home CD players can play CD-R (recordable on once only) and CD-RW discs, basic DJ CD decks may not have that feature. With the Internet giving access to a lot of rare music, you'll want your CD decks to play burnt CDs without skipping.

Chapter 8 has detailed descriptions of CD deck functions, and how to use them.

Musing on MP3s and PCs

MP3s are computer music files that have been *compressed* (reduced in size) but still retain most of the original sound quality. This makes them easy to download and send over the Internet, and they take up very little storage space on computer hard discs and personal MP3 players, like iPods (a popular MP3 player).

To give you an idea of how this compression helps, my iPod is only 60 gigabytes in size, but it contains enough music that I wouldn't hear the same tune play for six weeks! I'd need over 800 CDs to hold the same amount of music.

As MP3s start off as computer files, you have a few different ways to utilise them:

- ✔ **Create traditional CDs.** You can burn MP3s to a CD and play in the same way as a traditional CD that plays on any CD player. You can only fit 74 minutes of music on one CD using this method. Most CD-burning software has a setting that can automatically convert MP3s so that you can burn them as traditional CDs.

- ✔ **Make MP3 CDs.** By keeping the music compressed in MP3 format, you can fit a lot more tunes on one CD. Depending on the length and bit rate of each of the tunes, you should be able to fit over 100 tunes on one CD. MP3 CDs have the added bonus of letting you sort the music into folders, which can help when trying to find 1 tune out of 100.

  These MP3 CDs won't play on every CD player or DJ CD deck, though. Be sure to check when buying your equipment if you're planning on using MP3 CDs. DJ CD decks that play MP3 CDs are normally identical in design and layout to CD decks that won't play MP3s; you just have to pay a little more for them.

- ✔ **Use hard-drives.** Lots of CD decks such as the Denon DNHS5500 or the Pioneer CDJ400 and CDJ2000 let you bypass the need to burn CDs, and enable you to connect external hard-drives via USB (Universal Serial Bus) containing all your music files. Some have internal hard-drives too, but connecting external drives is a more versatile way to manage and work with your tunes. These decks normally have comprehensive menu systems to help you find the right track quickly.

- ✔ **Use software.** Digital DJing has swept through the DJ community, allowing DJs to store thousands of music files on computers and use a variety of methods to control DJing software to play back and mix the music together.

  The advantage of using a computer to mix is that the software normally contains the entire DJ mixing package. In a series of windows, or one well-designed window, the software gives the user at least two input players on screen and a mixer. So all you need is a lot of music files and your PC's soundcard connected to an amplifier, and you're a DJ! Digital DJing can get a lot more complicated though; Chapter 9 covers the various options.

✔ **Try out DJ toys and gadgets.** Many DJ toys and gadgets are available that move DJing away from the DJ booth and into the palm of your hand. Products like the Tonium Pacemaker, the Nextbeat and even an app for your iPhone let you mix music wherever you are. These gadgets tend to use MP3s because of file sizes, but the products with bigger, internal hard-drives let you mix uncompressed, CD-quality tunes if that's your desire. Chapter 9 describes these toys and gadgets in more detail.

Mixing It Up with Mixers

The mixer is the glue that keeps the night running smoothly, and the dancers dancing without falling over. The purpose of the mixer is to change the music that you hear through the speakers from one input to another without any gaps. Chapter 10 contains more information on everything to do with mixers.

The most basic features a mixer must have for DJ use are:

✔ **A cross-fader:** On most DJ mixers the important control that helps to change the sound from one input to another is the cross-fader. As you move the cross-fader from left to right (or reverse), the sound you hear through the speakers gradually changes from one deck to the other. If you leave the cross-fader in the middle, you hear both songs playing at the same time. How you change the music from one song to the other is a massive part of how you're regarded as a DJ.

✔ **At least two input channels:** Each should have a switch to select a *phono input* (for turntables) or a *line input* (for everything else).

✔ **Headphone monitoring with Pre Fade Listen (PFL):** PFL (or cue) lets you hear the music through the headphones without it playing through the speakers. This is important when you want to find the right start point for the next tune, and is vital when you're beatmatching.

✔ **LED indicators:** These display the sound level coming into and going out of the mixer.

✔ **Gain controls:** You use these in conjunction with the input LED indicators. They're extremely important for keeping the overall volume of the mix smooth, creating a professional sound to the mix.

✔ **EQs (equalisers) for the bass, mid and high sound frequencies:** These three simple controls help you add creativity, and improve the sound quality of the mix, transforming lacklustre transitions from one tune to another into great-sounding, seamless ones.

Budget mixers (around £50) aren't likely to have EQ controls. These aren't 100 per cent necessary if you're a party DJ who doesn't create long, over-lapping mixes, but for the sake of around £30 more, you can find a mixer that has everything I recommend at an affordable price range from manufactures like Numark, Stanton and Behringer.

With these functions you have a lot of control over your mixes and can go a long way towards sounding like a pro. A whole range of features and functions can help you adjust and improve your mixes, but they aren't as vital as the six I describe in the preceding list.

Monitoring Your Music with Headphones

Don't underestimate the importance of a really good set of headphones. When you're in the middle of a noisy DJ booth, your headphones are the only way to ensure that the mix is as smooth as your hairstyle.

Though not a major factor when practising DJing in your bedroom, in the live arena using clear headphones that don't distort when you turn them up really loud is extremely important. If you can't easily and clearly hear the records you're playing now and want to play next, your mix has the potential to go really wrong, really quickly!

When choosing a good starter set of DJ headphones, concentrate on comfort and sound. Make sure they're soft and nice to wear, and that when you use them you can hear a good bass thump and the high frequencies are clear. If you get a chance to test them at quite a loud volume, carefully do so (you don't want to damage them, or your ears), just to make sure that they don't distort or that the mid-range frequencies don't drown out the bass beats.

If you choose to buy budget headphones so you can afford better turntables, I strongly recommend that you spend your first DJ pay cheque on a good pair of DJ-specific headphones – you'll only encounter problems with poor head-phones and may not get any more pay cheques! Check out Chapter 11 for loads more about headphones.

Powering Things Up with Amplifiers

The sound signal that comes out of the mixer is barely strong enough to power your headphones, so you need something to increase (amplify) this signal so that it drives some speakers (makes 'em work). You can amplify your music in four different ways (Chapter 12 has more on these options):

- ✔ Buy a separate amplifier and speakers. This choice can be a bit costly, but it's a great way of doing it.

- ✔ Plug the mixer's output cable into the CD or AUX port in the back of your home stereo (if you have one). I prefer this method at home when starting off, because it cuts down on the amount of equipment you need – and money you have to spend – and it means that you may already have a built-in tape or MiniDisc recorder to record your mixes.

- ✔ Use powered speakers – speakers that contain a built-in amplifier. Provided that they're sufficiently powerful to let you hear the music loud enough, they'll suffice.

  For professional use, my preference is a great monitor by JBL (which DJs use in booths a lot).

- ✔ Use the speakers on your Mac or PC, which are often powered speakers, like the previous option. Instead of connecting the speakers directly to the mixer, you can connect your mixer to a computer's soundcard first. This method has the added bonus of being able to record to your computer anytime, for easy uploading of your mixes to the Internet.

Figuring Out the Furniture

Furniture is probably the most overlooked and least thought about aspect of your DJ setup. Some people spend weeks researching the best decks and mixer to buy and completely forget that in the end they need something to put them on.

Two items of furniture for you to consider are:

- ✔ Something to put your decks and mixer on
- ✔ Somewhere to keep your records and discs

Considering ergonomics and stability

When looking for a DJ desk, you need something that's solid enough so the needle doesn't jump or the CD doesn't skip when your cat breathes on it. Even more important is the height level of your decks and mixer.

If you need to bend down to use your equipment, you'll end up like the Hunchback of Notre Dame after all the hours of practice you'll be putting in. So make sure that your equipment is at a height that enables you to practise with your body erect and your shoulders back, in line with your spine. I have a great friendship with Dr Dan, my chiropractor, due to years of not following my own advice!

Correct ergonomics for any desk (and that includes a DJ 'desk') are that you don't need to reach, stretch or bend to use the equipment. Ideally, you want to stand tall, with your shoulders back and your elbows at 90 degrees when DJing. Protect your neck, too, by looking down at the controls rather than craning your neck downwards like a goose!

Although everybody's height is different, these ergonomic principles mean that if you're using something like a computer desk, you probably need to find some bricks or a couple of breezeblocks to raise your decks up to a comfortable height.

Selecting store-bought stands

A few desk units are specifically designed for DJ use, with an adjustable height, a flat top for your decks and mixer, and some big cabinets underneath to keep your records in. My concern with keeping everything in the same unit is that if you're flopping all your records around in the cabinet when trying to find a tune, moving 50 records from left to right creates a hell of a wallop, and is likely to skip the needle.

Check out any online DJ store (and eBay), and you find a great range of DJ desks and stands. Nearly all of them are flat-pack so you need to assemble them yourself – make sure you pack some patience with your screwdriver!

I've found that the king of the flat-pack, IKEA, do a great unit (in the 'Billy' range; see www.ikea.co.uk) that your decks can fit on/in – the only problem is that the shelves would never take the weight of 2,000 tunes. Hard plastic shelving from DIY stores can step in to hold your CDs and records, but make sure the unit is level, and store your records so that the opening is against a wall. I had a terrible accident with Timo Maas's *Ubik* when it dropped out of its sleeve because of a wonky shelving unit – let's just say it's half the record it used to be . . .

I've gone through a few different setups. My first was to have everything on an ironing table, which was very precarious! Then I used a big unit that my dad had built in the 1970s, but I now use a bespoke desk I built myself. My decks and mixer are 'Recessed' inside the top section, and my CD decks and laptop are held up with dedicated stands bought on eBay. (My website, www. recess.co.uk, has photos and guidance on how to build such a desk.)

Killing vibration with bricks and air

Another point to consider with your furniture is how to minimise vibrations. CD decks that don't have good anti-skip can stop playing properly if something bumps into them, or if way too much bass vibration travels from the speakers, through the desk and onto the CD deck. As a vinyl DJ, although there's a good chance your needles will skip if you bump into your desk, the main concern with speaker vibrations is feedback, or *howl round*.

The purpose of the needle is to translate vibrations from the record groove into sound. Feedback happens when the sound from your speakers reaches the turntable (through sound vibrations), and is re-amplified – which reaches the turntable, and is re-amplified. This re-amplification creates a snowball effect (a re-re-re-re-re-re-amplification), creating a ringing noise that rapidly gets louder and louder, which is known as *feedback*. It hurts your ears and your speakers, so try to avoid it.

Whether you're a CD or vinyl DJ, avoid putting speakers on the same unit that your decks are on. If you can't avoid that arrangement, try to minimise the vibrations by sitting decks on something that absorbs the vibration. As in many bedrooms of budding DJs across the world, I used to sit my decks on top of bricks for this purpose.

If you're looking for a classier way of doing the same thing, you can use specially designed 'feet' for your turntables. Made out of metal, they replace the normal rubber feet that are on each corner of the turntable to absorb vibrations more effectively than a brick can. These Isolator feet can be quite expensive (around £90 for four). A fantastic alternative if you can afford £30 is the Freefloat 'cushion' that you sit the decks on top of (Figure 2-2 shows the Freefloat deck stabiliser). This cushion not only stabilises the decks, but has the added advantage of looking a lot better than some bricks 'borrowed' from a building site!

Figure 2-2:
The
Freefloat
deck
stabiliser.

Locating Your DJ Setup

Where you set up your decks in the bedroom has probably already been decided by the current position of your bed and television, but if you have loads of space to tinker with and can consider positioning yourself anywhere in the room then the main factor is to stay near to your speakers. Chapter 12 has a section on positioning your monitors, but as long as you're within a few feet of the speakers, you don't have to worry about audio delay or acoustic problems.

One thing that's always amazed me is that some DJs feel the need to set up their decks so that they're facing a wall. Try turning everything around so that you're looking out across the room. This positioning helps with visualisation, when you start to imagine yourself playing in a big club, but it also looks a lot more impressive when your mates come to see you show off your skills. You need to keep the cables tidy so they're not all hanging off the back of the desk, but this aspect gives you a much better feel of being in the DJ booth.

Chapter 3

Shopping for Equipment

. . . .

In This Chapter

▶ Trying out the right gear for you, and sticking to your budget

▶ Making the choice between high street and the Internet

▶ Choosing to buy new versus second-hand

▶ Checking that your kit works properly

. . . .

*Y*ou've soul searched, and you've read ample magazines (and books, I hope!) and browsed enough websites to last you a lifetime on the subject, so now you're ready to take the plunge into buying equipment.

Buying equipment used to be straightforward. Your choice was limited to one specialist shop, a bit out of town, that would sell DJ gear. The guy running it would be a bit shifty, and you'd leave feeling ripped off and dirty.

The situation has now changed. With so much competition in the DJ equipment market, stores can't afford to put off the buyer, and with attractive package deals, free postage and good support, the days of the prickly, aloof salesman are long gone.

Taking Stock Before You Shop

Speaking from my own personal experience, people who have a dream don't want to listen to advice from others telling them to think carefully before spending their money. And if you feel as excited as I did when I got my first DJ setup, then I may not be able to convince you that doing so is important – but I'll try. Before you take the padlock off your piggy bank, do one last piece of investigation.

Trying before you buy

The first thing to consider is: are you ready to spend money on your dream? You're likely to be investing a lot of money into something that you don't know you'll be any good at (though by the time you've finished this book, you'll be great). So before you consider opening your wallet to buy your dream setup, try to find out whether you can go anywhere to use some DJ equipment first, or download a demo version of DJ software and have a play with that, so you can get used to the basics of DJing.

Ideally, you want to use the setup of a friend who has a couple of turntables and CD decks, a digital DJ setup and loads of records, CDs and MP3s ready for you to rifle through and have fun with. You'll get an idea of the equipment you need and how it works, but more importantly, you'll probably develop an affinity for one medium or another, which is a lot of help when choosing between CD and vinyl or whether to go digital. Your friend may not have this perfect setup though, so ask around and find out whether any other DJs you know will let you try out their kit too.

The friendlier DJ equipment stores let you demo some of their equipment if you look as if you're going to buy it, but not many of them have a room in the back with a full DJ setup for you to try out your skills. By all means ask the store for a prolonged demo, but don't hold your breath.

A big advantage when using other people's equipment, or a 30 day demo of DJing software, is that you'll have more time to save up for your dream setup. When you're happy that you know what you want and are bursting to buy, now's the time to blow the dust off your wallet or purse and go shopping.

Budgeting your money

How much money you have and how you spend it vastly alters the choice of equipment available for you to buy, including whether you opt for new or second-hand.

Have a realistic budget. You're not going to get good DJ equipment for £50 unless you know someone who needs to sell quickly. DJing isn't a bargain basement pursuit; set aside as much as you can and avoid going for the cheapest deal out there. Remember the saying 'Buy cheap – buy twice' when it comes to this kind of thing because if you get really cheap, unsuitable equipment now, you'll need to buy better equipment in a few months' time when you get better at DJing. Save yourself money by only shopping once for your DJ setup.

If you do have a very small budget to work with, the best way to make it work for you is to split it into two chunks: one large chunk for your turntables or CD decks (if they're the format route you're taking) and a smaller chunk for your mixer. It's more sensible to spend as much as you can on your input devices because even the best mixer in the world can't fix CD decks that skip, or turntables that don't hold a constant speed when playing. A basic mixer may be very basic, but is still sufficient when you're developing your initial skills as a DJ, and even if you do have to 'buy twice' for your mixer, it's far cheaper to upgrade the mixer than it is to upgrade two terrible turntables or CD decks.

A wide range of equipment is on the market, and I highlight a few popular manufacturers in this section, but of course they're not the only ones out there. Each budget level covers some broad options available to you when buying brand new turntables or CD decks. Remember, you'll still need to buy a mixer, no matter how basic.

- ✔ **£200+:** You can buy a very basic mixer and a basic set of turntables or CD decks within this budget. If you have only £200, I believe that your best option is to pick up basic Numark, Stanton or Gemini direct drive turntables or CD decks second-hand. You can discover how to mix on these decks, but if they're very basic and have had a lot of use they may not be the most reliable decks in the world, meaning that they may eventually hold back your progress.

- ✔ **£400+:** For around £400 you can get new, intermediate level turntables or CD decks. CD decks in this price bracket come with a better range of functions than the basic models, and you get a more reliable, stronger motor if you buy turntables. You won't have much money left after the decks, though, so you may still have to buy a very basic mixer.

- ✔ **£800+:** By the time you've got £800 to spend on your DJ setup, I hope that you took my advice about trying out DJing on someone else's equipment first! That said, you can get some intermediate level turntables/CD decks and a good mixer for £800 or my preference of top level decks like Technics 1210 turntables or Numark's high-end range of turntables, or good Pioneer, Stanton or Vestax CD decks. Along with these, you should be able to afford a slightly better than basic mixer.

- ✔ **£1,500+:** Budgets that stretch to £1,500+ open up the world to you. I prefer the top of the range turntables or CD decks from Vestax, Pioneer and Denon, which can cost between £700 and £3,000 for two. And my choice of mixers are by Pioneer, Rane and Allen & Heath, which cost between £500 and £1,500.

If you're about to spend six months' worth of hard-saved money on equipment, make sure you've got some left to spend on all the records and CDs you want to play on them. I spent about £40 per month on records when I first started DJing, but that soon ballooned to hundreds, so consider how this new hobby can affect the rest of your lifestyle.

Crossing over with digital DJing

If you're considering choosing a digital setup where you use a hardware controller or turntables, CD decks and a mixer to play and mix music on a computer, the previous budget considerations are just as important.

Not even counting budgeting for a computer/laptop if you don't already have one, you also need to set aside a large chunk of your budget to buy your chosen software title. This can range from £70 to £200 for the software, £200 to £500 if audio interfaces and control CDs and vinyl are on your shopping list, and well into the thousands if you're buying hardware controllers like the Allen & Heath Xone 4D.

Chapter 9 has more information about digital DJing and some of the different solutions to let you mix music with computers.

Buying Brand New

Buying your decks and mixer brand new has many advantages. As well as having the choice of the latest, greatest gear, your equipment comes to you untouched and working perfectly. If any problems crop up, the stores should replace faulty kit, and if your equipment fails after the end of their returns policy, you have the backup of a manufacturer's warranty to sort out anything that goes wrong. Not that anything ever goes wrong, of course . . .

The obvious downside to buying your DJ gear new is the price. But with high-street stores and online stores competing with each other, driving prices ever lower, if you hunt long enough and are patient you can find some great deals.

Resale value is the other downside to buying new. Consider a pair of Technics 1210 MkII turntables. Brand new, they cost around £700, but second-hand, you can find them for £400 or less, which is a considerable loss (but a bargain if you're the buyer!).

Cruising the high street

As DJing has become more popular, DJ shops have smartened up their stores and selling styles. Most cities now have at least one place that sells DJ equipment, and if you're in a large city you can find a few of them, all competing for your money.

Try before you buy and cry

I learnt a hard lesson regarding not trying before buying, and not paying enough attention to a magazine review. I was trying to choose between two very popular mixers and had read that although one of them had better features, the controls weren't laid out very well and were difficult to use (especially in the dark) because they were crammed too close together. I stood in the shop staring at both of the mixers, and didn't have the sense (or this book) to think to ask to try them both (even just to twiddle the knobs). I bought the more expensive, better featured one, of course, and assumed that the guy in the magazine must have fat hands.

The first time I accidentally hit the wrong switch the magazine review came crashing back into my mind! There's nothing like the silence of accidentally switching over to the line input to make you really regret some choices.

A high-street store offers three things you won't get anywhere else:

- ✔ **The chance to use a range of different equipment.** The ability for you to have even a quick demo on the equipment in the shop sets local stores apart from online stores, and gives you the chance to compare many different pieces of kit.

  You may have read in magazines and books that one style of turntable is better than another, or that single CD decks are better than twin units, but until you're able to stand in front of them, touch them and use them, you won't be certain yourself. Second guessing your choice after spending a whole load of cash on your kit based only on a review isn't ideal.

- ✔ **The personal touch of being able to ask a sales rep questions.** There's no doubt about it, getting face-to-face, immediate advice from someone and being able to hold a conversation about what you want is extremely helpful when you're buying equipment. The guys or gals you're talking to at your local DJ store have sold a lot of kit in their time and typically really know their stuff.

- ✔ **Immediate gratification.** I don't know if having immediate gratification is important to you, but it sure is for me. If I buy something as expensive as DJ equipment, I want it now. I want to be able to take it away with me and use it as soon as I get home. If the piece of equipment I want is only a small amount extra in a shop, and if I'm really jazzed about getting it, I'd much rather go into a shop, buy it and take it home there and then, than have to sit at home the next day hoping that every car that drives past the house is the delivery dude.

Opting for online shopping

Whether you use a high street shop that also sells online or an online reseller that doesn't actually hold any stock, you can expect dramatic price drops from online stores. With so many websites trying to get your business, a bit of patience and comparison can save you money.

Most sites have fantastic customer support and are really good at answering customers' questions via email. However, the drawback to online shopping is that you can't have a face-to-face conversation and get answers immediately to your myriad questions. Although some websites offer live web-chat or telephone assistance to try to get around this hurdle, they can't compete with you being able to walk around a store with a salesperson.

Ironically, even though an Internet store can seem faceless and anonymous, their after-sales customer service is usually as good, if not better, than high-street stores. An online shop is only as good as its reputation, and when shoppers start writing bad things, other people listen. The DJ community is a tight-knit one, and online stores need to avoid causing ill feelings, word of which can then spread like wildfire.

In addition to great customer service and attractive prices, Internet stores enable you to build your own package in an attempt to lure you away from high-street stores. A *package* is where the store offers you the turntables (or CD decks) and a mixer together at a reduced price. High-street shops typically can't mix-and-match packages quite so freely due to stock limitations. They can order other equipment in for you, but if you have to wait anyway, you may as well go online and get it cheaper!

Whether they physically hold the stock or not, Internet stores have access to every piece of kit available, which opens up the possibility to get any combination of turntables or CD decks and mixer you can think of. With access to an equally large range of headphones, amplifiers, cables, needles and so on, the choice and price you can get online, if you already know what you want to buy, is really attractive.

A number of manufacturers sell their own combinations of decks and mixer and aim them at beginner DJs. These can be convenient ways to buy basic kit on a small budget, but the downside to these packages is that you may outgrow the very basic equipment when your DJ skills demand more functions to help you work with the music. The safest option is to arm yourself with research and build your own package.

Many people are going into the high-street DJ store and asking all the right questions, finding out the best equipment for their use and then buying it all online through a cheaper store. No rule prevents this, just morals and a little dent in your karma. And if your local high-street store goes out of business, who are you going to talk to then?

Buying Second-hand

The advantage of buying your DJ gear second-hand is that you get a better standard of equipment for your money. Rather than needing to buy a basic set of decks and mixer brand new, you can afford a better set second-hand.

The disadvantage is that you don't know how well the person selling the kit has treated it. You can find some key things to look out for when buying second-hand later in the later section 'Making Sure That Your Kit Works', because you can never be too sure that the turntables haven't spent the last ten years of their use being drowned in beer and cigarette ash!

You can use three different places to source your second-hand equipment:

- ✔ Auction websites
- ✔ Classified adverts in newspapers, shop windows and online
- ✔ Second hand and pawn shops

Bidding on auction websites

Auction sites like eBay are a great way to find a bargain, and the seller/buyer rating system gives you a relatively safe way to buy (or sell) your equipment. You need a little patience, but as long as you know what you want before you start looking, you can find some great deals.

When buying on an Internet auction site, you can be forgiven for worrying about two basic things:

- ✔ The seller won't send the goods to you after you've paid.
- ✔ The seller hasn't been accurate in the item description.

Looking at the feedback rating of a seller gives you an idea of whether you need to worry about not receiving your goods after payment. Take time to check out what previous buyers have written about a seller, and if you're not convinced that the seller has sold enough to warrant you dealing with him or her, be extremely cautious before handing over a whole load of cash!

Don't feel bad about emailing the seller to ask any questions that aren't covered in the item's description. Ask him or her to confirm the working order of the equipment, its general condition and whether they're prepared to accept responsibility for items that don't work correctly upon arrival with you. In the unlikely event of the seller 'bending the truth' with the item description, email evidence proves invaluable if you need to make an official complaint about the seller to the auction site.

The last point you need to consider when ordering anything from online auction sites is the postage and packaging costs. Two decks and a mixer need a lot of protection to survive being loaded into the back of a van in a cardboard box. You may think the postage costs are quite high, but the mountains of bubble wrap and foam required may be inflating the costs of carriage. Some sellers may try to make extra money by boosting the price of postage, though, so if you suspect anyone of attempting this practice on you, send a quick email asking the seller to include a receipt for the cost of postage.

Scanning newspapers

Newspaper classified sections have been hit pretty hard by auction websites over recent years, with people entering less items for sale. Fortunately, because not as many people look at newspaper second-hand sections any more, there's less of a chance that someone else spots and buys your dream DJ setup before you do. Also, because people normally sell items in newspapers at a fixed price or a 'nearest offer', you can secure the item immediately, rather than entering a bidding war!

Items sold in the classified section of a newspaper or shop window are probably quite local to you too. You can save a little money by picking up what you're buying rather than paying for postage, and you can take a look at the equipment first and see it working before handing over your money.

I'm getting all grown-up on you now, to warn you about the dangers of going to strangers' houses – be careful. Always let someone know where you're going, and try to take someone with you just in case the seller starts to raise the price, which can make the situation confrontational and even aggressive.

Internet classified websites like Craigslist and Gumtree offer a combination of the fixed price nature of a newspaper classified and the ability to search the entire country (or world) for someone selling a specific piece of kit. Caution still needs to be your watchword when buying something through these websites. Make sure what you pay for is what gets delivered to you!

Dipping into second-hand and pawn shops

Take advantage of people (sadly, DJs) who've fallen on hard times and go looking in a second-hand shop or a pawn shop. Over the past ten years a new wave of second-hand stores have appeared that have transformed the traditional murky pawn shop into a modern shop that rivals many high-street stores. They often have better displays, a large selection to choose from and a few even have expert salespeople who can help you with any questions you have.

Some second-hand shops aren't set up for you to check out the equipment before you buy, but I strongly suggest that you request to see as much of the equipment in working order as possible. I went to buy a mixer from a pawn shop once, and asked to see it working before I paid for it. They plugged it in, turned it on and a plume of smoke came out the back. So I went somewhere else, quickly.

Making Sure That Your Kit Works

If you're given the opportunity to try out the equipment before buying second-hand, try to be as thorough as possible, testing and checking all moving parts and any controls known to be vulnerable to malfunction.

Listen to the voice inside your head; your first impressions are nearly always correct. If you look at the equipment and can see that it's been well kept in a clean environment, chances are you'll find no problems. If it's dirty, dented and scraped, and been kept in the damp basement of a messy teenager, give the equipment a thorough test, as I describe in the following sections, before you part with your cash! (Rubber gloves are optional . . .)

Checking cables

Wiggle all cables and check all connections. On turntables, mixers, amplifiers and headphones make sure that you move the cables around and listen out for connection problems. You'll know if you have a problem because you'll hear crackling sounds or the music will cut out entirely for a moment.

Testing turntables

Here's how to test a turntable:

1. The first thing to check out on a turntable is the accuracy of the motor. (Chapter 6 covers everything you need to know about the workings of turntables.) The red light that shines onto the dots on the side of the turntable platter is a strobe light and helps you to check whether the motor fluctuates in speed when it's playing (see Figure 3-1). To test this, set the pitch control to 0, and look at how the dots on the side of the turntable move.

Figure 3-1:
The power switch on a turntable, with the strobe light underneath it shining onto the calibration dots on the deckplatter.

At 0 pitch on Technics decks, for example, the row of dots second from the bottom should appear completely stationary; at +6 per cent, the top row of dots should appear stationary. If the dots move a little, you may be able to adjust the motor to fix this. If the dots move erratically, speeding up, then slowing down and then going in the opposite direction, the motor has a major problem.

2. Assuming that you're happy with the motor at the four calibration speeds (shown in Figure 3-1, next to the control: –3.3, 0, +3.3, and +6 per cent), start to move the pitch control smoothly from 0 pitch into the +

(faster) region. As you increase the pitch, the second row of dots on the side of the turntable start to move from right to left, and as you increase the pitch fader even more, the dots start to move faster and faster. This change in the dots should indicate a smooth increase in speed; if the increase is erratic, something's wrong with the pitch control or the motor. Repeat this method for the slower pitch region.

3. As you check how the pitch control affects the speed of the turntable, try to notice how the fader feels as you move it. If it's sticking in places and is hard to move (apart from 0 pitch, where it clicks into place), the pitch fader is probably really dirty. You can buy degreaser spray that cleans out dirty faders, but start to ask questions about how well the owner maintained the turntable and why the kit is in such a state of disrepair.

4. The last thing to check on the motor is that the 45 and 33 buttons do their job. A few people have forgotten to check this, only to get the deck home and find that the turntable only plays at 45 no matter how hard they hit the 33 button with a hammer.

5. If you have the time, lift off the deckplatter (the bit that turns around with the record on it) so you can take a look underneath. If that area is really dirty then you may find that the motor is dirty too. Ask whether you can unscrew the cover and take a look at the motor if this is the case – although you may annoy the person who's selling the turntable with this rather invasive request.

6. Take a look at the deckplatter while you've got it in your hands, and make sure that it's not warped or bent. Place it on a flat surface to check that the platter makes contact with the surface all the way round. If (heaven forbid) you're looking at belt-driven decks, take a look at the belt too, which is located under the deckplatter. Check carefully for signs of stretching or damage. Belts are easily replaceable and don't cost much, but damage and wear indicates that the turntable has had a lot of use over time.

7. Finally, examine the *tonearm* (the arm that holds the needle over the record). The biggest problem you may find is a wobbly tonearm assembly. If the seller is a chatty chappy, you may have already found out how he used the decks. If the seller used them in clubs and took them to the clubs in cases, be extra vigilant when checking the tonearm. Though a turntable case is a nice sturdy item, it doesn't actually offer much protection for the tonearm, which is the most delicate part of the turntable.

You have two basic ways to check the tonearm for damage. In both cases, if the tonearm has a height adjustment control, make sure that it's locked (see Chapter 6 if you want to know more about the height adjustment feature):

- **Wiggle it.** Be very gentle, but try moving the assembly. Does it move while you wiggle it? If it does, it's likely to be damaged.

- **Float the tonearm.** This method is the more precise way to check for damage to the bearings in the tonearm assembly. You may want to remove the needle from the cartridge, just in case you get this bit wrong; even better, ask whoever you're buying from to do this check.

  With the antiskate control (used to cancel out the pull of the tone-arm towards the centre of the record) set to 0, turn the counterweight (the weight on the back of the tonearm) so that the tone-arm floats in mid air. (For more information on how to do this check out Chapter 6.)

  Move the tonearm toward the middle of the record and once there start to increase the antiskate control. As you increase the antiskate, the tone-arm should start to move back toward its resting place. If it doesn't move, or if it jams in one place, the tonearm assembly is likely to have serious and expensive problems.

If the turntable's tonearm fails either test, run for the hills. The repair job for this fault is very expensive and troublesome, and not one you should undertake yourself.

8. While you're looking at the tonearm, have a quick peek at the needle and cartridge. You can replace needles, but you may not want to pay for a new one so soon, so if it's bent or squashed, ask for a little money off the price. On the cartridge, look at the wires that connect into the headshell. Check for signs of corrosion or loose connections.

If you're willing to buy decks that have been quite heavily used, you may want to think about getting them serviced. A good technician can usually get everything back to normal again, but that comes at a price, so be warned that the cost of repair added to the cost of the turntable may just cost the same as a brand new turntable!

Vetting CD decks

Checking how the pitch control affects the playback speed on CD decks is harder than on a turntable, because you don't have a visual reference like the strobe light on a turntable. However, CD decks don't tend to suffer from the same motor problems as turntables, so you really only need to check that the pitch control and pitch bend functions work properly and are free of dirt.

Here are a few tips for checking out CD decks:

- ✔ Make sure that the pitch control increases and decreases the speed of the tune in a constant, smooth way and that the pitch bend buttons temporarily change the pitch when you press them, and the pitch of the tune returns quickly to the set pitch when you release the buttons.

- ✔ Try to use every function on the CD unit. If you researched the CD deck well enough before choosing to buy it, you probably know what functions to expect. To be on the safe side, bring a checklist for that particular model and make sure that the functions all work.

- ✔ Inspect the CD loading system. If the CD deck loads with a tray, make sure that it's not bent, that no bits are missing and that it goes in and out smoothly. If the CD slots directly into the deck, try inserting a CD a few times and make sure that the deck doesn't spit your CD back at you. (Although, maybe it just doesn't like the music you're playing . . .) If the CD deck uses a top-loading method to accept the CD, make sure that the deck closes properly, and as with the other loading methods ensure that the CD plays properly when it's in there!

- ✔ If the CD deck has a good antiskip function (which prevents the CD from skipping when there are a lot of vibrations), get a demonstration of that working properly. Ask the seller to do this demo, rather than thumping the deck with your fist a couple of times or throwing it across the room. Make sure that you're satisfied with the antiskip, and that it does actually prevent the CD from skipping when faced with vibrations.

Monitoring mixers

Make sure that you get a chance to see the mixer turned on and in action – you don't want to get it home and see smoke pouring out of it! (Turn to Chapter 10 for more on mixers.)

Before you play anything through the mixer, connect the turntables/CD decks to the mixer and listen. If you can hear any kind of electrical hum from the equipment or through the speakers, turn off the decks so only the mixer is on, and if you can still hear a loud hum, check the connections (especially the earth connection) for any problems. The noise may be a harmless operational hum given off by the mixer, but if you're not convinced that this sound's good, it probably isn't harmless!

After you've listened to the mixer with nothing playing through it, put on a record/CD and check that all the controls do what they're supposed to. The master level, the gain control, the EQs, the channel faders, the cross fader, the booth controls and effects section; absolutely everything needs to be checked for each channel on the mixer. Listen for any signal (sound) dropout or any crackling sounds as you turn knobs and move faders.

When checking the faders, pay particular attention to the cross-fader. The cross-fader should have a smooth fluid motion from one side to the other, and you need to check for faults in the fader's control of the audio.

The first thing to listen for is any crackling as you move the fader from one side to the other, but more importantly, listen for any music bleeding in from the other channel. If you're playing music into channel 1, and nothing is playing on channel 2, move the cross-fader over to channel 2, where you'd expect it to be silent. If you can still hear channel 1 playing faintly while you should have silence, you've got a problem with the cross-fader.

Depending on the mixer you're looking at, you may still want to buy it if the mixer has a user-replaceable cross-fader. Ask the seller to knock off some money so you can buy a new one. A worn cross-fader may be a sign of extensive wear and tear to the mixer, but then again, it may just be a worn cross-fader after months of use by a scratch DJ. Go with your instincts.

If you have headphones and a microphone available, try them out with the mixer. Wiggle the cables of the headphones and microphone while they're plugged in and listen for any loose connections causing the signal to cut out.

Use all the headphone cue controls, making sure that you get a good, clear sound from each channel, and if the headphone section includes a headphone mix or split cue, test them to make sure that you don't have signal cut out here either. Plug in the microphone and check that the controls and the inputs are clear of any crackles, and if the mixer has a talk-over function, which dips the level (volume) of the music so you can be heard talking over it, be sure that it works properly.

For mixer outputs you'll probably see a Master Out, a Record Out and, if you're looking at a good mixer, a Booth Out or Zone Out. Test all three of the outputs through the amplifier, and make sure that no breaks in signal occur when you wiggle the wires.

Don't overlook the Line/Phono switches when checking out a second-hand mixer. Ensure that the switch from Line to Phono for each channel works without crackling, and check for silence when you switch to either Line or Phono when they don't have an input. For example, if you have turntables plugged into the mixer, when you switch to Line, make sure that you can't still hear the turntable playing.

If the mixer has any of the other features that I mention in Chapter 10, such as BPM counters, cross-fader curve adjusts, punch buttons or hamster switches, check that they all work too.

Assessing headphones

If the gear you're buying includes headphones, listen carefully to them at varying volumes. Move the cable around to make sure you don't hear any breaks in the signal, and check the connection of the cable to the mixer to ensure that it's securely fitted to the ear pieces, and if you move around a lot that you don't lose sound.

Turn the volume up in the headphones for a few seconds. Be careful not to play the music so loud that you may damage your hearing, but still try to play the sound at a volume loud enough to check whether the music distorts. Distortion can naturally occur on headphones when you play music too loud, but they need to take a lot of volume before starting to sound fuzzy.

Sounding out amplifiers and speakers

Look at the amplifier and speakers (if provided) in the same way you did the mixer and headphones in the previous section. Check that you don't get a loud hum coming through the speakers, check that all the controls are working properly on the amplifier and make sure that the speakers don't distort at moderate sound levels. As always, give the cables a little wiggle and check that the connections don't crackle or the signal cuts out.

If the speakers are in an open cabinet that lets you view the drivers (another name for the actual speaker), then inspect them for tears, dents or even stains. If the cone on the speakers is ripped or badly dented, this damage can cause the music to start distorting really quickly and the speakers may fail completely if you play the music too loud, so don't even consider buying them. If you see stains, liquid may have got inside the speaker, which as well as weakening the speaker cone may be on its way to corroding cables and circuit boards inside.

Chapter 4

Retro Chic or PC Geek? Buying Records, CDs and MP3s

. . . .

In This Chapter

▶ Buying your tunes the smart way

▶ Considering the legalities of MP3s

▶ Caring for your CDs and records

. . . .

*I*f your decks, mixer and headphones are the tools you use as a DJ, consider your records, CDs and MP3s as the nails, screws and glue you need in order to perform your best work.

In this chapter, I cover what to look for when buying your tunes, how to make sure that your hard-found records and CDs stay in great condition for as long as possible and how to keep on the right side of the law with MP3s.

Sizing Up Records, CDs and MP3s

Music is expensive, so you need to make sure that you're buying the right tunes, by the right people, from the right place. Therefore, you need to consider all options when you're about to spend your hard-earned money.

Circling around vinyl formats

Records (circular discs made out of vinyl) come in a few different formats:

> ✔ **7-inch singles:** Not as popular as they were a few years ago, but still hanging in there, 7-inch singles tend to have the main release on one side (the A-side) and a different tune on the other, B-side. The A-side

may be a specially edited version of the original tune for radio (known as a *radio-edit*), which cuts it down to a minimum length and content, and this process could remove parts of the tune that you'd really want the crowd to hear. The B-side may contain a tune that you don't like or don't want to play to a crowd.

7-inch singles are small, so they're quite fiddly to work with, and the cut-down version of the main tune on the A-side combined with the lack of remixes of the tune mean that club DJs don't often use this format. However, many northern soul, ska and reggae DJs still find that the 7-inch is king for releases of their music.

✔ **LPs:** An LP (long play) is a larger record (12 inches in diameter) that contains an entire album by an artist. Wedding and party DJs who still like to use vinyl can use LPs because the album version of a tune is more than likely the one most people are familiar with, and there may be a few tracks on the LP that the DJ would like to play.

The downside to using LPs is that they're quite hard to use when beat-matching or scratch DJing due to the amount of space dedicated to each song. With only an inch or two's worth of vinyl available to play the entire track, you may find that the map of the tune (see Chapter 14), which the different shading of the black rings creates, is fairly difficult to see, and the tightly compacted groove is more prone to picking up scratches, pops and crackles.

✔ **12-inch singles:** These singles are designed and produced with the DJ in mind. Typically, you get two or three remixes of the same tune on the one record, offering a lot more choice and versatility with how you play the tune. There may be a different tune on the B-side too – but not often.

Remixes are variations of the same tune, sometimes by the producer who created it or sometimes by other producers who change the sound of the original tune entirely (like Tiesto did to Sarah McLachlan's 'Silence'). The layout changes record to record, but often the main mix that the record company feels may be most popular sits on an entire side of a 12-inch single, with the remixes on the B-side.

Polishing up on CD options

CDs can come in different sizes too, the most common being 12 centimetres in diameter, but a smaller version (originally marketed as a CD single) comes in at only 8 centimetres. CDs this size find their place as CD-ROM business cards and promotional, gimmick CD releases. The full size, 12-centimetre diameter CD comes in a few different flavours:

The party DJ: Sticking with familiarity

The great thing about being a party or wedding DJ is that you only need to play the tunes (and the mixes of the tunes) that everybody knows. Playing a deep house remix of 'Brown Eyed Girl' is probably just going to throw people off the dance floor, so you don't need to spend the time looking for rare mixes of tunes that club DJs do.

Go to a record store, buy a few compilation CDs, bolster your collection with tunes that you can't source on a good compilation CD and you'll have a great set list for a fantastic night.

✔ **CD singles:** CD singles are like the middle ground between a 7-inch and a 12-inch single. CD singles normally contain the main release of a tune (often still the radio-edit), the full mix of a tune (if appropriate) and the B-side that would be on the 7-inch single, but most importantly, CD singles regularly contain one or two of the remixes that you find on the 12-inch versions.

✔ **CD albums:** Albums on CD are similar to LPs in that they give you more songs from the artist, but they only give you one mix (the original) of the tune to play. Unlike albums on vinyl, however, size and reliability problems aren't an issue with CDs, so if you're happy using an album from an artist, nothing's stopping you doing so on CD.

✔ **Compilation CDs:** Compilation albums with 20 or more separate, individual tunes from different artists on them can help the party or wedding DJ build a large music collection for a small amount of money.

One compilation CD can contain the entire track list for an evening. Buy two copies of the same CD so that you can mix from one to the other, and you'll have a record collection for £20, whereas the individual tunes together would probably cost you £100!

One point to be careful about when buying compilation CDs: the tracks on them might be the dreaded radio-edited versions, not the full length tunes that you want to play.

✔ **Mixed CD compilations:** Whether you're looking for pop music, commercial dance music or rock and pop tunes, you may come across a lot of premixed CD albums that contain a whole load of tracks that you'd like to get your hands on.

The problem with mixed CDs is that lifting only one tune out of the original DJ's mix to use in your own set is hard to do because of the overlapping between the intro and outro of tunes. If, for example, a mix CD contains 'Jump' by Van Halen and the DJ mixed Foo Fighter's 'Everlong' into it, the end of 'Jump' and the intro of 'Everlong' will mix together. If you want to play Everlong in one of your mixes, and choose to start it from the very beginning, you'll still hear Van Halen playing. You need to have a clean version of Everlong (just the tune on its own) in order to keep this a nice-sounding mix, which you don't have on a mixed compilation CD.

Byting into MP3s

The Internet plays a huge part in your life, changing the way you receive music, movies and television. MP3 has firmly taken hold as the way to listen to and buy music. Available throughout the Internet on pay sites (and, unfortunately, illegal sites), MP3s are a quick and cost-effective way to get your music, and with iPods and iPhones becoming style icons, MP3 is the fashionable way to listen to music.

Considering compression

On a typical CD you can fit only 74 minutes of CD-quality music. If you burn your MP3s onto a CD at 192 kbps (kilobits per second) stereo, which is the best trade-off for sound quality versus file size (although I prefer 320kbps), you can get over 500 minutes worth of good quality music stored onto a CD. If taking a wallet filled with CDs instead of massive record box to a club is an eye opener (and weight off the shoulder) for vinyl DJs, just think what MP3 CDs mean! You can walk into a club with a pair of headphones and just two CDs filled with hundreds of MP3s, and be a DJ!

MP3s are able to cut the file sizes down by *compression*, throwing away sound frequencies that don't make much of an impact on the sound quality of the music. This method is perfectly acceptable to a lot of people, and with a good pair of headphones on your iPod you soon get used to this drop in audio quality and your brain adjusts to accept this level as the standard sound of the music.

But the compression in MP3s can have a huge effect on how the music sounds in a club. The low, sub-bass frequencies and the very high frequencies are the main casualties of MP3 encoding. The higher frequencies help with the clarity of the music, but more importantly, the sub-bass is what makes your whole body shake as the bass beats thump.

 Sub-woofer amplifiers and careful attention to EQ settings can emulate sub-bass information from the frequencies left in the compressed tune, but the key to keeping MP3s sounding good on the dance floor is in the compression setting. MP3s compressed at 320kbps are preferable, but try not to go lower than 192kbps and you should be okay.

Staying on the right side of the law

Explaining the legalities of downloading and using MP3 tunes is very simple. If you go to somewhere like iTunes or Beatport to buy and download your MP3s, you're doing so legally. If you use peer-to-peer software to share MP3s, downloading a few gigabytes' worth of music without giving any money towards the artist, you're doing so illegally.

From a moral standpoint, as a DJ you're an artist yourself and you need to share responsibility with your fellow artists. Take an example of (imaginary) new producer DJ Steve who's just released his first single. Suddenly, the single's a smash hit and tens of thousands of DJs all over the world are downloading his track to play in nightclubs, but he doesn't have a strong financial foundation to absorb such a loss of revenue. All this time, you're getting paid to play his music that you didn't pay for, while he starves . . . Okay, maybe I'm being a little heavy handed here, but as a DJ who gets paid to play, you'll be treading on very thin ground by playing stolen music, both legally and morally.

Depending on the country you live or perform in, you may need to investigate digital DJ licences. Check out whether you need a licence to stay legal, so investigate what you need to do as a DJ and check that the bar, club or any other venue you play at owns any legal licence required. In the UK, an organisation called PPL (Phonographic Performance Limited) deals with this; see www.ppluk.com for more information. Search for 'digital DJ licence' online to find out whether you need one in your country.

Researching and Buying Your Tunes

In many cases, the place you research what tunes to buy and where you buy them from are exactly the same place. Online download sites and high street stores can all give you lots of information about the music available.

Buying MP3s

MP3s have taken over as a music format, not only for the DJ but also for a huge amount of the population, for the simple reason that because you most commonly buy them online, they're easy, instant and cheap to buy.

Downloading iTunes software from www.apple.com/itunes and accessing the iTunes store is a fantastic way to purchase and download a wide variety of popular and rare genres of music. The great benefit is that you can buy single tracks on an album you like instead of the entire album. Spending 99p on one track you like instead of £15 on an entire album saves a lot of money in the long run.

Avoiding musical holes

If you're relying on a review or recommendation to pick out a tune you haven't heard, or have only heard a preview of online, try to find a way to listen to the whole thing to make sure that it doesn't have a 'musical hole' in the middle. (Radio shows, clubs and online stores may help with this.)

What I mean by a musical hole is that a tune can be beautiful for the first couple of minutes, but then turn to musical mush in the middle. For some ungodly reason, the artist decided to kill everything and play 20 seconds of a car alarm going off.

This point has further implications if you're buying tunes to play that evening in a club or at a party. Unless you really trust the person who's recommending the record, be sure to listen to it from start to finish, just so you know that 'Merry Christmas Everyone' isn't going to suddenly start playing halfway through. I'm not kidding; I played a record that did that. In the middle of summer. I could have curled up into a ball and cried . . .

For a similar approach aimed more towards the electronic dance music DJ, download sites such as Audiojelly (www.audiojelly.com), DJ Download (www.djdownload.com) and Beatport (www.beatport.com) work in a similar way to iTunes and have a large range of dance tunes available.

 Most online music download sites enable you to preview the track before buying it, just to make sure it's the tune or mix that you want to buy – and that you like it! These previews are usually a small snippet of a tune, so if you haven't heard the entire thing, be careful – you may be running the risk of it going somewhere strange! A little research (see 'Choosing what to buy', later in this chapter) can help with this, however.

Purchasing CDs and records

Three avenues are open to you when it comes to buying records and original CD releases:

- ✔ High street music stores
- ✔ Online music stores
- ✔ Auction websites

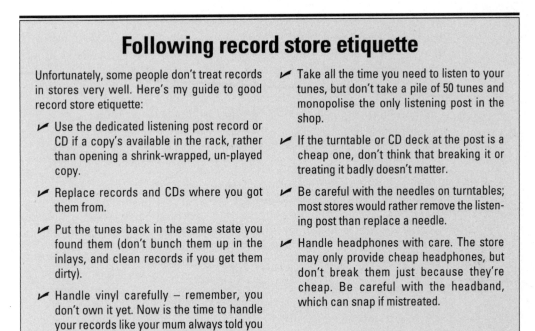

Following record store etiquette

Unfortunately, some people don't treat records in stores very well. Here's my guide to good record store etiquette:

✔ Use the dedicated listening post record or CD if a copy's available in the rack, rather than opening a shrink-wrapped, un-played copy.

✔ Replace records and CDs where you got them from.

✔ Put the tunes back in the same state you found them (don't bunch them up in the inlays, and clean records if you get them dirty).

✔ Handle vinyl carefully – remember, you don't own it yet. Now is the time to handle your records like your mum always told you to, by the edges – no fingerprints please.

✔ Take all the time you need to listen to your tunes, but don't take a pile of 50 tunes and monopolise the only listening post in the shop.

✔ If the turntable or CD deck at the post is a cheap one, don't think that breaking it or treating it badly doesn't matter.

✔ Be careful with the needles on turntables; most stores would rather remove the listening post than replace a needle.

✔ Handle headphones with care. The store may only provide cheap headphones, but don't break them just because they're cheap. Be careful with the headband, which can snap if mistreated.

Visiting high street music stores

High street music stores may have suffered a decline in recent years due to the number of online stores that are able to sell the same music for a lot less, but you'll still find them in busy shopping malls and city centres. The CD DJ can find new releases in these stores more easily than the vinyl DJ. If you're looking for new releases on vinyl, you need to hunt for some specialist stores that cater for DJs like you in or near to where you live.

All good record stores have a *listening post* (a spot in the store with a turntable/CD deck and a pair of headphones for you to listen to records and CDs before buying them), or they have a deck sitting in the back, on which, if you ask nicely and look as if you're going to buy something, you can review your music choices.

Don't feel as if you have to rush listening to the record just because someone's standing over you, waiting to listen to CDs and records. You're about to spend quite a lot of money, so take your time to ensure that you're spending it wisely. Listen to as much of the record as you can, and check for scratches and dirt on the surface of the CD or vinyl – be aware that a lot of people don't know how to treat records properly, especially ones they haven't bought yet.

Surfing into online record stores

The Internet's a wonderful thing. I've found everything from poker chips to a house online. For the DJ hunting down new releases on vinyl and CD, or if you don't have a record store nearby, the Internet is a treasure trove. In the years before the Internet, the poor DJ would trudge from store to store and hunt through the Yellow Pages trying to track down a few elusive CDs and records. Now all you have to do is boot up, sign in and surf for it!

Using the Internet as a store front is an exceptionally convenient way to sort through a store's music stock, and as a result, hundreds of high street stores are on the Net.

Prices are usually cheaper than the high street store because online retailers don't have as high overheads. You may miss out on the personal touch when you compare shopping online with going into your local, specialist record shop, but you can get over this downside by ensuring that you do your research first.

Specialist websites like Hard to Find Records (www.htfr.com) and Juno Records (www.juno.co.uk) carry huge back catalogues of stock as well all the latest tunes. If you're also hunting for commercial and popular tracks don't pass by websites such as Amazon (www.amazon.com), Play (www.play.com) or HMV (www.hmv.co.uk). Most of these sites have options to let you preview the tunes before buying them, and many of them are also MP3 download sites.

With every online store, whether you're browsing for shoes, garden furniture, rucksacks or iPod accessories, getting reliable customer service for buying and receiving items is the most important aspect of the store. If you find you have difficulty buying a tune because you can't navigate the site well enough, you won't return to it or buy anything. If delivery takes a long time, is too expensive or – heaven forbid – the store sends you the wrong item, you'll think twice before returning to that store.

With many online stores, if you order enough then delivery is free. Even when you do have to pay a postage cost, the overall cost of what you're buying online can amount to what you would've paid in the store anyway. And by the time you add on money for petrol and parking or a train fare, and consider the time spent looking for the tune in a store, you're probably happier to wait a day or two for it to arrive. Most online stores post to anywhere in the world, so you have to wait only a day or two for your goodies. But make sure you know your currency conversions!

Using auction sites

Sites such as eBay (www.eBay.co.uk) are a great resource to find tunes that you thought were long gone. As with buying anything online, however, try to make sure that the records (and CDs) are in proper, playable condition. Be sure that:

✔ You don't get ripped off by postage.

✔ The seller has good feedback.

✔ The CD is an original and not a copy burnt to a recordable CD.

✔ You get some kind of assurance that the seller does have the record or CD (I've sadly been stung this way when buying a rare promo record).

See *eBay For Dummies* (Wiley) by Jane Hoskyn, Steve Hill and Marsha Collier for loads more about using eBay.

Choosing what to buy

You can find a lot of music on the market, and you need a way to find the good eggs and avoid the bad. Start reading music and DJ magazines and pay particular attention to the record reviews. You may make a couple of mistakes and go on wild goose chases, but eventually you're likely to find a reviewer with the same taste as you. You can trust what he or she says about a new record so you can pay particular attention to that tune next time you go shopping. You needn't die by a reviewer's advice, but write-ups are a good place to start.

Try listening with an open mind to specialist radio shows, such as Pete Tong, Judge Jules and Zane Lowe on Radio 1 (www.bbc.co.uk/radio1) where you can listen again to the show online and read the tracklist. Going back and listening to the show again is a good idea because you can get distracted the first time around and miss the little hook in a tune that turns it from okay to wahey! And face facts, sometimes the DJ says the title or artist a bit too fast to catch so you need to hear it again, or read an online tracklist.

Online DJ charts (such as those at www.dmcworld.com/charts) can give you a great deal of information about what's popular in a variety of different genres. DJ homepages, online forums and MP3 download sites like Beatport contain charts from popular DJs too, so you can take a look at what your favourite DJ is currently playing and pick out tunes you might like to play.

Eventually, to supplement the advice you get from radio shows, magazines and websites, you may end up standing in front of a huge rack of records or CDs, or navigating an online MP3 store library, reading the blurb the store has written about a tune and trying to decide whether you'll like it or not.

You can supplement what the store writes about a tune by considering the label and artist. When you've bought enough music, listened to enough radio shows and read enough magazines, you'll start to show an affinity toward certain labels and artists. If most of the records you like are released on a similar range of labels, always focus on them first. Even the big labels sign a few turkeys, but going back to a familiar label is a good way to thin out a lot of rubbish that gets released.

If you've liked the last five or six tunes by an artist, there's a good chance you'll like the newest one on the rack in front of you too. But as well as your favourite artists' own work, check out who's done the remixes of their tunes. If you look at other tracks remixed by these producers, you may find that although you've never heard of the main artist, you really like the tune, whether it's the original or the remix.

Eventually, your selection of artists, labels and remix producers all create links to other labels, re-mixers and artists that sprawl out like a web of knowledge, helping you pick out tunes that you wouldn't normally look at.

The guidance of a knowledgeable guy or gal behind the counter can prove invaluable for getting hold of the latest, greatest tunes, and when you spend enough money (and time) in a specialist record store, the staff there can get to know your tastes, recommend tracks and start handing over the tunes that they reserve for their preferred customers.

Weighing up Classic and Current

The genre of music you're DJing with has a great impact on how you build your music library. Wedding and party DJs need to play a mixture of new music along with a lot of older tracks to keep varied guests interested. It helps to go to a few parties and weddings and take notes of the kind of things they're playing, or look at online catalogues for inspiration when building your arsenal of tunes. Rock, indie and pop DJs play a lot of current tracks, but throw in older, classic tracks to get the dance floor rocking.

House and trance DJs can fall between the tracks when it comes to building a library. If you've grown up with certain tunes, quite possibly the ones that made you want to be a DJ, you'll want to own them for yourself to play and mix, which is great. As a beginner, owning records that you're familiar with, that you love to hear and that mean a lot to you is a positive thing. Especially if your progress with beatmatching has hit a plateau, you still love listening to the music you're playing, and that can keep you pushing on to get better.

However, you do need to think about what happens when you try to get work as a DJ – how many places are going to be happy for you to play only old tunes? Depending on the club or pub where you end up playing, they may demand set-lists comprising only current music, and you'll play any classic tunes in your library only at home, for your own amusement.

I was lucky. My first DJing gig was called 'A Decade of Anthems', which meant that I could play whatever I wanted, new or old. But if your sights are set on the big clubs that only play the newest, greatest tunes, you may end up spending a lot of money on old music that you'll never play live.

If you get the chance to drop in a classic tune once in a while during a set, it can be very effective. Check out the crowd to gauge their reaction to what you're playing (see Chapter 21 for more info on reading the crowd), and ask yourself whether they seem like a knowledgeable bunch that would respond to a classic tune. If the answer's yes, try playing a really good, older tune, but be careful because reading the crowd wrongly can clear a dance floor faster than a good night in a bad curry house!

If you don't have a paying DJ job yet, think hard about the tunes you're buying; don't buy anything just because it's brand spanking new and top of the charts, or it's the big tune at the moment. You'll play it once or twice at home, include it in a couple of demo-mixes and then demote it to the bottom of the pile because its initial appeal has completely worn off.

No matter whether you're a rock, party, pop or trance DJ, when you start to get more work, you need to buy and play tracks that are popular or get played frequently in clubs. However, if you don't think that you'll ever play a track when you're yet to perform outside of your bedroom, don't buy it just because it's popular.

Of course, you can't know which tunes are going to stand the test of time. Some tracks may surprise you by lasting a while, but if you feel you're compromising your musical integrity by buying a tune, you can bet that you won't be playing it after a month or two.

Protecting Your Records and CDs

You may have the best DJ setup in the world, the best turntables, needles, amplifier, mixer, effects units and CD players ever made, but if your records and CDs are scratched and dirty, they'll sound just as bad on top-quality equipment as they would on basic equipment.

Storing records

How you store your records when you're not playing them is extremely important for keeping them clean and protecting them from getting scratches. Put your records back in the inner and outer sleeves, and if possible store the record so that the opening doesn't point upwards, because dust and dirt that floats through the air makes a beeline towards the record (due to static electricity and gravity).

If you have the patience, go one step further by rotating the inner sleeve by 90 degrees inside the main sleeve, so even if dirt and dust did get into the main sleeve, the opening of the inner sleeve is on the other side and dust can't get in to dirty the record.

Cleaning CDs, records and needles

Think of your records and CDs as you do your teeth. If you can prevent damage occurring by cleaning them before and after use, they'll last a lot longer and you won't have that feeling of doom when everything starts to go wrong. (I'm a hypocrite by the way; I always put off going to the dentist, waiting for toothache to make a visit necessary . . .)

- ✔ **CDs:** CDs are easy to clean. A soft, lint-free cloth wiped in a straight line from the centre out removes any dust on the disc. If you've spilt something on the CD, you may want to give it a clean by wiping the CD (in the same direction) with weak soapy water. Then wipe it with clean water to rinse and pat it dry with a soft cloth.

  Try to stay clear of CD cleaning machines, which clean the CD in a circular motion. I don't recommend cleaning them in that way; always wipe from the centre of the CD outwards in a straight line.

  Prevention is the best cure, so always return your CDs to the CD case or wallet after use. Don't be lazy and leave your played CDs lying around the DJ booth, where people can spill beer onto your hard-found music.

- ✔ **Records:** Various cleaning solutions are available for keeping your records sparkling, and a few promise that if you clean the record once with the solution you'll never need to clean it again. Some people swear by using lighter fluid to clean the record, others say that alcohol or soapy water (rinsed very well afterwards) works wonders.

  I find that a wipe with a carbon fibre brush (designed for this purpose) in a circular motion round the record before and after playing is more than enough. In truth, though, in the middle of a darkened DJ booth, a quick wipe with your T-shirt is probably the best your record can look forward to!

✔ **Needle:** The reason you need to be so careful about keeping your record clean is because of the friction caused by the needle travelling through the record groove, which creates a lot of heat (up to 150 degrees centigrade). This heat softens the vinyl, and dirt in the groove gets welded onto the side of the needle and gouges its way through the walls of the groove. This chain of events is the major cause of all the pops and crackles that can appear on your beloved records. Well, that and throwing your records onto your bed when you've played them . . .

Repairing vinyl

If one of your tunes has a scratch that makes the needle jump, you're probably better off looking for a new copy. But if you really want to try to salvage the record, you can try a technique with a sewing needle before throwing the record in the bin. I was taught this about 18 years ago by a friend who scratched my Van Halen album, and it's stuck with me ever since (though the friend wasn't so lucky . . .). All you need is a small sewing needle, a magnifying glass and a lot of care and patience to do this without ruining your record even more. Here's what you do as a last resort option:

1. **Play the record to locate the exact position of the scratch and look closely at whether the needle jumps forward or backward.**

   If the needle jumps to a previous part of the record, the scratch runs from right to left. If it skips to a part you've not heard yet, the scratch goes from left to right across the record.

2. **Take the record off the turntable and place it on top of a soft, protective cloth on a flat surface.**

   In a well-lit room, look through the magnifying glass to see where the scratch is on the record. Now pick up the sewing needle. (You may want to wind some tape around the needle so that you can hold it more securely.)

3. **Drag the sewing needle along the groove from one or two centimetres in front of the scratch to one or two centimetres behind it.**

   Drag in the opposite direction to the scratch. If the needle jumps backward when you're playing the record, you need to drag the sewing needle in an anticlockwise direction. (And if it jumps to a point later in the tune, drag the needle in a clockwise direction.)

   While dragging the needle along the groove, apply a little pressure as you start, increasing to a moderate pressure as you reach the scratch and then releasing the pressure for the next couple of centimetres. Any reduction in audio quality is less noticeable by a gradual change in pressure. You may have to go through five or six groove lines to cover the entire scratch.

   Note: If you're at all clumsy, this method isn't for you.

Instead of carefully dragging through a needle, some DJs simply press down pretty hard on the turntable's cartridge while slowly playing the record through the scratch to achieve a similar effect. If the scratch isn't too deep, this technique can repair it. However, if the scratch is too deep, it can just make things worse, so it's a bit of a lottery really!

Fixing warped records and CDs

Your records and CDs can become pliable under heat, which can cause them to warp. Vinyl can also warp just through stress, so your records are likely to warp when left at a strange angle with weight on them. Some compounds in vinyl and CDs aren't affected by heat, making repairs quite difficult, but if you can't play them anyway then you may want to try the following method, which was first adopted for vinyl but works just as well for CDs that become pliable under heat.

1. **Clean the record/CD.**

2. **Place it between two clean sheets of glass.**

    Make sure that everything is clean before doing this, or you may fix the warp only to find that you've scratched the record!

3. **Warm up the record or CD when it's inside the glass sandwich by using a hairdryer or leaving it out in the sun.**

    The hairdryer is better because you can work out how long and how hot you need to get the glass in order for this technique to work. You can't be too sure how much heat the sun gives off (I live in Scotland, and the sun's not that hot here!) so you can't guarantee replicating the same temperature using the sun when treating other warped tunes.

4. **No matter how you heat it up, after it's warm apply an even weight on the glass over the record/CD and leave it for a few days.**

5. **Come back to it and see whether the record or CD is flat again.**

Another similar method involves putting a record in the oven to generate the heat. I tried it once. The results weren't pretty . . . Be careful with how much heat you apply; too much and the record will look like Salvador Dali made it.

If you want to test out fixing warped tunes before having a go on your precious records and CDs, go to a second-hand record store and search (or ask for) a couple of warped records or CDs that you can use as test cases. After you've perfected the technique with them, you can fix your own.

Repairing scratched/cracked CDs

Record stores carry many products that you can use to protect your CDs from scratches in the first place, or repair them if they've been scratched. Just don't try to be smart like me and use Brasso to clean the CD. That idea doesn't work too well . . .

Some people swear by fluids and gizmos that remove part of the protective surface of the CD to smooth out the scratches. I'd be very careful using this approach, though: you don't want to run the risk of removing too much of the surface – your CD player may not be too happy playing thin CDs.

If you've accidentally cracked one of your CDs and you don't want to buy (or can't find) a replacement copy, you may still be able to play the CD. You probably can't play the parts of the CD that are cracked (and remember, a CD plays from the inside-out) but the rest of it may still be okay. Be careful, though: if the cracks are too plentiful then when you play the CD it may disintegrate.

Some audio-ripping software has an advanced error correction built into it, which may let you archive broken discs before throwing them in the bin, but in the end you may find that buying a new copy of the CD is easier, or if you can't find it on CD, you could find it as an MP3 to then burn to a CD.

Backing up digital libraries

No matter whether you're a PC or a Mac user, don't rely on the promises of operating systems to look after all your MP3s and digital music for you. Every week, or after every major import of music, back up your tunes and your library database to an external hard-drive, and keep it somewhere safe. If possible store your backup in a different room (or building) from where you keep your equipment and music library, just in case your DJ room goes up in flames or gets flooded.

I have my music library on an iPod, which I use to listen to all my tunes. The added bonus of this is that it functions as a backup for all my tunes, and I email myself my library database once a week so I have an online backup of it in case anything goes wrong. See Chapter 9 for more about digital DJing.

Part II
Stocking Up Your DJ Toolbox

The 5th Wave   By Rich Tennant

"It's my mixer that sets me apart from other DJs."

In this part . . .

You need to make an informed decision about which equipment is best for you and your DJing style and, more importantly, how it all works when you get it home! Part II takes a foray into format considerations, covers the features and functions of turntables, mixers, CD decks, headphones, and amplifiers, as well as explaining the different designs of needles and cartridges for turntables, the wonders of slipmats and ways to be a digital DJ.

To wrap up this part of the book, Chapter 13 is dedicated to how to set up and connect all of your equipment, and how to troubleshoot the connections if something goes wrong.

Chapter 5

Keeping Up with the Tech-Revolution: Format Choices

. . . .

In This Chapter

▶ Looking at the blurry line between CD and vinyl

▶ Diffusing the argument with hybrids and computers

. . . .

Cain and Abel, the Capulets and the Montagues, Apple and Microsoft, Britney and Christina; throughout time, history and literature have told of the wars between two similar sides; wars that exist because of what the two sides have in common, not because of how different they are. When CD decks first came onto the scene, vinyl purists all over the world cried foul. CDs were seen as a great threat to the vinyl DJ and DJs started to take sides between the standard vinyl method of DJing and the CD upstart.

If you're unsure what format to use as a DJ, this chapter covers the major differences between DJing with CDs or vinyl and then suggests how utilising your computer destroys those differences.

Clashing CDs against Vinyl

The argument for using turntables or CDs boils down to two different things: functionality of equipment and the availability of the music you want to play.

Finding your format

You may dream of being a vinyl DJ using two turntables, a mixer and a box of records to create your sets, but unfortunately, the genre you want to play may not let you. During the 1970s and '80s this wasn't an issue, because music was released across all formats: vinyl, tape and then CD. But as records became less popular, CD and MP3 downloads became the main way to buy music and the availability of records you could buy reduced considerably.

Reflecting on vinyl

As sales for the home consumer market have fallen over the years, vinyl has been aimed almost exclusively at the club music market because of its long associated history. Music genres such as house, trance, drum and bass, hip-hop and techno still release the majority of their tunes on vinyl.

Some rock, classical, folk and country music is still released on vinyl, and a bit of a resurgence is going on in the indie/alternative scene in the UK for 7-inch singles, but when you compare the range of music that's released across all the different genres, only a tiny percentage of it is available on vinyl.

Unreleased music was one of the big areas in which vinyl reigned strong. Record companies would send promotional recordings (known as *promos*) to DJs in hopes that they would get early exposure and gain popularity at gigs. Recently, however, CDs and MP3s have become more popular for promos because they're cheaper and more convenient to send out than pressing a thousand records. Record companies still hand out vinyl to the chosen few, and you know that you're in a position of reckoning when you're a working DJ who receives promos on vinyl.

Keeping up with CDs

Record companies release hardly any music nowadays that isn't available on CD. Every music genre – rock, folk, classical, country, pop – is waiting for you on a shiny, 12-centimetre disc. Even if it's not available to buy in store on CD, you can buy an MP3 online, burn it to CD and play it immediately.

As a CD DJ, if you receive any promos on vinyl, or a small label has only released a test pressing of a tune on vinyl, you can easily transfer them onto CD. All you need is a good quality, direct-drive turntable that plays accurately at zero pitch (refer to Chapter 6), a good set of needles and a computer with a soundcard and CD burner and you can transfer all your records to CD. You may even want to incorporate the turntable into your DJ setup for some variation!

If you have lots of vinyl that you're transferring onto CD and you're a beat-matching DJ, use a BPM (beats per minute) counter to set the BPM for each tune in the same genre to the same BPM as you transfer them (125 for house, 135 for trance and so on). This way, when you play back tunes with a similar genre from CD, beatmatching is really easy because you won't have to change the speed of your tunes by much (if at all) in order to match the beats. (Check out Chapter 15 for more about beatmatching.)

Unfortunately for the vinyl DJ, recording from CD to vinyl doesn't work out quite as cost effectively. If, for instance, you're a rock DJ, you'll find that most of the tunes you want to play aren't available on vinyl; so to be a rock DJ who uses vinyl, you need a way to transfer the music you want to play onto vinyl. Vinylium make the Kingston Dub Cutter to add onto a standard Technics turntable or you may be able to find the Vestax VRX-2000, both of which etch the music into blank 12-inch records. But at around £5,500 for the Dub Cutter and more than that for the Vestax, you'd better be making a lot of records to get your money's worth!

Choosing Analogue or Digital

Analogue audio (which you encounter as a DJ when you play records on turntables) played through the right sound system may sound warmer (more pleasant with a feeling of depth) than an original CD played through the same sound system. But the fragility of vinyl, which suffers through time from cracks, pops, skips and jumps, is a flaw that (in my opinion) gives music released digitally on CD an edge over analogue audio.

The only time a CD release sounds different is when you use a different sound system to play it. A CD never wears out, it never degrades and, as long as you take care to prevent deep scratches on the surface of the disc, you don't need to worry about the CD skipping or jumping.

MP3s burnt to CD are a different proposition. To keep the digital file sizes small, MP3s are heavily compressed, removing some of the higher and lower audio frequencies that aren't too audible in the first place.

How good the music ends up sounding is down to the level of compression. If you heavily compress the music and remove too many audio frequencies to keep the file size small, the music can sound as if it's been recorded under-water. But with the correct compression setting (I recommend 192 kbps (kilobits per second) stereo as a minimum, but 320 kbps stereo is preferable) and a good sound system, it can be hard to tell the difference.

You can burn an MP3 to CD in MP3 format, which fits a lot more music onto the disc (check whether your CD deck can play MP3 CDs first) or you can 'up-convert' MP3s and burn them as a traditional CD. However, this up-conversion doesn't transform an MP3 into CD quality music. All it does is allow you to play MP3s on a normal CD player – if it sounded bad before, it'll still sound bad . . .

Functionality: My Way Is Best!

If you get the chance to compare a record and a CD (an original CD release from a store, not an MP3 burnt to a CD-R) in a club environment, there's very little to choose between them, and it can be hard to tell the difference when listening back to recordings of mixes too. So if you had enough money to buy any equipment on the market, only a few sensible arguments are left when choosing between formats.

Turntables and records are heavy and cumbersome

Turntables are solid and heavy for a good reason; if they weren't, the needle would skip with all the booming bass you play through the club's sound system.

Having lugged around a couple of bags and boxes filled with vinyl to clubs, I'll concede that a wallet with 100 CDs inside is a lot lighter than the same amount of tunes on vinyl, but I could do with losing a few pounds anyway, and look upon 'night club weight training' as a booster to gym visits.

On an affectation level, I'm embarrassed to say that I felt really cool walking into clubs with two big boxes filled with records. Everyone I passed in the crowd knew I was the DJ (and if they didn't, I'd make sure to bash their knees with the record boxes a couple of times). If you walk into a club with a little wallet filled with 100 CDs, the crowd may think that you're just there to read the meter!

I was kidding about the boxes and the knees. I'd never do that . . .

The shifting sands of time and development

Early CD decks were based on the domestic CD player, and although they added a pitch control and a jog wheel to search through the tunes, they weren't anywhere near as versatile or functional as turntables. Since those early models, technology has improved the CD deck so not only does it compete with turntables in all areas, but it leads the way in functionality and creativity. Options like pitch bend, master tempo, scratching, seamless looping, hot cues, effects and mixing between two tunes on the same CD have all shifted the dividing line that once existed between vinyl and CD.

CD DJing is firmly mainstream. Back in 2007 Judge Jules (one of the UK's biggest DJs) said he'd only use CD DJ decks when playing in clubs because the effects and controls give him enormous creativity in the DJ booth. Add to this the ability to remix a tune on a laptop en route to a gig, burn it to CD and play it that evening and he's able to provide an incredible, entertaining and unique performance each night.

Turntables don't have built-in effects

Until CD players included built-in effects, this point was never an issue. If you wanted effects, you'd buy a separate effects processor like the Pioneer EFX-1000 or you'd get a mixer with built-in effects. Personally, I'd much rather have the effects externally, or on the mixer rather than on the turntable or CD player, but my opinions aside, effects, loop controls and multiple cue points (places to start playing from) make CD decks more versatile than a single turntable. See Chapter 8 for more on these functions.

You can't see the music on CD

The great thing about vinyl is that all the different shades of grey and black rings on the record let you see where you are in the tune. If you look closely at the changes between the darkness of the rings, you can work out how long it will be until the breakdown, chorus and so on, and you know when to start your mix accordingly.

As a CD (which is a shiny disc without shading information) just spins around inside the deck, you have to take the time to discover the structure of your tunes, remembering when changes happen, and read the time display in order to make perfect mix placements. Unless, that is, you have a CD deck with a waveform display.

Manufacturers realised that this issue was a big flaw for the beatmatching DJ, and have started to show a representation of the music's waveform on readouts of CD decks (see Figure 5-1). The waveform is larger for loud parts and smaller for quiet parts, so you can tell by the dips and troughs when the tune is about to change to a quieter or louder part. You still need to know the structure of the tune, and the waveform is more of a ball-park reference than a precise guide, but it has transformed mixing on CD from blind memory of a tune structure to a visual trigger of your memory.

Using CDs lacks aesthetic performance

On expensive, professional CD decks like the ones made by Pioneer and Denon, with large platters and vinyl emulation, this isn't really the case any more. For those who like to see a DJ do more than just press a couple of buttons on cheaper CD decks, these professional CD decks give the DJ creative flexibility, all with loads of visual flair when working the controls.

Personally, the sight of a DJ teasing a record out of its sleeve, cleaning it on his or her T-shirt, placing the needle in the groove and then man-handling it to get the beats matched still does it for me. But as the design, control and versatility of CD decks evolve, the argument about the lack of aesthetic performance isn't as strong – provided you spend the money.

Bars don't have turntables for DJs any more

As vinyl has become less popular and more DJs shift towards CD DJing, sadly a lot of bars realise they can claim back space by removing bulky turntables and replacing them with twin CD units. If you're a vinyl DJ, you can't do much about this unless you're allowed to bring along your turntables. One option is to transfer your entire collection onto CD for occasions like this, but that can take a lot of time.

Whether clubs still have turntables depends a lot on the genres that they play. House/trance clubs should still have a set of turntables waiting to be used, but if you're a rock, pop or indie DJ, you might not be so lucky.

Turntables are more expensive than CD decks

This all depends on what you're buying. I've found that one of the most expensive vinyl-only turntables is the Technics SL-1210M5G, which is around £700; but one of the most expensive CD decks on the market is the Pioneer CDJ2000 at £1,500 *each*! Even the industry standard CDJ1000MkIII from Pioneer is around £850. Compare money with features, though, and turntables can still be a lot more costly than CD decks.

A pair of £100 turntables will probably be belt-driven, have motors that won't hold their pitch very well, will most likely cause feedback when you play them too loud due to the thin plastic bodies and you'll probably get fed up with them in a year or so and want to buy a different pair. On the other hand, if you have £100 to spend on a CD deck you should find one that gives you a reliable pitch control and pitch bend with possibly a loop function too. The antiskip on them might not be the best, but these basic functions on a cheap CD deck can give you more control and confidence mixing the music than a cheap, belt-driven turntable ever could.

If you have £200 to spend, you find that the features on the CD decks you look at outclass what's on a turntable of the same price. Although the turntable you can afford now has a high torque (power), direct-drive motor like the one on the Numark TT500 and may offer a pitch bend and large ranges of pitch variance (sometimes over 50 per cent faster or slower), I still don't think that a turntable competes with a CD deck in the same price range.

For starters, at £200 you can afford twin CD decks, so you'd only have to pay £200 to get both of the input devices instead of paying £400 for two turntables! Or I recommend that you get something similar to the Numark AXIS 9, with loads of built-in effects, multiple cue points, a beat counter, seamless looping and the chance to do some scratching on CD too!

If you compare the £700 Technics SL-1210-Mk5G mentioned previously to a CD deck in a similar price range, you find that the CD deck still beats the turntable hands down on features. For £700 you can get the Denon DNHS5500CD, and this thing rocks. It's got a motorised deckplatter, so it can feel like using a turntable, built-in effects, ability to connect external hard-drives and iPods to play MP3s and it can even mix into itself with the two-decks-in-one feature.

So if you want to compare top prices, CD decks are more expensive but you get a lot more bang for your buck. Refer to Chapter 3 for more on buying and budgeting for equipment.

Can't We All Just Get Along?

Two factors blow the whole CD versus vinyl argument completely out of the water.

Hybrid turntables let you have it all

Hybrid turntables, which play both CDs and records on the same unit, have blown the wind out of the sails of the CD versus vinyl argument.

These turntables come at a hefty price (between £500 and £700), but Numark and Gemini have both brought out hybrid turntables that let you use the deckplatter like a giant jog wheel to control CDs as if they were vinyl, and when you want to play a record you do so on the same piece of equipment.

If you're thinking of going down this route, bear in mind that you'll rarely find hybrid decks in a pub or club. Not too much of a problem for vinyl DJs, because it's a skill that's easily transferable between turntable models; all that changes is the feel and response of the platter and the pitch control. But the CD controls on these hybrid decks may be nothing like those you use on CD decks in a pub or club, so be sure to do some research first, before standing in the DJ booth with a look of horror on your face!

You can say the same no matter what CD decks you use, but a bigger difference in controls may exist if you're used to using hybrid decks. Chapters 20 and 21 have some guidance into what to look for in the DJ booth.

The new kid: Digital DJing

Digital DJing's most explosive feature is that it can let you use your turntables or CDs to control music stored on a hard-drive using special DJ software. With digital DJing, the two dividing factors between CD and vinyl that I mention at the beginning of this chapter (the availability of music and deck functionality) become irrelevant.

By storing music on your computer's hard-drive and controlling it with your choice of turntables or CDs (or both!), you have almost no limitation to what music you can play with your chosen format. If you want to use turntables to DJ with but the music you want to play isn't available on vinyl, find the music online at an MP3 download site, load it into the DJ software and use your turntables to play the music as though it were on a record in front of you. Genius!

From a functionality point of view, most of the special features that CD decks have that turntables don't, like effects, BPM counters and loop controls, are contained within some of the DJ software programs. This gives you access to exactly the same creativity tools using your turntables and DJ software that CD DJs have, and means that in the right hands, with the right software, turntables are on an equal playing field with CD decks.

On my journey through formats I started as a vinyl DJ, but I moved to CD when the music I wanted to play was too hard to find on vinyl. But now I use a digital DJ setup, using my turntables and mixer to control Native Instruments 'Traktor' playing music stored on a laptop. As a result, I haven't even switched on my CD decks at home for over a year . . .

I cover digital DJing in detail in Chapter 9.

Chapter 6

Getting Decked Out with Turntables

All turntables are equal in that they play records but, like most things in life, some are better than others. Whether you're using turntables to play loads of different records, or want to use them to control MP3s in software, playing the same two records over and over again (see Chapter 9), you need a turntable that can cope with the physical demands of DJing. In this chapter, I go through the functions you need to look for when purchasing, setting up and servicing turntables.

Avoiding Cheap Turntables

Deciding what turntable to buy and use is largely based on your budget. When you go shopping don't go for the cheapest option so that you can save a little money. Investing in a better quality turntable puts you straight on the road to becoming a quality DJ. Actually, maybe reversing the point makes this clearer: the worse your turntable, the harder it is to become a good DJ. And this advice isn't aimed at just the beatmatching DJ. If you're a rock, indie or party DJ, and you're planning to use turntables, it's just as important to buy quality turntables that won't skip or feedback in loud environments.

The main things to watch out for on cheap turntables are that they tend to have belt-driven motors rather than direct drive motors (see the following section), and they often skimp on essential DJ features such as removable headshells, tonearms with adjustable counterweights and long pitch sliders.

Spend as much money as you can on the turntable – only then think about purchasing the rest of your equipment. Great decks remain great decks no matter what mixer and headphones you use, but not even the best mixer or the clearest headphones can make cheap, belt-driven decks better.

Motoring in the right direction

Belt-driven decks do seem like an attractive option when you're looking to become a DJ because they're so much cheaper than their direct-drive big brothers. Of course, some people claim that their belt-drive decks are fine to mix with, scratch with and so on, and I'm sure that they think they are. But the first time these folks use a good direct-drive deck, they change their minds and (reluctantly) accept that they've been thinking only with their wallets or purses and have been fooling themselves. (A few people still stand by their belt-driven decks, but they're either stubborn as a mule or have super-human powers of adaptability.)

Belt-driven turntables

Inside a belt-driven turntable is a small motor with a rubber band linking it to the underside of the *deckplatter* (the part you put the record on). It's similar to how turning the front cog with your bike pedals makes the back wheel turn. This method of powering the turntable results in low *torque* (power to the turntable), meaning that the deckplatter often grinds to a halt when you hold the record stopped.

The other downside is that the speed the turntable plays at can fluctuate, speeding up and slowing down. If you're a DJ who'll be trying to beatmatch the bass beats of two different records (see Chapter 14), the fluctuation of speed makes keeping the bass beats playing at the same time, for anything over ten seconds, extremely difficult. You may blame your own beatmatching skills rather than realising it's the turntable's fault.

Direct-drive turntables

Where belt-driven turntables have a rubber band transferring power from the motor to the deckplatter, which then spins around a centre spindle, in direct-drive turntables the centre spindle is attached directly to the motor.

The improved torque that this results in means start-up times of well under half a second, and the power from the motor is more than enough to keep the turntable spinning under the slipmat as you hold it still, preparing to start a tune or when performing complicated scratches.

The turntable speed is solid and reliable on a direct-drive turntable. Though you can get pitch wobbles around the zero pitch mark (see the sidebar 'The Bermuda Pitch Zone exists'), you can be confident that any beatmatching errors are your errors, not the fault of a weak transfer of power through a rubber band. You may regard this fact as a double-edged sword – but the moment you realise you can't make excuses and blame your performance on bad turntables, your DJing skills start to improve!

Watching out for pitch control design

Watch out for cheap turntables that use a small (2-inch/5-centimetre) pitch fader or rotary knob to adjust the pitch of the record. You won't often find either on direct-drive decks, but super-cheap belt-driven decks sometimes have them. These pitch faders are too small to make the fine adjustments you need to keep the beats of your records playing in time, and this can make beatmatching insanely difficult.

Look at the standard design of a turntable (the Technics 1210 in Figure 6-1) and notice the large pitch control down the side of the deck that lets you make minute adjustments to the pitch. Make sure that the turntable you buy is based on a similar design.

Figure 6-1:
The
Technics
1210 DJ
turntable.

Short-term gains, long-term pains

If you're happy doing things the hard way, you may find that at least one good thing comes out of learning to DJ on belt-driven turntables. In the short term, you'll become an extremely accurate, attentive DJ when beatmatching.

I've found that beginner DJs who start by using top of the range turntables from Technics, Vestax and Numark can have a really easy time. The motor is so powerful and reliable that they don't need to worry about speed fluctuations throwing off their beatmatching skills. When these DJs have to use a poorer set of turntables at a party, for example, they may find that their concentration and levels of attention aren't as good as those DJs who were forced to develop on bad decks, and may have difficulty keeping their beats matched because they're not used to the problems of bad decks.

I must stress, however, that eventually, the good DJs develop attention and accuracy just through time spent practising and developing their own skills – no matter what turntable they use – so this isn't an excuse to buy cheap, belt-driven decks.

One club that I worked at developed a problem with their turntables due to a customer of the club spilling beer over them. While they were getting repaired, the club owner decided to hire a pair of belt-driven turntables. Due to the heat of the club, the belts started to stretch, causing the decks to be even worse at holding their pitch, which made beatmatching extremely difficult.

Fortunately, I was used to decks that played in this way, because one of the pubs that I'd worked at had decks with motor problems, which felt just like shoddy belt-driven decks and really used to annoy me. From using those decks frequently I developed the intuition and concentration to hear beats slipping out of time before they were noticeable to the dance floor, and wasn't too fazed by such a problem when it happened in the club that night.

The other DJ wasn't quite so lucky . . .

Identifying Key Turntable Features

A DJ turntable has many key features. Some of them are similar in function to a home hi-fi's record player, but added functionality to these controls and designs is what truly separates a DJ turntable from a hi-fi's record player. This section covers what these features do so that you not only buy the correct turntables but also know how to make use of them.

Start/Stop

Automatic hi-fi record players start playing when you place the needle on the record and only stop turning when you take the needle off and replace the arm on the rest, or when the needle gets to the end of the record and automatically returns to the rest.

This isn't helpful for the DJ – you need manual control of how the motor starts and stops. You sometimes need to stop the turntable but still leave the needle at a specific place on the record. This is usually when you've taken time to find the place to start the record from (the *cue* point) but don't want to start the tune for a couple of minutes. The Start/Stop button gives full control over how and when the turntable starts and stops. Pressing Stop when the record is playing can be a great DJ technique too (see Chapter 16).

On/Off

The On/Off switch on a DJ turntable is normally on the bottom-left corner of the deck, next to the Start/Stop button. The switch is raised above the deckplatter, and a strobe light is positioned underneath (see later sections in the chapter for information about the deckplatter and strobe light). Though used mostly for the mundane task of turning the turntable on and off, you can also use the switch creatively in the mix (see Chapter 16).

33/45/78 RPM

Nothing's particularly special about the RPM (revolutions per minute) button on your DJ deck; when you press 33 and the pitch control is set to zero, the record makes 33 revolutions in one minute, and when at 45, the record revolves 45 times in one minute. If you don't know what speed you should set your turntable to, look at the record label or cover, which tells you whether to play it at 33 or 45 RPM. Or simply try listening to the record. If you're playing Barry White and it sounds like the Chipmunks, you're playing the record too fast; try pressing the 33 button!

If you have older records set to play at 78 RPM, some turntables have a sneaky hidden setting: when you press the 33 and 45 buttons together, the turntable plays at 78 RPM. If you need this feature, check that the turntables you're looking to buy has it before parting with your money.

Strobe light

The strobe light is the soft red light at the side of the turntable (normally bottom left corner, integrated as part of the On/Off switch). It's not just a pretty red light – it's a strobe light that you use to calibrate and check the accuracy of the turntable's motor, as I describe in detail in Chapter 3.

Deckplatters

The *deckplatter* is the part of the turntable that spins round and is what the slipmat and the record sit on. Home hi-fis have a rubber mat firmly glued onto the platter, which is useless for DJing with, because the deckplatter needs to be made of smooth metal to let the slipmat slip (see Chapter 7 for what a slipmat is and how to make it slip better).

When you buy Technics decks they come with a thick rubber mat sitting on top of the deckplatter, which fortunately isn't glued down. If your decks came with a similar thick rubber mat on top of the metal deckplatter, simply lift it off, exposing the deckplatter, and keep the rubber mat somewhere safe. I find down the back of the wardrobe is a safe enough place.

Target light

The target light (shown in Figure 6-2) sits on the edge of the deckplatter and shines a light along the grooves of the record where the needle traces, enabling you to see the grooves more clearly. Why do you want one? Apart from letting you see where the needle is (or where you'd like to put it), the target light helps you locate different parts of a tune. If you take a look at a record under good light, you can see groups of different shaded rings on the record. These rings are the map of the tune: the darker rings are the quieter parts and the lighter rings are the louder parts. Being able to see where the needle is in the record can help you work out when new parts are about to kick in, helping with perfect mix placement (see Chapter 16).

Like your health, you don't really think about this little pop-up target light until you don't have it. If it's broken, or the decks you have don't come with one, it can be hard to see these rings in a well-lit room, let alone in a dark DJ booth.

Pitch control

The pitch control adjusts the rate at which the turntable turns. If you move the pitch control into the + area (towards you on a standard DJ turntable), the record plays faster; and if you move the pitch control towards the – area (away from you), the record plays slower. Different turntables have different ranges, but you typically find that pitch adjustment ranges are between 8 or 12 per cent in either direction.

Figure 6-2:
The target
light on a
Technics
1210. A
helpful little
fella.

Although the record plays faster the more you increase the pitch control, it's called a pitch control, not a speed control, so the more you increase the speed, the higher the pitch of the music gets. So you may start to beatmatch two tunes you think will sound great together, but when you increase the pitch on one of the tunes, the two tunes may sound out of tune, like your dad singing in the shower along with the radio. See the section 'Master Tempo/Key Lock', later in the chapter, for one way around this issue (and take the batteries out of the radio to stop your dad singing in the shower).

The numbers

The numbers on the pitch control can be confusing. These numbers don't refer to BPMs (beats per minute, the usual measurement of tempo) of the music you're playing, but rather a percentage difference of the speed of the turntable. The only time the numbers correlate exactly with the BPM is if the tune you're playing has a BPM of 100. If you move the control to +1, you increase the pitch by 1 per cent of 100, which is 1 BPM; and the same for the other numbers (5 per cent would be 5 BPM and so on).

If you're playing a 150-BPM tune and decrease the pitch to –1 per cent, then the tune now plays at 148.5 BPM (1 per cent of 150 is 1.5). A 130-BPM tune with the pitch set to +5.5 per cent increases by 7.15 BPM – so you can assume that tune now plays 'around' 137 BPM, and adjust the pitch on other tunes so they play at the same speed too.

The Bermuda Pitch Zone exists

The decks that I learnt on used to change the pitch the wrong way for a 1 per cent region; if I moved the pitch fader to +1 per cent, the music slowed down, and the music sped up if I moved the pitch fader into the – region. Fortunately, after the +/–1 per cent area, the pitch control went back to normal – otherwise, I'd have gone mad!

Even my Technics 1210s suffer from this problem, but not as pronounced as with the decks I learnt on. The 1210s just hover around zero pitch between +/–0.5 per cent, and then go back to normal again.

Fortunately, turntable manufacturers have noticed and rectified the problem – first Vestax and then Technics on their 1210 MkIII have made the pitch fader completely smooth, with no click point as you pass through zero pitch to cause this problem.

You can 'hack' your turntables to disable the quartz lock feature that's the cause of the problem, but you'll have to search on the Internet for these hacks because I don't want this book to create an epidemic of broken turntables!

Unfortunately, the pitch control isn't an exact science. The difference that even 1 millimetre of change can make to the speed of your record is enough to throw off your beatmatching. Even though the fader sits somewhere near the 2 per cent area, you may actually be playing at 2.2 per cent, and that 0.2 per cent can make a huge dent in your beatmatching skills. So use your ears and listen to what the beat is doing, rather than only relying on the numbers on the pitch control.

For more about how calculating BPMs can help with beatmatching, check out Chapter 14. The Cheat Sheet at www.dummies.com/cheatsheet/djinguk has the mathematical calculation for working out BPM percentage changes.

Accuracy

The other problem with the pitch control is that through time its accuracy starts to shift, so when you set the pitch to 4.5 per cent the turntable is actually only running at 4 per cent. But even worse is the area around the zero pitch mark on the turntable (what I like to call the 'Bermuda Pitch Zone', because it's easy to get lost in there for days!). On problem decks, when you set the pitch control to zero the control clicks into place. When you move the pitch control away from this zero pitch click point the motor sometimes has trouble knowing which way you're moving the pitch control, and can do the opposite of where you're setting it, or sometimes belligerently remains at zero pitch for a short distance either side of the click point.

Counterweight/height adjust

The counterweight is a metal weight that rotates on the back of the tonearm, which, when turned anticlockwise to add weight, increases the down pressure of the needle on the record, making it less likely to skip when you're moving the record back and forth, either to find the start point of a record (the *cue*), or when scratching. You can find detailed information on calibrating and using the counterweight properly in the later 'Counterweight' section.

The higher you set the tonearm, the steeper the angle at which the needle points down into the groove, exerting even more down-force and making it even less likely to skip. A lot of scratch DJs adopt this setting to give increased needle stability. Be careful, though – if you've set your tonearm height to the top and the counterweight on at full, you'll wear out your records and your needles really fast.

You may have read about or heard of DJs who like to put the counterweight on back to front, to get a little more down pressure onto the needle; this action is very bad for your needle and your records, damaging and wearing them out really quickly. For the scratch DJ who accepts accelerated wear as part of the consequence of scratching, this is fine. But as a beatmatching, mixing DJ, never put on more weight than the needle manufacturer suggests. If you need to add that much weight, chances are your technique is wrong, your needles are already damaged or dirty, or you're using the wrong needle altogether (Chapter 7 covers these issues).

Antiskate

When a record plays forwards, a *centripetal* force pulls the needle in the groove in toward the centre of the record. *Antiskate* cancels out this pull by adding an equal force that pulls the needle out toward the outer edge of the record, keeping the needle in the middle of the groove with no sideways force to wear out the walls of the groove.

Although antiskate helps to keep the home listener's vinyl copies of Mozart in pristine condition, when DJing the function can be redundant because you don't only play the record forwards; between scratching and back cueing, you also do your fair share of playing the tune backwards. When you play a record backwards, the force that normally pulls the needle into the centre of the record when playing forwards is now pulling out toward the edge of the record (it's become a *centrifugal* force). If an antiskate setting is already pulling the record out to the edge, more force than normal is acting on the needle, making it even more likely to jump out of the groove. All this really means is that most DJs tend to leave antiskate set to zero.

Removable headshell/cartridge

The needle you use is very important depending on the style of DJing you do. DJs who want to scratch need to set up their needles for maximum stability, and beatmatching DJs need to ensure that they get the best sound and versatility from their needles and cartridges. The ability to adjust the angle at which the needle points into the groove or change the entire headshell from (for example) a standard Technics design to an all-in-one Concorde design are important factors for achieving individual DJs requirements that separate the DJ turntable from the home hi-fi record player, which typically doesn't allow this kind of customisation.

From a practical point of view, removable headshells can be a life-saver if you damage a needle during a set in a club. If something happens to the needle on the turntable, and you have a spare headshell to hand, instead of fiddling around trying to remove the needle from the cartridge to replace it in a dark, loud DJ booth, while under pressure to get the next tune ready to mix in, you can whip off the headshell containing the damaged needle and screw on a new one, all within five seconds. For more information about needles and cartridges, head to Chapter 7.

45 RPM adaptor

In the days before CD and hard-disc jukeboxes, 45 RPM, 7-inch singles were crammed into a jukebox. Manufacturers produced these records with an extra large hole in the middle (25 millimetres in diameter, compared to 5 millimetres on 33 RPM LPs) so that you could mechanically move them from the rack and sit them securely on the unit that played the record in the jukebox. Because the singles used in jukeboxes were the same as those on sale to the public, a 25-millimetre adaptor placed onto the centre spindle increased its diameter so you could play the record properly on home turntables that had a 5-millimetre centre spindle.

Now relegated to a recess in the top-left corner of the turntable, this shiny piece of metal has become (virtually) obsolete due to the demise of traditional jukebox records. However, if you play older records (ska or northern soul stuff especially), or newer reggae/ragga 7-inch singles, you'll find that you may still need to use this adaptor on some of those records.

Customising Your Sound with Advanced Turntable Features

The basic features on a turntable enable you to play a record and change the playing speed. For most DJs, that's more than enough. But for some, gadgets, buttons and switches all go hand-in-hand with creativity and individuality and personal styles, so they look to turntables with enhanced features.

When you look at the gadgets and controls on your turntables, just bear one thing in mind – where are you going to be DJing? If you only ever intend to make mix CDs and run your own parties using your own equipment, then feel free to go nuts, but if you're planning on playing in clubs, have a quick think about how much you use these add-ons and the likelihood of them being available on the clubs' setup.

This argument is similar to the one about relying on beat counters to develop your beatmatching skills (see Chapter 10). The advanced functions such as reverse play, quartz lock, digital displays and pitch bend/controls with 50 per cent variance are all useful, adding a nice dimension to your mixes when at home, but because 97 per cent of clubs still use Technics 1210s (with nothing more than a pitch control that's a bit wonky around zero pitch and an otherwise rock-steady motor), ask yourself whether your advanced turntable DJ skills will travel well to these clubs. If you can only mix well on advanced turntables, you're in for a tough time when you can't use any.

I'm not saying don't get turntables with advanced features on them. I'm not even going to lie and say that you'll never work in a club that has decks with these features, but in the same vein as beat counters, don't rely on these advanced features to make you a good DJ.

Pitch range options

Once upon a time, your choice of pitch range was limited to 8 per cent faster or slower (unless you opened up and started screwing around with the innards of the turntable); that was when Technics 1200/1210s ruled the roost. But things have moved on. Now 12 per cent pitch variance has become a standard on many turntables, but advances in pitch control mean that the DJ can have 50 per cent pitch variance on offer, or more!

Simplicity is reliability

I believe that the Technics 1200 and 1210 MkII turntables have gained popularity over the years in no small part because they're extremely reliable. They're reliable because there's very little in them to go wrong – just a motor, a few electronics to control the power and speed of the motor, and the audio output.

Adding extra features to turntables can increase the chance of breakdown and malfunction. However, in my opinion, manufacturers such as Gemini, Vestax and Numark have elevated turntables to another level of functionality by offering the DJ extra creativity (for a price), while ensuring a long life-span for the equipment by increasing reliability and build quality.

You aren't likely to play a tune at 50 per cent that often, but you're certain to want to play a tune faster than 8 per cent. Some scratch, funk and drum-and-bass DJs like to over-pitch their tunes, making them sound completely different. (Try to steer away from using tunes with vocals when you do this, though, because the vocalist will sound as if she's been inhaling helium!)

 Sliding the pitch control up or down to 50 per cent at the end of a tune is a good technique to use (sparingly) to get from one tune to another, but increased pitch options are more about offering the DJ another level of creativity than about everyday use.

Pitch bend and joystick control

Pitch bend was first introduced on CD decks. When beatmatching, if the beats start to slip out of time, instead of temporarily speeding up or slowing down the turntable by pushing the record, spinning the spindle, touching the side of the deck or briefly boosting/cutting the pitch fader setting by 4 or 5 per cent, you get two buttons on the turntable, or a joystick, which control small bursts of speed. When you use the + or – pitch bend buttons or controls, the turntable speeds up or slows down by a small amount. When you release the buttons, the deck returns to the original speed setting.

CD DJs, who are used to using buttons instead of using their hands to control the speed bumps on their tunes, welcome these controls when they first use vinyl. You still need to set the pitch control and start the record at the right time, but if you're more familiar using buttons to correct the speed of CDs, the concept and the technique of using the turntable's pitch bend is the same, making the migration from CD to vinyl all that bit easier for the CD DJ.

Predictability

The knack of adjusting the speed of the record with your hands is something that you pick up after a few hours, but sometimes you come across a record that feels stiff to move or flies away too fast and turns a lot faster than you thought, almost spinning out of control as you try to speed it up. The constant, definite change that you always have to hand as you press the pitch bend buttons, no matter what record you use, means that your mixing is easier, quicker and sounds better.

Cleaner records

Pitch bend is also a good alternative to pushing or slowing down the tune with your fingers because it protects your records from excessive fingerprints and grime. As a DJ you're actively encouraged to touch your records, but a method that keeps your records as clean as possible is a good thing.

 When you're considering buying turntables with pitch bend, try to see the feature in action first. Some turntables have a really clumsy control over the speed boost/lag, and can zip up the speed of your tune by too much, too fast, sometimes rendering the control pointless because you can never make small enough adjustments to get the bass beats back in time.

Tempo Reset/Quartz Lock

Earlier in this chapter, I describe the 'Bermuda Pitch Zone', which is where the pitch control goes a little wonky through the zero pitch range on turntables that click into place when set to zero. To get around this problem, turntable manufacturers started to make turntables with *clickless* pitch faders that glide through the zero pitch area, moving smoothly all the way through the entire pitch range. The problem with a clickless fader, though, is that you can't be sure when you're at exactly zero pitch any more. Some turntables still show a green light as you pass zero, but a better option is the Quartz Lock or Tempo Reset button, which resets the pitch to zero pitch, no matter where you set the pitch control.

Some people use this Quartz Lock almost like a pitch bend when the record is playing too fast. Hit the button once to slow the tune down temporarily and then again to bring the tune back to the speed you set it at. This technique is a bit hit and miss, though, and not as accurate as a pitch bend or using your hands. I like to use it by slowing a record right down by 50 per cent (or more) to really drag out the last couple of beats of a breakdown, then I use Quartz Lock to instantly return to zero pitch rather than an acceleration as I move the slider. The downside to this is if I was playing the tune at 5 per cent before slowing down to –50 per cent, the tune will now be playing at zero per cent, 5 per cent slower than before.

Master Tempo/Key Lock

Master Tempo – first available as an add-on to turntables by a company called Vinyl Touch, then available on Pioneer CD decks and now an option on a number of advanced, digital turntables – enables you to change the speed of a tune, but not its pitch.

The pitch control isn't just a speed control. As you increase or decrease the pitch control, the pitch of the music gets higher or lower as a consequence of the tune playing faster or slower. Pressing the Master Tempo button means that you can affect only the speed, leaving the pitch of the music as it was recorded.

Some decks take this a stage further, like with the Key Lock on the Numark TTX1 turntables. You can use the pitch control to select whatever music pitch you want the tune to play at, press the Key Lock button and then adjust the tempo while retaining your original pitch setting. Check out the info on harmonic mixing in Chapter 16 for more.

These controls can be quite temperamental, though – not just on turntables, but on CD decks and in software too. If the pitch setting is more than 4 or 5 per cent and you activate Master Tempo or Key Lock, you can sometimes add digital noise to the music, making the track sound as if it's playing underwater. Tunes with strong vocals tend to suffer the worst from this problem, whereas simple, musical tracks can withstand quite a large change.

You won't find any hard and fast rules for using the Master Tempo and Key Lock features, so you simply need to keep experimenting to work out how far you can push each of your tunes.

Digital display of pitch

The pitch control is an essential tool on a turntable, but its analogue nature means that you can't be 100 per cent sure that when you set the pitch to 3.5 per cent it's has actually changed by 3.5 per cent. Sometimes the smallest pitch change is all you need to make the beats of two tunes play at the same time; with a pitch fader that has no display you have to guess whether the pitch changes at all when you move the fader by a millimetre.

A digital display on the turntable shows you exactly where you've set the pitch, and whether you've adjusted the pitch by a small enough amount to make the beats play in time. This info helps you mix with confidence, taking away some of the guesswork that comes with analogue pitch controls.

Adjustable brake for Start/Stop

Traditionally, when you press Stop on the turntable, the record stops in about half a second. Some decks enable you to adjust the brake, which changes the time that the record takes to stop, giving you more control if you decide to use Stop as a mixing technique (see Chapter 16).

The half-second Stop is really nice, but even prolonging that to one bar of music (which equals four beats) can add another dimension to the mix, or you can set a really long brake time and emulate the power-off as I describe in Chapter 16.

In some instances, you can tighten the brake up so much that when you press Stop the record plays backwards!

Reverse play

Instead of adjusting the brake to make the turntable play backwards on advanced turntables, sometimes turntables have a handy little button (often located next to the pitch control) that does exactly the same thing. Simply press the Reverse button and the deck plays backwards. You get a slow-down-to-stop, start-up delay as you do this operation, but if your timing's right when pressing this button, it sounds great.

Some CD decks give you the option of instantly reversing the direction of the music, rather than needing to account for this delay as the record changes direction. See Chapter 8 for information on DJing with CDs.

Different shaped tonearms

For years the standard shape of the tonearm on a turntable was an S shape. The S-shape creates a variety of different forces upon the needle as it's pulled into the centre of the record – a tracking force, an inside force and a vertical force – which not only adds to the wear on the record but also, due to so many different forces, you can understand why the needle might jump out of the groove when scratching. In the late '90s Vestax pioneered the ASTS straight tonearm for DJs, which only has a tracking force affecting the needle. By cancelling out some of the lateral forces, the turntable achieves maximum stability, and the needle is less likely to skip out of the groove when you're in the middle of a really complicated, frantic scratch move.

The straight tonearm isn't aimed at only the scratch DJ, though. The reduction in forces acting on the needle in the groove means that you get a lot less wear on the vinyl, your records last and sound good for much longer and the needle is less likely to pop out of the groove when you're trying to locate the cue point in the record.

A lot of turntables come with only an S-shape or only a straight tonearm, but some decks from companies such as Numark now include both styles in an interchangeable format, so you can change the design of tonearm as often as you change your socks.

Turntable modification companies can create a fixture similar to the headshell joint that enables you to easily swap from one design to the other, depending on your mood (or that day's style of mixing).

Removable cabling

For years turntables came with the *RCA cables* (you may know them as *phono cables*) hard-wired into the electronic gubbins inside the casing. This setup meant that any damage to the cables involved opening up the casing and re-soldering the connections (if possible) or sending your precious turntable off for repair.

When equipment manufacturers realised that this was problematic for DJs, they started to make turntables with RCA plugs on the back, just like the inputs on the mixer. These turntables now have removable cables that you plug between the turntable and the mixer, and if anything happens to damage the cables they're easy to replace. The new design can also prevent further damage to your turntable because if you drop something on the cable, instead of the tug on the cable pulling the turntable onto the floor, the RCA plugs may act as a shock release, unplugging themselves through the force on the cable and saving the turntable from damage.

Digital outputs

As well as addressing the mechanics of the cabling on the back of the turntable, manufacturers also looked at the range and quality of output connections that they offer to the technology-driven DJ. Not content with the analogue signal sent through the RCA outputs, digital outputs such as USB and S/PDIF (which I describe in more detail in Chapter 13) are now on offer for you to connect turntables to a mixer or PC with a similar input.

Battle or club design

Look into the history of DJing and you see that club DJs have the turntables positioned as per the manufacturers' expectations, but scratch DJs turn them around 90 degrees, anticlockwise. The reason that scratch DJs turn their decks around is so that the needle is clear of their hands as they move like lightning from deck to mixer to the other deck and back again, all in the blink of an eye.

The downside to this orientation is that the power control, pitch control and Start/Stop button (all of which scratch DJs love to use) are now awkwardly placed. Companies such as Numark and Vestax saw a gap in the turntable market and designed turntables with Start/Stop switches at both corners, and pitch faders that you move from one side of the deck to the other, making it more comfortable for the scratch DJ to use the decks.

If you're a beatmatching DJ with no interest in scratching, turning up to a club that has the turntables set up with this 'vertical alignment' for scratch DJs can be extremely annoying. It's not as easy to access the pitch control, it's a bit harder to take the needle on and off the record and it simply isn't as comfortable to beatmatch with the turntables set up like this. Some time spent using turntables with this orientation soon gets you over this hurdle, so when you research a venue where you're due to play be sure to look at how the turntables are positioned and put in any required practice at home with this setup if need be.

Built-in mixer

Okay, I'm going out on a limb here: I believe that the Vestax QFO (see Figure 6-3) is the ultimate in advanced scratch turntables. Suggested, tested and tweaked by DJ QBert (a famous scratch DJ), this turntable is a feature-packed single deck aimed at performance scratch DJs, with a built-in mixer for performing scratches, reverse play, Quartz Lock and a straight tonearm. But best of all, you can take off two of the feet, put a strap on the remaining two feet and wear it like a guitar!

How practical the QFO is as a turntable for everyday use (especially at the cost of £750) is questionable, but if you're looking for the ultimate turntable gadget then this is it.

Figure 6-3:
The Vestax
QFO
turntable.

Setting Up Turntables

The various features I describe in this chapter can make turntables appear to be complicated creatures if you know nothing about them. Whether you're using your turntables to play loads of different records, or just the same two over and over again when controlling music in software (see Chapter 9), you need to set up three different elements before use:

- ✔ Deckplatter
- ✔ Tonearm
- ✔ Peripherals

Deckplatter

If you're using direct-drive turntables, all you have to do is make sure that you've removed the thick rubber mat that may have come with the turntable and then place the slipmat directly on top of the deckplatter and the record sits on top of the slipmat.

If you've just bought brand new belt-driven turntables, you may find that the belt hasn't been linked between the motor and the deckplatter. Carefully lift off the deckplatter and look underneath; if the belt isn't linked to the motor, it's probably taped to the underside of the deckplatter. Stretch the belt between the motor's capstan (the bit of the motor that turns) and the under-side of the deckplatter. If in doubt, check the manual for instructions!

Tonearm

The tonearm holds the needle. If you set the tonearm up poorly, the needle can jump out of the groove when you're trying to find the cue point (see Chapter 14). Worse than that, though, a poorly set up tonearm can perma-nently damage the needle and your records.

As well as leaving the antiskate set to zero for DJ use, the tonearm may require adjustment in two different ways:

- ✔ Counterweight
- ✔ Height

Counterweight

The *counterweight* is a weight on the back of the tonearm that controls how much down-force the tonearm applies to the needle to keep it in the groove. The amount to add is suggested by the manufacturer of the needles and cartridges that you're using (Chapter 7 tells you more about needles and cartridges, and has a table of common counterweight settings).

The key to achieving your desired setting begins with a technique known as *floating the tonearm* (Figure 6-4 shows the correct, floating position; notice how the tonearm is completely parallel to the deckplatter, pointing neither up nor down).

To float your tonearm, follow these steps:

1. **Remove any records from the turntable.**

2. **Starting on one of the turntables, carefully lift the tonearm off its rest towards the middle of the deckplatter.**

3. **While holding the headshell to keep the needle from crashing down onto the slipmat, turn the counterweight clockwise with your other hand so that it starts to move towards the back end of the tone arm.**

4. **As you move the weight backwards, frequently check to see whether a shift in weight has caused the tonearm to point up instead of down.**

Figure 6-4:
The tonearm perfectly balanced, with the needle removed from the cartridge to avoid damage.

5. **When the tonearm starts to point up, turn the counterweight anticlockwise by a small amount in order to find the setting where the needle floats in mid air, neither pointing up nor down, as shown in Figure 6-4.**

6. **After you've found this floating point, return the tonearm to its rest and use the tonearm clamp to lock it into place.**

7. **Now hold the silver part of the counterweight and use two fingers to grip the black ring on the front of the weight. The ring, which has numbers on it, turns independently to the rest of the counterweight.**

8. **Turn only the black ring until the line pointing down from the number zero lines up with the line on the tonearm beneath it. Figure 6-5 shows you how to control the black ring.**

The tonearm is now set to the floating position and has been *zeroed*. If your needle manufacturer suggests that you add 3 grams of counterweight onto the tonearm, turn the entire counterweight (so the black ring also turns) anticlockwise until the number 3 on the black ring lines up with the mark below it on the tonearm.

Figure 6-5:
One hand
supports
the back of
the counter-
weight while
the other
rotates only
the num-
bered ring.

Height

The height adjustment on most decks is a ring at the bottom of the tonearm assembly that raises or lowers the tonearm as it turns clockwise or anti-clockwise. A small mark on the assembly shows you how much height you've added, and unless you're a scratch DJ who uses a raised tonearm height to add even more down-force to the needle, your best bet is to follow the height suggested by the makers of the needle and cartridge you're using.

When you're altering the height of the tonearm, leave the tonearm in the tonearm rest with the clamp on to hold it in place. Otherwise, one wrong move and the needle may bounce across the record/slipmat/deckplatter.

Look out for the lock switch on the tonearm – without releasing this lock, you can't change the height, and if you try to force the ring, thinking it's stuck, you may do permanent damage to the tonearm assembly. Also be aware that when left in an unlocked position, the tonearm moves slightly and may fool you into thinking that you've damaged it.

Peripherals

The last items to attend to when setting up your turntables are the feet and the lids. Keeping the lids attached to the turntables when you're mixing is a bad idea; they get in the way and you may knock them, causing the needle to jump. Don't be lazy: take them on and off each time you use your decks.

The rubber feet on your turntables don't act as mere vibration dampeners. Because the feet screw in, adjusting how tightly they're attached affects the height of each of the four corners of the turntable, which is ideal when compensating for the badly built DIY furniture that your decks sit on. Grab a spirit level if you want to be precise, and adjust the feet to make sure that your decks are level. If they're not level, the needles may skip.

Servicing Your Turntables

Make your turntables last as long as possible by showing them a little bit of care and attention from time to time. You can find information all over the Internet for fixing various broken parts on your decks, but a little cleaning and lubrication can keep the gremlins at bay.

As a general rule for all your equipment, when you're not using it, keep it covered. If your turntables have plastic lids, put those back on when you're not using the turntables. If you keep the decks in flight cases, put the lid back on. If you have neither of these, put a clean bed-sheet (or something soft, clean and lint-free) over the decks when they're not in use, to catch any dust before it gets a chance to settle on your faders, motor and tonearm.

- ✔ **Motor:** If you keep the motor properly lubricated, it can run smoothly for years. All you need to do is remove the deckplatter and put a small drop of sewing machine oil on the centre spindle. Use lubricating oil such as sewing machine oil rather than covering the entire insides of your deck with a slobbering of WD-40 spray!

    After you've lubricated the motor, replace the platter and spin it round with your hand. You can use the turntable immediately, as long as you didn't pour half a can of oil all over the inner workings of the deck.

- ✔ **Tonearm:** You need a can of compressed air and a can of degreasing lubricant to thoroughly clean and lubricate the tonearm assembly (the degreaser dissolves any dirt you can't clean by hand or air alone). Don't worry if you think these sprays are expensive; you're going to need them for your mixer too (see Chapter 10).

Cover the rest of your equipment with a sheet you don't mind getting dusty and then spray the tonearm assembly with the compressed air to remove any surface dust (the sheet is so you don't just move the dust from one deck to another). Spray the grease dissolver over the bearings in the tonearm to remove any ground-in dirt and keep them lubricated.

✔ **Pitch fader:** Use the compressed air to blow any dirt out of the pitch fader. Use the cleaning lubricant to dissolve any dirt residue in the fader if you think that you have a problem, but using the compressed air is usually adequate to clean the fader.

✔ **Headshell:** If you ever suffer from signal dropout from the cartridge (which is when the music starts to break up and cut out), use a pencil or a pin to clean any dirt off the contacts. I've heard of DJs licking the contact points on the headshell and the cartridge to try to clean off any dirt, but as well as being disgusting, your saliva (mixed with the beer you've been drinking) ends up damaging the contacts in the long run.

Check that the screws holding the cartridge are tight, that the needle is clean of any dirt build-up and that it sits securely inside the cartridge.

✔ **Under the platter:** If your turntable comes with a removable deckplatter, lift it off and wipe around the underside with a lint-free cloth, and make sure to pick up any dust or dirt that may get trapped underneath. Using the spray can of air may be a bad idea because you can blow the dust farther inside the deck chassis. Although a little dirt may not cause a problem with the electronics, it's not a good idea to keep forcing more and more dust inside the turntable.

Chapter 7

Perfecting Your Decks: Slipmats and Needles

. . . .

In This Chapter

▶ Understanding what slipmats are for

▶ Making sure that your slipmats slip

▶ Knowing the differences in needle designs

▶ Picking the right needle and cartridge for your DJing style

▶ Prolonging the life of your needles (and records)

. . . .

*W*hen choosing a turntable to DJ with, Chapter 6 encourages you to look for one with a good pitch control, an adjustable tonearm, a strong motor and a solid design – qualities that set the DJ deck apart from a home record player.

However, you still need to look at two more areas before your turntable is a true DJ tool: slipmats, and what types of needles and cartridges to use.

Sliding with Slipmats

As well as acting as an antistatic device, the slipmat is a key factor in transforming your new turntables from just a really good pair of record players to fully functional DJ decks.

The *slipmat* is the same shape and size as a 12-inch record, and sits between the record and the *deckplatter* (the part of the turntable that rotates to make the record rotate). Slipmats are normally made out of felt, and if you've taken my advice in Chapter 6 about making sure that your turntables have a smooth, metal deckplatter, you find that the low friction between the felt and the metal keeps the deckplatter turning underneath the record when you hold it in a stopped position. This simple function of the slipmat is extremely important when you want to start a record playing at an exact time, and is essential for successful beatmatching.

If the deckplatter has stopped turning underneath the record, when you let go of the record to start playing it again it can take almost a second to get up to full speed, meaning you've started the record later that you'd planned. With the slipmat helping the deckplatter continue to turn under the stopped record, the record takes little or no time to get to full speed, and your records start exactly when you want them to.

This friction-free slip is also essential for the scratch DJ so that he or she can move the record back and forth easily, without the drag and inertia of the full weight of the deckplatter moving backwards and forwards with the record.

The setup you want to achieve with the slipmat goes like this:

- ✔ The deckplatter (the part with the bumps on the side that turns round) is at the very bottom.
- ✔ The slipmat goes on top of the deckplatter.
- ✔ You place the record directly onto the slipmat.

When you first buy your turntables, they may come with a thick, heavy rubber mat on the deckplatter with the slipmats placed on top. Remove this big rubber mat so you have the same setup I describe in the preceding bulleted list. If you leave the rubber mat on, the slipmat won't slip over the rubber mat, and the deckplatter will grind to a halt when you try to hold it stopped.

Choosing an appropriate slipmat

The two design concepts that affect how well your slipmat slips are its thickness and weight, and what kind of design is printed on it.

The best slipmat is made from a smooth, compacted felt, and is thin and light. If the slipmat is too thick and heavy, and the felt too rough (or too fluffy), the extra friction drags on the deckplatter, making it turn a lot more slowly under a stopped record, or making it stop completely.

The image printed on the slipmat can be a great expression of your personality. Search any online record store and you find a whole load of slipmats with different logos, designs, photos and colours printed on them. Slipmats like these are great to look at, but try to steer away from cheap versions that are covered in print because, depending on what technique the printer uses, your slipmat may stick to the record and cause drag problems, or the design can wear off and look bad, and may actually harm your records.

My first set of slipmats came second-hand (as did the turntables), and the print had started to come away and go slightly brittle, which ended up scratching some of my beloved tunes. I got around this problem by turning the mat upside-down, so the logo was in contact with the deckplatter and the felt touching the record. This method had the added bonus of reducing the friction even more, and made the slipmat a lot more . . . slippy.

Winning the friction war

When you hold your record still, the power of the motor (known as *torque*) directly affects how easily the deckplatter continues to turn underneath. If you have a weak motor or (*gasp*) you chose belt-driven turntables (Chapter 6 has more on choosing a turntables), the motor may have a hard time keeping the deckplatter turning even with the best friction-killing slipmats.

If you do find that your turntables grind to a halt when you hold the record stopped, before laying blame on your decks take a look at your technique. You don't need to press down hard on the record to hold it stopped: just rest one or two fingers towards the outer edge and that should be enough. Too much pressure adds resistance, stopping the deckplatter turning.

If you're convinced that it's a friction issue between the slipmat and the deckplatter and need to reduce the friction, you can buy commercial products such as Flying Carpets, which you put between the slipmat and deckplatter. However, before you spend even more money, try out this home remedy using some wax paper instead.

A circular piece of wax paper, cut to the same size and shape as the slipmat and then placed between the slipmat and the deckplatter, is a great way of reducing friction and resistance. If you don't want to go out and buy wax paper for this purpose, take a look through your records and look at the inner sleeves that protect them. You may find a sleeve made out of wax paper with one of your records. Just remember to keep that record protected with something else if you take away its inner sleeve.

Here's how to make a friction-killer:

1. **Place the wax paper or inner sleeve on a flat cutting surface.**

   Carpets, dining room tables and the bonnet of your car are all suggestions of surfaces *not* to use.

2. **Using your existing slipmat as a template and a sharp utility knife as a cutting tool, cut a 12-inch (30-centimetre) circle out of the wax paper.**

   3. **Mark the centre of your cut-out by putting a pen through the centre of the slipmat, then cut a tiny hole at that point for the centre spindle on the turntable to go through.**

   4. **Place this wax cut-out between the deckplatter and the slipmat, and try it out.**

   You'll find that the record slips more easily now.

Getting Groovy with Needles and Cartridges

The *needle* is the part on the turntable that sits in the groove of the record. As the record plays, various bumps and ridges inside the groove cause vibrations in the needle that the cartridge translates into electrical signals, which are then sent from the turntable to the mixer, and you hear music. This is how the groove makes you groovy.

You need to know what the different kinds of needle and cartridge are, and how to pick the correct ones for your DJing style. The needles you use as a DJ are a lot stronger than the ones you find in home turntables because they need to take a fair bit of abuse. Back cueing (playing the record backwards while trying to find the place to start), scratching, the inevitable whoops when you rip the needle right across the record and repeatedly taking the needle off and placing it somewhere else on the record with a thump can all take a toll on even the most robust of needles.

The good news is that any needle and cartridge designed for DJs can go on any turntable. You don't have to use Stanton needles and cartridges on Stanton turntables; you don't have to use the Technics headshell that comes with Technics turntables. Manufacturers of DJ turntables have been smart enough to design a universal connection from the cartridge to the tonearm, so that you can use any cartridge on any turntable. This flexibility stands as long as you haven't just bought a basic, cheap, hi-fi turntable with an all-in-one, moulded tonearm and cartridge, or gone for a high-end design that uses different connections. Figure 7-1 shows the back of some cartridges with the same connection.

Figure 7-1:
The same connection on the back of different cartridges.

Your cartridge and needle considerations come in pairs (fitting, because you usually buy them in pairs). Firstly, there are two main designs for how the cartridge eventually attaches to the tonearm, and then you also have to choose between two different styles of needle:

✔ **Headshells with the cartridge and needle screwed on:** This design is the one that nearly always accompanies your turntables when you buy them. This doesn't mean it's a poor design, it's just the design that covers all bases. One of the most popular and enduring scratch DJ needle setups is a Shure M44-7 needle and cartridge attached to this headshell, and you find the Stanton 500AL (see Figure 7-2) in clubs and bedrooms all over the land.

The top of the cartridge is screwed to the headshell, and the needle plugs into the cartridge (the needle is the front, white part shown in Figure 7-3). Four coloured cables make the electrical connection from the cartridge to the headshell, which then plugs into the tonearm to make the final connection.

Figure 7-2:
A Technics
headshell
with Stanton
500AL
attached.

Figure 7-3:
A disassem-
bled needle
and car-
tridge with
a Technics
headshell.

✔ **Built-in headshell:** This design does away with the separate headshell; instead, the cartridge, which is the main body of this unit, plugs directly into the tonearm. The needle is still separate, and easy to remove and replace, but the sleek all-in-one design makes this cartridge a very attractive part of your turntable.

This style of needle and cartridge has a strong link in clubs for the beatmatching DJ, but is just as suitable for scratch DJs. To name only two, the Numark CC-1, pictured in Figure 7-4, is the signature model of the Scratch Perverts, and the Ortofon Concorde QBert was developed through DJ Qbert (both world-class scratch DJs).

Figure 7-4:
The Numark
Carl Cox
needle and
cartridge.

After you've decided on the design of your needles and cartridges, the next thing you have to think about is whether to buy elliptical or spherical needles. A lot of manufacturers supply both shapes for the same cartridge, and you can get them for both the designs I mention in the preceding bulleted list, so the choice is down to your preference rather than availability.

✔ **Spherical:** A spherical needle has a rounded tip that only makes contact with the straight sides of the groove, so the contact between the needle and the groove is extremely small (see Figure 7-5).

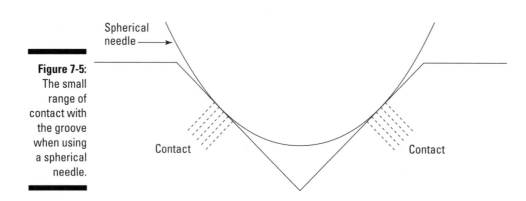

Figure 7-5:
The small range of contact with the groove when using a spherical needle.

The small contact area creates a very strong *tracking force* (the force created between the needle and the sides of the groove) so the needle puts up a fight against jumping out of the groove, making spherical needles an excellent choice for scratch DJs. However, the concentration of the tracking force means that the record wears down more quickly, and the small contact area with the groove means less of it causes the needle to vibrate, resulting in reduced sound quality.

✔ **Elliptical:** Elliptical needles make more contact with the sides of the groove because of their cone shape (shown in Figure 7-6), producing much better sound quality because they can pick up more information from the groove. However, the trade-off for this improved sound quality is that the tracking force is now spread out over a larger surface area, making it easier to knock the needle out of the groove. This makes elliptical needles unsuitable for really vigorous scratch moves (see Chapter 17), but they're perfect for the beatmatching DJ who demands great quality of sound.

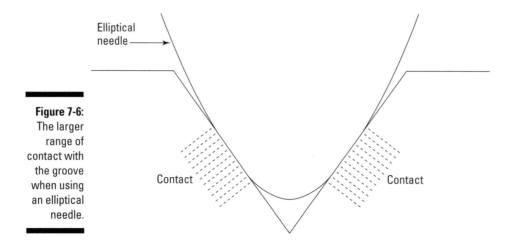

Figure 7-6:
The larger range of contact with the groove when using an elliptical needle.

Digital DJs who use timecoded vinyl to control music playing on computers (see Chapter 9) are usually safer with elliptical needles. Although sound quality isn't an issue, because the needles only need to carry a simple high pitched timecode signal, spherical needles would cause excessive wear to the groove and would be a great cause for concern because these DJs play the same two control records over and over again for the entire set.

If you're buying new turntables, find out whether they come supplied with needles and cartridges. Most stores include the basic Stanton 500AL cartridge and needle set with turntables, but do check – never assume. Imagine this scenario: you're waiting excitedly for your decks to be delivered, but when they arrive you find that needles and carts haven't been included, so you have to wait before you can use your new decks – and all because you forgot to check when you ordered.

Feeling the Force with Counterweight Settings

The *counterweight* affects the tracking force of the needle in the groove. The heavier the counterweight, the stronger the force, so the more secure the needle is in the groove – but the quicker your records wear out.

In Chapter 6 I describe how to set up your tonearm properly for DJ use, and how to add the correct amount of tracking force with the counterweight. Firstly, needle manufacturers dictate how much counterweight you add on the tonearm. The documentation you receive with the needles and cartridges tells you the suggested tracking force and suggested tonearm height for the needles you've bought. However, some of these figures aren't aimed toward DJ use, where you need stability; they're sometimes calculated for the greatest longevity of your records instead.

As a brief guide for you, here are the most popular counterweight settings for common DJ needles:

Needle	*Counterweight (in grammes)*
Stanton 500AL II, Stanton Discmaster II, Stanton 605SK	2–5
Shure M44-7, Shure Whitelabel	1.5–3
Numark CC-1	3–6
Ortofon Concorde DJ S	2–4
Ortofon Concorde Night-Club S	2–5

If you find that the needle still skips when you're scratching or trying to find the start point of the record, first check your technique. If you're quite rough as you move the record with your hands, it may be that you're the one making the needle jump out of the groove. You don't have to be forceful to move the record; you can move it back and forth just as quickly with a light, fluid motion as with a harsh, rough, jerky movement. When you push and pull the record, follow the curve of the record, rather than pushing and pulling in a straight line. This straight line force is a common cause for the needle popping out of the groove.

If you think that the needle is jumping because not enough counterweight is on it, try gradually increasing the counterweight until the needle stops skipping. Take your time and increase the counterweight by small amounts each time. And when the needle does stay securely in the groove, try taking a little weight back off again; you'll probably find it's still okay.

Though vinyl is designed to be long-lasting and not wear out too quickly, if you find you've had to use the full counterweight on the needle to keep it from jumping out the groove, you must understand that the added tracking force will wear out the record and the needle quicker than usual.

Nurturing Your Needles

Knowing when you need to change your needles requires a mix of professional help and general knowledge. The only way to truly know whether your needles are worn out and in need of replacement is to look at them through a microscope. Not many people have a microscope sitting next to their turntables, so you may want to do a bit of research now and get in touch with some of the specialist stores in your area to see if they can check your needles for you.

However, you can look for the following simple things yourself:

- ✔ Are the needles picking up lots of dirt from records?
- ✔ If you play a quiet part in a record, the next time you play the record does it pop and crackle because of damage caused by a worn needle?
- ✔ Do the high frequencies (especially the hi-hat cymbal sounds that normally play in between bass drum beats) sound fuzzy?
- ✔ Have you had your needles longer than a year, and used them for a couple of hours nearly every day?
- ✔ Does you gut instinct tell you that your needles need replacing?

If you can answer yes to half of these questions, especially the last one, then the chances are you need to replace your needles. If you're using relatively cheap needles such as Stanton 500ALs, trust your instinct and buy some new needles. But if you're using something like the Ortofon Night-Club E, which cost £45 each, get them checked out first by a professional, rather than immediately going out to spend £90 on a pair of new needles.

Because you plan to DJ with these needles, their lifespan is inevitably shortened, but you can do a couple of things to extend their usefulness:

- ✔ **Keep your records clean.** You'd think that if Mr Diamond and Mr Dust got into a fight with each other, Mr Diamond would win. Unfortunately, that's not the case with your diamond-tipped needle and the dust in the groove of your record. If you consider that by the time you play three or four records, the needle has played through a couple of miles' or more worth of record groove, if a piece of dirt is constantly grinding away on the diamond tip, the needle's going to wear down much more quickly than if it were playing on a clean record.

- ✔ **Keep the weight down.** The more counterweight you add, the quicker the needle wears down. It's as simple as that.

Your needles and your cartridges are literally the first point of contact for the music you're playing. Take care of your needles, and make sure that you replace them when they're worn. No matter how good the rest of your equipment is, if your needles aren't picking up all the information they should from the record, your music won't sound as good as it can.

You can only make poop from poop. Bad sound in equals bad sound out. Enough said.

Chapter 8

Spinning with CDs

. . . .

In This Chapter

▶ Considering designs of CD decks

▶ Locating the right tune and cue point using different CD deck controls

▶ Starting the CD and making pitch corrections

▶ Trying out additional CD deck features

. . . .

T he great thing about mixing with CDs if you beatmatch is that the only way the beats of two tunes can drift out of time is if you haven't correctly set the pitch. When the pitch is right and the beats are in sync, all you have to worry about is the mix, not dodgy motors on cheap turntables.

This chapter discusses the various controls on CD decks and how CD DJs use them to do the same thing as vinyl DJs, and use them to take mixing to another level of creativity.

Knowing the Requirements of the DJ's CD Deck

A CD deck meant for DJ use is different from the one that sits sandwiched in a home hi-fi system. The main differences are:

▶ The layout of the CD deck

▶ Controls and displays to help you search and find exact start points in tunes

▶ Pitch controls that enable you to alter the speed at which the CD plays

▶ Rugged designs that prevent the CD from skipping

DJ CD decks have many more improvements (see the later section 'Taking Advantage of Special Features') but these design features are what separates domestic from DJ.

Laying out the design

CD decks come in a few different designs, and although the functions and ease of use vary depending on the layout of the CD deck, these various designs allow you to mix music no matter what genre you play. Rock, pop, indie, house or wedding DJs can use any of the CD decks I mention in this section. The only DJ who may demand something specific is the scratch DJ.

Twin CD decks

Twin CD decks (shown in Figure 8-1) are split into two halves. The top part is a control panel, with two sets of time displays, playback and cue controls, a pitch slider and pitch bend, and a jog wheel for each deck to help search through music on the CD. Together, these controls let the DJ find the right place in the track, start it playing, set the pitch controls to match beats if beatmatching, return to the cue point, start the tune with a press of a button and adjust the speed briefly with the pitch bend if the beats aren't properly matched.

The control panel is linked by a cable to the other half of the unit: two CD players that use a 'tray' system (like a home CD player) to take the CDs in and eject them when you're done.

Image 8-1:
The Numark
CDN22 Twin
CD deck.

Twin CD with a built-in mixer

Twin CD decks like the Numark CD MIX series (shown in Figure 8-2) take the twin CD design one step farther; instead of a separate twin CD unit and a mixer, everything comes together as one piece of equipment. This design is good on paper, but as the mixer that's included with this kind of setup is quite basic (especially in the case of the CD MIX), you limit yourself in creativity by going down this route.

This design is good for the party/wedding DJ, who only uses the mixer to set the volumes of both the CD players, and performs a very simple, very quick mix from one CD to the other. But because the mixer is basic (mainly because of a lack of EQ controls) it doesn't give you full control over the sound of the mix.

This CD and mixer combination does look good financially when you start as a DJ, but beatmatching DJs will soon yearn for a new mixer, and this is a problem because even though you can send the outputs of the CD decks on this combined CD player/mixer unit to another, separate mixer, you're still stuck with the original mixer lumped together in a big box of plastic and metal with the CD decks. The mixer is always part of your setup, whether you use it or not.

Image 8-2:
Numark's
CDMIX 1;
good value
unless you
want more.

Single CD Decks

Single CD decks don't tend to use the tray design that the twin units use. Older CD decks used a top-loading design, where the top of the deck was hinged and opened up for you to insert the CD, but the newer CD decks use a slot on the front of the unit, which automatically takes in and spits out the CD using motors (similar to the CD player you may have on your car stereo).

The controls on offer on single CD decks are similar to the twin units, except the pitch slider may be a lot longer (which offers you finer control) and the jog wheel is bigger, helping you find cue points (start points) on the CD with ease. Single CD decks may also have a host of other controls to enhance the mix such as loops, reverse play and hot-cues (see 'Taking Advantage of Special Features', later in this chapter).

Scratch DJs and CD Decks

Innovations in CD technology have given the scratch DJ an avenue to scratch on CD, but doing it well, with ease, comes at a price.

The first thing that affects how well you're going to be able to scratch on the CD deck is the size of the jog wheel you use to perform the scratch. Scratch DJs need large jog wheels that they can scratch on as though they were normal records. This means that the jog wheels on twin CD decks, which are sprung and only turn 90 degrees left and right, aren't suitable for the scratch DJ.

In the same way, I've found that single CD decks with relatively small jog wheels, although still used by scratch DJs, make it a lot harder to perform complicated scratches.

The most important thing the scratch DJ needs from a CD deck is for the CD to sound like a record when being scratched. Unsuitable CD decks just stutter and stop when the DJ turns the jog wheel, but the ones suitable for scratch DJs sound identical to a record player when you play the music backwards and forwards with the jog wheel.

Many scratch DJs prefer the pro level CD decks that come with large jog wheels, such as the affordable Stanton C.304, or the more expensive Pioneer CDJ-1000MkIII (shown in Figure 8-3) and Denon DN-S3500.

Image 8-3:
The Pioneer
CDJ-1000
MkIII single
CD Deck.

Navigating the CD

The biggest difference between vinyl DJing and CD DJing is how you find a start (*cue*) point in a tune, and then how you start the tune playing. With vinyl, finding the cue is easy: pick the right side of the record that your tune is on, look at the groove, place the needle near to where you want to start, move the record backwards and forwards to hear the precise cue point and then hold the record stopped at that point. The hardest part when DJing with vinyl, especially beatmatching, is starting the record at the right time so the beats play in time with the beats on the other tune instantly.

CD DJing is the complete opposite. After you've found the correct cue point, starting the tune in time is extremely easy; all you need to do is press the start button, and if you're beatmatching just press it in time with the other beats. Locating the precise cue, however, can be a bit more difficult. Finding the cue on a CD means locating the right track on the CD, *scanning* (fast-forward or rewinding) through the track to find the general area you want to start from and then *fine-tuning* the cue by playing the CD forwards or backwards by the smallest of amounts.

Although this doesn't sound particularly difficult, CD decks don't have a visual reference other than the time display to help you know where (or when) you are in the tune in order to set the cue. Wave displays, which have a series of peaks and troughs to show the louder and quieter parts of the tune, can help with this problem, but you only find them on the more expensive CD decks such as the Pioneer CDJ1000MkIII as shown in Figure 8-4.

Figure 8-4:
The Wave display on the CDJ1000 MkIII.

 Keep the inlay covers or written tracklists with your CDs to help you find what the track number for a certain tune. Don't just print on the CD itself, though – reading what's on the CD when it's spinning inside the CD player is rather hard! Putting all your CDs together in a case with the tracklists makes reading the track names and numbers easier, and saves time and frustration when trying to find the track you want to play next in the mix.

Different CD decks have slightly different sets of controls to find the cue, using one or (more commonly) a mixture of the following designs:

- ✔ Buttons
- ✔ Jog dials
- ✔ Platters

Buttons

CD decks with very basic controls only use buttons to navigate the CD. You use one pair of + and – buttons to go through the track numbers on the CD to locate the correct tune to play and a second pair to search through the CD and fine-tune the cue point.

The longer you hold down search buttons, the faster the CD plays in either direction. If you just tap the search button, the CD plays frame by frame (a frame is the smallest time change that the CD deck can give you), which enables you to locate the exact cue.

 Repeatedly tapping the search button makes the music play in slow-mo, but because the CD deck repeats each frame you stop on over and over again until you move on, the sound you hear is like a broken CD. This digital noise can initially lead to difficulty in hearing where you are in the tune, making it hard to set a precise cue. Listen out for a change in the sound that's playing; when the sound has more bass to it, you're likely to be on the bass drum. (The cue point you want to set is likely to be one of the bass drums in the tune – see Chapter 14.)

Using buttons to find the cue is quite laborious and takes patience and a good memory of the tune to do quickly. However, developing the knack for finding the cue this way doesn't take long, and although the cheaper, budget CD decks tend to use only buttons, as long as you can find the precise cue when you need to then nothing's wrong with this basic design.

Jog dials

The jog dial on a twin CD deck is between 7–12 centimetres in diameter, and is normally made of two parts: an outer ring and an inner disc (see Figure 8-5).

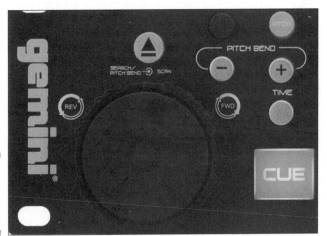

Figure 8-5:
The jog dial on a twin CD deck.

CD decks with jog dials still tend to use buttons to find the track you want to play on the CD, but a sprung outer ring on the dial replaces the search button you find on cheaper CD decks to find the general area in the tune you want to start from. How far you turn the ring left or right changes how fast the tune searches backwards or forwards. When released, the ring returns to the centre position, playing the music at the speed you set with the pitch control.

An inner disc inside the outer, sprung ring makes fine-tuning the cue a lot easier. Most of these CD decks are designed so that their inner disc gives a little click as it turns, with each click representing a frame in the music. By spinning this disc backwards and forwards quickly, you can play the music in slow-mo and then turn the disc more slowly to play the music more slowly and find the exact frame. When scanning through the track frame by frame, you do still hear a digital repetition of the frame you're on, so this still takes concentration, knack and a good ear to hear properly, but it's a lot easier than only using buttons to do the same thing.

The jog dial on a twin CD deck is small and quite fiddly to use, but single CD decks that use a similar, sprung jog dial tend to have much larger dials because the top of the deck has more room – and this increased workspace makes fine-tuning the cue easier.

Platters

CD decks used to try to keep up with and emulate turntables, but the introduction of large control platters now means CD decks have matched and surpassed the functionality of the vinyl turntable, revolutionising the world of CD DJing.

Motorised, rotating platters (as found on the Denon DNS3500 – see Figure 8-6) or manual platters that only turn and affect the music when you touch the platter (as found on the Pioneer CDJ1000MkIII that I use) help CD DJs find the cue in the same way as a vinyl DJ, by controlling the CD just like a record on a turntable, spinning the platter back and forth to find the general area of the tune. But more importantly, when locating the cue, these decks emulate the exact sound you'd hear if you were using vinyl rather than the stuttering, digital, broken CD sound you get on other CD decks.

You can still use track Skip and Search buttons to locate the general area in a specific tune, and then use the platter to fine-tune the cue point like you would with a record on a turntable, playing it backwards and forwards until you find the exact place.

Figure 8-6:
The Denon
DNS3500
platter.

Adjusting the Pitch

As with vinyl DJing, locating start points and starting the tune in time is only part of beatmatching. The other important part is using the pitch control to adjust the speed to make the bass beats of the new tune in the mix play at the same time as the one currently playing through the speakers.

The good news is that the pitch slider on CD decks acts in exactly the same way as on a turntable (refer to Chapter 6). Pitch controls have improvements, such as adjusting the range from 4 per cent to 100 per cent or more, but the principle is the same: moving the slider towards you (into the + area) makes the tune play faster; away from you (the – area) makes the tune play slower. (Check out Chapter 14 for more on the basics of using pitch control when mixing.)

However, if you set the pitch control slightly too fast or too slow and the beats start to drift, you can't push the CD like you can with a record (even if you could touch it, the CD would skip). So *pitch bend* controls are on hand to get the tracks back in time. These controls may be different depending on the CD decks you're using:

- **Buttons:** Usually found on twin CD decks but sometimes used on single decks, two buttons (one marked + and one marked –) temporarily speed up or slow down the tune when you press them. The longer (and sometimes harder) you press the button, the greater the pitch bend you achieve. When you let go of the button, the CD returns to the speed you originally set with the pitch control.

- **Small jog ring:** Found on a number of twin CD decks, there's usually a button or switch that changes the function of the sprung outer ring from 'search' to 'pitch-bend'. You turn the jog ring to the right to go slightly faster, and to the left to go slower. How far left or right you turn the ring affects how large a pitch bend you get. When you return the ring to the centre position, the CD plays at the set pitch again.

- **Large jog wheel:** Depending on your CD deck, the large jog wheel may work in exactly the same way as the small jog ring. In the case of the expensive CD decks with platters, you can temporarily adjust the speed that the tune plays at as if it were a piece of vinyl.

  With vinyl, if you need the record to run faster you can make the record turn faster, or if you need to slow it down you add some resistance to the side of the deck. It's exactly the same with CD decks like the Denon DNS3500, which have motorised plattters: push the platter to play it faster, or run your finger along the side to slow it.

  The Pioneer CDJ1000 uses a ring around the edge of the platter as a pitch bend. Turn it clockwise to speed up the tune, or anticlockwise to slow it down. Importantly, it's only when the ring moves that any change happens to the CD and how fast you move the ring directly affects the amount of pitch bend. So quickly spinning the ring forward or back by a couple of inches is normally all it takes to get the beats back in sync.

No matter what method you use to adjust the error in beat sync, remember to change the pitch control to reflect your adjustment. If you needed to briefly slow down the tune and the beats are drifting further and further apart, make sure that you reduce the pitch control slightly, and increase it if you needed to speed up. Otherwise, because you haven't set the speed of the tunes exactly in time, you'll need to keep using the pitch bend to get the beats back in time. If it was just a starting error you needed to fix, just use the pitch bend and don't worry about altering the pitch control unless you hear the beats starting to drift out of time.

Smoothing Out Vibrations

The good news is, you don't need to do or know much when it comes to dealing with vibrations caused by loud bass sounds and physical knocks.

When you buy your CD decks be sure to do a little research and make sure the ones you're choosing have a good antiskip feature. Nearly all CD decks designed for DJing have some level of antiskip; you can hit or throw some CD decks across the room without the CD skipping; others can deal well with sound vibrations, but if you're too rough with them the CD judders and skips.

When you've chosen your CD decks, consider where you place them. The first thing to consider is what they'll sit on while you use them. Choose something heavy and solid that won't transfer any sound vibrations into the chassis of the CD deck, which may cause it to skip. Also try to put the decks somewhere you won't easily bump into them. (Sitting them so they overhang your desk at waist height is asking for trouble.)

Lastly, put some thought into speaker location. Avoid placing your speakers on the same piece of furniture that your CD decks are on, because bass vibrations may travel through the solid surfaces and cause the CDs to skip.

Working with the Cue

No matter what format you use to DJ with – CD, vinyl, computer software or an app on your iPhone – the basic concepts of DJing and of beatmatching remain the same: find a precise starting point (the cue); if beatmatching, set the pitch control so that the beats of your tunes play at the same speed; start the tune playing; and then make sure the beats play at the same time if you're beatmatching. The choice you make about what format to use only affects the mechanics of how you go about each stage.

I describe how to use the pitch control and pitch bend function to beatmatch on CD decks in Chapter 14, but finding the cue, starting from it and returning to it on CD needs a dedicated explanation.

The four steps to properly work with the cue are:

1. **Locate the cue.**
2. **Store the cue.**
3. **Check the cue.**
4. **Start the tune from the cue.**

Locating the cue

No matter what controls your CD deck has (see 'Navigating the CD', earlier in this chapter), you need to locate the precise cue. If you often start from similar parts of the track, take note of what the time display reads and write that info next to the track title on the inlay sleeve.

Some CD decks (like the CDJ1000 and CDJ2000) have memory cards that can save the cue points that you set on your CDs. This means that you can return to a stored cue point almost immediately after you pop the CD into the deck.

If you haven't written down or stored a cue point for a tune yet, here's how to use the controls to find the cue:

1. **Use the search controls to get close to where you want to set the cue, and if the tune doesn't automatically start playing when you release the search control, press Play so that you can hear the music.**

2. **When you're near to the cue point, press Play again to pause the music, then use the jog controls (buttons, dials or platters) to slowly go through the tune to find the exact start point of the first bass drum of a bar or phrase, or whatever piece of music you want to start from.**

When fine-tuning the cue, if you want to start on a bass drum you'll hear the sound change to have more bass frequencies as the drum hits. Experiment with setting the cue before or on this sound, to see how this affects your timing when you press play. It may only be 100th of a second difference, but it can make all the difference between starting beats in or out of time.

Storing the cue

After you've found your cue point, you need to store that position to the CD deck. On some CD decks, when the CD is in pause mode and you've located the exact cue, you simply need to press Play to set the cue point, and if you ever need to return to it, just press the Cue button again. Pioneer CD decks are different in that you press the Cue button to store the cue when you've found it. Interestingly, the Denon DNS3500 CD decks have a button that lets you choose between either of those methods, so you can set the cue in the way that's most familiar to you. Read the manual that comes with your CD decks so you know what method you should use to store the cue.

Checking the cue

Start your tune, and if you find that you haven't set the cue accurately enough, return to the cue point and use the jog controls to fine-tune the cue and store this new, updated cue.

After you've found and successfully stored the preferred cue, you need to return the CD to that cue point, ready to start the tune in the mix. This may just be a case of pressing the Cue button, but sometimes the state the CD deck was in before you pressed Cue affects what happens afterwards. On some CD decks, if you're in play mode when you press Cue, the CD returns to the cue point and restarts playing from there, or if you're in pause mode then pressing Cue returns you to the cue point and the CD stays paused. However, on Pioneer CD decks, pressing Cue in pause mode resets the cue to where you are at that instant.

This is why it's exceptionally important that you learn how your CD decks operate. Read the manuals that came with your CD decks so you don't accidentally press the wrong button at the wrong time!

Starting the tune

Starting tracks on CD is a lot easier than on vinyl. When the tune that's playing through the speakers gets to the part you want to start the new tune, press Play on the new tune and then go to the mixer to mix between them.

If you're beatmatching, listen to the bass beat from the other tune. Try to block out the rest of the music and focus on the boom from the bass, almost like meditation – helping you press Start on the new tune at the same time as the one that's currently playing. Pressing the button exactly on the beat takes practice, but it's nowhere near as hard as starting tunes on a turntable.

If you prefer a challenge, and still want to start tunes like vinyl, CD decks with motorised platters can let you do this. Find the cue point, hold the platter still and then let go, or give a little push to start the tune.

Taking Advantage of Special Features

DJ CD decks improve on home CD players by including pitch controls, rugged designs and better navigation, but that's not where the improvements end.

MP3 playback

As music becomes easier to buy and download online it makes sense that a lot of the music you'll purchase as a DJ will be files you download from iTunes or other online stores like Beatport or Audiojelly (see Chapter 4 if you need tips on buying online).

CD players that allow you to play downloaded music that you've burnt to *writable CDs* (CD-R or CD-RW) aren't unique to the DJ CD deck – home and car CD players have been able to do this for a long time. However, a feature that negates the need for a CD disc and reads music directly from USB hard-drives, iPods and flash cards is a great addition to DJ CD decks.

CD decks such as the Pioneer CDJ2000 (pictured in Figure 8-7) and the Denon DNHS5500-CD still allow you to play CDs and CD-Rs, but connecting external hard-drives give you access to thousands of tunes, all without needing to worry about ejecting and storing individual CDs.

Figure 8-7:
The CDJ2000 is packed full of features including MP3 playback.

The important thing to investigate when looking at this kind of CD deck is how well the display and controls let you navigate the large library you're using. If you have a CD with eight tracks burnt onto it, it's hard to get too lost finding a track; even if you're unsure what one you need to play, you only need to skip through eight tracks to find it. If you've just connected an iPod containing 6,000 tunes, it might take a little longer to go through them one by one . . .

Most CD decks that allow connection of external hard-drives account for this, though, and have large screens to help you sift through your library in even the darkest, dingiest of DJ booths.

Master Tempo

Master Tempo isn't unique to CD decks; it's available on a lot of turntables too. It enables you to speed up or slow down a tune without changing the key that the music was recorded in. So if you play Barry White and *pitch him up* (speed up the tune) by 16 per cent, he still sounds like Barry, whereas decks without Master Tempo make him sound like a chipmunk.

Some CD decks do this better than others. The more you speed up the track, the harder it can be for some CD decks to keep the pitch the same, and some can suffer terribly from digital noise problems if you try scratching with Master Tempo turned on. If you think you'll use this feature a lot, be sure to get a demonstration of it working on the CD deck you're buying.

Hot Cues

Normally labeled *1, 2, 3* or *A, B, C*, Hot Cues are extra cue points that you can set *on-the-fly*, which means that you don't have to stop or pause the CD in order to set them. Doing so takes a little hand/ear coordination, but setting and then returning to these cue points is very simple.

You can then use hot-cues to jump around the CD, instantly playing different parts of a tune, or even jump to a Hot Cue that you've set in another track on the CD! Repeatedly pressing the same Hot Cue button returns to that cue point each time you press the button, playing the same part over and over.

Loop

The *loop* function plays a discreet part of a tune from an in point (that you can set anywhere in the tune) to an out point (that you also need to set). When you hit the Loop button, the music plays from the in point to the out point, then in to out over and over again, until you stop the loop.

Looping intros and outros or sections of a tune can extend the mix and subtly remix the tune to make something different, or looping part of a buildup to extend it adds variety to the mix. If the buildup is a drum-roll, set it as a loop and edit the length of the loop so it gets shorter and shorter; the shorter the loop gets, the more frantic the breakdown sounds and you can work the crowd into a frenzy before finally ending the loop or hitting a Hot Cue button and crashing back into the powerful beats of the tune.

Loop controls vary in their ability to help you get it right. If you're looping one bar of beats, and haven't hit the in and out points exactly on the beat, you'll hear a stutter/jump of beats each time the loop restarts. Some CD decks automatically adjust the loop for you; others let you edit the loop points and fix any issues; whereas with some CD decks you need to get it right first time, every time.

You can use loops creatively to keep a good part of a track repeating, or you can use this feature as a safety net. If you haven't had time to set up the next track in the mix yet and you're approaching the end of a tune, you can repeat a section of the end of the tune, giving you the time to set up and mix in a new tune. (This shouldn't ever happen, but you might spend too long talking to the wrong person and run out of time.)

If you're the type that always runs out of tune, you could try saving a Hot Cue earlier in the track and then trigger it to jump back and repeat the last minute. This can be easier than using loop controls, because if you're about to run out of tune it's easy to get flustered and begin to panic, which can make it difficult to set accurate in and out points in a loop – but you do need to plan ahead.

Sample banks

Similar to the loop function, instead of setting in and out points, you can record a section of the music into *sample banks* (memory contained on the CD deck) to play back as and when you like.

You can use these samples in as many ways as you can think of. You can loop them or play them on their own, and on some CD decks you can also play them over the CD that you took the sample from, letting you remix a track or mix into another tune on the same CD deck! The creative possibilities are endless.

Reverse play

Reverse play is possible, and a nice gimmick with vinyl, but CD decks give you a lot more control. For starters, some CD decks let you choose whether you want the CD to go into reverse just like a turntable or instantly. If a record is at zero pitch at 33 revs per minute (rpm), it needs to slow down from 33 rpm to zero and then accelerate from zero to 33 rpm in reverse. Some CD decks offer the same de-acceleration and acceleration sound, but also the choice to instantly reverse the tune without any delay. The Denon DNS3500 gives an incredible level of control over reverse playback.

BPM counters

Instead of needing to buy an external BPM counter or a mixer with beat counters built into it, many CD decks calculate and include the BPM of a tune you're playing in the time display area.

Like any BPM counter, it can be easy to rely on this calculation rather than use your ears when beatmatching. Try to avoid falling into this trap, otherwise the first time you use equipment that doesn't have a BPM counter you won't be able to beatmatch very well.

Digital DJ software control

Denon, Numark, American DJ, Pioneer and many other DJ CD deck manufacturers have models that can control music playback in software that supports MIDI (musical instrument digital interface) and USB connections, instead of relying on timecoded control discs. Check that the digital DJ software you use allows this before buying CD decks for this purpose.

Having Fun Experimenting

Many more features are available on CD decks, and each year a new piece of equipment with a brand new innovation escapes into the DJing community, so it's easy to lose track of what your CD deck is capable of.

If you're unsure about what your CD decks can do, or how best to utilise their functions, read the manual, go to clubs to see them in action and check out video clips on websites. Between reviews on manufacturers' websites and personal reviews on magazine websites and on YouTube, you should be able see the deck you love doing all the things you didn't know it could do.

Or just toss the manual under the bed and experiment for a while. Then, after you're thoroughly confused, try to find that manual again . . .

Chapter 9

Bits and PCs: Digital DJing

. . . .

In This Chapter

▶ Discovering various digital DJ setups

▶ Choosing and controlling the right software for you

▶ DJing on the move

. . . .

*I*n my opinion, *digital DJing* – using computer software to play music stored on a hard drive – is as big a revolution to DJing as when someone realised that using two turntables and a mixer could keep the music playing all night with no gaps.

With digital DJing, the equipment the DJ uses no longer restricts the music available to play. Vinyl DJs who previously needed to tirelessly hunt out music available on vinyl can now download tracks to their hard drives and use their turntables to control the DJ software. CD DJs can take charge of their libraries, binning the countless CDRs they've strewn across the DJ booth by keeping all their music on one hard-drive instead.

Alongside greater access and control of music, the creativity and accessibility that digital DJing opens up is outstanding. Whether through a vast host of built-in effects, loops and samples to enhance the sound of a mix for creative DJs or an auto-beatmatch function that can keep new DJs inspired if they hit a plateau while learning how to beatmatch properly, digital DJing is helping to create and motivate a new generation of DJs.

Designing Your Digital DJ Setup

The three things you need to consider when putting together a digital DJ setup are:

- ✔ A computer
- ✔ Any external hardware to control computer software
- ✔ The software for DJing

Processing computer hardware

The computer is the heart of your digital DJ setup and as such it's vital to make sure it's as powerful, stable and capable as possible.

Mac versus PC

If you're lucky enough to be shopping for a new computer to use for your digital DJ setup, the decision to use a Mac or a PC probably comes down to what you're more familiar with and which one you prefer. I've used a Windows laptop and a Macbook Pro in my setup, but have stuck with the Mac.

The more popular, market-leading DJing software titles that I describe later in this chapter, such as Traktor, Serato and Ableton Live, release their programs for both Windows and Mac operating systems. However, some DJ programs (like PCDJ and BPM Studio) only work on computers with Windows operating systems, so if you've decided on the software you want to DJ with before thinking about the computer you'll use it on, do some research to check whether you'll be forced into using a Mac or PC by the software specifications.

Few DJing programs don't work with Windows, so this caution is aimed more at the Mac user, but Windows users still need to check that the software works with the installed operating system. Some titles have been slow to adopt Vista and Windows 7; others need at least Windows XP Service Pack 3 or later; and if you've still got that old Windows 95 PC, it might be time to dust off your wallet and go shopping for a new one.

Desktop versus laptop

The most common design of computer to use in a digital DJ setup is a laptop/ Macbook style due to its portability and compact nature. Full size work-stations, PCs and Mac Pros work just as well as laptops – sometimes better due to a larger screen, increased memory and faster processor speeds – but they're not very portable when hopping from club to club, and finding room for a separate keyboard, mouse and monitor might prove tricky in a DJ booth or in your bedroom setup.

Memory and processor considerations

If your computer is old, check that you have enough processing power and RAM along with suitable hardware (such as supported soundcards and USB ports) to run the software you want to use.

For PC DJs, most software recommends a minimum of a 1.5GHz processor (how fast your computer can 'think' and do what you want it to do is measured in Hertz – Hz) and 1Gb (gigabyte) of RAM (think of RAM like a car-park: the more spaces, or RAM, your car-park has, the more cars can go about their business; but with fewer spaces, less cars can park, or less applications can run smoothly on your computer, and a bottleneck will build, slowing down traffic and your computer).

PC DJing software usually needs Windows XP Service Pack 3 or later to run properly. For most DJing programs, Mac users need an Intel Mac with similar processor and RAM minimum requirements as the PC DJ. The most recent OSX operating system is likely to work fine, but check the software requirements to be sure no compatibility problems exist.

If you can choose a computer that has features well above the recommended minimum of the software, you'll find you have a smoother DJing experience. You might want to record your mix as you perform or have an Internet browser window open at your chosen MP3 store, in case you need to buy a tune to play to the crowd in front of you. Increased memory and processor power lets you do this without risking glitches and sound problems in the DJing software. It's like giving you more floors to your car-park, and getting the cars moving around faster.

Stability

Stability largely depends on how fast your computer is, how well you maintain it and what other programs and processes are running in the background. But whether you're buying the DJ software on its own, or a new computer too, do some research on Internet forums (and on the specific DJ software websites) to make sure the software works in harmony with your hardware.

I experienced problems with my HP laptop where if I had the Wi-Fi card turned on the music would cut out intermittently – which doesn't go down very well in the middle of a club! I don't tend to hook into Wi-Fi during a set to download music to play (or update my Facebook status like a few DJs I know), so it's not an issue for me. But loads of DJs (especially party and wedding DJs who get wide-ranging requests) love having the option to download any music to play instantly, so Wi-Fi access can be an important complement to their music library.

Macs aren't immune to hardware problems either. Earlier Macbook Pros required you to connect USB soundcards to the socket closest to the power input in order to maintain enough power to keep the music from cutting out.

Do some research before and after you buy your setup to avoid being plunged into silence during a DJ set. Software websites are usually very good at giving setup and troubleshooting advice. The Native Instruments website has a comprehensive list of tweaks for Vista and XP operating systems; go to www. native-instruments.com/support and search for 'tuning tips', or just search their forum and knowledge base. Even if you're not using their Traktor software, the troubleshooting ideas on their website may solve any problems you might be experiencing with the DJ software you've bought.

Controlling the Digits

Digital DJing is based around software running on a computer with a common layout of the software display similar to what you'd see in a DJ booth: at least two decks to play the music, with a mixer in between, and a library of your tunes underneath it all (see Figure 9-1). However, what makes digital DJing so fascinating is that you aren't shackled to a keyboard and mouse to control the software.

Figure 9-1:
The Traktor Scratch Pro interface – two decks, a mixer in between and the library of tunes below.

Mouse clicks and keyboard strokes are the most basic way to navigate and adjust the various controls and options in DJing software. However, by adding some external hardware, digital DJing evolves into a true performance, for your experience as the DJ and for the people on the dance floor too.

Setup options available for the digital DJ include:

- ✔ Use a laptop only (or a computer with keyboard, mouse and display) with DJing software installed – you control everything with the keyboard and mouse.

- ✔ Add a better soundcard and a DJ mixer to the laptop, leaving the mouse and keyboard controlling only playback of the music.

- ✔ Use a DVS (Digital Vinyl System) to control the playback of music using any turntables or CD decks, with the option of adding an external mixer too.

✔ Combine control over playback of the music and a mixer in an all-in-one piece of hardware.

✔ Connect CD decks via USB or MIDI (musical instrument digital interface) to control playback of the music. Adding an external mixer minimises keyboard and mouse use.

Laptop/computer only

By far the simplest setup is in Figure 9-2. Install software, connect the output of your computer's soundcard to an amp and navigate the music library, adjust playback of the music and control the mixer all with the mouse and keyboard.

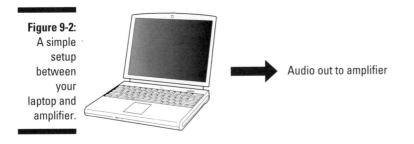

Figure 9-2: A simple setup between your laptop and amplifier.

Audio out to amplifier

Nothing's wrong with DJing this way – you can do everything that any other digital DJ can do. You just might need a little more time to navigate menus, click and drag cue points back and forth, find the right key to press to activate an effect and then to move the mouse slowly enough when controlling the cross-fader and EQs on the internal mixer in the software so that the mix still sounds good. And in my opinion, a DJ just using a mouse and keyboard to perform the mix gives a bit of a lacklustre performance. For all I know, I'm looking at a manager checking email, not a DJ mixing up a storm!

The connections and requirements for this setup are relatively simple. All you need is:

✔ A laptop (or a computer with a display, mouse and keyboard) with a soundcard so you can output to an amplifier

✔ DJ software

✔ Music files

✔ Amplifier and speakers

✔ A cable to connect the soundcard output to the amplifier (check the connections on your setup)

A downside to this option is that the output of a laptop is likely to be just a headphone socket. This can be a low level sound output that needs amplifying more than a normal Line level output and could result in a lot of interference and noise being amplified too.

The bigger downside, however, is that as a DJ you want to be able to send the main mix sound to an amplifier, but also be able to listen to the next tune you want to play in your headphones (without it being sent to the amplifier too; check out Chapter 12 if you need more information about why this is important). A laptop-only setup is unlikely to let you do this because it probably has only one output (the headphones) and even if it has a Line output and a Headphone output, it's unlikely that you can play a different tune through each one through the software. In order to make this happen, you need to add some hardware.

Enhancing the basics by adding hardware

You can buy a new soundcard (most likely to be an external, USB soundcard) that can split two different signals sent from the DJ software and that has at least two outputs, one of them being a headphone connection. With this more advanced soundcard, you'll be able to send the main mix to the amplifier and listen to the next tune in the headphones, as Figure 9-3 shows.

Figure 9-3:
A laptop with an external soundcard. You can connect the two outputs to an amp and headphones, or both to a mixer.

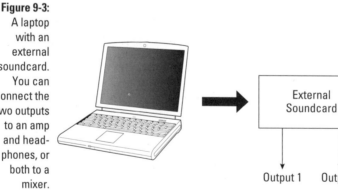

Adding this kind of soundcard to your laptop setup also means you can add a DJ mixer to your setup too. This means you can mix between tunes using traditional DJ hardware with a lot more control (and performance value) compared to using only the keyboard and mouse.

By using a soundcard that can accept two input signals from the DJ software and that has two outputs, you can send Deck 1 of the software to Channel 1 of the DJ mixer, and Deck 2 to Channel 2 of the mixer. You mix the music from both decks using the mixer like a conventional DJ would, and the output from the mixer is then sent to the amplifier to rock the dance floor!

It's rare you'll find DJ software that can't send two output signals to a sound-card, but if you're unsure about the functionality of your chosen software title, or if it has any specific recommendations for what soundcard to use, do some research on the program's website or on Internet forums first.

DVS using records and CDs

DVS ((Digital Vinyl System) is how digital DJing has found its place and exploded into clubs and bedrooms all over the world.

DVS setups are similar to the arrangements I explain in the previous sections, except instead of needing to use a keyboard and mouse to control and adjust playback of the music in the software, you can use traditional turntables (or CD decks) to do the same thing, as Figure 9-4 shows. If you use a mixer in this setup, the only time you need ever go near the laptop's keyboard or mouse is to select the next track to play or to enable any effects. Even then, adding hardware controllers like the Kontrol (see the later section 'Adding Hardware Controllers') means that you don't even need to do that either!

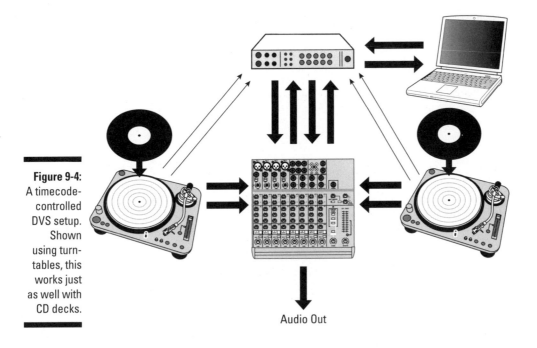

Figure 9-4: A timecode-controlled DVS setup. Shown using turntables, this works just as well with CD decks.

Audio Out

The DVS option in Figure 9-4 is based around records or CDs that play special timecode data into a special soundcard. The DJ software reads the timecode data and matches it to the music you want to play. So if you move the needle on the record one minute in and start it playing, the track you've loaded into the matching deck in the software starts playing from one minute in. If you stop the record turning, the music stops playing too, or if you play the record backwards, the music playing from the computer plays backwards.

Nearly all software that you can use in a DVS setup has fantastic vinyl emulation sound (whether you're using CDs or vinyl), so not only does the music stop playing or play backwards, but also it sounds exactly the same as if the music were playing on that record instead of from a computer. This enables scratch DJs to scratch with DJ software and it sounds no different to if they were scratching a record with real music on it instead of timecode squeal.

In a DVS digital DJ setup, a separate mixer isn't essential, because you can still use the software's built-in mixer (if it has one) to mix the music. But most DJs with a DVS setup won't stop at using only CD decks or turntables; they'll add a mixer to their setup too, so it faithfully emulates a traditional DJ setup.

Connections and requirements

Nearly all DJ software that you can buy as a DVS setup uses a specific sound-card designed by the software manufacturer. For example, I use the Audio-8 *hardware interface* (what they call the external soundcard) when DJing with Native Instrument's Traktor, and then have to unplug it and connect the Serato SL made by Rane when using Serato to DJ with (see 'Picking Out the Software', later in this chapter, for more about DJing software choices).

Unfortunately, in most cases, you won't be able to buy just the software, a cheap soundcard and a few cables and then use your turntables to play MP3s on your laptop. With wide-ranging price ranges between different DJ DVS setups, though, you should be able to find one within your price range, so hopefully the rigid hardware specifications don't become too much of a problem.

Connections are important but can seem complicated, with the external soundcard acting as a connection junction between turntables, CD decks, the mixer and the computer. You connect the outputs of the turntables (or CD decks) to the soundcard (using RCA to RCA cables) and the soundcard to the computer via USB, transferring the timecode data from the CD or record to control music playing on the computer. The music is then sent back to the soundcard, and you connect the outputs of the soundcard to the mixer, with the output of the mixer sent to an amplifier. It may sound confusing, but once you work out the chain of what's happening, and look at the writing on the soundcard, it's not that bad!

Some soundcards (like the Serato SL) have two inputs and two outputs so you can control and send only two tunes from the computer to the mixer using these connections (just as if you'd connected two turntables or CD players directly to the mixer playing normal records or CDs).

The Audio-8, used with Traktor, has four inputs and outputs, which in my case means I can use both of my turntables and both of my CD decks at the same time, controlling four tunes and mixing between them with my four-channel mixer – not something I do often, but it's nice to have the option!

DJ software manufacturers realise that you may have a large library of normal CDs and records, so they usually have a function that lets you bypass the software to enable you to send the music from real records and CDs directly to the mixer to use in the mix. If you want to use existing records and CDs in your DJ sets, check that the software, hardware and cables let you do this before spending loads of money only to leave your old library useless.

Adding Hardware Controllers

Although DVS pushed the boundaries of digital DJing, external controllers are probably the most fast-moving and exciting side of digital DJing hardware now.

All-in-one hardware controllers

Simplifying connections and equipment needs, hardware controllers from the likes of Behringer and Hercules (and many more) release you from a reliance on the keyboard and mouse to control software in the same way a DVS setup can, but mean you only need a laptop, some software and the controller.

Combining playback control, a mixer, effects and the audio interface, these hardware controllers are incredibly convenient and sometimes cost-effective ways to DJ. Different makes and models offer different levels of functionality. Lower priced offerings from Behringer or the Hercules DJ console offer an affordable yet full level of control, and more expensive mixers like the Allen & Heath Xone:4D, which controls similar functions to the cheaper alternatives, give greater flexibility and options for creativity.

Most of these hardware controllers allow you to add other input devices too, so not only can you play music stored on the computer, but if someone hands you a CD with music he wants you to play, you can throw it into a CD deck (if you have one with you) and mix it into music playing from the computer.

Control and effect

A hardware controller like the Kontrol, which is designed to work best with Traktor (shown in Figure 9-5), gives you full control over the effects in the software but also has a section to control playback of the music. DJs with DVS setups who want to be able to control effects with hardware instead of mouse clicks can make great use of this kind of controller, as can laptop DJs who want to expand their control over the software but don't want to be saddled with a cumbersome all-in-one controller.

Figure 9-5:
Traktor
Kontrol.

Putting CD decks and mixers in control

Instead of using timecoded records or CDs to control music playing in software, special CD decks like Pioneer's CDJ400, 900 and 2000 along with Denon and Numark CD decks connect to DJ software directly via MIDI or USB to control playback of the music. With no CD or record to play, stability and reliability is 100 per cent locked in when using these pieces of kit, with internal gubbins inside the CD decks themselves doing all the controlling.

You still need to decide whether you want to use the internal mixer in DJ software or an external one (I suggest using an external mixer), and you need to make sure your CD decks work with the software you want to use.

This method takes a lot of the confusion out of the connections of equipment. USB connections to the computer control the music in the software, and standard audio outputs of the CD decks are sent to a mixer in case you want to play a real CD instead. You still need a soundcard to connect the music from the software to the mixer, but overall the connections are nowhere near as complicated as the DVS connection method.

Your way is the best way . . . for you

The decision whether to add hardware to your DJ setup is entirely up to you. If you can still create a great sounding mix with your chosen setup, and you love using it, then it's the right one for you.

The kind of DJ you are may affect how big your setup is. Party DJs may be happy with just a laptop; DJs who work in a bar and want a bit more control but still keep things compact may just add a mixer to the laptop. Club DJs are likely to want to use the more expanded options, using hardware controllers or DVS setups for full control and performance reasons.

Picking Out the Software

Pick the right software title for you depending on how much money you have in your pocket and how you much control you want over the software.

Keeping it simple with jukebox software

Although most DJs want to use DJ specific software, if you don't really need or want to get too involved in the mechanics of mixing, you can easily set up jukebox programs like iTunes, Windows Media Player or SilverJuke, which offer different levels of control.

From a hardware point of view, this is the most basic digital DJ setup: just a laptop connected to an amplifier. Load all your tunes into the music jukebox program, create a playlist of music you want to play, enable any cross-fade options that may be available so that the songs overlap a little (in iTunes, check 'Crossfade Songs' under the Playback preference) and then walk away. iTunes takes care of everything, randomises the order in which the tunes play, mixes them together and even keeps the overall output volume the same if you enable Sound Check.

If you want a little more control over the playlist, get hold of the latest version of iTunes and select the DJ option. This lets you add tunes and change the order of play while the music's playing. You still don't need to worry about sound control or mixing the tunes together – you just have greater control over what music plays and in what order.

As good as it is, the iTunes approach is in danger of putting a lot of DJs out of work as bars decide it's cheaper and more reliable to have a pre-loaded computer at the end of the bar playing a set list of tunes than a DJ who has an opinion. Stop these bar managers in their tracks by being the best DJ you can be!

Software designed for DJs

From free titles like Mixx and Zulu to expensive, industry-standard options like Traktor and Serato, most digital DJing software titles tend to have interfaces designed around the same basic setup shown in Figure 9-1, earlier in this chapter.

What's added to this basic design separates DJ software titles from one another. Very basic software just has the players (with pitch controls and cueing section), a mixer and the library, with no effects, no waveform display to help you find the beats in the music and no option to connect external hardware to control the software.

However, recent software releases address these issues, with features packed in to help you create a fantastic sounding mix. Even Mixx and the free version of Zulu have built-in effects, auto-beat-sync and a waveform display to help you with cue points and beatmatching.

Considering auto-beat-sync

Auto-beat-sync is a very seductive feature. By automatically dealing with beatmatching for you, and sometimes even finding perfect placement points so that bars and phrases match, it's all too easy to simply let the software take over so all you have to do is move the cross-fader to mix between tunes (and most software can take control of this too!).

If you're busy adding effects, dropping in samples and scratching up a storm, and want to give yourself more time to be creative by removing the mechanics of beatmatching, auto-beat-sync is a useful tool. If you're not doing any of this and have loads of time to beatmatch properly, but your constant reliance on auto-beat-sync means all you do is move the cross-fader from side to side every four minutes, leaving the computer to take care of beatmatching and placement, you're cheating yourself out of learning a great skill. You're still DJing, but you're only half a DJ.

Waving for help

A *waveform* (shown in Figure 9-6) is a visual representation of music. When the music is loud and powerful, the waveform is bigger; when it's quieter, it's smaller. So bass beats (which are loud and powerful) show as sharp spikes in the waveform. By looking at the waveform and spotting where these big spikes are, you can work out when bass beats are going to play. For example, in Figure 9-6 a section of music has no bass beats for a short period, but when you see the big spikes, that's when the bass beats start to play.

Waveform displays do more than let you know what's about to happen in the next few seconds. By zooming out and viewing the entire waveform for a tune, you can tell where the music changes through its different parts of structure (check out Chapter 15 for more about the structure of your music).

This way, you can make sure the next tune you want to mix in starts at the correct place to allow for perfect placement (see Chapter 16).

Figure 9-6:
A tune's
waveform
in Traktor
Scratch
Pro – the
peaks are
bass beats.

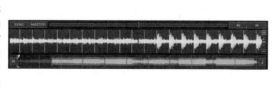

Serato aids beatmatching by showing the waveforms of two tunes playing side by side. Spikes of different frequency in the music are a different colour in the waveform, which means you can see what's a bass beat and what's a combined bass/snare beat. Looking at how closely similar colours of the waveform play next to each other when you're adjusting the pitch of the cued tune (the next one you want to add to the mix) can help unlock the mystery of which tune is playing faster than the other. And when similar coloured spikes are locked side by side, you'll hear that the beats are matched, with the bass beats playing at the same time. It takes a little getting used to, but with enough practise, it's easy to do.

Perfect placement, getting bars and phrases matched, takes more attention, and still needs you to listen to the parts of the tune that work best together, but the two waveforms side by side can give a boost to the DJ who's struggling to grasp beatmatching.

The waveform isn't just for beatmatching DJs; scratch DJs benefit from it too. You can locate the sample that you want to scratch by looking at the waveform. By watching the waveform move back and forth while scratching, you can ensure you're returning to the correct sections of that sample (Chapter 17 has more on scratching).

Taking Control

What can make you lean towards one software title or another is how you can control it. Software that you can only control by a mouse or keyboard can be quite hard to use quickly and creatively, but software that lets you use external controllers, or even your turntables or CD decks to play the music, open up great options, both creatively and as a DJ performance in front of a crowd.

Most software works with USB hardware controllers from Behringer, Hercules, Vestax, Denon, Pioneer, Numark and many more, but check first before buying the software and hardware, just to be sure.

A growing number of options also allow DVS control (see 'DVS using records and CDs' earlier in this chapter), and this is what most DJs look to use. The two leading lights in my opinion are Serato and Traktor. Both titles are sweeping through clubland as clubs install the hardware you need to use them properly into their DJ booths.

I have both Serato and Traktor, simply so I'm never stuck if I'm in a club that uses one or the other, but at home I use Traktor because of the expanded functionality. Without the link to Live (see the next section), Serato is designed as an easy-to-use, reliable music playback and mixing title, giving little added value like effects, whereas Traktor has built-in effects and unending customisation to help you set it up to create the best mix you can.

Livening up software choice

DJ solutions that emulate a twin CD setup are great for traditional DJs who want to mix from one tune to the other, add samples, scratch and add effects to the music, but Live by Ableton (for Mac OS and PC) uses more of a sequencer approach to put the mix together, taking mixing on computer a step further by allowing you to remix any of the tunes live during the mix.

You can use Live through each stage of the musical process; so you create the music and then perform that creation to the crowd as a DJ. The software is so versatile that you can remix the tunes on-the-fly, live to the crowd, and add MIDI controllable instruments to the mix, to create a completely unique remix and a DJ set that nobody else has ever heard or may ever hear again.

You need to do a fair bit of prep-work before you can beatmatch with Live, which is one argument that some people have against using it to DJ with. Instead of having a pitch control to affect the speed of your tracks, Live uses a warp function that helps to change the tempo of the tune. The warped songs in Live link to the program's internal beats per minute (BPM) clock, so changing the BPM of a tune from 135 BPM to 138 BPM is effortless, and takes no time at all during a performance. For this technique to be effortless, though, you need to give the software reference points to know how to adjust a tune's BPM quickly. In Live, these are called *warp markers*, which you add to the waveform display in the Live software.

The setup process sounds quite complicated, but it isn't. If you ripped your entire CD collection into Live for a mix, you'd only need to take a little time to analyse the tracks and prepare each of the songs with warp markers in order for Live to be able to change the BPM when you're beatmatching.

In the past, some people have accused Live DJs of cheating, lacking the skill to beatmatch, and say that sets performed on Live are preconceived and no better than a mix tape played through the sound system. However, Sasha, John Digweed, and Gabriel & Dresden are typical of the DJs that use Live: they've all proven that they're already masters of their craft, and use Live to expand their creativity rather than cheat the DJ skills. Because the beatmatching is essentially done for you by Live, DJs are left to focus more on what tunes they want to mix, and how they put together mixes between tunes and create the effects and track layering that build up a unique sound to the mix.

A whole host of controllers and options are available for whatever stage of the music process you use Live for, so you aren't faced with a DJ staring at an iMac, clicking a mouse. With audio interfaces and controllers for making music, and mixer and output interfaces to control Live for DJ performances, you can't accuse anyone of lacking in aesthetics when using a computer with Live and a few controllers attached to it. Check out `www.ableton.com` for more information.

Bridging the gap

One of the most exciting developments in recent times for Live is its partnership with Serato. Using software called The Bridge from Serato, you can use Serato to mix tunes together using a DVS setup (see the earlier section 'DVS using records and CDs') but also utilise the remixing capabilities of Live to turn the mix into something incredible. This union of Serato and Live using The Bridge turns Serato from a rock-solid playback title into a must-have for the creative DJ.

Exploring Alternatives

Huge digital DJ setups incorporating two CD decks, two turntables and a mixer might be good if you're looking to perform a big, complicated mix, but other options are available, ranging from the very simple DJ option on iTunes to mixing with iPods, iPhones and MP3 gadgets. Unfortunately, DJ Hero on the Xbox or PlayStation isn't really DJing . . .

DJing with iPods and USB drives

If you'd like to keep a toe in the digital DJing waters, but don't really want to go as far as lugging a computer around with you, try these alternatives.

DJing with hard-drives

You can use USB hard-drives that hold thousands of music files in a few different ways.

If you DJ using software on a computer you can use an external hard-drive to expand your storage space. If your internal hard-drive is only 50Gb in size, you can store around 10,000 tunes. By adding a 1Tb (1,000 gigabytes) external drive, you now have the ability to store approximately 200,000 more tunes!

It's not only DJs who use DJing software who can gain from this expansion of music storage. CD decks like the Pioneer CDJ2000, the Denon DNS1200 and many more from the likes of Numark, Gemini and Citronic allow you to connect a USB drive and play, control and (if applicable) effect the music on the hard-drive in the same way as if you'd inserted a CD into the player.

The iBooth

An iPod is, in essence, just an external hard-drive. However, the music library database it contains is what makes this a lot better than a simple USB hard-drive that has 200,000 tracks placed in one folder.

You have a few iPod solutions, the most basic being using two iPods connected to a mixer, but because this doesn't allow you to change the pitch of the music (which you need to do when beatmatching) it isn't the ideal choice.

DJ equipment manufacturers have come up with several solutions to DJing with iPods that range from a simple connection that uses the iPod in exactly the same way as an external USB hard-drive to connecting the iPod to a CD deck or mixer and allowing access to the library of music, but with limited playback capability.

However, for functionality versus cost, Numark's iDJ2 (shown in Figure 9-7) leads the way in iPod DJing in my opinion.

Figure 9-7: The Numark iDJ2 offers a digital solution for iPod DJing and regular DJing.

The future's bright . . .

I imagine the ultimate design for a digital DJ hardware setup is something that encompasses all needs: a Swiss-Army knife of DJ mixers and controllers that would allow the DJ to stay digital, or continue to use turntables and CD decks if so desired. Although combinations of functionality exist already, the ultimate mixer for a digital DJ would be something that allows full control of DJ software, the ability to play, navigate and have full control over music from hard-drives and iPods, a mixer section comparable to the most expensive Pioneer or Allen & Heath mixer, with everything linked together via simple single cable connections instead of complicated patch and splitter cables.

Although something like the Numark MixDeck comes close, the ultimate mixer isn't out there quite yet. But believe me when I say it won't be long!

The most impressive feature the iDJ2 offers is the ability to play two tracks from the same iPod at the same time. With an LCD screen helping to navigate and manage your iPod's library, a complete mixer with EQ controls, cue controls, metering (to make sure you keep the sound output at its best) and a cross-fader curve adjust, it helps the iPod DJ create stunning mixes.

The ability to connect turntables and CD decks as well as USB hard-drives to the iDJ2 means that it's ideal for DJs who want loads of music and format options available to DJ with. Check out www.numark.com/idj2 for more about the iDJ2.

Though still functional for a lot of DJs, be aware that the previous model, the iDJ, didn't allow you to alter the pitch of the music – vital if you want to beatmatch your tunes. So if you want to beatmatch, and you're shopping for one of these iPod solutions, make sure you get the iDJ2, not the iDJ.

Mixing on the move

DJs no longer need to be chained to a DJ booth in order to mix up a great set. Portable, handheld DJ devices and applications (*apps*) on smart-phones won't replace the traditional DJ booth, but for short, sharp, entertaining DJ sets, they've opened up the glass door to let the DJ perform outside of the booth.

A few DJ gadgets are out there, but in my opinion the Tonium Pacemaker is one of the most fun and effective portable mixing consoles available. It has everything you need to beatmatch, mix, effect and record your mixes jammed into a handheld device along with storage for over 15,000 tracks. It's incredibly intuitive and creative to use, and the end results, I think, are stunning.

For something a bit more substantial, but just as portable, the Nextbeat by Wacom can either be desk mounted for standard DJ booth use, or if you want to add a performance aspect to your DJing it has a removable controller that lets you walk out onto a stage, into the crowd or just over to the bar, and mix a fantastic set while ordering a drink.

iPhone apps can help you pick a restaurant, magnify the menu, book a taxi home and then track a bike route to help you burn off all those calories the next day! Even better than that, though, if you hunt through the App Store (you'll need to download iTunes from www.apple.com/itunes to access this) you'll find apps that let you emulate the DJ booth with your iPhone.

Apps like Quixpin DJ (see Figure 9-8) have loads of features, with two input decks, a full featured mixer with cross-fader curve adjust and all important pitch controls to aid beatmatching. A comprehensive set of different output modes through the headphones let you listen to the next tune before you add it into the mix (see Chapter 12) and if you utilise an audio splitter out of the headphone socket you can connect your iPhone to a DJ mixer and use it as two separate decks!

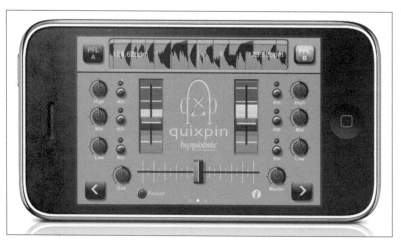

Figure 9-8:
The Quixpin DJ app for the iPhone.

iPhone apps aren't just about the full mix experience either. Apps that work as BPM counters, virtual single turntables (so you can add a third device and do some scratching with it), music production apps and even controllers for software like Serato and Traktor have all helped to turn the iPhone into the third hand that you sometimes need in the mix.

And these apps aren't just for iPhones: Windows Mobile and Android phones have a few apps available that are capable of DJing too. Search on the Internet to see whether any applications exist for your phone.

As with the bigger Digital DJ setups, audio connections are very important when using portable devices to DJ with. Before parting with your money, check that you're able to connect your device to an amplifier, but also check you can connect headphones to listen to the next tune without people hearing it through the amplifier.

Other things to keep an eye out for are that your portable device is fully charged if running on batteries, and if it relies on Bluetooth or Wi-Fi connections to operate or send/receive music, test all the connections before trying to mix in front of a crowd. Otherwise, you'll just be someone standing on a stage in front of a crowd holding a phone with a panicked expression.

You could phone a friend for help while the phone's in your hand, though . . .

Chapter 10

Stirring It Up with Mixers

· ·

In This Chapter

▶ Finding out about the mixer's most common features

▶ Looking at the advanced options available

▶ Choosing the right mixer for your DJ style

▶ Keeping your mixer in tip-top condition

· ·

Mixers are a very demanding breed of animal. They come with many functions and features, and can manipulate the music in many ways. But in the end, mixers only do what you tell them to do.

This chapter explains how the vital controls on a mixer function and how they relate to your DJ mixing style. Understanding that much sets you on your way to buying the right mixer.

Getting Familiar with Mixer Controls

In your journey as a DJ, you'll come across a vast range of mixers. Some you may already know about, and some you won't ever have seen before. If you understand what the features are on a mixer, and how to use them, you need never accidentally press the wrong button and cut out the sound.

Well, *never* may be too strong a word . . .

Inputs

The common DJ mixer accepts three different input methods:

- ✔ **Phono** inputs for turntables
- ✔ **MIC** inputs for microphones
- ✔ **Line** inputs for everything else

Professional digital mixers also have S/PDIF, USB and Firewire inputs to connect digital sources (such as CD, MiniDisc and PC inputs) and keep the music playing at the best possible quality. For information on how to connect these, and the standard inputs in the list, head to Chapter 13.

Phono inputs

Records are recorded in a special way in order to fit all the information onto the vinyl. The mixer needs to translate the signal it receives from the turntable in a completely different way to a CD player or any other device, and it's the Phono input you use for this translation.

Line inputs

All other equipment (CD players, MP3 players, MiniDisc players, the audio output from your computer and DVD player and so on) sends out a Line signal to the mixer. When you want to use any of these, you use the Line input on the mixer.

On a two-channel mixer, both channels have a Line and a Phono input connection. This means that you can connect two turntables and two CD players to a two-channel mixer, and use the Line/Phono switch to select the CD player or turntable input for either channel.

Mic inputs

As well as accepting playback devices like turntables and CD players, most mixers also have XLR or quarter-inch jack inputs for connecting a microphone. There's usually a separate volume and EQ (equaliser) control to affect the bass, mid or high frequencies in your voice so that you can sound great speaking to the crowd.

Outputs

Basic mixers usually have two outputs, with better mixers having at least three outputs.

- **Master Out** connects to an amplifier. The LED display on the mixer relates to how strong a music signal you're sending out of the Master Out to the amplifier. The stronger the signal, the less you have to turn up the amplifier. Too strong a signal, though, and you may cause the sound to distort because the amplifier can't process it properly.

- **Record Out** is for sending music to a recording device like a CD burner, digital recorder or computer. The output LEDs on the mixer have no bearing on how strong a signal you send to the recording device through this connection. Only the channel-faders (the vertical faders) and the gain control (which changes how strong a signal comes in from the turntables or CD players) affect how strong a signal you send to a recording device.

✔ **Booth Out** sends a signal to a separate speaker in the DJ booth so that you can hear the music too! This is vital in a large club where the main speakers are far away. The delay in sound between those speakers and your ears can make beatmatching very difficult.

For more on each of these outputs, and how to connect them to their intended recipients, check out Chapter 13.

Multiple channels

Although you can have two turntables and two CD players plugged into a two channel mixer and flick from Line to Phono, having a dedicated channel for each input is more convenient. You also need more than two channels on your mixer if you want to use three CDs or three turntables, because you can't plug a turntable into the Line input and you can't plug a CD deck into the Phono input on a mixer.

A mixer with three or four inputs can cater to most DJs' needs, and if you need more than four channels to use all your equipment, I'd be more worried about the electricity bills than where to plug it all in!

Cross-faders

The *cross-fader* (see Figure 10-1) is a simple horizontal slider that enables you to change the music played out of the mixer from one input device to another. The cross-fader is a lot like the control on your shower that lets you adjust how much hot and cold water comes out. You can have only cold, only hot and many, many different combinations in between.

Figure 10-1:
A cross-fader on a mixer.

After you've towelled off thoroughly, go to your DJ setup. Tune A plays into Channel 1 on a two-channel mixer (and is usually the turntable or CD deck positioned on the left side of the mixer) and Tune B plays into Channel 2 (on the right-hand side of the mixer).

With the cross-fader positioned to the far left, you only hear Tune A. When the cross-fader is all the way to the right, all you hear is Tune B.

However, the cross-fader comes into its own when it's anywhere in between. If the cross-fader is in the middle, the output of the mixer is both Tune A and Tune B, and if the cross-fader is to the left of middle, you can hear more of Tune A than Tune B (and vice versa).

How much louder Tune A is than Tune B is dictated by something called the *cross-fader curve*. The cross-fader curve controls how quickly one tune gets louder as the other one gets quieter when you move the cross-fader from side to side. The following figures show some common cross-fader curves you'll encounter. Figure 10-2 shows a simple cross-fader curve.

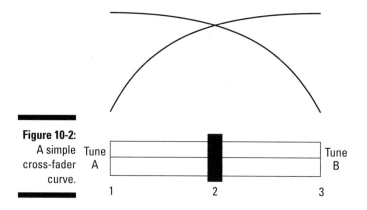

Figure 10-2:
A simple cross-fader curve.

✔ At Position 1 marked on the cross-fader, Channel 1 is at full and Channel 2 is silent.

✔ By Position 2, both tunes are playing at around 90 per cent of their loudest volume.

✔ By Position 3, Channel 2 is at its loudest and Channel 1 is silent.

The cross-fader curve in Figure 10-3 helps to stop both your tunes blaring out of the speakers simultaneously at near to full volume.

✔ At Position 1, Channel 1 is full and Channel 2 is off.

✔ At Position A, Channel 1 is still full; Channel 2 is starting to come in (playing at about 10 per cent of its full volume by this stage).

✔ At Position 2, both tunes are at 80 per cent of their normal volume.

✔ By Position B, Channel 2 is now playing at full volume and Channel 1 is playing at 10 per cent volume.

✔ And by Position 3, Channel 2 is playing at full volume, with Channel 1 silent.

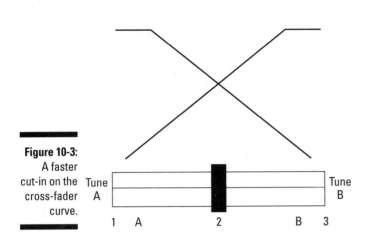

Figure 10-3: A faster cut-in on the cross-fader curve.

Although this curve is similar to the first example, the straight line in this 'curve' gradually brings in one tune while removing the other one, whereas the swooping curve in the first example kept the tunes playing together for longer at a higher volume level.

Figure 10-4 shows the cross-fader curve preferred by many scratch DJs due to the speed at which you can cut in (make audible) the second tune at full volume.

- ✔ Position 1 shows Channel 1 playing full and Channel 2 is off.
- ✔ At Position A, both channels are playing full volume, and it only took a small amount of cross-fader movement to get there.
- ✔ This situation stays constant until Position B.
- ✔ At position 3, Channel 2 is full and Channel 1 has been removed.

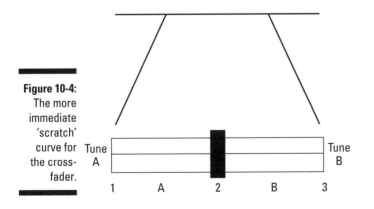

Figure 10-4: The more immediate 'scratch' curve for the cross-fader.

You can also get a straight X-shape curve, which fades one tune out while bringing the other tune in at exactly the same ratio throughout the move. If Tune A is playing at 10 per cent, Tune B is at 90 per cent – if Tune A is at 73 per cent, Tune B plays at 27 per cent, and so on. (That's likely to be the cross-fader curve of your shower control too.)

A number of mixers come with just one kind of cross-fader curve, but most mid- to high-range mixers have a way to change the cross-fader curve by selecting pre-defined curves with a switch or with a control that enables you to create any kind of curve you like.

Channel-faders

DJ SPEAK

Channel-faders are the up and down faders that control how loud the music comes out of the mixer when the cross-fader is all the way over to one side, allowing the full power of a channel to play.

Taking another visit to your bathroom, think of channel-faders like the taps on the bathroom shower. Even though the water mixer (the cross-fader) is set to only let out cold water, if you don't turn on the cold tap, nothing comes out. So although the cross-fader lets you mix hot and cold water to the right temperature through the showerhead, the channel-faders control how much hot and how much cold water is available to mix together in the first place.

Getting back into the DJ booth then, the ability to vary the volume of the two channels, as well as mixing with the cross-fader, gives incredibly precise control over the mix. If you use the channel-faders in conjunction with the cross-fader to their extremes, you get the kind of curve shown in Figure 10-5.

Figure 10-5:
The cross-fader curves are unlimited when you use the channel-faders as well as the cross-fader.

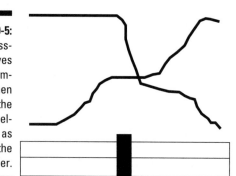

Chapter 16 covers how to use your channel-faders to help your mixes sound really professional.

Headphone monitoring

The headphone section on the mixer is simple, but extremely important. Plug your headphones into the quarter-inch jack socket (if you're using a mini-jack, similar to the one on the end of your iPod headphones, you need a converter from the mini jack to quarter-inch jack to do this). Use the headphone volume control (which you don't need to set to full, please) along with the cue controls to listen to individual channels on your mixer (or a few of them together at the same time).

Headphone cue controls are split into two functions:

✔ Choosing what plays into your headphones

✔ Controlling how you hear the music in your headphones

Each channel on the mixer has a *Cue* or *PFL* (pre-fade listen) button assigned to it. When you press it, you can listen to the music in that channel without needing to play it through the main speakers. This function means that you can listen to any combination of any of the channels on the mixer at any one time. You can listen to Channel 1 on its own or with Channel 2 playing at the same time – or have Channels 1, 2, 3 and 4 all playing in the headphones. That might not sound very good, though.

You use headphones to find the start point of the next tune you want to play (called the *cue*), but beatmatching DJs also use them to make sure that the beats of both tunes are playing at the same time. This is called beatmatching, and it's the fundamental concept of house/trance DJing. Go to Chapter 14 to discover how DJs use headphones to match beats, and how the following ways of listening to music in the headphones can give you more control over the beatmatching process:

✔ **Headphone mix** enables you to play both tunes in stereo in your headphones, and a mini cross-fader or rotary knob gives you control over how loud each tune plays over the other (exactly like a cross-fader, except for your headphones). Headphone mix is especially useful because you can check how the two tunes sound playing together before letting the dance floor hear, and check that the beats of both tunes really are playing in time without anyone else hearing.

✔ **Split cue** sends one selected channel into the left earpiece of the headphones and another one into the right earpiece (as if you're listening to one tune in the headphones and have one ear to the dance floor). Split cue is a lifesaver when you don't have a monitor (speaker) in the DJ booth and the delay in sound from the dance floor speakers makes it hard to check whether the bass beats are playing at the same time.

EQs and kills

The *EQ controls* on a mixer enable you to increase or decrease three broad musical frequency bands: high, mid and low. The amount of change is measured in decibels (abbreviated as dB), and although mixers let you increase the EQ bands by +12 decibels or more, the amount they take out is actually of more importance to the DJ.

A cut setting on an EQ *pot* (a professional term short for *potentiometer*, which describes a rotary knob) removes the EQ frequency band from the tune completely. So when you cut the bass from a tune, all you hear is the tinny *hi-hats* (the *tchsss tchsss* sound made by the cymbals on a drum kit) and the *mid-range* (which carries the vocals and main melody of a tune).

The difference between an EQ pot and a *kill switch* is that an EQ enables the DJ to vary the amount of frequency to cut out, from just a little to the entire band, whereas a kill switch instantly removes the bass frequency at the push of a button, and then puts it back in when pressed again. No grey areas here!

EQs on a mixer serve two purposes. Firstly, they let you make the tune you're playing sound great; if the bass is too loud through the speakers, you can reduce it using the bass EQ, and if the music sounds a little too shrill, reducing the high and mid controls can fix the problem.

But apart from sound processing, EQs are essential for the seamless mix DJ who wants the transition (mix) between tunes to be as smooth as possible. If you get a chance to study DJs such as Paul Oakenfold, Tiesto and Sasha closely, you see just how much they use the EQs to aid their mixes. Chapter 16 has a whole section dedicated to using EQs to create seamless mixes, and Chapter 21 has a section about sound processing with EQs.

Input VU monitoring

Your mixer has a VU (volume unit) display to show the strength of the signal going *out* of the mixer, and an important enhancement of this feature is the option of checking the strength of the signal coming *in* to the mixer.

The normal output display on a mixer is two lines of LED lights, one showing the strength of the left-hand side of the stereo music, the other showing the right-hand side. Some mixers offer the DJ an option to change this display into the left line of LEDs showing the input strength of Channel 1, and the right line displaying Channel 2's input strength. Or, in the case of mixers like Pioneer's DJM-600, a separate line of LEDs next to each channel's EQ controls shows the strength of the input signal – leaving the Master Output display to always show how strong a signal you're sending out of the mixer.

Gain controls

Gain controls aren't just another volume control. Don't regard them as a way to affect the volume *going out* of the mixer: look at them purely as a way to affect the music *coming in* to the mixer.

If the input level LED for Channel 1 is at zero decibels, occasionally flashing into the red +3 decibel area, and Channel 2's LEDs show that its input signal is well below zero decibels, you use the gain control to increase the input level of Channel 2 to match Channel 1. If you mix from Channel 1 to Channel 2 without matching the input levels, you'll notice a drop in volume even with both channel-faders set to full. Gain controls (and input level LEDs) let you get this level right at the input stage, instead of panicking at the output stage when it's too late.

If your bass EQ is set to *cut* or *kill* when checking the channel's input level, it can appear a lot weaker than it really is. When you then bring the bass frequencies back into the music, your speakers won't be very happy with you, because you'll be playing far too loudly, and you may damage them (or at the very least, your reputation!). For more information on how to use input levels to create an even volume to the mix, head to Chapter 13.

Balance and pan controls

The *balance control* alters which speaker the sound comes from. When the control is to the left music only comes out of the left speaker, the reverse for the right-hand side and when the control is in the middle music comes out through both speakers, much like the balance on your home stereo.

However, some mixers have balance controls (sometimes called *pan* controls) on each channel rather than having a control that affects the mixer's Master Output. Why do you want balance controls on each channel? Sometimes (for example) if you have one channel panned all the way to the left and another all the way to the right, and bring the cross-fader into the middle, the effect of having one tune playing in one ear and another in the other ear can sound really good (if you've chosen the right tunes and both bass beats are playing at the same time). This feature works well with plain beats, especially if you constantly change the balance settings during the mix.

Hamster switch

Mixers used by scratch DJs often have a *hamster switch*, which simply reverses the control of the cross-fader (but the channel-faders remain the same). So instead of hearing Channel 1 when the cross-fader is all the way to the left, you now hear Channel 2, and vice versa. Check out Chapter 17 for more information about scratching and why the hamster switch exists – and why it has such an odd name.

Punch and transform controls

If you have the cross-fader completely on Channel 2 (what I call *closed off* onto Channel 2), pressing the *Punch* button changes the output to Channel 1 until released. Note, however, that some mixers don't take account of where you leave the channel-faders, only where you set the gain controls, so make sure you set those gain controls properly otherwise you may experience a huge drop (or rise) in volume when you punch in the other channel!

Transform controls were designed as an advancement to the technique of cutting a mixer's channel in and out of the mix (quickly hearing it, then not hearing it) using the Line/Phono switch. When using turntables, flick this switch over to Line and the music cuts out (for CD, flick it to Phono). The problem is that you often hear a clicking or popping sound when you switch, so transform controls were designed to do the same thing but won't pop or click when you use them. (The Punch button does the same thing as the transform controls if nothing is playing through the other channel).

Built-in effects

Although some mixers offer sound effects such as sirens and horns, I don't really mean this type of effect. Rather than having to use an external effects processor, mixers like the Pioneer DJM-600 have built-in effects like flanger, echo, delay, transform, pitch, loop and reverb assignable (able to add the effect) to each channel or the Master Output. These effects are a great way of adding a new sound to the music, or during the transition between tunes.

The most common effects you find on mixers are as follows:

- **Delay** repeats a selected part of the tune while the rest of the tune is still playing. Especially useful for repeating musical hooks in quieter parts of tracks or for doubling-up bass beats to play three bass beats where only two would normally play.

- **Echo** is similar to the delay feature, except the music fades away when repeating to create an echo effect. Useful again in quieter parts of the tune (or at the very end of your DJ set).

- **Auto pan** swaps the music from the left to the right speaker (and back).

- **Transformer** cuts the entire sound in and out at a speed you set. A good way to create a stuttering effect as the music builds up or during a scratch (see Chapter 17 for how to manually perform a transform).

✔ **Filter** manipulates the sound frequencies of the music to alter its tonal quality by removing and then replacing a range of frequencies. The filter isn't the same as using the EQs on the mixer to kill and replace frequencies, though, because a specific sound is also added to it.

If you've ever been to the beach and held a shell to your ear, the ambient, resonating sound you hear from the shell is similar to the sweeping effect as the filter removes and replaces frequencies in the music – as if the shell had a tiny DJ crab inside it . . .

The filter effect doesn't always sweep in and out. Certain filters enable you to select a range of frequencies, add the resonating filter effect and then keep the music in that same state until you turn off or alter the filter.

✔ **Flanger** makes a 'swooshy' sound like playing music through a jet engine as it climbs and falls, while retaining the full frequency range (and usually boosting the bass frequencies) of the music. The most over-used effect ever (but really cool the first time you use it!).

✔ **Reverb** adds reverberation to the music so that it sounds as if you're playing in a massive hall. Turn it up to full and the sound is like listening to music inside the toilets at a club.

✔ **Pitch shifter** can change the pitch of the music. Useful to try to match the pitch of another tune, but mixers vary in their ability to do this well.

You encounter other built-in effects, as well, of course. I took this list of effects from the Pioneer DJM-600 that I use.

Effects Send and Return

The Effects Send and Return enables you to send just one channel from the mixer to be processed by an external effects processor (like the Pioneer EFX-1000, for example), to add whatever groovy effects you want, and then it's returned in the blink of an eye for you to use it in the mix. All the while, the other channels on the mixer are unaffected. A detailed description of Send and Return connections with an effects processor is in Chapter 13.

Built-in samplers

Samplers are great because they enable you to take a short vocal sample or a few bars of beats from a tune and extend or introduce a mix by playing these samples. DJ mixers with built-in samplers can record short samples – for anything longer, you need to buy a separate sampler.

An example of how you can use a sampler is with the 1990s song 'Nighttrain' by Kadoc. At the very beginning of the record, James Brown says 'All aboard, the Nighttrain'. By recording that vocal sample into the sampler, and playing it a while before you start the mix, you create anticipation of what's yet to come. I used to do this as a scratch (see Chapter 17 for how), but the sampler made this a lot easier and simpler to do.

The better samplers have loop controls on them, where the sample you take is looped seamlessly over and over again, meaning you can really extend the mix. A good use of this technique is to record four bars of beats into the sampler and loop them to extend the outro of a tune, or to add beats over a breakdown to keep the energy going to the dance floor.

Built-in beat counters

Beat counters give you a visual display of how many beats per minute (BPM) are in a tune you're playing. Two channel mixers with built-in beat counters may have a counter for each channel. Multiple channel mixers can have a counter for each channel, or two counters that you can assign (choose to use) to any channel you like. This can be helpful for beatmatching DJs. By visually comparing the BPMs of two tunes, you know how much to speed up or slow down the next tune to match the BPM of the one currently playing.

A beat counter that displays the BPM to one decimal point (for example, 132.7 BPM) is more accurate than one that only shows whole numbers. If one tune is playing at 131.6 BPM and another is playing at 132.4, and the counter simply rounds up and down those figures to show them both as 132 BPM, it's wrong by 0.8 BPM, which is a huge difference when beatmatching.

Beat counters can be a real help to the beginner to let you understand what's happening with the beats and tune your ear to gauge when a tune is running too fast or too slow, but they can also be a real hindrance. If you're going to refer to a beat counter as you develop your beatmatching skills, you need the discipline *not* to rely on it. Otherwise, the first time you stand behind a mixer that doesn't have a beat counter (which is going to be quite often in clubs), and are expected to beatmatch using just your ears, you'll find it very hard and possibly get into a lot of trouble!

Beat light indicators

Beat light indicators are little LED lights that flash in time with the beat of the tune. By looking at the lights of two tunes flashing together (or not together), you can tell whether the beats are playing at the same time.

Beat light indicators are very nice to watch in the dark, but personally, I think that they're next to useless when compared to your ears.

MIDI controls

Although MIDI (musical instrument digital interface) can connect a mixer to an effects processor, allowing control over how you activate these effects, the biggest application of MIDI control has become how it helps to control various aspects of software on a computer directly from the DJ's mixer.

Using MIDI connections, you can trigger samples, control effects and playback and locate cue points on the mixer instead of via the mouse and keyboard (or other separate hardware). The capabilities of MIDI on a DJ mixer grow with each new equipment release and have become limited only by the scope of the software.

Choosing the Right Mixer

Different mixers suit different kinds of DJs. If you're looking to spend a lot of money on your mixer, make sure that you're buying one with the right functions on it depending on your mixing style:

- **The seamless mix DJ** needs a mixer that helps every mix sound perfect by controlling the sound levels and the sound frequencies of each tune during the mix.

- **The scratch DJ** needs to chop and change from track to track using a slick cross-fader on the mixer.

- **The effects DJ** isn't content with the sound of the tunes as the original producers intended, and wants the option to add a series of different sounds and effects to the music, making a new sound unique to that performance.

- **The wedding DJ** uses a mixer as a means to change between a wide range of different styles of music.

The seamless mix DJ

The club or house mixer is used by house DJs, trance DJs, drum-and-bass DJs – anyone who wants full control of how the music sounds when they're mixing to create the best transition from one tune to another. So another name for this type of DJ is a seamless mix DJ.

If you're a seamless mix DJ, the important features you need on a mixer are:

- EQs to fully control the sound of each tune, with the ability to cut or kill the frequencies to help tidy up the mix.

✔ Multiple channels so that you can use more than two CD decks, MP3 players, or turntables at the same time.

✔ Headphone monitoring, which needs to be as comprehensive as possible, with headphone mix, and ideally split cue for when no DJ booth monitor is available.

✔ Easy-to-use (and see) metering that shows the input level strength as well as the mixer's output level.

✔ Beat counters and built-in effects, though not essential, are a great tool for the seamless DJ.

The house mixer can be quite large, and has the controls spread out to remove the risk of accidentally pressing something if the mixer controls were crammed together.

The scratch DJ

Although scratch DJs can use same mixers as seamless mix DJs, *battle mixers* are designed specifically for scratching. With only two channels, they make good use of space to allow the DJ unobstructed control of the channel-faders and of a robust, fluid cross-fader.

Although by no means essential, extra controls such as Punch and Transform buttons, along with hamster switches and cross-fader curve controls, are becoming standard tools for the scratch DJ. You can find built-in effects and BPM counters on a lot of scratch mixers, though I think I'd fall over if I had to use all that lot and scratch at the same time!

The design of the battle mixer is as important as the features it offers (see Figure 10-6). Because the most important controls on a scratch mixer are the cross-fader and the channel-faders, these three controls take up a lot of space and are kept clear of any obstructions. To this end, the headphone input is located on the front of the mixer (often along with the cross-fader curve adjust) so it's not poking up from the mixer, where you're going to smack it with your hands one day!

The most important part of any battle mixer is the cross-fader and how it performs. Because you make a lot of fast movements with the fader when scratching, any resistance on the cross-fader is not a good thing, so you need to have as slick and fluid a cross-fader as possible.

Scratching is incredibly taxing on a cross-fader, so it needs to be durable and replaceable (or at least cleanable until you can afford a new cross-fader). New designs of non-contact, optical and magnetic cross-faders from manufacturers such as Rane and Stanton are increasing the lifespan, durability and ease of use of the cross-fader. But don't worry, the standard cross-fader on a battle mixer is good enough for developing the basic skills.

Figure 10-6:
The Vestax
VMX-002XL.
Note the
headphone
socket on
the front
(bottom
right).

The effects DJ

The EQs and design of the club mixer for the seamless mix DJ are perfect for the effects DJ, although frequently, the effects DJ demands more than the built-in effects available on the club mixer.

In this case, the Send and Return function on the mixer may be especially important because it enables you to send individual channels to an effects processor and add whatever effects you want, without having to affect the entire output of the mixer.

However, the effects DJ is becoming more likely to embrace the effects processing built into software in a digital DJ setup than needing to use an external sound processor. In this instance, a mixer with good MIDI capability on it will be of great creative benefit, giving instant access to effects in the software and enhanced control over playback of the music.

The rock/party/wedding DJ

The music these DJs play is more important than the way they mix it together. A lot of creative DJs out there play this kind of music that demands features similar to the seamless and effects DJ, but a large number of these DJs care more about the music and just want to be able to fade from tune to tune. As such, an expensive, feature-laden mixer isn't required for most party DJs. Multiple channels can be useful if you're going to use more than two CD players, MP3 players or turntables, but normally a simple setup requiring two or three input channels at most suffices.

Controlling the sound using EQs when mixing from tune to tune to make it seamless isn't such an important feature for the party DJ compared to the seamless DJ. However, EQs can help remove some bass or add some high frequencies when you're trying to overcome bad sound in different sizes of venues. A global EQ on the amp, which just affects the entire sound output, is probably enough, but you may also consider the option to change the sound for each tune played and therefore need EQs for each channel on the mixer.

EQ controls on the microphone are important to help to sharpen your voice as you talk over the music, enabling you to control the evening with clarity.

It goes without saying that the microphone you use should be a good quality one in the first place. One of the workhorse microphones that (in my opinion) you'll never go wrong buying is the Shure SM58; it sounds great, is simple to connect and it's almost indestructible (though please don't try to prove me wrong).

Built-in beat counters are all but redundant, because the party set list has wide-ranging BPMs. From Tom Jones' 'Delilah' at 64 BPM to Ricky Martin's 'Livin' La Vida Loca' at 178 BPM, the variance is so large that it's near impossible to beatmatch them! Check out Chapter 16 for a good trick on how you can manage this, though.

As to built-in effects, apart from using the reverb effect on your voice when speaking to the people on the dance floor, they won't be of much use to a lot of party DJs. Although I'd love to hear a flanger effect running through 'Build Me Up, Buttercup' . . .

Servicing Your Mixer

Although your turntable or CD player is the piece of equipment with the most moving mechanical parts, the piece that's most likely to suffer from problems first – if you don't keep it clean and treat it well – is your mixer.

You need to look at two things in order to keep your mixer in proper working condition. Clean all the dust away from the rotary controls, and clean and lubricate the faders.

You need the following tools to clean your mixer properly:

- ✔ A can of compressed air
- ✔ Lubricant
- ✔ A screwdriver

Follow these steps to clean your mixer:

1. **If you can, pull the knobs off the rotary controls on the mixer.**

   Take them all off at the same time, place them next to the mixer and lay them out in the order that they've come off, so that you can replace each knob back onto the control it came from.

2. **Spray around each of the controls with the compressed air to blow away any dust that may be lodged in them.**

   You may also want to wipe the mixer carefully with a lint-free cloth to remove any stubborn dust particles after spraying.

3. **If you have a mixer that enables you remove the channel- and cross-faders, use a screwdriver to take them out one at a time (so you don't mix up where to replace them).**

   Dirt that may have worked its way in can cause crackles and sound bleeding (hearing the music quietly when it should be silent). To clean out dirt and dust, blow the compressed air into every crevice in the fader. Then spray the fader with a lubricant and replace it in the mixer.

   However, sometimes your faders still make crackle noises, are too stiff and start to malfunction, in which case many mixers are designed to allow you to buy replacement faders from your preferred DJ store.

4. **If your mixer doesn't have removable channel-faders and they sound crackly, try spraying compressed air and then cleaning lubricant into the slot in the mixer where the channel-fader pokes through.**

   However, you may be too late, and may not be able to reverse the damage yourself, meaning you'll have to send the mixer to get repaired – or more likely, buy a new mixer.

To keep this servicing to a minimum, keep your mixer clean and free of dirt, keep it covered when not in use and give the faders a quick lubrication every couple of months.

Chapter 11

Ear-Splitting Advice about Not Splitting Your Ears: Headphones

*T*he funny thing about headphones is that they're probably the most important part of your DJ setup because you can't mix properly without them, but, strangely, many DJs treat them as an afterthought.

The only time I've ever really panicked in the DJ booth was when I couldn't hear clearly through the cheap headphones I was using. I couldn't hear any bass, couldn't hear how the beats were playing together, and was effectively mixing 'blind' (or should that be 'deaf'?). If you've followed the same cheap path that I did, when you do start to demand more and want to get more suitable headphones, put some thought into what you need, and don't just get caught up in current fashion trends.

And no, your iPod earbuds won't do . . .

Choosing a Good Set of Headphones

As you advance your DJ skills you start to become aware of all the things that are holding you back from progressing. Cheap decks and a basic mixer are nearly always the first things to upgrade, but consider what your current headphones sound like. Can you hear a good, solid bass thump? Or are the mid-range frequencies drowning out the rest of the music so you can't find cue points for your rock tunes? Better headphones will improve your mixing and beatmatching a lot faster than a new mixer can.

The following six factors can help you when deciding what to buy:

- **Weight/Comfort:** Ideally, you're looking for headphones that are light-weight so they don't hurt your ears after sitting on your head for a couple of hours. That's not to say that lightest is best, though. If the headphones are too light, they may fall off when you lean forward to look down at the mixer, or they may be so light that they don't sit tightly over your ears, letting in a lot of external noise as a consequence.

  Because you may be wearing them for four hours at a time, the ear cups need to be soft and sit comfortably on your ears. The headphone band that joins the two ear pieces needs to be comfortable when worn on your head in a normal position, but still be just as comfortable when you twist the band backward to free one of your ears to hear the monitor (speaker) in the DJ booth.

- **Closed-back:** *Closed-back headphones*, like those shown in Figure 11-1, have seals around the outer parts of the ear cups so they don't let as much external sound through to your ears. In the DJ booth this enables you to clearly hear the next tune you want to play in the headphones despite the noise coming from the dance floor.

  The best style of headphones are closed-back and sit nice and tight on your ears, a bit like ear mufflers but with speakers inside!

Figure 11-1: The Technics RPDH1200 headphones with the closed-back design to the ear cups.

✔ **Wide frequency response:** At school you were probably taught your hearing ranged from 20 hertz (the deep, deep bass sounds) to 20,000 hertz (really high, hissy sounds). In reality, your hearing is closer to 20 hertz to 16,000 hertz, although children and dogs can hear up to 20,000 hertz.

Quality DJ headphones typically cover the frequencies from 5 hertz to 30,000 hertz, so they cover the bass and sub-bass ranges all the way through to the stuff only dogs and sound engineers can hear!

✔ **Low impedance:** If you don't know anything about impedance, it's okay, you don't need to, but it's all about electrical resistance. You only need to know to try to match the impedance of your headphones as closely as possible to the impedance of the mixer you use. A large mismatch can lead to distortion, unwanted noise and sometimes a drop in the maximum volume your headphones can play (all things you really don't need when DJing).

Fortunately, this isn't something to lose a night's sleep about, because most DJ equipment manufacturers are well aware of this issue and design their equipment within the same impedance range.

✔ **High sound pressure level:** *Sound pressure level* is just a way to describe how loud your headphones (and speakers in general) can play. You want your headphones to be able to play loud to let you cope with noisy DJ booths, but please remember you don't have to turn up your headphones too loud (see 'Remembering that the Volume Doesn't Have to Go Up to 11', later in this chapter).

Have a realistic budget when upgrading your headphones. If your current pair only cost £10, you won't benefit much by getting a pair for £30. Save up more money and start looking to spend around £100 on a set of Sony, Sennheiser, Technics or Pioneer headphones, which I think are the market leaders. Don't be fooled by fashion. Few people (apart from fellow DJs) care that you have the latest, best-looking headphones; they only care about the music!

Realising no one cares about headphones

I remember one night when Alex P did a guest spot at a club where I had a residency, and the other DJ (Dave Armstrong) and I were left wandering through the club, feeling a bit bored while waiting for him to finish (because, remember, DJs don't dance). At this time, the new Sony MDR-V700 DJ headphones had just come out, and they were the fashionable choice of the discerning DJ – including the two of us.

Thinking we were being really cool and funny, we both put on our headphones and wandered around the club, talking to people we passed, and had a bit of a laugh. I look back at the image now of two guys with matching headphones on their heads in the middle of a nightclub, with Dave trying to chat up all the girls, and I cringe. That said, I think Dave got some phone numbers . . .

These considerations play a major role in deciding what headphones you eventually buy, but other features are available that may yet swing your decision from one pair to another.

Single-sided, coiled cords

Coiled cords are the curly ones that you sometimes see guitarists use (Brian May from Queen uses a coiled guitar lead). By coiling the cable, manufacturers are able to offer a lot more length to the DJ without the danger of a long, dangling, straight cable that can bunch up on the floor and trip you up. You attach single-sided cables to only one earpiece, and the cable travels from one ear-cup to the other through the headband.

Only after spending an evening in the DJ booth with a pair of headphones that don't have single-sided cabling do you realise why this simple design is so important. By the end of the night's mixing, after repeatedly putting on and taking off your headphones, putting them down, picking them up, dropping them under the decks and so on, you'll have spun the cable round enough to almost strangle yourself as the two cables twist around your neck. A single-sided cord has nothing to wrap around, and stays out of the way, keeping you breathing happily for the rest of the evening.

A single-sided, coiled cord, such as the one on the Technics RPDJ1210 headphones that I use, is perfect for giving you a long, coiled cable, which allows you to move around in the DJ booth, and the single-sided cord means that you don't end up garrotting yourself by the end of the night!

Swivelling earpieces

Sometimes the headband on the headphones can feel slightly uncomfortable when you pull one of the ear cups back behind your ear to listen to the live sound. Swivelling ear cups mean that you can pull the ear cup behind your ear, but the headband stays across the middle of your head.

This setup is advantageous not only because of comfort, but because it reduces the stress on the headband. Cheap, plastic headphones (like the cheap ones I started with) can snap after you twist them backwards too many times.

User-replaceable parts

Sennheiser's HD25 and HD25SP headphones are designed to be completely modular, with each piece user-replaceable. This design means that you need never stress about these headphones breaking or malfunctioning. Provided you have the spare parts in your DJ bag, all you have to do is replace the broken part, and keep on mixing.

Having been in the position where someone wrenched the cable out of my headphones one evening when he stood on them (my fault for leaving them on the floor), the opportunity to instantly replace the cable would've been fantastic. But because I didn't have headphones with user-replaceable parts, I had to mix with only one ear working for the rest of the night.

Sticking it to your ears

Figure 11-2 shows an example of a 'stick' headphone that has only one ear cup. By wedging the cup between your shoulder and your ear, you can cut out more external sound and hear the music a bit more clearly through the one earpiece. However, I still prefer traditional headphones, which let you do exactly the same thing and still give you the choice of hearing the music in stereo – and you won't end up with a strained neck from craning it to one side. DJs such as Fatboy Slim and David Morales have used this style of headphone with great success, and their heads don't loll to one side, so absolutely nothing is wrong with this design.

Figure 11-2:
The Stanton
DJ Pro
3000 STK
'stick' head-
phones.

Remembering that the Volume Doesn't Have to Go Up to 11

Please forgive the Spinal Tap quote (check out the film *This is Spinal Tap* if you don't understand the 'Up to 11' reference!), but the only person who knows you're playing the headphones at full volume is you – you can't show off to anyone because no one else can hear. You don't need music to be loud to enjoy it, and you certainly don't need to look forward to wearing hearing aids in your future.

As a drummer from age 10 who also used to go to loud rock concerts, some-one who used to go to clubs at least four times a week (and dance right next to the speaker, because it was somewhere to keep the drinks!) and a DJ from age 21 through to the current day, I've always surrounded myself with loud music. I pay the price for that now by having a constant ringing in my ears (something called *tinnitus*). Although it doesn't affect what I hear, you don't want to wake up in the middle of the night and just hear a ringing in your ears, believe me. Do everything you can to protect your ears. You are *not* invincible.

In addition to causing irreversible ear damage, if you play the music in your headphones too loud, you'll find mixing a lot harder. Beatmatching and find-ing cue points (see Chapter 14) are easier when you find the perfect level to listen to the headphones while the amp is still blaring out at 130 decibels.

When *beatmatching* you need to listen to two tunes at the same time to work out whether their bass beats are playing at the same time. The most common technique (single ear monitoring) involves listening to one tune in one ear through the headphones and the other tune in the other ear from the speakers or monitor in the DJ booth. Playing one tune so that it plays louder than the other makes it harder to concentrate on the bass drums from both tunes.

For more information on the single ear monitoring technique, and guidance on how to check that you've set the levels (volumes) of both the amplifier and the headphones correctly, go to Chapter 14.

Using Earplugs

Earplugs can make a world of difference to your future hearing and the qual-ity of your mixing. I encourage you to use earplugs when practising in the bedroom so you're used to using them when it comes to DJing in a club. I only wear one earplug during a mix, protecting the ear that listens to the music from the monitor, while the other ear has some protection from the headphone that's covering it.

The decibel level in a club can be upwards of 100 decibels (decibels, abbreviated as *dB*, are a way of calculating how loud sound is), and as a DJ who gets work four or five times a week (if you're lucky) you're exposed to this level more often than any clubber. So although I recommend using one ear plug in your ear open to the monitor when you're mixing, I strongly suggest that you plug the other one in when you've taken the headphones off, in order to protect the other ear.

Even though I don't have an earplug in my headphone monitoring ear, that ear benefits from the protection given to the other ear. Because the earplug reduces the loudness of the music that enters the ear that's open to the monitor, you can reduce the volume at which the headphones are playing. If you didn't lower the volume of the headphones, it would be harder to concentrate on the music from the monitor, making it harder to beatmatch.

The noise levels and acoustic sound inside a club can make hearing specific parts of a tune quite difficult, no matter how good the monitor in the DJ booth is. Maybe you want to hear a subtle change in the melody, or you want to hear the hi-hat cymbals as they change, or you just want to hear the bass drum beats stand out from the rest of the tune. You can sometimes have difficulty picking out these parts with the combination of sound from the dance floor and the monitor, and you may (wrongly) consider turning up the monitor in the DJ booth to try to hear the music better.

You experience this difficulty because the sound waves from the dance floor and from your monitor in the booth mix together, making it harder for you to pick out and concentrate on the parts of the song you need to. Using an earplug means that the sound waves have to travel through the foam or rubber before they get into your ear canal, so the music sounds a lot clearer. Wearing an earplug is like running a brush through tangled hair. It's much easier to separate the hair if it's been brushed (or filtered in the earplug case), and pick only the parts you'd like to concentrate on. (Just make sure that the person whose hair you're stroking is happy with this!)

The basic foam earplugs that you get from the chemist cost about £1 for three pairs and aren't designed specifically for listening to music. They're designed more for getting to sleep when the person sleeping next to you is doing an impression of a sawmill. They do a very good job at cutting out high volume levels but aren't good at retaining the quality of the music (they don't let through the high frequencies very well, so they're like sending the person with tangled hair to get it all cut off to fix the problem).

If you think that the cheap foam earplugs aren't letting you hear what you need to hear in the music, you have two options – buy more expensive ear plugs off the shelf or get some professionally made for you:

✔ **Off the shelf:** You can find lots of great designs for earplugs that try to maintain the quality of the sound that enters your ears; like Elacin Er-20s (which I use) or Hocks Noisebrakers (shown in Figure 11-3). Noisebrakers embrace the laws of physics to bounce the sound coming into the earplug back out again, which has the effect of not letting anything over 80 decibels into your ears without sacrificing the quality of what you're listening to. They cost about £15, so are a step up in price from the basic foam ones, but they do work well, and save your ears while still making it easier to mix.

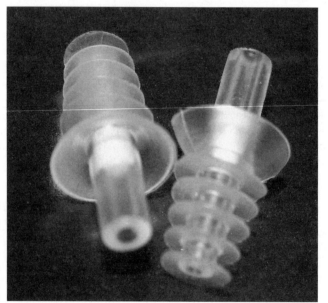

Figure 11-3:
Hocks
Noise-
brakers
earplugs.

✔ **Custom made:** Custom-made ear plugs from companies such as Etymotic and Advanced Communication Solutions (ACS) are costly (around £165 for the ACS ER-15s), but they have a superior ability to maintain sound quality while reducing the volume level (see Figure 11-4). The company uses an impression of your ear cavity to make an earplug that fits snugly into your ears, and your ears only.

Figure 11-4:
ACS custom-made ER-15 earplugs.

For more information about earplugs, check out www.earplugstore.com, and for more information about tinnitus and taking care of your ears, check out www.deafnessresearch.org.uk.

Chapter 12

Letting Your Neighbours Know That You're a DJ: Amplifiers

In This Chapter

▶ Choosing the right amplification for your wallet and environment

▶ Getting to grips with connecting it all up

▶ Keeping the sound down to save your hearing, and your neighbours' sanity

*E*ach stage of the DJ equipment chain is vital. Without the amplifier and speakers, you'd be the only person to hear how good a DJ you are. In this chapter, I cover the various methods of amplification, the best way to connect and place your speakers, and how to play at a volume that won't get you ejected from the neighbourhood.

Choosing Suitable Amplification

You need to choose a method of amplification that's suitable to the size of room you're playing in, and also for the size of your wallet – which are both important factors. The key word here is *suitable*. If you're just in your bedroom practising at a moderate volume, you won't have much need of a £3,000, 1,000-watt amplifier and set of speakers, so save your money!

The different ways you can amplify the signal from the mixer so you can hear it through speakers are via:

✓ **Your home stereo:** For the bedroom DJ who has a good-sounding stereo with a spare input into which you can plug the mixer.

✓ **Powered speakers (each speaker has a built-in amplifier):** If you don't have a home stereo, or the one you have doesn't have a spare input, powered speakers are perfect as an all-in-one solution.

✓ **A separate amplifier and speakers:** This combination is the best choice if you have a large room/hall/club that you need to fill with music.

Settling on your home stereo

Your home stereo (or hi-fi) is probably the easiest and cheapest route to go down when you're just playing in the bedroom for practise, because you probably already own one. As long as you have a spare input channel on your hi-fi, and you can position the speakers close enough to your DJ setup that you can get a good sound from them, your home stereo is a very good option. Though a hi-fi may not be as loud as a separate amplifier, if you're playing in a modest-sized bedroom, it should be more than loud enough.

Don't sneer at the idea of using a hi-fi. They can have great sound quality, produce very loud volumes and may have a built-in recorder to record your mix sessions.

If you get the chance to buy a new hi-fi for this use, search for one that has a manual graphic equaliser on it, rather than relying on some pre-set nonsense about Hall, Big Hall, Stadium and Bread Bin to approximate the different sounds that those areas would make. A manual *EQ* (equaliser) lets you adjust the sound to your taste, by controlling a range of different sound frequencies individually. If you plan to use the hi-fi to record your mix, full control of the sound is especially important (see Chapter 19 for guidance on recording great sounding mixes). Even if it means another £20, you won't regret your choice. Hi-fis with pre-set EQs are great for domestic, easy listening at home; but you're a DJ – you're far from domesticated.

The hi-fi also needs a spare input on the back of it to plug in your mixer. If you only have CD and Phono inputs on the back, you have to use the CD input (Phono inputs are only for direct connection of a turntable). If you already have a CD player plugged into the hi-fi, you'll need to unplug the CD player and plug in your mixer each time you want to use do some DJing, which can get tiresome, so try to pick a hi-fi with a separate AUX (auxiliary) input to plug your mixer into if buying a new one.

The length of the cable between the hi-fi unit and the speakers can also affect your choice of purchase. For example, I have a Sony hi-fi with less than a metre's worth of speaker cable between the base unit and each of the speakers. I have no plans to use it with my decks, but the length of cable provided is useless for DJ use because I can't get the speakers either side of the decks without needing to sit the base unit on top of my mixer!

Purchasing powered speakers

If you don't have an amplifier or don't want to tie up an input on your hi-fi with your mixer, *powered speakers* (also knows as *active monitors*) are a good alternative. Powered speakers are the same as normal speakers, except they don't use a separate amplifier; each speaker has its own, built-in amplifier so you can connect the output of the mixer directly to the speakers.

Consider power needs if using this kind of amplification. You may need to connect each speaker to its own power supply, or power both speakers from one power unit. Make sure that wherever you intend to sit the speakers you have a power point close by.

If at all possible, to maintain audio quality don't cross the power cable over any of the audio cables, because this may cause electrical interference. You probably won't have any problems if you do, but if you can get into the habit of properly laying the cables between two pieces of equipment now, you'll know to keep the speaker cable away from power leads if you're ever connecting a lot of speakers and amplifiers for a party or club night. The volumes involved at those events may reveal the electrical interference.

Powered speakers are very popular in the DJ booth as booth monitors. The volume control for this monitor is usually situated somewhere accessible on the side or back of the cabinet, which is perfect because you can turn it up or down whenever needed (especially if the mixer doesn't have a separate booth level control on it). Powered monitors in the DJ booth also don't tie up an entire amplifier for the sake of one speaker, making good financial sense. See 'Working with Monitors', later in this chapter, for more about booth monitors.

For bedroom use, powered speakers can range in quality (and price) from budget monitors such as those by Ion and Numark, which cost around £40 a pair and have an acceptable sound (though to my mind they're lacking a bit in bass thump), to great-sounding powered speakers such as those made by KRK, Alesis, JBL and RCF, which can cost anywhere between £300 and £6,000 for a pair!

Good quality, surround-sound powered speakers that you usually use with computers can sometimes be an option too.

Opting for separates

A powerful amplifier with huge separate speakers can be overkill in the bedroom. Five hundred watts of music can be more than you need even in a large hall, so if you buy a high-rated amplifier and speakers and turn up the volume to full, don't be surprised if your neighbours come knocking on the door!

Both the amplifier and the speaker have a power rating, which is measured in *watts* (abbreviated as *W*). The higher the number of watts, the louder you can play the music. Generally speaking, the rating on the back of your *amp* (short for amplifier) tells you the maximum sustained output that the amp can produce. On speakers, however, you may see two ratings, the *average* and the *peak* rating. The average rating (also known as *RMS*) refers to the maximum sustained output that your speakers can handle. The peak rating refers to how much power they can handle momentarily without risk of damage.

In non-tekky talk, think about a trampoline. How low the membrane on a trampoline is to the ground when you're standing still on it would be the average rating: it's happy at this level, and nothing's really going to go wrong with it. When you start jumping on the trampoline, as you land the membrane gets a lot closer to the ground momentarily. How close the membrane can get to the ground before suffering damage is the peak rating of your trampoline.

The peak value is always higher than the average value, and is why manufacturers like to print the peak in their documentation – it makes the speaker look more powerful.

When matching up an amplifier for use with your speakers, it's safer to make sure that the power of the amplifier is less than the average rating of the speakers. No matter how loud the amp goes, it shouldn't be able to blow the speaker this way. If you *do* want to choose an amp that's more powerful than the average output of the speaker, make sure not to buy an amp that's more powerful than the peak rating of the speaker. Even if you make a promise to yourself that you'll never turn the amp up to ten, you can't say the same for your friends, or your drum-and-bass-loving cat.

Allowing a power margin for error

Choosing the power rating of the amps and speakers, especially when considering a lot of power for a hall, or club setup, takes a little forethought and margin for error.

If you're looking to buy a setup that would give you 200 watts of power, the best option isn't buying a 200-watt amplifier and speakers with an average rating of 200 watts, nor is it buying two 100-watt amplifiers to make up a total of 200 watts of sound.

The preferred way to set up this amount of power is to buy three 100-watt amplifiers and three sets of 100-watt speakers, and run them all at two-thirds of their output level. Running two amplifiers at full volume for too long is running the risk of one, or both, breaking down – but three amps at two-thirds of their power will run happily for a long time. And even if one of them did blow, you'd still only lose one-third of the power, instead of all or half of the power in the other two examples.

Table 12-1 is a general guide to the room size, occupancy and power rating you may need for different situations. This guide isn't a set-in-stone rule, and you may want more than suggested to give you a little 'headroom' of power, in case you want to go louder.

Table 12-1   Amplifier Power Needed for Different Room Sizes

Room and Occupancy	Power Needed
Empty(ish) bedroom (you, your bed, your decks and the cat)	20–40 watts
Full(ish) bedroom (a few friends came for a visit)	40–60 watts
Big room or small, half-full hall (back room in a pub)	80–150 watts
Large hall, half full (local Scout hall, and so on)	150–300 watts
Large hall, lots of people (phew, they came!)	500–800 watts

You may have noticed that the number of people in the room affects the amount of power you need. People are very greedy. Not only do they raid your fridge for beer and food, but their bodies also absorb sound waves, robbing some of the volume from the room. The more people that turn up, the louder you have to play the music to be heard at the same volume! The good thing is that even though you have to turn up the sound a bit, the soaking of the stray sound waves by the crowd can improve the sound on the dance floor.

As well as counting the people on the dance floor, when you're choosing the amount of amplification for an event take a look at what's around you; the decor and the floor are just as important as the size and capacity of the room. A room with wooden floors and wooden or mirrored walls bounces sound waves around the room, making the music sound a lot louder. A room with carpet flooring that has big, thick curtains in it does just the opposite, absorbing a lot of the sound waves; so you may need a touch more power.

If you want to know how to connect multiple sets of speakers into your amplifiers (which is essential knowledge for club systems and some mobile DJs), check out www.recess.co.uk.

Working with Monitors

Your booth monitor is your link to what's really happening on the dance floor and can make the difference to your night going well, or going to you-know-where. Without hearing the exact audio that's coming from the mixer at the exact moment it comes from the mixer, you'll have a really hard time beatmatching. In the bedroom, the 'dance floor' sound and the music you hear in the 'monitor' are the same thing (usually because they *are* the same thing), but in a club, the two sounds are a bit different.

The booth monitor is like your health. You don't miss it until you don't have it any more. It not only lets you gauge how the music sounds playing to the dance floor, but also helps with the accuracy of your beatmatching.

Working with the speed of sound

This is where the DJ booth monitor comes in. The monitor is often a pair of speakers either side of the DJ, but in some cases, is just a single speaker positioned to the left or right of the DJ. A monitor right next to your ears cuts the audio delay from ¹⁄₁₆ th of a second to ¹⁄₂₅₆ th of a second (if it's a metre away), which is more than acceptable.

Positioning your monitor

Unless you live in a mansion, you're unlikely to have to deal with any delay in the bedroom from your speakers to where you have your decks set up. If you do live in an oversized room that's causing delay similar to working in a club, ask your butler to bring one of the speakers closer to you. Sarcasm aside, if bringing a speaker closer to you isn't an option, then you can hook up a separate booth monitor (maybe a powered speaker) to play right next to your DJ setup, or you can add another pair of speakers to your existing setup and place them next to your homemade DJ booth.

The monitor needs to be close enough to counteract any delay from the dance floor, but also overpower any music from the dance floor that you may still hear in the DJ booth. Keeping the speaker close and facing you gives you the best clarity. Too far away and you may find it harder to pick out a solid bass thump or the crisp hi-hats and snare drum that you use as reference when beatmatching (see Chapter 14).

The perfect position for a monitor in the DJ booth is 1 to 2 metres from the mixer, slightly in front of you, at head height and with the speaker turned in to point directly at you. Assuming that your speaker has the *bass driver* (the big speaker) at the bottom and the *tweeter* (which plays the high frequencies) at the top, this position is perfect for getting the best sound quality from your monitor.

If the monitor is too high, the bass driver dominates the tweeter, drowning out a lot of the high frequencies from the music. If the monitor is too low, aimed at your waist, the bass is lost, leaving a shrill, unclear sound dominated by the high-frequency tweeter that's at head height. Turning the monitor on its side so both the tweeter and bass driver are at the same height helps to prevent either eventuality.

For your bedroom setup you may not have as much room or control over where you can put the speakers. The two things to keep the same as in the club DJ booth are that the speakers are in front of you and pointing toward your ears, and that you try not to set the speakers on the same piece of furniture that your decks are on. If the vibrations from the speaker cause the turntable to vibrate, you'll generate feedback. If you're using CDs, you may cause the CD player to skip with the bass vibrations.

Noise Pollution: Keeping an Ear on Volume Levels

Many reasons come to mind as to why you shouldn't play your music loud all the time, but hearing damage (which I cover in Chapter 11), neighbour relations and the quality of your mixes are paramount.

Protecting your ears

Keeping the volume of your monitor at the lowest functional level protects your ears and reduces any risk of distortion from the headphones or the monitor.

One of the most popular ways to cue up the next tune (get it ready to play) and match the bass beats of two records is to use a technique called *single-ear monitoring*. This technique is when you have one ear open to the music from the monitor, playing the *live* sound from the amplifier, and the other ear has one of the headphone cups on, listening to the *cued* song that you wish to play next. (For more information on this, check out Chapter 14.)

The volume of the music that comes into your head from the monitor needs to match the volume at which the headphones are playing into your other ear. Due to the proximity of the headphone to your ear, this is about perceived volume rather than trying to match the actual decibel level coming from the monitor in the DJ booth – because to do so would make you go deaf.

You only have to play the monitor loud enough to drown out the music from the dance floor, which helps the accuracy of your beatmatching. You may be surprised at how little it takes. After you've reached that level, try not to increase the volume, even if you're really getting into the music!

Neighbourhood watch

Keeping the music at a sensible level so that you don't go deaf or harm your mixing skills is important, but you also have your sense of social responsibility to think of. Not only may the rest of the people in your flat, house or building start to get a little irked when you play pounding bass beats at full volume for hours at a time, but the people in surrounding buildings may soon get fed up with the dull thudding noise coming from your house.

Getting spooked into turning down the bass

When I lived at home with my mum, I had a huge setup in my bedroom with six 100-watt speakers dotted around the room, which was on the ground floor of the house (no wonder with all that noise!). I used to spend hours playing my tunes, working out new mixes, having fun and improving my skills. I didn't always play the music really loud, and I hardly ever played it at full volume, but I had a huge subwoofer that made a heck of a thump every time the bass drum pounded.

Understandably, my next-door neighbour got fed up feeling the vibrations of the beats through the floor in his house – 30 feet away! Because a dual-car garage linked the houses, the vibrations travelled through the foundations of my house and into his house. All this disturbance led to him banging on the window of my room for ten minutes, getting increasingly frustrated while waiting for me to turn around and notice him. When I eventually did turn around and saw a (less than happy) face staring in through the window, it scared the life out of me! I thought it was a ghost against the window. I turned the bass down after that fright.

Realising that you only need one speaker

When you're DJing at home, you really only need the one speaker, and that's the one you use for the 'live ear' when using single ear monitoring to beat-match (your equivalent of a DJ booth monitor).

When a neighbour pointed out how annoying the bass of my subwoofer was, I put switches on all of my speakers so I was able to leave only the monitor speaker running. This meant that I could play the music just as loud as before, but because only one speaker was playing the volume that other people could hear was a lot lower, yet my perceived volume of the monitor stayed the same. Turning off the unnecessary subwoofer helped a lot too!

If you only have two speakers, you may not need to add switches to isolate one speaker. If your amplifier (or hi-fi) has a balance control, just pan the music so that the music only plays out of your preferred speaker (though if you use a hi-fi to record your mixes, this may result in the recording only playing out of one speaker too).

If you're thinking of adding switches to isolate your speakers, do some research into the best switch to use. I must admit, I used light switches, but they're not designed for audio signals and can add too much resistance to the signal from the amplifier to the speaker, even when just passing through the circuit. This resistance may only cause a drop in sound quality or volume, but in the worst case it may break your amplifier. Something as simple as the Hama LSP 204 (shown in Figure 12-1) can do the job a lot better for up to 100 watts of sound.

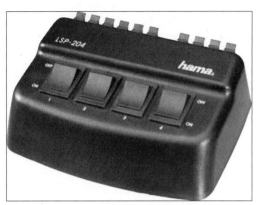

Figure 12-1:
Hama
LSP204 is a
great way to
control four
different
speakers.

Chapter 13

Plugging In, Turning On: Set-up and Connections

*Y*ou've spent a heap of cash on your new turntables, CD decks and a mixer, bought an amplifier loud enough to deafen the back row in a stadium and everything's turned on and ready to go – except you can't hear anything.

You simply have to know the chain of inputs and outputs to check that you've plugged all your equipment into the right place.

This chapter assumes you're connecting turntables, CD decks or MP3s directly to the mixer – digital DJ setups are a bit more complicated, so be sure to read Chapter 9 for information about these connections.

Getting Familiar with Connectors

DJ SPEAK

Before you connect your equipment together, getting familiar with the connections you're using is a good idea. The most common connection types you come across are RCA (also called *Phono*), XLR and quarter-inch jacks (also known as *TRS*). In order for music to play in stereo, you mostly encounter two of each of these for connecting your equipment. One cable and connector carries what you hear out of the left speaker; the other carries what you hear out of the right speaker. Quarter-inch jack plugs are also available as a single, stereo connector (as seen at the end of your DJ headphones).

Some turntables, CD decks and mixers use digital connections to keep audio quality at maximum. In order to make use of them, your mixer must have a digital input too. USB (universal serial bus) and Firewire are connections you see on computers, and along with S/PDIF (Sony/Philips Digital Interface Format) these digital connections combine both sides of the stereo sound and send it through one cable. The mixer then separates out the stereo sound and plays it back at crystal clear quality.

RCA/Phono connections

RCA connections are also known as Phono connections, but I'll continue to call them RCA to stop any confusion with the Phono/Line terminology for inputs on the back of the mixer.

RCAs are the most common connections you use as inputs and outputs to your DJ mixer. They come in pairs, one for each side of the stereo signal, and each of them is a different colour. The left signal cable is usually white, though it can be yellow or black, but the right-hand side of the audio signal is always red. The two 'R's make remembering which cable plugs into where easy; simply remember that Red = Right.

S/PDIF digital connections on DJ equipment often use the same RCA style of connection. These are usually coloured yellow (just to add confusion!).

XLRs

Used for amplifier connections and microphones, XLRs are the preferred connection for professional audio equipment because they're capable of reducing interference when using long cables, and because they lock into place so they can't accidentally pop out if a drunken customer falls on them.

XLR connections (see Figure 13-1) come in two different flavours:

- ✔ **Unbalanced** XLRs are the more common *pro-sumer* (a mixture of professional and consumer) XLR connection. An unbalanced XLR simply sends the audio signal through the cable, and any unwanted electrical or radio interference that's picked up by a long cable is carried along with the music to the speakers or recording device.

- ✔ **Balanced** XLRs are used in professional audio equipment, and attach to the cables in a way that cancels out the unwanted sound interference.

XLR microphone (mic) inputs and master outputs on DJ mixers often work with cables and connectors that are both balanced and unbalanced, but when buying a new microphone, amplifier or mixer it's best to check the specifications of the equipment you use if you're unsure of the connections.

Figure 13-1:
Two XLR
connectors;
one for the
left, the
other for the
right.

Quarter-inch jack

A quarter-inch jack (also known as a TRS jack), is what you find at the end of
your DJ headphones (though not the one on the end of your iPod headphones;
that's a 3.5-millimetre jack). Quarter-inch jacks also come in balanced and
unbalanced varieties. Balanced connectors are mono, so you need two of
them, but an unbalanced connector can carry a stereo signal so it only needs
one cable and jack plug. If you need to know whether the jack you're holding
in your hand is mono or stereo, look at the black bands on the tip; one band
means it's mono, two bands mean it's a stereo jack, as shown in Figure 13-2.

Figure 13-2:
Left: A mono
quarter-inch
jack (TRS)
connector.
Right: A
stereo quar-
ter-inch jack
connector.

It's not always the clubber's fault

Blaming an accident on the customers of the club that you play in is quite easy, but as a DJ you have to be careful of doing things that can break connections yourself. I remember one evening while playing at a bar I had the lid of the record box neatly balanced on the DJ booth. I knocked it with my hand and it fell down the back, bounced onto the cables coming out of the mixer, pulled out the Master Output cable and plunged the place into silence for about three minutes while I tried to work out what I'd done. Thank goodness I worked there as a barman; otherwise they'd have thrown me out on my ear for being so careless! Soon after, the bar started using XLR connectors that locked into place.

Plugging Into the Mixer

The first time you take a look at the back of a mixer, it can look quite daunting with all the different inputs and outputs, but after you've plugged in a couple of pieces of equipment you find out just how simple it is back there. For more information on mixers and any functions you may be unsure of that I mention in this section, refer to Chapter 10.

Connecting turntables to a mixer

Turntables are unique in their connection because they're the only item of DJ equipment that plugs into the Phono input on the mixer and they have a thin *ground* wire (also called an earth) connection that you need to connect to prevent electrical hum and static from the turntables.

Connection is simple:

1. **Take the two RCA cables that come out the back of the turntable and plug them into the Phono input on the mixer.**

   The red RCA is the right-hand side of the music signal, and white is the left-hand side (see the earlier section 'RCA/Phono connections').

   If your turntable uses detachable cables, connect the RCA cables to the correct colours on the turntable outputs as well as the mixer inputs.

2. **After you've connected the cables properly, set the Line/Phono switch on the mixer for the channel you've just plugged into to Phono.**

3. **Connect the ground (earth) wire.** It's usually a thin cable with a piece of bare wire exposed at the end, or a thin U-shaped metal hook.

Your DJ mixer will have something similar to a thumb screw on the back to which you connect the ground wire. Cinch the ground wires from both turntables between a washer on the screw and the body of the mixer (as shown in Figure 13-3).

Be sure that you have a secure connection for both turntables to this ground point by checking that the metal ends of the wires make connection with the ground point's metal washer or screw. You'll know if you haven't properly grounded the turntables because you'll hear static or a really nasty, loud hum playing through the speakers.

Figure 13-3:
Two ground
wires
screwed to
the back of
the mixer.

Connecting CD decks to a mixer

CD decks usually use two RCA outputs to connect to the mixer's analogue Line RCA inputs.

However, if your CD decks have digital outputs and your mixer has a digital input (both are usually an RCA connection), use a single RCA cable to connect the CD deck to the mixer and keep the music digital.

When connecting CD decks to the mixer through the analogue outputs and inputs (a pair of red and white RCA cables), be sure not to plug one of them into the digital connection by accident. If you hear only one side of the music and you have a digital input or output, this mistake could be why.

Connecting iPods and personal MP3s players to a mixer

Unless you're using one of the Numark iDJ mixers or another mixer specifically designed for mixing with iPods, you need to use a cable that converts the output of your iPod (or any other MP3 player) to two RCA plugs. You can get a cable that's based on the dock connector of the iPod that splits into two RCA plugs (this is how a lot of people play their iPods through a home hi-fi) but without that, and for most of the other MP3 players, you need a cable that splits the headphone output into two RCA plugs.

You can buy these cables from most electronic spares stores, or simply type '3.5 mm stereo jack to RCA' into any search engine or eBay (www.ebay. co.uk), and you'll find one for about £5. Just make sure that the jack on the end of the cable you go for is stereo (it'll have two black bands on the tip), and that it's a 3.5 millimetre jack, otherwise it won't fit into the MP3 player's headphone output.

As with the CD decks, simply plug the RCAs from this cable into the Line input on the back of the mixer, making sure that the channel you use for this input on the mixer is switched over to Line.

 Headphone outputs are normally weaker than a typical Line output, so you may have to set your MP3 player to a high volume or increase the gain on the mixer by more than normal in order to play a strong signal through the mixer, so you can keep the volume of the MP3 music similar to the music from your CDs and turntables.

Connecting a computer as an input device

To connect the audio outputs of a computer to the mixer so that you can mix the computer music with your CD players and turntables, you use the computer's soundcard output. The soundcard processes the digital music data and converts it to a Line signal to be sent to the mixer (the reverse also happens, see 'Connecting a Mixer to your PC/Mac', later in the chapter).

If you have a soundcard with analogue RCA outputs, use a cable with two RCA connectors on each end and connect the RCA outputs of the computer's soundcard to the RCA Line inputs on the mixer. If you have RCA style digital S/PDIF outputs on the soundcard and a matching input on the mixer, use one RCA cable to connect between them both. If the soundcard has a 3.5-millimetre jack output marked 'Line', you'll need the stereo 3.5-millimetre lead to RCA cable I mention in the previous section 'Connecting iPods and MP3s to a mixer'.

If you're using a laptop or have a computer with a very basic soundcard, you may notice that the only audio connections you have are a headphone output and a microphone input. You can use the headphone output as long as you have the RCA to 3.5-millimetre jack cable, but like the MP3 player headphone output you'll need to adjust the gain on the mixer to get a strong signal.

A wide range of analogue to digital USB and Firewire converters are also available to buy. Edirol (shown in Figure 13-4), Alesis, Behringer and a whole host of other makes have products at varying prices (and quality) if you don't have a good enough soundcard on your computer.

Figure 13-4:
The Edirol audio to USB by Roland with analogue inputs and outputs connected to a USB connection.

If you want to connect your computer directly to an amplifier, the connection is identical to connecting to a mixer. Connect the output of the soundcard to an available input on your amplifier.

Always check the software and computer hardware you use for any special input or output connection instructions to enable it for DJ use. Manuals are there for a reason: don't start disconnecting and screaming at cables only to find out you were meant to click 'Out' in the software!

Choosing your mixer inputs

If you just use two turntables, CD decks or MP3 players, and have a two-channel mixer, connection is simple. Connect the CD deck/MP3 or turntable to your left to Channel 1 and the one on your right to Channel 2.

If you have more than two channels on your mixer, take a look to see whether any of them are aimed at a certain input device. Channels 1 and 2 on a four-channel Pioneer DJM600 mixer have specific connections for Pioneer CD decks as well as standard Line/Phono inputs. They have the connection for Pioneer's fader start controls that make the CD start when you move the fader. So if you want to use that function on your Pioneer CD decks, you'll need to connect to Channels 1 and 2. The Pioneer DJM800 has fader start connections on all four channels, but turntables only connect properly to Channels 2, 3 and 4.

If your mixer doesn't have any specific channel requirements or functions, you can connect to any two channels on the mixer, though it's still an idea to connect the left deck to a lower channel number and the right deck to the higher number (for example, use 1+2, 2+3, 3+4, 1+3, 1+4 or 2+4).

If you use two CD decks and two turntables, and have a four-channel mixer, you may want to connect in the same way the decks are arranged in front of you. Suppose that you arrange your equipment in this order:

   Turntable 1 – CD 1 – Mixer – CD 2 – Turntable 2

A simple setup is to connect Turntable 1 to Channel 1, CD 1 to Channel 2, CD 2 to Channel 3 and Turntable 2 to Channel 4 on the mixer, which may cause less confusion about what channel controls what equipment. Just make sure that you switch the Line/Phono switch to Line for the CD decks and Phono for turntables.

The mixer you're using may have other ideas! For instance, with the special CD control inputs on the Pioneer DJM600, if you want to use fader start controls you need to connect to Channels 1 and 2 for CD decks and 3 and 4 for turntables.

If you only have a two-channel mixer, you can still use two turntables and two CD decks. Plug Turntable 1 into the Phono input on Channel 1, and CD 1 into the Line input on Channel 1. Then plug Turntable 2 into Phono on Channel 2, and CD 2 into Line on Channel 2. You then just need to switch the channels from Phono to Line (or vice versa) to use the right piece of equipment. However, it's important to remember that you won't be able to mix from Turntable 1 to CD 1 or mix from Turntable 2 to CD 2 because even though they're different machines, they're both playing into the same mixer channel.

Your headphone jack isn't a headphone rest

Please don't get into the habit of hooking your headphones over the headphone jack when you're not using them. A club I worked in had the mixer at an angle and also had very little room in the DJ booth, allowing hardly any room to put anything down. So when I wasn't using my headphones I'd hook them over the headphone jack, which seemed sensible to me. That was until I aimed a bit high and hit the power switch with the headband from the headphones, plummeting the club into silence, and I almost blew a speaker when I turned the mixer on without turning the volume down . . . oops. Also, the weight of hooking headphones over the jack connection can cause damage to both the mixer and the headphones, which may lead to sound problems (the headphones may cut out and go silent).

Plugging in your headphones

Plugging in your headphones is as simple as finding the hole marked 'headphone' on your mixer and plugging them in, but I want to mention it here so that I can bring up the use of 3.5-millimetre adaptors. These adaptors let you convert headphones with a small 3.5 millimetre jack into the big, 6.35-millimetre (¼ inch) size that your mixer needs.

A 3.5 millimetre jack is the same as the one on your iPod earbuds. Though it may be tempting to use your earbuds for DJ headphones, they're not really suitable because they don't sound too good when played very loud, and they let in a lot of external sound from the dance floor and DJ booth. For more about picking suitable DJ headphones, check out Chapter 11.

Some mixers have the headphone connection on top of the mixer; others have it on the closest side to you, or even both. Choose your connection and plug in. Simple.

Connecting effects units to a mixer

You can connect effects units to the mixer in two ways:

- **Between the mixer and the amplifier:** Direct connection is the most basic, and easiest way to connect your effects unit. Take the Master Output of your mixer (two RCAs) and plug them into the Line input on the effects unit. Then, take the output of the effects unit (still two RCAs) and plug them into the input of the amplifier.

  The drawback to this method of connection is that the entire audio signal will be effected by the effects unit; you won't be able to play one channel from the mixer clean (without effects) while the other one gets a whole load of crazy effects applied to it.

✓ **With Send and Return connections:** You can send music from an individual channel on the mixer to an effects unit using the Send and Return option. With this, you can apply an effect to only one channel, leaving other channels to play unaffected through the speakers.

You can send the signal from the mixer to the effects processor (and return it) in two different ways:

- If the effects processor can accept multiple inputs, you can use a mixer with a separate Send and Return for each of the channels. Controls on the effects processor (and sometimes on the mixer) let you choose what channel on the mixer to apply the effect to. With the correct controls, you can 'effect' any number of channels while 'un-effecting' any number of channels. This method is by far the most versatile approach to using an effects processor, but does tend to require a large mixing desk instead of a compact DJ mixer.

- Some DJ-specific mixers with multiple channels may have only one pair of Send and Return connections but have a control on the mixer that assigns what channels are sent. The DJM-600 that I use lets you send any one of the four channels or the entire Master Output to an effects unit, so though it's not quite as versatile as the option to include or exclude any number of channels, this way can still give you clean audio from one channel while 'effecting' another, which is good enough for me.

The connections for Send and Return vary, but on the DJM600 it's a pair of mono quarter-inch jacks for each direction. One pair connects from Send on the mixer to the input of the effects unit, then another pair connects from the effects unit to Return on the mixer. You may find some units use RCAs for this purpose or stereo quarter-inch jacks, so take a close look at your mixer and the effects unit so that you know what cables you need.

Connecting mixer outputs

After you have all the inputs connected to the mixer you need to look at how to connect your mixer to an amplifier in order to hear the music, and maybe also connect to a recording device (tape, MiniDisc, CD, PC and so on) so that you can capture the moments of greatness you'll achieve in the mix.

Your mixer has two (or sometimes three) outputs:

✓ **Master Out** is the connection to use when connecting to an amplifier. Using a stereo RCA cable, connect one end to the Master Out on the mixer and the other end to an input on the amplifier. If the amp has more than one input channel and you're also sending items like a TV, PlayStation or another CD player to it, you may want to add sticky labels to change the normal 'Input 1, Input 2' labels that'll be on the amp, to help you remember what channel lets you hear what.

More expensive, professional mixers may use a second Master Output that uses XLR connections rather than RCA connections.

The Master Out is affected by the *Master Level Control* on the mixer, so if you turn that down, the volume of the music from the mixer reduces.

✔ **Record Out** is reserved for outputting to recording devices. The reasons you use this output rather than the Master Out are because

• The Master Out is probably going to an amp anyway.

• The Record Out bypasses the Master Level Control, so if you turn the Master Output down (maybe to take a phone call), the music level you send to the recording device won't change.

Like the Master Output, connect the Record Outputs to the recorder's inputs using a stereo RCA cable, making sure to continue to plug the red RCA output to the red RCA input and the white output to the white input. (For information on how to set the record levels on your recording device, see Chapter 19.)

✔ **Booth Output** is where you feed the mixer into a separate amplifier and speaker in the DJ booth, known as the *Booth Monitor*. Chapter 14 has important information about setting the volume of the Booth Monitor and the headphones to allow you to mix properly.

The connection is the same as Record Out and Master Out: connect one end of a stereo RCA cable to the Booth Output on the mixer and the other end to the Booth Monitor's input.

Connecting a mixer to your home hi-fi

Connecting to your home stereo (hi-fi) is similar to connecting to an amplifier. You make the connection using a stereo RCA cable from the Master Output on the mixer to the hi-fi – but you need to pay attention to the input you choose to use on the hi-fi. On the back of a hi-fi you probably see some of these inputs: Line, CD, TV, DVD, Aux and, if you have an old (or really good) hi-fi, a Phono input too.

If a CD or MP3 player is already connected to the hi-fi, a TV is connected to the TV input, and the DVD input is in use too, you're left with Aux (Auxilliary) or Phono (which is meant for turntables only). Therefore, you should use the Aux input to connect your mixer. Even though the music may be coming from turntables, by the time it's played through and outputted from a mixer, the signal's transformed into a Line level signal.

Of course, if you don't have a CD player or TV plugged into the hi-fi, you can use the TV and CD inputs too. Just stay away from the Phono input unless you're connecting turntables directly to the hi-fi.

Connecting a mixer to powered speakers

Sometimes powered speakers only have a jack input (like the headphone output on your mixer), so check whether you need to buy an RCA (the output from your mixer) to jack cable for each of the speakers (left and right).

You can find more information on using amplifiers, powered speakers and home hi-fis to play your music in Chapter 12.

Connecting a mixer to your PC/Mac

Whether you're using the computer as an amplifier or plan to record the mix to edit it or upload it to the Internet, the connection between your computer and your mixer is similar to all the other equipment you'll connect. Connect the output from the mixer to the input on the computer's soundcard (see 'Connecting a computer as an input device', earlier in the chapter, for detailed information on the connections and what you use a soundcard for). Use the Record Output if you're only using the computer for recording and the Master Output if using the computer as an amplifier (this frees up the Record Output for a recording device).

If your soundcard came with instructions and software for setting up the computer to be able to accept a Line input, please refer to the manual carefully. If it's a Windows controlled soundcard, you can activate the Line input through the Volume Control or Recording Devices window – found either by double clicking the speaker icon in the taskbar or through the Hardware/ Sound properties in the control panel. Mac users can access audio input controls through the Sound section of System Preferences.

You may want to turn off any other recording inputs (de-select them in the Record Control) or mute other playback devices in the Volume Control Window (by selecting Mute) to make sure that Windows system sounds or sounds from other programs aren't accidentally combined with the sound from your mixer. Nothing's worse than being halfway through a great mix only to have Homer Simpson say 'D'oh!' over the music when you get an email. Come to think of it, that might be quite cool . . .

Troubleshooting Set-up and Connections

Sometimes you're sure that you have everything plugged into the right place, you've turned everything on and everything's playing, but you just can't hear anything. To wrap up Part II of this book, and the equipment information as a whole, the following is a list of troubleshooting issues that may help to answer any of your connection and turntable setup problems.

Everything's connected, a record (or CD) is playing, but I can't hear any music through the amplifier

Ask yourself the following questions:

- Are the LEDs on the mixer flashing up and down to show that the mixer is receiving some music? If not, there's currently no signal.

- Have you used the correct inputs on the mixer for your MP3/CD players or turntables and set the Line/Phono switches accordingly? (Line for CD and MP3, Phono for turntables.)

- If you're currently playing one channel of music, have you made sure that the cross-fader is on that side and the channel-fader is up at least to 75 per cent? And if the cross-fader has an assign function to control any of the channels, is it switched to control the correct channel?

- If the mixer LEDs are flashing, have you made sure that you've connected the mixer's Master Output to a Line input on the amplifier?

- If the amplifier has the capability for multiple inputs, have you made sure that you've set the input switch or button to the correct input?

- Are the Master Level and the Input Level on the amplifier set at a point where you should hear music?

- Are the speakers connected?

- Have you tried connecting something else to the amplifier to check that it isn't a problem with the amplifier or the input channel you're using?

I can hear the music from the amp now, but I can't hear anything through the headphones

Try the following steps:

- Firstly, check that you have your headphones plugged in, turned up and switched to monitor the correct channel.

- Try turning all the headphone cue switches on. If you can hear music now, you were pressing the wrong cue button or you've connected your equipment to a channel you didn't intend to use.

- Plug your headphones into another piece of equipment with a headphone socket (such as the amplifier) to make sure that this problem isn't a malfunction with your headphones.

One of the turntables sounds really bad: it's distorting and the high frequencies sound fuzzy

The first thing to do is to look at your needles. Are the needles caked in dirt? (Carefully remove the dirt from around them.) Are they really old? (Replace them.) Are they inserted into the cartridge properly? (Check and re-insert them.)

If you think it's a malfunction, try swapping the headshell from one turntable to another or try swapping the needle from one headshell to the other. In case you have a connection problem rather than a needle or headshell problem, try swapping round the turntable connections to the mixer.

Why do my needles keep jumping when cueing?

If you're having a problem with your needles jumping around, try working through these possible solutions:

✔ Refer to manufacturer guidelines on where to set the height and counterweight of your tonearm. If you're given a range of numbers to set the counterweight within (between 3 and 5 grams, for example), set the counterweight to the lowest number first and then gradually increase the weight until the needle stops skipping.

✔ Check the settings provided with the needle and cartridge for the height of the tonearm and make sure that it's completely parallel to the record. If you need to set the weight or height to more than the recommended amount, your technique or needles could be at fault:

• Make sure that you're cueing the record back and forth in the curved direction of the record. If you push and pull horizontally, rather than in a curve, this action may make the needle jump.

• Old, worn needles are more prone to skipping.

I hear a really strange humming noise coming from my turntables

You may not have connected the ground wire. Make sure that it's securely attached to the earth/ground connector on the back of the mixer.

Why is everything distorting badly when I play a CD?

Check whether you've inserted the outputs of your CD decks into the Phono inputs of the mixer by accident. This causes distortion. Plug into the Line input.

Why is everything really quiet when using my turntables, even when everything is turned up to maximum?

Make sure that you've plugged your turntables into the Phono input. If you've put them into the Line input, they'll be very quiet.

Everything sounds nice through the mixer, but distorts through the amp

Ask yourself the following questions:

✔ Have you turned up the input level on the amp too high? Turn it down a bit; see whether that helps.

✔ How strong a level are you sending out of the mixer? Take a look at where the LEDs on the mixer are flashing; try not to play the music above + 5 decibels on the scale because it may cause some nasty distortion.

✔ Have you plugged into the Phono inputs of the amplifier by accident? Change the connections to plug into one of the Line inputs.

Music is playing through the mixer, but I can't get any music into the PC

Try the following steps:

✔ Make sure that the speakers on your computer are turned on and all volume controls (including the computer's) are turned up.

✔ Check the connections and ensure that you've plugged the output from the mixer to the Line input of the soundcard. You may find a Mic input right next to the Line input, so double check that you didn't plug into the wrong place when you were fumbling behind the PC.

✔ Check the meters on the recording software. They'll be bouncing up and down if they're receiving a signal.

✔ Check the Record Control (which you can access through the Volume Control icon on the taskbar). Double check that you've selected Line input and that the input level is set to at least 75 per cent.

✔ Have a quick read of the manual that came with the software and the soundcard to see whether you need to do something special.

The meters are flashing like mad in the software, I'm able to record what's going in, but nothing is coming back out of the PC

Check that you've connected the Line Out from the soundcard and not plugged into the Mic or Line In by accident.

Check the Volume Control found in the taskbar. Make sure that you haven't accidentally checked the mute box thinking it was the select box from the Record Control (I do this all the time).

Why doesn't my recording device seem to record anything when connected directly to the mixer?

Have a look at your connection. There's a good chance that you didn't connect the Record Output to the Line In on the recorder.

Ask yourself three questions:

✔ Did you accidentally use the Booth Output to send to the recording device, but turned the Booth Output volume off? If so, switch the cables over to Record Out, which is preferable to turning up the Booth Output.

✔ Is the input level control on the recording device switched to accept the Line input, and turned up to an appropriate level?

✔ Does your recording device need to be in Record mode in order to register any input? This isn't a common case on home tape and MiniDisc recorders, but on a lot of professional equipment if a CD/DAT/MiniDisc is in the machine then you need to press the Record button on its own to get the device into record mode (the machine only starts recording when you press Record and Play together). This tells the electronics to accept a signal in rather than just play a signal out.

Part III
The Mix

The 5th Wave   By Rich Tennant

"He's taught me all I know about scratching."

In this part . . .

DJ skills are two-fold. Beatmatching is the core skill of the electronic dance music DJ – all DJs who play this genre of music need this skill. Chapter 15 in this part tells you all you need to know about beatmatching. Chapter 16 covers further mixing skills, including mixing music from other genres.

The second part of your DJ skills are the most important, and apply to all genres of music – choosing the tunes to play, the order to play them, and how and when to mix between them.

If you want to add another layer of creativity and performance to the mix, scratching is covered in Chapter 17, with guidance on how to start your journey as a creative DJ or a dedicated scratch turntablist.

Chapter 14

Grasping the Basics of Mixing

- -

In This Chapter

▶ Discovering the essence of club DJing

▶ Working out the tempo of your tunes – beats per minute

▶ Finding the first beat of a tune with confidence

▶ Starting your tunes so the beats play in time

▶ Using the pitch control to match tempos

▶ Getting to grips with headphone cueing techniques

- -

DJs play music. They play music that people want to dance to, and play music that keeps people on the dance floor. As a DJ, if you can't do that simple thing, you're not going to be a big hit with the crowd.

House and trance DJs employ a technique called *beatmatching*, which makes the bass drum beats of two different records play at the same time. That way, when they change from one record to another, the people on the dance floor don't have to adjust their dancing rhythm.

In this chapter, you discover all the tools and skills you need to beatmatch. The secret of successful beatmatching is simple: good concentration and lots of practise – no special tricks required. The great news is that after you've made the investment of devoting your time and concentration to mastering beatmatching, the skill sticks to you like glue.

Knowing What Beatmatching's All About

Matching beats is a very simple concept, but it's an important core skill. Although certain kinds of music don't lend themselves to beatmatching (rock music, for example, tends only to use beatmatching once in a while as a special trick), if you want to play in a club where the DJ's expected to beatmatch records to mix them together, you'd better develop the skill!

The reason beatmatching is so essential for the trance and house DJ isn't only to aid with smooth, seamless transitions from tune to tune, but also for the physical effect on the people on the dance floor.

When these DJs progress through the set, playing different tunes and different styles, the music gradually plays faster and faster until it reaches what I call the *sweet spot*. This sweet spot occurs when the bass beat from the music matches the speed of the heartbeats of the people dancing. This speed can be anything between 130 and 145 beats per minute (BPM) for most music, but can be more depending on the music genre.

When the speeds of the pounding bass beats and the thumping heartbeats get closer and closer, the combination of pulsating rhythms begins to do strange things to the body and emotions of the people on the dance floor. With time, this euphoric moment is commonly signified by a *hands in the air* moment on the dance floor. It makes me sweat a bit, but that's just me . . .

Importantly, even if you consider this phenomenon as some kind of voodoo mind control, you need to understand that you should play at a tempo where people are enjoying themselves and comfortable dancing on the dance floor.

Other genres of music can affect the people on the dance floor too – but usually only on a song by song basis. The right rock tune at the right speed can really blow off the roof – but this isn't the same thing as the pounding, pulsating beats of a series of great trance tunes putting the people onto the dance floor into a euphoric, trance-like state.

Discovering How to Beatmatch

Your choice of format doesn't matter – CD, vinyl, MP3 or anything else – the mechanics of beatmatching are the same. It's just the controls that are different.

In this chapter I describe how to perform beatmatching with reference to vinyl and CD DJing. However, please check Chapter 6 if you need more information about using controls on turntables, and Chapter 8 if you need more details about using CD decks. Digital DJs may find the on-screen layout and controls very similar to a CD deck, but check out Chapter 9 for more on digital DJ setups, so you can be sure you know what to do depending on your equipment.

Choosing skills over thrills

As technology advances, especially with digital DJing, the option to let technology take care of the skill of beatmatching rather than doing it yourself is available more and more, and can be very tempting.

One school of thought says letting technology take care of the hard stuff means you can concentrate on the music you're playing, but trust me, beatmatching is only hard at the beginning. When you get good at it, you'll be able to beat match two tunes in 20 seconds or less.

Setting up your equipment

A few basic settings and requirements can help you master the fundamentals of mixing comfortably (jump back to Chapter 10 if you're not sure about some of the mixer controls):

✔ Make sure that your DJ setup is switched on and hooked into an amplifier (check out Chapter 12 for more on connecting up). Don't worry about headphones for now; you get to them later.

✔ Use two copies of the same tune (preferably something that has a simple, constant beat from the very beginning). The reason for using two copies of the same tune is that when both pitch controls on the turntables are at zero (known as the *green light* area), both tunes play at exactly the same speed. This fact means that you don't have to worry about one tune playing faster than the other, and makes getting to grips with starting your tunes and keeping them in time a lot easier.

✔ Set your mixer so that you can hear both records at the same time and at the same volume. (Typically, this requirement means moving the crossfader into the middle, and setting both of the vertical channel-faders to maximum, with the gain and equaliser, or EQ, controls set the same on both channels). The reason you set the mixer to hear both records at the same time is so that you only have to worry about working with the tunes – you don't waste time and concentration trying to adjust the controls on the mixer. This method may sound messy at first, and your dog may leave the room in protest, but don't worry – you'll move on to proper mixing soon, and the dog needed some exercise anyway.

By using two copies of the same tune, you may experience a phenomenon known as *phasing*. When two identical sounds play over each other, their sound waves combine and cancel each other out to make it sound like your music is playing through a jet engine. This can seem a little distracting at first, but as you begin to hear this phasing sound, you're getting the bass beats closer and closer to playing together, so you eventually realise that this is a great help when learning how to beatmatch. When you move on to using two different tunes, you won't need to worry about phasing any more, unless you want to use it instead of using a phaser or flanger effect on a mixer (check out Chapter 10 for information about effects on mixers).

Locating the first bass beat

Every journey begins with a step, and every beatmatch begins with a beat. To start with, find a tune with a solid, clear bass beat right from the beginning. (In a perfect world, all records would start with a constant bass beat, making beatmatching a lot easier.)

'For an Angel' – for a new DJ

For years I've used the same record when helping people develop their DJ skills: Paul Van Dyk's 'For an Angel'. It's quite an old tune now and my two copies were getting very worn before I went digital (especially at the beginning of the record). The reason I love to use this track is that it has really clear, solid-sounding bass drums throughout, and they start from the very beginning.

Whether you've chosen a record with the beat at the beginning or picked a record that has its first beat 45 seconds in, the following points can help you locate the first bass beat so that the needle is *cued up* (ready to play) or the CD is waiting at the very instant the first beat is about to play:

- ✔ **Listening for the beat:** The first option is to simply start the tune from the beginning and wait until you hear the first beat. When you hear the first beat, place your finger on the record to stop it and slowly play it backwards by hand. As you play the record backwards, you hear the part of the record you've just heard playing in reverse. (Don't be overly concerned about revealing any Satanic messages when doing this; dance music doesn't tend to contain any.) If you use a tune that starts with a beat from the beginning, the last thing you hear playing backwards is that beat. The instant the beat goes silent is where you want to leave the needle.

  CD DJs: Pause the CD when you hear the first beat and then play the tune backwards (your CD deck will have a certain way of doing this; check out Chapter 8 for more) until you get to the beginning of the bass beat. Then store that point as your *cue* (start) point – often by pressing the Cue button, but check what to press on your CD deck in order to do this.

- ✔ **Winding to the beat:** If you're impatient or in a rush, you can turn the record around really fast with your finger until your hear the *brrrrrrrrrp* noise of beats playing really fast and then play the record backwards until you find the very first of those beats.

  CD DJs: If you have a CD deck with a large rotating platter that emulates the sound of a turntable, you can do the same as vinyl DJs. If you only have buttons that skip through the tune, press and hold the Search button until you hear the bass beats starting to play very fast, and then play the tune backwards until you locate the first of those beats.

- ✔ **Looking for the beat:** Take a close look at a record and you can see a lot of different shades of grey and black rings (the target light on your deck shows up this shading). The darker parts of the record means that it doesn't have as much information cut into the groove and is likely to not contain a beat. Look at the beginning of the record where the rings change from dark to light – the lighter shaded area contains more sound information and is probably where the beat starts. Place the needle where the dark and light rings join. If you can hear the beat, spin the record backwards until the beats stop, or if you still hear the introduction, play the record forwards until you find the first beat.

CD DJs: If you have a *wave display* on your CD decks or software, which has a series of peaks and troughs to show the louder and quieter parts of the tune, refer to your wave display to find where the big peaks begin – that's likely to be where the beats start.

Starting your tunes in time

When you're happy with finding the first beat in a tune, choose a deck and get ready to start. (I'm left-handed so I seem to always start on the left.)

Vinyl DJs:

1. **Place your finger on the outer inch of the vinyl.**

   Notice I didn't say *press* – just place your finger, you only need a little pressure.

2. **Press the Start button.**

   Due to the wonder of slipmats, the turntable turns underneath the record while you're still holding it (if it doesn't, shame on you for buying cheap equipment).

   Now the easy part.

3. **Take your finger off the record.**

   Glorious bass drums should now flood through your speakers.

   CD DJs: No need for three steps for you – just press Play!

Deciphering drum patterns

Although most house/club music follows a pounding bass beat, not all dance music has this simple and basic rhythm. Drum patterns are as varied as the music they accompany, ranging from a simple bass/snare beat to the complicated patterns of dubstep, drum and bass and jungle. You can often distinguish different music genres as much by their drum pattern as by the

music. The drum pattern alone is enough to be able to recognise breakbeat, R&B or two-step garage.

If you're interested in finding out more about drumming and drum patterns, I heartily recommend *Drumming For Dummies* (Wiley) by Jeff Strong.

4. **While the tune is playing, listen to it.** Don't simply *hear* it – take a moment to really listen to what's happening (this is called *listening with an active ear*). Really concentrate on listening to the bass drums.

   You should pick up that the bass drum has two different sounds. One of them is just a bass drum on its own, and the other one is normally the bass drum combined with another sound (sometimes a *clap* – or a snap sounding drum called a *snare drum*). Listen – notice the difference in emphasis between the first beat of the bass drum (represented by **B** in my DJ beat notation that follows) and the second beat of the bass drum (represented by **BC** to show that's **B** combined with another sound):

   B   BC   B   BC   B   BC   B   BC

5. **When you're comfortable with the sounds of the beat, move over to the other deck and check that the pitch is set to zero. Vinyl DJs: go back to the previous steps 1 and 2.**

   The first beat that you've located on your tune and are ready to start from is normally the bass drum on its own. What you're about to try is starting this first beat at the same time as the single bass beat plays from the tune that's currently playing through the speakers.

   Have a listen again. Make sure that you know what bass beat sound you want to start on. At this early stage, you may find that counting the beats in your head is helpful: '1 – 2, 1 – 2, 1 – 2' or 'bass – snare, bass – snare, bass – snare'.

   The record is poised, ready to go; the deckplatter is still spinning underneath; you're now sure that you know the sound of the beat you want to start on.

6. **Let go of the record (*CD DJs:* Press Play).**

Chances are, one of three things happens.

- ✔ **You get it right first time – both beats play at the same time.** Well done! Give it a few more goes to make sure that you've really got the knack.

- ✔ **In your haste, you let go/pressed Start too early and the two bass beats sound like a galloping horse when they play together.** Don't worry; it's easily done. Take the needle off (*CD DJs:* Return to your cue point; check out Chapter 8 if you're unsure how), head back to Step 1 and have another go.

- ✔ **You're over-cautious, wait too long, start the tune too late and the beats sound like a train-wreck together.** Again, very easily done. Just go back to the first step and try it again.

The good news is that a small timing error may not be all your fault. Before you get too frustrated at not getting your tunes to start in time, check out a couple of external factors:

✔ **Give a little push.** When using vinyl, you may find that waiting too long happens more often than not, which is common and happens to the best DJs. The good news is that the delay may be nothing to do with when you let go of the record but more to do with the motor in the turntable.

In your attempt to start the beats in time, even though the slipmat does its job and the deckplatter still turns underneath the record, if you just lift your finger off the record to start it playing, the motor can still take a fraction of a second to get the turntable up to full speed (known as *lag*).

The more powerful the turntable's motor, the quicker it gets up to speed, but even the best of decks can introduce a tiny delay. (All you CD DJs are allowed a smug smile at this point.)

To get around motor lag, don't just let go of the record – give it a gentle push too. How much of a push you have to give the record is just as much a knack as starting it at the right time, but like everything else with beatmatching, you'll get the knack with practice.

✔ **Make sure that you've really got that beat!** The other common cause of not starting the beat in time is not having the needle or CD cue point at the very beginning of the first beat.

For CD DJs this is just about listening properly to the sounds of the beats as you try to find the very beginning of the bass beat. For vinyl DJs and CD DJs who use deckplatters with vinyl emulation, to get used to finding exactly where the beat is play a second or two duration of the tune backwards and forwards, as if you were scratching slowly. The beat will make a *boom – woomp – boom – woomp* noise as you rock it back and forth.

To improve the timing when you eventually release the record, perform this rocking (scratching) motion at the same time as the other tune plays its bass beats. Scratch forward when the other tune only plays a bass beat, and backwards as the other tune plays the bass and snare/clap beat. Then, when you want to start the tune, just let go instead of continuing to scratch to the beat.

With all the noise around you in a DJ booth, you can have difficulty hearing the first bass beat if it isn't a solid thump. By rocking a record back and forth through the needle, you're giving your brain more information to help it pick out the bass sound from all the other noise.

Try this rocking technique a few times as you practise starting the record in time. You'll be amazed at how quickly you get used to working the vinyl (a fancy-pants way of saying using and touching the record).

Your parents may have told you never to touch records and to treat them with care, which is right for their Beethoven LPs but not for DJing. Moving the needle off and on the record, finding the first beat and starting it playing at the right time are skills that go toward making you more comfortable with your DJ tools. Just keep your hands clean and show some care (don't drop the needle from a great height or rip it right across the record) and your tunes will be with you for a long time.

Adjusting for errors

When you make a timing error starting the beats, starting over again is perfect when you're developing your skills, but it's not how experienced DJs deal with theses errors.

Try starting the beat again – but from now on, if you make a timing error, use the following methods to bring the bass beats *back in time* (make them play at the same time):

✔ **Starting too soon:** If you started the new tune too early, its bass beats will play before the bass beats on the tune to which you're trying to match the beats. So you need to temporarily slow the new tune down a little to get it in time.

CD DJs should have pitch bend controls on their CD decks which do exactly this. If you have pitch bend buttons, press and hold the – pitch bend button until the beats play in time, and then release the button to return to the correct speed. If, like me, you use something like the Pioneer CDJ-1000 with an outer ring that you rotate to make the tune play faster or slower in short speed bumps, spin it backwards to slow down the tune.

Vinyl DJs can place a finger on the dimpled ring running around the side of the spinning turntable to add a little friction. This added friction slows the speed at which the turntable turns and eventually slows the record down enough so that the beats play at the same time. When the beats now play in time, take your finger off the dimples to return the record to normal speed. The amount of pressure to add to the dimples takes a little getting used to, and if you're ticklish try not to giggle – it doesn't look professional!

✔ **Starting too late:** When you start the tune too late, and the beats on the new tune play after the one to which you're trying to match, vinyl DJs can try a couple of methods to speed up the record:

• Tightly grab the turntable's centre spindle that pokes through the record with your thumb and middle fingers and turn that around to make the turntable turn faster than normal.

• My preferred method is to place your finger lightly on the label at around the 6 o'clock position, and push that round to help the record play faster.

CD DJs: Use your pitch bend controls to temporarily speed up the tune.

A technique some DJs use to fix starting errors on CD decks or turntables is to use the pitch control as a pitch bend. Briefly boosting or cutting the speed using the pitch control works well at this stage, because you only need to return it to zero in order to make the tunes play at the same speed again, but by the time you start using the pitch control to play your tunes faster or slower (see 'Using the Pitch Control', later in this chapter), it'll be a lot harder to return the control back to where you originally set it.

Nerves and carelessness don't mix

I remember my first night playing live in front of real people (eek!). I was so nervous that when I tried to speed up the record by pushing the label, my hand slipped and I ripped the needle right across the record (which is why I now start at the 6 o'clock position, nowhere near the needle!).

Fortunately, you tend to only do this kind of thing once . . . it's incredible how quickly being that embarrassed helps you learn from a mistake like that!

Experiment with all the methods and find the one that you're most comfortable with. Importantly, you need to find the error adjustment method that suits you the best, giving you consistent, positive results.

No matter which method you use, try to be gentle when making these timing adjustments. If you press down too hard on the side of the turntable, it'll grind to a halt! Or if you push the label around too hastily, you may knock the needle out of the groove or zip forward through the tune by 20 seconds. Some CD decks pitch bend more the harder you press the button, so work out how heavy-handed you need to be.

Knowing which record to adjust

When you need to alter the speed of a tune to make the beats go back in time, you almost always adjust the tune that isn't playing through the speakers yet – the *cued track*, which you normally listen to in your headphones. If you were to speed up or slow down the *live* track that people can hear, they'll start shouting 'Sack the DJ!' (a phrase that strikes fear into the heart of any DJ). If both tunes are playing through the speakers when you're in the middle of mixing one tune into the other, adjust the quieter of the two tunes.

There are cases (usually a tune with a constant note playing) where speeding up or slowing down the quieter tune sounds terrible because of the pitch hiccup to the notes playing, but practice gives you the experience to know which one to change.

Using the Pitch Control

After you're comfortable starting your tunes in time (see the earlier section 'Starting your tunes in time'), the next step in beatmatching is to follow the same process using the same two tunes, but this time one of them starts off playing at a different speed to the other one so you can get used to working with the pitch control.

At this stage of getting to grips with beatmatching, the advantage of using the same two tunes as the first exercise is that you can compare the pitch controls of both decks to help match the speeds. The downside is that you still play the same tune over and over. Don't worry, you'll move on to other tunes soon.

Understanding BPMs

In order to use the pitch control correctly, it's useful to know how it affects the speed of the music, and how to calculate these changes of speed.

Beats per minute (BPMs) are a way to describe how fast (known as the *tempo*) your tunes play. The name gives it away; the BPM is the number of beats that occur in one minute.

As a *very broad* generalisation, house music is recorded with a BPM between 110 and 130 BPM, trance music ranges mostly between 130 and 145, and hard-house/happy hardcore can be well in excess of that. Other genres of music, like rock, pop, jazz and so on, have wider ranges of BPM. Even looking at just one artist like Aerosmith, 'Crazy' is a ballad at 54 BPM, whereas 'Young Lust' rocks out at 189 BPM!

Calculating BPMs

When you try to beatmatch two different tunes, knowing the BPM of each one helps you to make an educated guess about how much you need to adjust the pitch control.

You can adopt two main approaches for calculating BPMs:

- ✔ **Use a beat counter.** A beat counter is a useful DJ backup tool that automatically calculates and displays the BPM of the tune for you. Stand-alone beat counters can cost between £70 and £200. If you're thinking about BPM counters and you haven't chosen your mixer yet, it makes good financial sense to look at a mixer with built-in BPM counters. Instead of buying a basic mixer and an expensive stand-alone BPM counter, use the combined money to afford a really good mixer with built-in BPM counters.

- ✔ **Calculate the BPM yourself.** The free approach. It doesn't take long, and is easy to do. Set the tune to zero pitch and get a stopwatch ready. Hit start, and count how many bass beats you hear for 30 seconds. If you counted a beat as you started the watch, subtract one and double the figure – that calculates the beats per minute for that track.

For example, if you counted 67 beats in 30 seconds and counted a beat as you hit Start, the BPM would be $66 \times 2 = 132$. If you counted 60.5 beats in 30 seconds, and started counting from the first beat after you started the stopwatch, the BPM would be $60.5 \times 2 = 121$ BPM.

You can count the beats for an entire minute of course, but you'll probably find that the difference between the 30 second and 60 second count isn't noticeable enough to warrant doing it for longer.

If you can get into a routine of calculating the BPMs of your records as you buy them, you'll always be on top of your calculations.

After you've been DJing for a few months and your skill develops, you'll find you don't have to worry about knowing exact BPMs any more. Quite quickly, you'll not only develop the skill to tell instantly whether a tune is faster or slower than the one playing, but you'll find you've developed an incredible memory of the general tempo of your records before you play them and won't need to refer to calculations.

Matching the pitch setting

The numbers on the pitch control don't in fact show how many BPMs you may add or subtract. The pitch slider on a turntable is numbered to show the percentage increase/decrease of the turntable rotation, and therefore the percentage change of the original BPM of the tune. On Technics 1210mkII turntables the pitch slider is zero when in the middle, +8 when moved closest to you and –8 when moved away from you to the farthest point (assuming you don't have your turntables sideways for scratching – see Chapter 17).

If you play a 130 BPM tune and set the pitch control to +4, you're not adding 4 BPM, you're adding 4 per cent to the original BPM. Four per cent of 130 is 5.2, which means the 130 BPM tune now plays at 135.2 BPM.

Don't count your life away

I used to spend a full minute calculating the BPM because I wanted to be sure that I was *really* accurate. Eventually, I figured that by the time I'd counted 120 records, I'd used up an extra hour of my life for no real reason! I'd rather have spent that hour mixing.

Here's an example of how to calculate where to set the pitch control on the *cued track* (the track you want to play next) in order for it to match the *live track* that's currently playing through the speakers to the crowd:

✔ **The live track is a 130 BPM track with its pitch set to +2 per cent.** This data means that the record is running at around 132.5 BPM (2 per cent of 130 BPM is 2.6, which I round down to 2.5 BPM).

✔ **The cued track is 138 BPM.** You therefore need to slow this tune down by around 5.5 BPM to make it close in BPM to the live track. Because it's best to deal in rough estimates with the first adjustment to the pitch control (see 'Taking your eyes off the pitch control', later in this chapter), this means taking the pitch control down to around –4 per cent to slow it down enough, and then you just need to do some fine tuning.

All hands (back) on decks

Enough theory – go back to your decks and try the following method, still using two copies of the same tune:

1. **Slide the pitch control on your live track to about +3 per cent.**

   (The numbers on Technics turntables go up in twos, so set the pitch slider between 2 and 4 if you have one of these.)

2. **Leave the pitch setting on the cued track at zero and start its first bass beat at the same time as the live track's single bass beat.**

   You'll notice that the beats start to drift apart and play out of time very quickly.

3. **Change the pitch to +3 per cent.**

   Fortunately, you can cheat for now. Because you can see that the live track is set to +3 per cent, you know that you need to set the pitch on the identical cued track to the +3 per cent mark in order to get the beats playing at the same speed.

4. **Have another go at starting the beats in time, but this time don't stop the cued track when it's playing too slowly.**

   Treat it in the same way as a starting error. You know (for now) that you need to set the pitch control to +3 per cent, so do so, and then use your chosen error correction technique (see 'Adjusting for errors', earlier in this chapter) to get the beats to play at the same time again.

You may get lucky and set the pitch precisely the first time, but most often you'll probably find that the beats start to drift apart after ten seconds or so, because even though you've moved the pitch control to the +3 per cent mark, the pitch control may not be totally accurate.

This is all just for practise of course – when you use two different tunes with different BPMs you won't have the option to cheat by just looking at the pitch control on the other turntable to know whether you need to speed up or slow down the new tune. So things start to get a little trickier. You need to be able to tell whether the cued track is running too fast or too slow in order to make the beats play in time again, using your ears, instead of your eyes. You work this out by listening to the sound that the bass drums make together.

Playing too slow or too fast

If you can hear that a record is slipping out of time before anyone else can and if you can react to it and fix it before anyone hears it, you'll be as good at beatmatching as any top-class DJ. However, knowing whether a tune is play-ing too fast or too slow is *by far the hardest part of DJing.* How to know this is the question I most commonly get asked, and the hardest thing for a lot of new DJs to figure out.

The reason people new to DJing have difficulty making this judgement is that they haven't spent the time training their ears to listen out for the audio clues that provide the answer. Spend time practising the following method, and listen to and concentrate on the sound that plays when a tune is running too fast or too slow.

In order to be able to tell whether your cued track is playing too slow or too fast, you need to change your mixer setting so that the live track's channel-fader is set to about three-quarters of the volume of the cued track's channel. You make this change because you need to be able to identify the cued track's bass beats while both tunes are playing through the speakers. If both tracks played at full volume, you wouldn't know which beat was playing first (espe-cially because at the moment they're currently both the same tune!). Having one tune louder than the other helps you distinguish one from the other.

The reason I suggest this setting is that it's similar to how I set my head-phones when beatmatching. I have the cued track playing loud, and assum-ing the mixer has headphone mix where I can also play the live track in the headphones, I play the live track at a much lower volume at the same time. See 'Introducing Your Headphones', later in this chapter, if you want to know why that's my preferred setting.

I've discovered that the best way to describe what to listen for is by using onomatopoeic words (words that you can associate with sounds): *l'Boom* and *B'loom.* (Please bear with me here . . . I haven't gone mad.)

Simply, when the cross-fader is in the middle, the cued tune is beating away at full volume: *Boom Boom Boom Boom* . . . The live tune is playing quieter than the cued track; instead of sounding like a loud *Boom*, it's a softer *loom* sound: *loom loom loom loom*. (Honestly, bear with me, it does makes sense when you put this into practice, I promise.)

This means that the two sounds you hear that let you know whether to speed up or slow down the cued track are:

- ✔ **B'loom:** When the louder 'Boom' tune (in this case, the cued tune) plays too fast, you hear its beat first – and the sound you hear is *B'loom, B'loom, B'loom, B'loom*

- ✔ **l'Boom:** When the cued tune is too slow and plays after the live track, it sounds like *l'Boom, l'Boom, l'Boom, l'Boom*.

Being able to hear the sounds of both bass drum beats with all the rest of the music playing takes a fair bit of concentration, but some spend time practising and you'll realise that I'm not as mad as I sound. It's slightly easier when using two different tunes, because the bass drums will probably sound different anyway, but regardless *B'loom* and *l'Boom* are your beatmatching buddies.

Go back to the previous step of playing the live track at +3 per cent and, starting at zero per cent, adjust the pitch on the cued track so the speeds are similar. Listen carefully to the sound that the bass drums are making when the beats are almost matched. Listen especially for *l'Boom* or *B'loom*, and try to work out whether your cued 'Boom' track is running too slow or too fast.

If you got it wrong and have slowed down a track that was already playing too slow, that's okay! Just remember the sound that you heard that made you think that the track was running too fast and re-associate that with running too slow.

This technique takes practice and concentration, and you may want to adopt a trial-and-error approach for a while. Go back to zero pitch on both of the tunes, slow one of them down and listen to the sound the bass beats make – then speed one up, listen to *that* sound and take note of the difference.

Taking your eyes off the pitch control

When you're used to hearing the different sounds that beats make when they're playing too fast or too slow, the next step is to match the beats by adjusting the pitch control without looking at where the other deck's pitch control is set, using only your ears as your guide.

Using identical tunes, increase the pitch control on the live one but this time with something covering the reading, so you know that it's increased but you can't cheat by looking at where the pitch control is set to. A bit childish I know, but from now on your cheating DJ days are over.

To match the pitch control on the cued tune to this new setting, I consider four different ranges of adjustment:

- Large, rough adjustments to get somewhere close

- Medium adjustments (about 1–2 per cent on the pitch slider) to get closer

- Small adjustments (about ¼ of 1 per cent) to finalise it

- Minute adjustments (millimetres) for fine tuning during the mix

For example:

- If the cued tune starts to play too slowly immediately, increase the pitch control by about 4 per cent and perform your preferred error correction method to get the beats playing at the same time (see 'Adjusting for errors', earlier in this chapter).

- If you then hear *B'loom* when you stop the error correction (which means you've sped up too much, but the beats aren't drifting apart as fast as they were in the last step), reduce the pitch a little, by about 1 per cent.

- If the beats now take about ten seconds to play noticeably too slow, and you begin to hear *l'Boom* sounds this time, increase the pitch by about ¼ of 1 per cent.

- If you're almost there, but after 20 seconds you start to hear *B'loom* again (the louder, cued tune is playing too fast), correct the error and decrease the pitch by the tiniest amount. Nudging it to move by only a millimetre is sometimes all that it takes.

Practising happy

Always think about the fact that you're spending the time practising because you want to be a DJ – and you want to be a DJ because, as well as a lot of other things, DJing really is a heck of a lot of fun.

If you start to get a little frustrated as you try to develop any of your beatmatching skills, stop. Take five minutes away from the decks. Get a glass of water (anything stronger may inflame matters!), and come back to your setup with one thought in mind – to have fun. Don't worry about any of that pesky learning/skill stuff. Don't record yourself, don't try to be something you're not, don't sweat it. Just play some music and smile like you mean it! In fact, this is *almost* the one time I'd say an auto-beatmatching function on your decks would be of help, so you can pretend you're really the one doing it, get your groove back and get rid of any negativity.

Introducing Your Headphones

When first developing your beatmatching skills (see the preceding section), playing both tunes through the speakers at the same time makes it a lot easier to hear clearly and instantly whether you've managed to get the bass beats to play in time. Sadly, you don't get that option when mixing for an audience or when recording a demo CD because, as you'll already know, it sounds awful. So I think that it's time to take the stabilisers off and start to work out whether the beats are *in sync* (play at the same time) through your headphones from now on. Your neighbours and dog will thank you for this.

Switching over to headphone control

In order to start making the best use of the headphones, you need to set up your mixer so that you only hear the live track playing through the amplifier's speakers, and you only start to hear the cued track playing through the speakers when you move the cross-fader toward the cued track's channel.

Set your mixer to these settings:

- Cross-fader all the way over to the live track's side
- Headphone cue buttons set to hear the cued track in the headphones
- Gain controls and EQ settings on both channels set identically (so both records play at the same volume, with the same amount of bass/mid/ high frequencies playing)
- Both channel-faders at maximum

The last setting is for ease of use while you're developing your skills because this, along with the EQ and gain settings, maintains an identical play-out volume for both identical records. As you get better as a DJ, though, you'll find that setting the channel-faders to maximum can cause volume problems instead of prevent them. (See Chapter 16 for more information.)

If you're unsure of how any of these settings affect the sound through your mixer, or for detailed explanations of the different cueing options, refer to Chapter 10.

Cueing in your headphones

Making the pitch adjustments to the cued track in the headphones while listening to the live track through the speakers isn't an easy thing to do at first. *Cueing* in your headphones (finding where you want to start in a track and also setting the pitch control during the beatmatching process) is another key skill of beatmatching that once gained stays with you forever. At first it can feel a bit like patting your head and rubbing your tummy, or juggling four chainsaws while singing – though not quite as dangerous.

Cueing with single ear monitoring

The most popular way to cue in the headphones is called *single ear monitoring*. Quite simply, you cover only one ear by the headphones playing the cued track, leaving the other ear clear to listen to the live track through the speakers. This way, you can hear both tracks and compare them in your head.

Cueing with headphone mix

You can use a *headphone mix* to help hear the *B'loom, l'Boom* sounds (see the earlier section 'Playing too slow or too fast') when *single ear monitoring*, or cover your ears with both cups of the headphones to check that the beats are playing in time.

When *single ear monitoring* with the cued track playing at a good volume in your headphones, the headphone mix lets you play the live track quietly over it (what I call *bleeding in*) so you can hear the *B'loom, l'Boom* bass beat clues in your headphones. If you hear *B'loom*, the cued track is running too fast; if you hear *l'Boom*, your cued track is running too slow. See the earlier section 'Playing too slow or too fast' if you need to go over this technique.

When you get halfway through the mix, and the cued track is now the louder tune through the speakers too, you may wish to swap the headphone cue controls so that the cued track now becomes the live track and is now the quieter one, and the tune that was the live track now plays louder in the headphones and becomes the cued track. What this means now is that when you hear *B'loom*, the tune you're mixing out of (which is now the cued track) is running too fast, and when you hear *l'Boom*, it's running too slow.

Apart from helping to spot the *l'Boom* and *B'loom* indicators, the other advantage of a headphone mix is that you can do a trial mix with both ears of your headphones on before letting anyone hear it. Some records just don't play well with others, and listening to a mix first in your headphones can be a great safety net for preventing a poor choice of tunes to mix together.

You may even find that the *B'loom* and *l'Boom* indicators are easier to hear through both ears, rather than single ear monitoring and you're happier with both ears of the headphones on when checking the beats are playing in sync.

If you're going to check the beats and maybe even perform the mix with both of your ears inside the headphones, periodically take them off, just so you can hear the music playing to the dance floor. You may think that you're performing the best mix in the world, when in reality the people on the dance floor can only hear distortion and noise.

Headphone mix isn't a vital option on the mixer, but every little bit helps – especially when beginning your beatmatching development!

Cueing with split cue

Another headphone monitoring option is *split cue*, where one ear of the headphones plays the cued signal and the other ear plays the live signal.

This technique is almost identical to single ear monitoring, where one ear is in headphones and one ear open to the live sound, except that the live sound is a lot clearer through headphones than from the speakers on the dance floor.

There's no right or wrong method for cueing in your headphones. The headphone cueing section on your home mixer can have an enormous effect on your cueing style, as can the room or club you're playing in. I suggest that you practise how to beatmatch with single ear monitoring first because it's the most common technique, but choose the method you prefer and make sure that you're 100 per cent happy with it.

Knowing how to use all three kinds of headphone cueing makes you a well-rounded DJ. If you can only mix using single ear monitoring, for example, the first time you play in a club that doesn't have a monitor in the DJ booth and you get a delay that's caused by the distance between the main speakers and the DJ booth, you're going to struggle. If you're faced with that occasion and if the mixer has the option, if you know how to mix with a split cue in the headphones, you're prepared for such a problem.

Centring your head with stereo image

Listening to two tunes at the same time and comparing their bass beats to see whether they're playing at the sam e time takes a lot of concentration. Your brain isn't normally in situations where it needs to listen and react to two things at the same time, so at first it tries to shut one of them out, meaning listening to two tunes at the same time may take some getting used to. The trick to getting this method right is how you set the volume in your headphones.

When you put your headphones on both ears just to listen to some music, you should notice that the music seems to be playing in the middle of your head. This sensation is known as the *stereo image* and is the voodoo magic of stereo sound.

If you monitor the live and cued track using single ear monitoring, the perfect volume at which to set your headphones is when you've created a similar *stereo image* in your head between the live speakers and the headphone as shown in Figure 14-1.

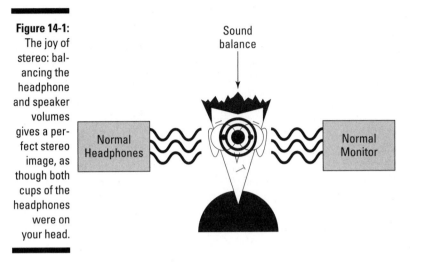

Figure 14-1: The joy of stereo: balancing the headphone and speaker volumes gives a perfect stereo image, as though both cups of the headphones were on your head.

DJs who use split cue can use the gain control to match the volume of the cued track in one ear of the headphones to the live track in the other ear. See Chapter 10 if you want more information about gain controls.

If the headphone or the loudspeaker is louder than the other, it becomes the more dominant sound, throwing off the balance of the stereo image, and your brain finds it much harder to concentrate on the bass beats from both records. Figure 14-2 gives you an idea of this imbalance.

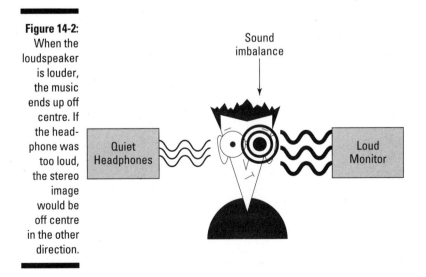

Figure 14-2: When the loudspeaker is louder, the music ends up off centre. If the headphone was too loud, the stereo image would be off centre in the other direction.

You can adopt this technique in reverse, which is why you turn up the TV volume when you're being nagged at home – when the TV is louder, it's harder to hear the person nagging you!

When listening to two copies of the same record, you really get the chance to discover what I'm saying in regards to stereo image. Set both records to zero pitch, start them playing at the same time (you're great at that now, I trust) and adjust the headphone volume louder and quieter. Close your eyes and listen to *where* the sound appears in your head. When you have a balance of volume between the live speaker and the headphone, the music creates a near-perfect stereo image in the middle of your head.

You won't often have the need to mix the same tune into itself, though, and when you play different tunes they won't create the same perfect stereo sound in your head. However, the bass beat is the key and is what you need to concentrate on. Even though the rest of the tune is different, all you need in order to create a stereo image in your head is the bass beat.

If you're having difficulty concentrating on the bass beats, or if the tune you're playing doesn't have a solid *Boom Boom Boom Boom* bass beat, listen to the bass and snare/clap combined beat instead (see 'Starting your tunes in time', earlier in this chapter). The snare drum or clap adds a sharper, clearer sound that some people find easier to pick out from the rest of the tune.

Practising with your headphones

To get used to using your headphones to monitor your tunes, go back to your DJ setup and, if you haven't already, set the mixer so you can hear the live track through the speakers and the cued track through your headphones.

Then go back to the beginning of this chapter and work on the basics of starting beats and matching pitch settings, from the basics of how to locate the bass beat to starting it at the right time, working out when you need to speed up or slow down a tune in order to match pitch settings and listening out for the *l'Boom, B'loom* indicators, all the time listening to the cued track in your headphones and the live track through the speakers.

When you're confident with cueing in the headphones and can comfortably tell whether the beats are in time this way, you can start creating long mixes without the beats of the tunes drifting apart, and will give yourself more time to spend creating impressive, professional-sounding mixes.

Using new tunes

At last. The confidence you've gained matching the beats of the same two tunes in your headphones means you can easily move on to beatmatching two different tunes.

Practice makes perfect

Practice makes a huge difference when developing your beatmatching skills. If you practise for two hours a night, you should be 75 per cent as good as anyone else at beatmatching by the end of one week – it's the last 25 per cent, perfecting it, that takes time to develop.

As a general timescale, when you become more comfortable with your music and your chosen DJ tool, be it CD, vinyl or digital DJing, by the end of a month practising beatmatching you'll find you'll be able to get the beats matched quickly without having to rush it or guess in order to start the mix before the other record runs out.

You may take months, maybe even years to perfect beatmatching and be confident that 99 per cent of the time you have the beats matched accurately and that they'll stay locked together for the duration of the mix. Just remember that during all that time spent practising, you get to listen to the music *you* love and the music *you* want to hear.

You may still want to use one of the tunes you've been practising with, but throw a new tune on the other deck. The good news is that you've already developed the skills and the ear to be able to match the beats of this new tune to the older one. The only things you have to think about are the sounds of the bass beats on this new tune, and whether its BPM means you need to speed up or slow it down in order to match the bass beats of both tunes.

If you take a while to get beatmatching right, that's fine. Tying to concentrate on two completely different tunes is a little more difficult, but give yourself time to practise and focus on what you're doing, and it'll fall into place very quickly.

Quick Beatmatching

I've left this technique until the end of the chapter because it's a last minute, emergency method for beatmatching when you don't know the BPM information that would normally help you with how to adjust the pitch control, and you don't have time to work it out.

You can use this method right at the beginning of your development when learning how to beatmatch, with both tunes playing through the speakers at the same time, or in a more traditional DJing situation, monitoring in the headphones. The outcome is just as effective.

1. **With the live tune playing through the speakers, set the pitch control on the cued tune (the next one you want to play) to maximum.**

   This takes all the guesswork out of knowing whether you need to speed up or slow down the tune to get the beats matched. Because you're starting the new tune way too fast, you know you'll just have to slow down the tune.

2. **With the cued track playing a lot faster than the live track, perform your chosen error correction method to slow the cued tune down enough that the beats are playing at the same time (or as close as you can get it). At the same time as you're performing this error correction, reduce the pitch control.**

   As you reduce the pitch control, you'll find you won't have to press quite so hard on the side of the turntable or press the pitch bend button quite as hard/long on CD decks to keep the tune playing slow enough to keep the beats matched.

3. **The closer you get to the correct pitch setting, the lighter and lighter your error correction needs to be.**

4. **When you feel you no longer need to error correct, stop – and stop adjusting the pitch control.**

5. **Make tiny error corrections and adjustments to the pitch control in order to keep the beats playing in sync.**

   When you stop hearing *B'loom* and *l'Boom*, which let you know your beats are out of sync, the beats will be matched.

Using this method, you should be able to get from Step 1 to Step 4 in about ten seconds. Step 5 may still take a little bit of time, but when you're in a rush, or just don't know your tunes well enough, this is an incredible quick fix for beatmatching.

Some people use this method for every mix they do, and nothing's wrong with that. However, in time, when you become more experienced with beatmatching and can easily remember more about the speed of your tunes, you won't need such a 'hail-Mary' approach to beatmatching.

Chapter 15

Picking Up on the Beat: Song Structure

*B*eing a good DJ means getting yourself a split personality. One half of you plays great tunes in the perfect order, and the other half of you creates the perfect mix from tune to tune.

You need more than straightforward beatmatching to create the perfect mix, especially if you're mixing rock, indie or party tunes, which don't lend themselves to beatmatching. How you adjust the EQs (equalisers) and overall sound level changes the dynamics of a mix (see Chapter 16 for more info), but the most important factor is choosing which parts of your tunes to mix over each other, and listening out for when your tunes progress from introductions to verses to choruses and to their outros.

Your knowledge of beat structures kicks in at this stage. Starting from the simple bar, which grows into a phrase, which blossoms into a verse, songs are mapped out in an extraordinarily ordinary fashion.

When you crack the code of how a tune is constructed, your instincts take over, you don't need to think and you can effortlessly create smooth transitions through your set that gets you praise for your skills.

Why DJs Need Structure

The simplest of mixes involves playing the introduction (intro) of a new tune over the last part (the *outro*) of the tune you wish to mix out of. In order to start this mix in time, the DJ needs to know when the outro is about to start. By analysing how beats and bars are put together to make up verses, choruses, introductions and outros (all of which I describe in detail in the section 'Studying Song Structure', later in the chapter) you won't miss a beat.

Knowledge of beat structure is vital for all kinds of DJs. Whether your style is to create minute-long, seamless transitions from tune to tune, or you simply start one tune as another ends, an understanding of how a tune is put together enables you to mix without any risk of gaps in bass drum beats, drops in the fun and energy of the night, or even worse – silence.

For more information on how different parts of tunes overlap to alter the sound and energy of the mix, check out Chapter 16.

Multiplying beats, bars and phrases

Just as a builder constructs a wall from hundreds of bricks layered on top of each other, and then adds that wall to other walls to make a house, a songwriter groups together the beats in a tune and adds these to further groups, and then joins these groups together to make larger structures, all of which are part of a bigger whole – the song. But before you start looking at how walls make a house (or how verse and choruses make a tune) you need to know how to build a wall – or create a chorus – out of beats and bars. If you can count to four, you can easily deal with beat structure, because the building blocks of nearly all tunes you'll encounter are grouped into fours:

  ✔ Four beats to a bar

  ✔ Four bars to a phrase

  ✔ Four phrases to a verse (normally)

Although typically made up of four phrases, the length of a verse can change depending on the decision of the songwriter.

The easiest way to explain how four beats become a bar and four bars become a phrase is with song lyrics. Unfortunately, I'd have to pay a lot of money if I wanted to use the lyrics to a recent, famous song, so I use the nursery rhyme 'Baa, Baa, Black Sheep' to show how the magic number 4 multiplies beats into bars and phrases.

To demonstrate the principle that you get four beats to a bar, look at the first line of the nursery rhyme, which is 'Baa, baa, black sheep', and lasts one baa, sorry, *bar* in length. You sing each one of these words on a different beat of the bar, and the first word has more emphasis than the next three.

A simple drum beat that accompanies this bar follows a basic pattern of 'bass' – 'bass/snare' (check out Chapter 14 if you need more information on drum patterns), as you can see in the following:

Beat 1 – *Baa* (bass drum)

Beat 2 – *baa* (bass drum and snare)

Beat 3 – *black* (bass drum)

Beat 4 – *sheep* (bass drum and snare)

Moving further into the nursery rhyme, this first bar is the first of the four bars that make up the first phrase:

Bar 1 – *Baa, baa, black sheep,*

Bar 2 – *Have you any wool?*

Bar 3 – *Yes sir, yes sir,*

Bar 4 – *Three bags full.*

This first phrase is grouped together with three others to create 16 lines (and therefore 16 bars) and create a full section.

Baa, baa, black sheep,

Have you any wool?

Yes sir, yes sir,

Three bags full. (End of Phrase 1 – four lines/bars in length)

One for the master,

One for the dame,

And one for the little boy

Who lives down the lane. (End of Phrase 2 – rhyme is eight bars to here.)

Baa, baa, black sheep,

Have you any wool?

Yes sir, yes sir,

Three bags full. (End of Phrase 3 – rhyme is 12 bars to here.)

One to mend the jerseys

One to mend the socks

And one to mend the holes in

The little girls' frocks. (End of Phrase 4 – total rhyme duration is 16 bars.)

Take another look at the 16 lines in the nursery rhyme. Although four different phrases make up the entire rhyme, you can group together the first two and the second two phrases as two different parts of the rhyme. Both halves start with the identical 'Baa, baa, black sheep, have you any wool, yes sir, yes sir, three bags full' phrase, but the next phrase is different.

You find the same principle in music: the second half of a verse may sound very similar to the first half, but in the final, fourth phrase, the sounds, drums and energy of any vocals or instruments increases to let you know that you're approaching the end of the entire verse rather than the end of the first half.

Hearing the cymbal as a symbol

Not all songs have lyrics to follow that let you know where you are in the tune. Even though music without lyrics sometimes has a change of the melody through the different phrases, you may need a little more guidance to help you pinpoint your position. If you've just dropped the needle, or started the CD at a random point with a view to starting a mix, you need to know how to work out where you are in a four-phrase (16-bar) pattern.

Luckily for DJs, record producers are very kind people and leave *end-of-phrase markers* (commonly cymbal crashes) at or after the end of phrases.

The four phrases given in the 'Baa, Baa, Black Sheep' example have three key, different types of endings:

- The end of the first and third phrase (probably identical)
- The end of the second phrase (the halfway point)
- The end of the fourth phrase (the final and most powerful point)

The ends of the first and third phrase are likely to have a cymbal crash as a simple punctuation point (often on the fourth beat of the fourth bar), but nothing too special.

The end of the second phrase, the halfway point, has a little more to it, because that first half exists as a discreet part of the story. This ending may have a small change to the drums, such as a mini drum roll, and end with a cymbal crash on the last beat or the first beat of the next (ninth) bar.

The end of the fourth phrase is the important one. This end-of-phrase marker lets you know that the tune is about to move onto a new section, from a verse to a chorus, a chorus to a breakdown or a breakdown to a verse, and so on. It's similar to the halfway marker, but more pronounced and powerful. The drum roll is longer, the vocals have more depth and the energy is a lot higher, swelling up to move onto the next section.

Everything changes

Markers at the end of each phrase are common in some genres of music, but don't rely on this fact; songwriters don't always provide markers at the end of Phrases 1 and 3. Knowing your tunes inside out really helps you at this stage.

If the tune has lyrics, then recognising the lyric cues for the end of phrases – when you've listened to the tune enough times – is relatively easy.

For a tune without lyrics, listen to how it changes from phrase to phrase, even without these end-of-phrase marker points. The main hook may start over, the melody may have a key change, another instrument may be introduced, another drum sound or synthesised sound may be added or you may pick up on a general shift in the volume or power of the music made by the addition of filters/compressors, a feeling to the music rather than something that you can actually hear and define.

Clever producers try to bend the rules and play with what you expect to hear, but in most tunes out there something changes or is added every four bars.

Counting on where you are

Start one of your tunes playing, listen to it and try to hear how the beats build into bars, bars build into phrases, phrases into halves of verses like the nursery rhyme and then how the verse moves into the next part.

To help you get to grips with this, start from the very first bass beat, and as the music plays count along with the beats, as shown in Figure 15-1.

Figure 15-1: Counting along with the beats.

BAR		*1*				*2*				*3*				*4*		
BEAT	1	2	3	4	1	2	3	4	1	2	3	4	1	2	3	4
SAY	**ONE** two three four				**TWO** two three four				**THREE** two three four				**FOUR** two three four			

Count the bar number as the first beat of the bar. The point of counting this way is simply so that you know which bar you're on.

The first beat of the bar has more emphasis to it, so when you're counting the beats, put more energy into saying the first number; '*ONE two three four* – *TWO two three four*', and so on.

At the end of the first phrase (four bars) of the tune you're playing, listen to what happens. On beat 4 of the fourth bar, or beat 1 of the next bar, you're likely to hear a cymbal crash or some kind of sound that acts as the end of the phrase. The marker sound for this first phrase is likely to be the same for all the first phrases of a section throughout the rest of the tune.

Carry on counting and listening to how each phrase ends, and take special care to compare how each of the phrases end and how this indicates where you are in the 16 bars.

Keep listening to the entire tune because the opening section (the intro) may only be eight bars long. As you listen to the rest of the tune, use your knowledge of phrase lengths and remember the different end-of-phrase marker styles to help you decide what makes up the intro, verse and the chorus, all of which I describe in detail in the later section 'Studying Song Structure'.

Actively listening to your tunes

Be an active listener; really listen to what's playing. Rather than just sitting back and enjoying the music, concentrate on the sounds that you're hearing: drums, vocal samples (an 'Oh yeah' at the end of a bar is a good indicator!), changes in melodies or the bass line, any strange whoosh or other electronic noises – any of these sounds can be the markers that the songwriter has left to let you know where you are in the tune. Even the absence of a marker at the end of Phrases 1 and 3 can be the very marker you're searching for! Listen hard and you'll uncover the secrets of markers.

When you've cracked the beats/bars/phrases formula of how a tune is built, when you can identify the different end-of-phrase markers and when you've developed these instincts to be able to tell when the music is about to change, you find that you no longer need to count out beats and bars.

I can't stress strongly enough that you should try to move away from counting beats as quickly as possible. Developing a reliance on beat counting in order to mix well can stifle your creativity and may end in disaster. Not only do you risk looking like Rain Man when you count the beats and bars as they roll by, but if something happens to throw your concentration and you don't know where you are in the tune, the potential to create a nightmare mix is too big. Dedicate the time and concentration to develop the memory and the skill that enable you to listen to a track halfway through and know where you are within one or two phrases.

Studying Song Structure

The people on the dance floor aren't really interested in how songs are made, although they do anticipate and respond to the different parts of the music – just as you need to, too. As a DJ, you have to know when the tune is playing a verse, a chorus or a breakdown – even if the song has no lyrics – in order to create seamless, error-free, professional-sounding mixes.

Introductions, verses, choruses, breakdowns and outros are the different groups of bars and phrases that go together to create an entire tune:

- **Introduction (or intro):** The part at the very beginning of the tune before the main tune kicks in. It can be as long or as short as a piece of string, but usually consists of a multiple of eight bars in length, with normally a change or addition of instrument or sound every four bars. At the end of the intro, the song includes an end-of-phrase marker (build up, drum roll or cymbal crash sound), letting you know that it's about to end.

  The most DJ-friendly intro for beatmatching DJs lasts for at least 16 bars, and is made up of just drum beats for the first 8 of them. The second set of eight bars may start to introduce music such as the bass line to the tune. Chapter 14 tells you why this is so useful for beatmatching DJs, and also describes how to deal with different types of intros.

- **Verse:** In tunes with lyrics, each verse usually has different lyrics. If the tune has no lyrics, the verse is harder to discern, and though it may contain the main musical *hook* (the catchy part of the tune that you hum in the shower), it won't be too powerful and energetic. In most cases, the verse lasts for 16 bars (four phrases), and is split into two sets of 8 bars where the melody repeats itself but builds up through to the end of the 16th bar.

- **Chorus:** The part in the tune that normally has the same lyrics each time it plays. The chorus is usually based around the melodic hook and it's the most energetic, catchy and powerful part of the tune. It's shorter and more powerful than the verse sometimes at only eight bars (two phrases) in duration and lifts the energy of the track (and the dance floor). You may find that the song includes a marker cymbal to crash between the two phrases, and it has a build-up out of the second phrase.

  Even music without lyrics has a verse and chorus. What you find is that the main hook that runs through the tune is quite subdued in one part, and then powerful, energetic and obvious in another part. The subdued section is the verse of the tune, and the more powerful, full-on section is the chorus.

- **Breakdown:** The part where you can have a little rest. It's a transition/ bridge from the end of the chorus to the beginning of the next part.

To create a nice bridge out of the chorus and back into the next verse, breakdowns tend to be less powerful. The bass drums drop out, and the bass melodies and a reduced version of the hook to the tune play. The last bar has a build-up, like the end of a chorus or verse, and you may hear an indicator on the last beat of the bar or the first beat of the next bar, to let you know that it's changed to a new part.

If the track includes a breakdown very early on, it's likely to be quite short, lasting four or eight bars, and is known as a *mini-breakdown*.

The main breakdown occurs around halfway through a tune, and probably lasts twice the duration of any mini-breakdown already heard. It's typically 16 bars in length and follows the same sound design as the mini-breakdown, but has longer to get in and out, probably has less sounds and instruments to begin with and includes a crescendo (a build-up, like a drum roll with the instruments getting louder and faster) for the last two bars or entire last phrase.

In indie/rock/party music, a breakdown in the middle of the tune is more commonly called a *middle 8*. It can follow the same principle I described in the preceding paragraph, dropping power only to build back into the tune. But often the middle 8 is a twist to the tune, lasting eight bars (hence the name) and building back into the main, familiar tune again when finished. The effect is the same, giving a break from the main sound of the tune, but the method can be different, compared to trance/house music.

✔ **Outro:** The last part of the tune. Chances are, the last major element before the outro is a chorus. This chorus either repeats until the end (which is a DJ-unfriendly fade out) or you have a DJ-friendly outro.

The best kind of outro is actually a reverse of the intro. The intro starts with just beats, introduces the bass line and then starts the tune. If, after the last chorus, the music distils into just the drums, the bass melody and a cut-down version of the main melody for 8 bars, and then the next 8 bars are the drums and maybe the bass melody, you have 16 bars on hand that make mixing into the next tune easy (head to Chapter 16 for more).

Outros can last for a long time, though – going on for minutes! Every eight bars, the tune may strip off another element, until all you have is the hi-hat and the snare drum. Rather than a waste of vinyl (or bytes), this outro is extremely useful if you like to create long, over-lapped mixes.

Repeating the formula

The main blocks of the song are linked together by repetition, and even more repetition, but with subtle changes throughout the tune:

✔ The next verse and chorus tend to be much the same as the first two. If the song has lyrics, different verses have different sets of lyrics, but the chorus probably won't change.

- Although the structure, melody and patterns remain the same, the music may introduce new sounds or effects processing to the original verse/chorus to create a new depth to the tune (changing the sound slightly gives the listener a feeling of progression through the tune).

- As the breakdown or middle 8 drops the energy of the tune to its lowest point, a lot of songwriters like to follow it with a chorus – the most energetic part of the tune. Once again, the song may introduce more instruments and sounds to give the chorus a slightly newer feel.

- Depending on how long the tune is, the main breakdown may be followed by more verses, choruses and mini-breakdowns.

Accepting that every tune's different

You'd soon get bored listening to tunes that were designed to the same structure, even if the music was all different. In music production, altering the length of an intro, adding verses or choruses, adding breakdowns and mini-breakdowns, changing their length and extending outros are all part of what makes a tune unique when still following the basic four beats to a bar, four bars to a phrase structure.

The brain is an incredible organ. When you listen to a track with an active ear, after three or four run-throughs your brain remembers the basic structure of the tune, and then relies on triggers (such as the end-of-phrase markers, vocals or even just looking at the different shades of rings on the record) that help you remember the structure of that track along with the 1,000 other tracks in your collection.

The trick to getting your brain to work for you is to listen to your music a lot. You can't expect to know the structure of a tune immediately; you need to listen to it a few times. Practising your mixing skills gives you an opportunity to get to know your tunes, but I recommend copying your tracks to an iPod/tape/MiniDisc/CD so that you can listen to your music at any time.

Always listen with an active ear to the structure, the melody, the hook and the lyrics. Your brain stores all this information in your subconscious, calling upon these memories and your knowledge of how a tune is constructed from bars and phrases, ensuring that you never get confused during the mix.

Developing your basic instincts

Your memory and instincts for your music develop in the same way as they do when you drive a car. When driving, you don't have to think 'Accelerate . . . foot off a little . . . steer . . . straighten up . . . brake . . . clutch . . . check mirror . . . change to third . . . clutch . . . change to second . . . accelerate . . .' and so on, you just do it. You develop your instincts as a driver through practice and experience. It's exactly the same with DJing.

You know that the first beat of the bar is emphasised, you know that the melody or line of a lyric is likely to start on the first beat of a bar and from listening to the tune you know the kind of end-of-phrase markers that a certain tune uses at the end of a phrase, at the end of half a phrase and when it's about to change to another element like a verse or chorus.

In the 'Baa, Baa, Black Sheep' example in the earlier section 'Multiplying beats, bars and phrases', when you hear 'Have you any wool?', your instincts tell you that you're in the second bar of either Phrase 1 or Phrase 3, because you know the lyrics so well.

The lyrics in the phrase that follows tells you what half of the verse you're in, so if the next phrase begins 'One for the master', you know that you're only in Phrase 2 – but if you hear 'One to mend the jerseys', you know that it's Phrase 4.

However, try to listen for the different end-of-phrase marker that can tell you if you're just halfway through the verse or about to enter a new part of the tune, so you don't have to rely on remembering a vast range of lyrics. Songs without lyrics still follow structures; you just have to listen for the changes in music and instruments, rather than the changes of lyrics.

Listening to a Sample Structure

After you know how beats become bars, and bars multiply like rabbits (or sheep for that matter!) to become verses and choruses, the best thing you can do is to go through the structure of an entire tune, and then describe each part in a bit more detail.

In my website to accompany this book (www.recess.co.uk), you can find a section that contains some audio examples. When you finish reading this chapter, I recommend that you download one of the tunes. Listen to it, and try to hear not only what happens to mark the change from the larger parts of the tune, but also what happens every four and eight bars.

The following structure may help you discern the structure of the sample tune:

- **Intro:** 16 bars
- **Verse 1:** 16 bars (four phrases)
- **Chorus 1:** 8 bars (two phrases)

- ✔ **Mini breakdown:** 8 bars
- ✔ **Verse 2:** 16 bars (four phrases)
- ✔ **Chorus 2:** 8 bars (two phrases)
- ✔ **Breakdown:** 16 bars
- ✔ **Chorus 3:** 8 bars (two phrases)
- ✔ **Verse 3:** 16 bars (four phrases)
- ✔ **Chorus 4:** 8 bars (two phrases)
- ✔ **Chorus 5:** 8 bars (two phrases)
- ✔ **Outro:** 16 bars

And remember – try to develop the skill to intuitively pick up beat structure through time and experience. Don't count bars!

Chapter 16

Mixing Like the Pros

In This Chapter

▶ Selecting the best placement points in your tunes

▶ Using your mixer's controls to their full potential

▶ Reaching the next level of beatmatching

▶ Mixing tips for different genres

*I*n this chapter, you build on your beatmatching skills (refer to Chapter 14) so that you can mix tunes at their correct points, and use the controls on the mixer to make the transition from tune to tune as smooth and skilful as possible. The mixing techniques in this chapter take time, experimentation and practice to get right before you can use them creatively. Understand the core concepts, but don't be bound by them, and discover the moments when breaking the rules is a good thing.

Recording your practice sessions when experimenting with the following techniques can be useful. In the heat of the moment, you may think that something didn't work, but when you listen back, it actually turned out great! Try anything, and if it sounds good to you then others may like it too.

Like all the techniques in this book, it doesn't matter what format you use – be it CDs, turntables, digital DJ setups or even MP3 DJ gadgets like the Pacemaker, the Nextbeat or an iPhone. It's not about what you use, it's about how you use it. The controls on these different pieces of equipment may be different, but beat structure and a need for perfect mix placement remains the same. Check out my website (www.recess.co.uk) for examples of the techniques I mention throughout the chapter.

Perfecting Placement

From Van Halen to Van Morrison, Silicon Soul to Soul to Soul, most tunes that you play follow the basic building blocks I describe in Chapter 15: four beats to a bar, 8 bars to a phrase and multiples of 8 bars to a section (a section is an entire intro, verse, chorus and so on, and typically lasts for 8 or 16 bars). One tune may have more choruses than another, or a longer intro, monster length breakdowns or extended outros, but this structure knowledge makes creating the perfect mix easier for you.

The perfect mix begins with perfect placement. Placement is simply the choice of what parts of the tunes you mix over each other. Perfect placement occurs when both tunes start or end a section at the same time – not only do the beats of both tunes match, but their structural changes match too. If the tune you want to mix out of (Tune A) is about to change from a chorus to its outro, an example of perfect placement would be to start the new tune (Tune B) so that its change from intro to verse happens on the exact beat that Tune A changes from chorus to outro.

Intros over outros

If Tune A has a 16-bar outro and Tune B has a 16-bar intro, simply overlapping the intro and outro is an option, but often intros and outros have no melody and are just a simple bass drum and hi-hats (the *tchsss*-sounding cymbal sound). Sixteen bars of that, though, can sound dull, unprofessional and boring. Figure 16-1 shows an example of a better sounding transition, where Tune A has two eight-bar choruses before the outro. You can create an overlap with the 16-bar intro of Tune B playing over the two choruses (marked Chorus 1 and Chorus 2) of Tune A. Then the outro of Tune A plays over the verse of Tune B.

In all the figures in this chapter, numbers in italics mean that the tune is at a lower volume, and numbers change size as the music fades in or out (gets gradually louder or quieter). Bold numbers mean playing at normal volume.

Figure 16-1:
16-bar intro
of Tune B
playing over
the last two
choruses of
Tune A.

Tune A:	Chorus 1	Chorus 2	16-bar outro	
Bars	**1 2 3 4 5 6 7 8**	**1 2 3 4 5 6 7 8**	*1 2 3 4 5 6 7 8*	*1 2 3 4 5 6 7 8*
Tune B:		16-bar intro		Verse
Bars	*1 2 3 4 5 6 7 8*	*1 2 3 4 5 6 7 8*	**1 2 3 4 5 6 7 8**	**1 2 3 4 5 6 7 8**

If both tunes had vocals in the chorus and verse, if you mixed between them so that the vocal on Tune A ended and Tune B's vocals started instantly, it may seem a little too quick. In this case, create a little rest, or an anticipation of what's to come. To introduce this pause, start Tune B at the end of Chorus 1, as Chorus 2 begins. This later starting point creates an eight-bar rest while the outro of Tune A mixes with the intro of Tune B, and then the verse of Tune B begins (see Figure 16-2).

Figure 16-2:
The outro
of Tune A
mixes with
the intro of
Tune B.

Tune A:	Chorus 1	Chorus 2	16-bar outro	
Bars	1 2 3 4 5 6 7 8	1 2 3 4 5 6 7 8	1 2 3 4 5 6 7 8	*1 2 3 4 5 6 7 8*
Tune B:		16-bar intro		Verse
Bars		*1 2 3 4 5 6 7 8*	1 2 3 4 5 6 7 8	1 2 3 4 5 6 7 8	1 2 3 4 5 6 7 8

Ideally, the outro of Tune A or the intro of Tune B is more than just plain drum beats. A bass melody or subtle background noise is enough to keep interest going in this mix for eight bars. A four-bar rest is better if you only hear drum beats. As with all these techniques, experiment to get the best results.

Melodic outro

Not all tunes have pounding bass beats from start to finish. Some have moody, beatless, melodic outros that sound great over an intro with a strong beat.

In Figure 16-2, the intro was slowly faded up to sneak into the mix. However, if you want to keep a constant beat going by mixing 16 bars of beat intro over 16 bars of beatless melodic outro, you have to start Tune B so that it instantly plays at full volume.

If Tune B has a good build-up out of the intro and into the verse, you can keep Tune A's outro playing at near to full volume until the end and then fade it out on the last beat before Tune B's verse starts (check out Figure 16-3).

Figure 16-3:
16-bar intro
of Tune B
playing over
the last two
choruses of
Tune A.

Tune A:	Chorus 2	16-bar melodic outro	(Tune A has now ended)	
Bars	1 2 3 4 5 6 7 8	1 2 3 4 5 6 7 8	1 2 3 4 5 6 7 8	
Tune B:		16-bar bass beat intro		Verse
Bars		1 2 3 4 5 6 7 8	1 2 3 4 5 6 7 8	1 2 3 4 5 6 7 8	1 2 3 4 5 6 7 8

Mixing beat intros over beatless melodic outros means you can't afford to make a starting error – you have to start the beat precisely in time. If you use turntables, spend lots of time practising starting records so you hear them instantly, to develop the confidence to start the beats on time, every time, without needing any error correction. (If you need to go back to the basics of starting tunes, check out Chapter 14). Waiting one or two beats to check that you're in time and then quickly moving the cross-fader to the middle (or worse, fading in the beats) sounds terrible, is unprofessional and usually ruins a mix (and your reputation). This technique is a lot easier for CD DJs who don't have to worry about motor start-up times like vinyl DJs. They just need to press a button in time with the beat to get it right.

If you're not confident with the instant start or don't want to mix the full 16 bars of intro over outro, start the beats of Tune B at the beginning of Chorus 2 (eight bars before the outro of Tune A begins) to make sure that your timing is immaculate. Then move the cross-fader to the middle after eight bars, as Tune A hits the outro (see Figure 16-4).

Figure 16-4:
Using the cross-fader to fade out Tune A's outro over the verse of Tune B.

Tune A:	Chorus 2	16-bar outro	
Bars	1 2 3 4 5 6 7 8	1 2 3 4 5 6 7 8	1 2 3 4 5 6 7 8 *(very quiet, if not out completely)*
Tune B:		16-bar intro	Verse	
Bars		1 2 3 4 5 6 7 8	1 2 3 4 5 6 7 8	1 2 3 4 5 6 7 8

The faint-hearted who need a safety net can slowly mix in Tune B's intro beats over the beats of Tune A's Chorus 2 using the EQs (equalisers) to smooth the transition (see 'Balancing it out with EQs', later in the chapter), which is far preferable to fading up the beats over a beatless outro.

Melodic intro

The reverse of melodic outros is a bit tougher, because mixing an intro with no beats means that with no drums to keep time when beatmatching, when the beats in Tune B eventually start you risk them playing at a completely different time to the beats from Tune A.

If the intro has a melody or a very soft rhythm, concentrate on that. Tapping your feet with this rhythm can help to keep your concentration. Practise this mix as much as you can, because when you do it live all the noise and distraction in the DJ booth can mean that you end up with a train wreck of a mix!

Mixing Breakdowns

You don't have to play a tune from the very beginning to the very end. Mixing two breakdowns over each other or an intro over a breakdown can sound great, and lets you shorten a really long tune. (Chapter 15 has more on breakdowns and mini-breakdowns.) Here are a few combinations to try:

✔ **Breakdown over breakdown:** No matter whether your breakdowns are 8-bars or 16-bars long, if both are the same length, start Tune B's breakdown as Tune A's breakdown starts, then gradually fade and EQ out Tune A so all that's left is Tune B's breakdown, which is about to build up into the beats again (see Figure 16-5).

Figure 16-5:
Two break-
downs mix
over each
other to
skilfully
introduce
the new
tune.

Tune A:	|	Breakdown	|
Bars	|1 2 3 4 5 6 7 8|1 2 3 4	|
Tune B:	|	Breakdown	|	Verse/Chorus	|
Bars	|*1 2 3 4 5 6 7 8*|1 2 3 4 5 6 7 8|1 2 3 4 5 6 7 8|1 2 3 4 5 6 7 8

✔ **Mini-breakdowns:** As breakdowns are normally at least halfway through a tune, you may not want to start Tune B at that point because it'll cut out so much of the tune. If you're lucky, there may be an eight-bar mini-breakdown in the first half of Tune B, probably after the first chorus, or it may be right after the intro, used as a way to emphasise the start of the main tune, in which case try my suggestion in Figure 16-6).

Figure 16-6:
A mini-
breakdown
introduces
a new tune
early on
rather than
halfway
through.

Tune A:	|	Breakdown	|
Bars	|1 2 3 4 5 6 7 8 |*1 2 3 4 5 6 7 8*|
Tune B:	|	Mini-Breakdown	|	Verse/Chorus	|
Bars	|	1 2 3 4 5 6 7 8 |1 2 3 4 5 6 7 8|1 2 3 4 5 6 7 8

✔ **Adding pace:** If you start Tune B eight bars earlier so that you mix out halfway through Tune A's breakdown, you add a feel of urgency and pace to the mix (see Figure 16-7).

Tune A:	| **16-bar Breakdown** |	(last 8 bars |
Bars	| **1 2 3 4** 5 6 7 8	are silent) |
Tune B:	| **Mini-Breakdown** |	**Verse/Chorus**
Bars	| 1 2 3 4 **5 6 7 8**	| **1 2 3 4 5 6 7 8 | 1 2 3 4 5 6 7 8**

✔ **Beat intro over breakdown:** This method, shown in Figure 16-8, is identical to starting a beat intro over a melodic outro (see Figure 16-3). You need the confidence to start Tune B with the cross-fader open to carry the beats through the breakdown. However, because this is a natural breakdown in Tune A, rather than an outro, you can fade in Tune B's beats if you use the EQs to kill the bass before starting the fade (see 'Controlling the Sound of the Mix', later in this chapter). The hi-hats from Tune B keep a rhythm going and you can quickly bring the bass in halfway through the breakdown. How well this method works and how good it sounds greatly depend on the tunes that you're using.

In that example, if you're still not confident starting the beats with an open cross-fader, start Tune B in the same place, wait until the end of the eighth bar and then quickly move the cross-fader to the middle. But if this sudden introduction of beats sounds a bit jarring, try killing the bass and gradually fade Tune B in over the first eight bars of Tune A's breakdown.

Tune A:	| **Breakdown** |
Bars	| **1 2 3 4 5 6 7 8 | 1 2 3 4** 5 6 7 8 |
Tune B:	| **16-bar intro** | **Verse/Chorus** |
Bars	| **1 2 3 4 5 6 7 8 | 1 2 3 4 5 6 7 8 | 1 2 3 4 5 6 7 8 | 1 2 3 4 5 6 7 8**

These examples are the simplest, most basic placement principles to take into consideration when mixing tunes. You can mix your tunes in thousands of different ways depending on where you start Tune B from, and where in Tune A you start the mix. Change where you start Tune B back or forward by 8 or 16 bars, and experiment with how soon or late to mix out of Tune A.

Listen to your tunes with an active ear for all the audio clues and markers (refer to Chapter 15) that let you work out the best places to mix in and out of your tunes. Two tunes may have the perfect mix – you just have to find it!

Controlling the Sound of the Mix

After you've mastered the mechanics of beatmatching and know the best places to mix in and out of your tunes, your true artistry comes from controlling the sound of the mix. The cross-fader, the channel-faders and the EQ controls on your mixer are the salt and lemon to your tequila, the candlelight to your dinner and the chocolate to your chilli; they all add extra zest and finesse to the mix. (I'm not kidding; add a little dark chocolate to your chilli – it's lovely.)

Bringing the cross-fader into play

How fast you move the cross-fader from one tune to another can dramatically alter the power of a mix. Smoothly moving from one tune to the other over the course of 16 bars can be very subtle if you're beatmatching, or extremely messy if you mix the wrong rock tunes together. Chopping back and forth from tune to tune adds a sense of immediacy, which can be really powerful at the right moment. These methods work with the right tunes, and can be the main way to mix for a lot of pop, rock, indie and party tunes. But as a beatmatching DJ, if all you do is whip the fader across quickly for each mix, you'll come across as a DJ who can't hold the beats matched for a long time and needs to mix out quickly.

Every mix has two halves. No matter how fast you move the cross-fader, you're not only bringing in a new tune but you still need to take out the old tune. Apply the same care and attention when moving the cross-fader to fully mix out of a track as you do when mixing in the new track.

A cross-fader move that lasts four beats or less is hard to get wrong – just time the move from one side to the other to last four beats (you'll be at the halfway point by the second beat). Moves that last longer than four beats when beatmatching need a bit more of a pattern and control to them.

The way to approach longer mixes is to move the cross-fader so that the increases occur on the hi-hat *tchsss* sound in between the bass drums. This method helps to hide the increase in volume from the new track, and makes taking out the old tune less noticeable.

Cymbal crashes and build-ups are great places to hide larger moves of the cross-fader. When something like that from either tune adds impact, move the cross-fader a farther distance than the move before. Be aware of a mix that starts to sound messy, though. If you're moving the cross-fader too fast, move it back a bit and let the music play for a bar without any increase (provided you have time in the tunes to do so).

You can also use crescendos and temporary bass beat drop-outs to disguise your cross-fader moves. *Crescendo* is a fancy way of saying build-up. A four-beat crescendo is over quite quickly, so you may want to have the two tunes mixed together for a couple of phrases beforehand with the cross-fader still favouring Tune A (the outgoing tune). Then, during the four beats of the crescendo, move the cross-fader over so that the new tune is dominant, at the end of the four beats, with the old tune playing in the background. When to finish the mix is up to you, but it's likely that this will be quite a fast mix.

The opposite is just as appropriate. Instead of a build-up, the last four beats of a phrase in Tune A may have no bass drum beat (but the rest of the music is still just as loud). Instead of mixing Tune B lightly into the background, keep it silent and then just as the last beat of Tune A's opposite-build-up plays (at the end of the phrase), quickly move the cross-fader over to the new tune. Moving the cross-fader all the way over in one beat can be an incredibly powerful mix, or you can move the cross-fader so that it favours the new tune (about three-quarters of the way across) and kill the bass on Tune A to keep it subtly playing in the background (see the section 'Balancing it out with EQs' for info on EQ control).

Unleashing channel-faders

Channel-faders are lonely little fellows. Lots of DJs put them up to full and leave them there forever. But these vertical faders have a secret, undercover role that many DJs don't tap into.

The primary role of the channel-fader is to work in conjunction with the gain control to control how loud the music from a channel plays out of the mixer. (If you're unsure of how to make this adjustment, check out Chapter 10.) With the input levels matched for both channels, you need to decide where to set the channel-faders when you want the tunes to play at their loudest.

DJs quite commonly set up their mixer so that the channel-fader needs to be set to its highest point (sometimes marked 10) for this optimum play-out volume. For beatmatching DJs who try to keep the volume of the mix a smooth constant from start to finish, this isn't the best setting. For scratch DJs, this highest-point setting is correct, and very important so that they can just flick up the fader to be at full volume.

Some DJs advise setting channel-faders to full so you won't accidentally knock them and increase the volume by accident. I say, be as careful about not knocking your channel-faders as you are about not ejecting CDs or taking off records while they're playing. You may do it once – but you learn quickly to be more careful.

The best way to set up your mixer is so that your channel-faders are set at three-quarters of the way to maximum (around 7 if your fader is marked from zero to 10). Using this technique means that when you mix in the next tune, if the tune is a bit too quiet even though the levels looked correct, you can quickly raise the channel-fader to compensate for the lack of volume.

Letting you in on a big, curvy secret

Cross-fader curves affect how much one tune gets louder and the other one gets quieter as you move the cross-fader from side to side (you can find examples of cross-fader curves in Chapter 10). However, sometimes the curve isn't subtle enough for a smooth, seamless mix and can cause the two tunes to play too loudly over each other, sounding messy and unprofessional. So you need to find a way to gain more control over the output of each tune during the mix. The channel-faders release you from the strict constraints of the cross-fader curve.

For a simple mix that gives you precise control over each tune's volume try the following:

1. **Set the channel-fader on the new tune (Tune B) to one-quarter of its loudest point.**

2. **When you're ready to start mixing in the new tune, move the cross-fader into the middle, following the techniques I describe in the section 'Bringing the cross-fader into play', earlier in this chapter.**

3. **Start to raise Tune B's channel-fader, continuing to increase it in time with the hi-hats. (The cross-fader is still in the middle.)**

4. **Keep an eye on the output meters and an ear on the sound of the mix, and as the Tune B gets louder slowly lower the channel-fader of the outgoing tune (Tune A) until Tune B is dominant and Tune A is playing at a volume that's best for that moment in the mix (likely to be similar to where the Tune B's channel-fader was when you started it).**

5. **When you want to fully mix out Tune A, move the cross-fader all the way over to Tune B's side.**

How you change the positions of the channel-faders, and the time you take to do so, is up to you. You can simply raise one fader while lowering the other, or wait for Tune B's channel-fader to be halfway up before you start to lower Tune A's fader. Make the adjustments depending on your own personal style, the output levels and what sounds best with the two tunes you're using.

If you prefer, you can leave the cross-fader in the middle (or do what I do and turn it off if you have that function) to bypass the cross-fader function alto-gether. This option gives you ultimate control over the individual volumes of your tunes during the mix. The only difference to the previous method is that you start with the channel-fader at zero for the incoming tune (Tune B), and end with the channel-fader at zero for the outgoing tune (Tune A).

Balancing it out with EQs

As with channel-faders, EQs have multiple roles. The first role is sound con-trol: affecting how the music sounds on CD or to the dance floor. You can also use EQs to add some variation and spice to a tune (check out the section 'Cutting in', later in this chapter). But their most useful role is in smoothing the sound of the mix.

Good EQ control can't do anything about a poor choice of tunes to mix together, but great EQ control can turn a passable mix into an incredible one.

Smoothing a transition with the bass EQ

The bass EQ is the one that you use most to create an even sound through the mix. When both tunes play with their bass at full, even if one tune is qui-eter than the other, the bass drums are too powerful and the bass melodies combine to sound messy.

The simplest but most effective technique is to kill the bass (reduce it to, or near to, its lowest point) on the incoming tune when you start to mix it in, and when you want to make this tune the dominant one increase the bass EQ at the same time as decreasing the bass EQ on the tune that you're mixing out of. This manoeuvre means that the amount of bass you hear through the speak-ers stays the same, but it comes from different tunes.

With the right tunes, taking your time over this swap can create a subtle, unnoticeable mix. Or swapping the EQs in one beat can cause a hands in the air moment by introducing the bass line from a tune that you know the crowd will love, emphasising a change in key (see Chapter 18), changing the power of the mix or punching in a change in genre.

Taking the edge off with the mid-range and high-end

Despite the fact that the high frequencies aren't as loud and obvious as the bass frequencies, they're just as important in controlling the sound of the mix. Two sets of loud hi-hats playing over each other can sound just as bad as two sets of bass drums and bass melodies. The technique is exactly the same as the bass EQ, except you don't need to cut the high EQ nearly as much. For example, on my Pioneer DJM-600 mixer I find that the 12 o'clock position is usually the best place to leave the high EQ for normal play-out.

When I want to cut out the high EQ to help the sound of the mix, I only need to move the knob to around the ten o'clock position (rather than the seven o'clock position for the bass EQ).

Because the mid EQ covers a larger range of frequencies, how much you use it with this technique depends on the tunes you're playing. You may not need to swap over the mid EQs if you don't notice a clash of sounds, or you may find that rather than cutting the mid EQ, you want to boost it. Sometimes, when the outgoing tune is playing quieter, I boost the mid EQ to play those frequencies louder than normal. If you have a melody or sound repeating in the background of the tune, this emphasis can lengthen and strengthen the mix, and even more so if you add effects to the music (see Chapter 10).

Always keep an eye on the meters and an ear on the sound of the mix while you're swapping any EQs. Strive to keep an even sound as the two tunes play over each other. If one tune is too loud, or both tunes have too much bass or high frequency, you may create a cacophony of noise.

Using Mixing Tricks and Gimmicks

Tricks and gimmicks are great to use once in a while because they add surprise and a little pizzazz to your mix. Avoid over using tricks, however, because the listener may think that you only use them because you can't mix between tunes properly. Use the gimmicks as transitions to increase energy, change the musical genre or key, or even just help a change in tempo.

With each of the following techniques, experiment with how long you take to move the cross-fader and where you position the cross-fader when you start the trick. Start by setting the cross-fader so that you can't hear the next tune until the start of the move, and then find out what it sounds like if you have the cross-fader in the middle when you start the move. Give thought to volume control as well because some of these tricks really don't work well with the channel-fader at maximum – you may deafen the dance floor or blow a speaker!

Spinbacks and dead-stops

Try out a technique called a *spinback*: beatmatch and start a mix between two tunes with perfect placement (see 'Perfecting Placement' at the beginning of the chapter) so that the tune you want to mix out of (Tune A) ends a section (probably a chorus or powerful outro) as Tune B (the new tune) begins the first phrase of a section. On the very last beat before this change, place your finger on Tune A and spin the record back, sharply. As the tune spins backwards, close the cross-fader over to Tune B within one beat, as shown in Figure 16-9 (SB stands for spinback).

Figure 16-9:
The spin-
back is
performed
on the
fourth beat
of the fourth
bar and then
instantly
mixes into
Tune B.

	Bar 1	Bar 2	Bar 3	Bar 4	Bar 1
Tune A:	**1 2 3 4**	**1 2 3 4**	**1 2 3 4**	**1 2 3** *SB*	*SILENT*
Tune B:	*1 2 3 4*	*1 2 3 4*	*1 2 3 4*	*1 2 3 4*	**1 2 3 4**

The spinback isn't exclusive to turntables, but you'll need a CD deck with a vinyl mode in order to make this sound right. CD decks without this mode just judder and stutter if you try to skip them backwards. A CD deck with vinyl mode activated should sound just the same as a record being spun-back.

To perform a *dead-stop*, instead of spinning the record back in the example in Figure 16-9, press the Start/Stop button on Tune A (the one you're mixing out of). This action makes the tune stop playing in about one beat (unless your decks have a function to change the brake speed and you've set it to last longer). As with the spinback, move the cross-fader over to Tune B by the time it plays the first beat of the new section (so the move only lasts one beat).

Similar to the spinback, the CD deck you're using affects how well the dead-stop works. A CD deck with vinyl mode works perfectly if you set the brake correctly, but one without just stops instantly when you press Stop.

Power off

A *power off* is when you turn off the power to the turntable (normally located bottom left with the red strobe light underneath it). When you turn off the turntable, it gradually gets slower and slower, until it stops.

If you have a CD deck with vinyl mode and can adjust the brake speed, set it to its longest amount and this does the same thing. If you don't have vinyl mode, don't try turning off the power . . . everything just turns off.

Power off is a great trick in the DJ booth if you have good lights and someone who knows how to use them. Ask your partner-in-mayhem to kill the lights slowly at the same time as you do the power off. Chances are, everyone will think 'Power cut!'. After a few seconds, slam in the next tune at the most powerful point, at full volume, as the lighting jock floods the dance floor with as much light as possible. It's a gimmicky, cheesy trick, but can take the dance floor by surprise, and – you hope – really jazz them up. It's very clichéd, but at the right time, works a treat.

A cappella

If you have an instrumental track that you think would sound better with something else over the top of it, look for an *a cappella*, a separate vocal track without any instruments behind it.

The problem with using vocals is that you need the vocal to be in the same key as the instrumental you want to play it over, otherwise it sounds out of tune. This makes speeches and other spoken words a great alternative. I have a copy of JFK's inaugural speech that I love to mix over long instrumental tracks. The line 'Ask not what your country can do for you . . .' is an incredible introduction into the most powerful parts of a tune.

Don't get so involved in your new creation that you forget to mix in the next track. Your blend of a 'Learn Italian' lesson over a great instrumental may be going down really well, but if you run out of time to beatmatch and mix in the next tune, you've wasted your time.

A third input device like an extra CD deck or turntable, or an MP3 player or laptop, lets you play the a cappella over the instrumental tune, beatmatch the next tune and start the mix with the a cappella playing the whole time. Or you can use audio software to pre-mix the creation on computer and then burn it to CD to play later, but you'll lose the spontaneous performance side of the live new mix, which is often what makes this so special and effective.

Cutting in

Cutting in beats from another tune gets its roots from beatjuggling (see Chapter 17). The idea is to beatmatch two tunes and move the cross-fader between them to temporarily cut in beats from one tune over the other. In the right hands, this method can be incredibly fast and complicated. Figure 16-10 shows a basic, slow pattern (underlined numbers are the beats you can hear).

You don't have to move the cross-fader all the way over when cutting in beats; you can go three-quarters of the way across so that you can still hear the original tune. I find placing a finger at the three-quarter point helps this, because you can just bounce the cross-fader off your finger – it stops the cross-fader getting any farther than three-quarters of the way across, no matter how fast or hard you cut in the other tune.

Figure 16-10:
Various
beats from
Tune B are
'cut in' to
Tune A to
add power
and a new
feel to the
tune.

	Bar 1	Bar 2	Bar 3	Bar 4	Bar 1
Tune A:	**123**4	**12**34	**123**4	12**34**	12**34**
Tune B:	123**4**	12**34**	123**4**	**123**4	**1234**

A variation on cutting in beats is cutting out frequencies of the tune. Dropping the power out of the bass for the last bar of a phrase before it changes to a new element can be extremely effective, and doing this when the crowd is extremely excitable and energetic can blow the roof off the club – which is no mean feat if you're in the basement!

Effecting the transition

You don't just use effects in the main body of a tune to make it sound different; you can also use them to help the transition from one tune to the next. One example of this is if you're performing a long mix between two tunes but are having problems changing the balance of power to the new tune, and want this change to happen as the first verse of the new tune starts.

In this case, adding a flanger, filter, reverb, beatmasher or transform effect to the last bar of music before this change occurs can add a new sound to this mix, helping the power transfer between tunes:

- ✔ Set flanger or filter effects to last for two bars, and instead of the music whooshing down and back up again when using it over just one bar of music, it will only whoosh down – taking the power out of the outgoing tune and helping you to finish the mix with the new tune playing louder.

- ✔ Use the reverb set to maximum to effectively kill the power of the outgoing tune. The incoming tune needs to be quite high in the mix for this to work, and you need to sweep in the effect (gradually increase the strength) so it doesn't sound too sudden. The metallic sound it gives to the outgoing tune is a nice, quirky effect.

- ✔ A fast transform over the last two beats of this bar (so it splits the sound into eight stutter sounds) can help this transition too.

- ✔ Beatmasher effects create drum rolls out of thin air. By combining the sounds of the beats, you can change the last four single beats of a bar into a fast drum roll to get to the next tune.

Experiment with:

- ✔ How long you use the effect
- ✔ How strong or long the effect is set to last
- ✔ Whether you sweep in and out the effect
- ✔ How loud each of the tunes are in the mix
- ✔ Whether you effect both tunes or just one of them
- ✔ Whether you keep the outgoing tune in the mix after this balance of power shifts.

The ideas in this section are no means all the available effects or techniques. Experiment with all your effects; where, when, how and what to use is entirely up to you. If it sounds great, do it.

Mixing Different Styles of Music

Some genres of music don't rely on rules like beatmatching and perfect placement: in order to get from tune to tune, the music the DJ chooses to play is much more important than the mix itself. Making the transition from one tune to another without beatmatching takes a special skill and you still need these transition techniques as a beatmatching DJ – to change genres, take over from someone else or change the feel of the mix.

That's not to say you can't try beatmatching rock music or some party tunes. Some tunes work well together, but the problem lies in the fact that rock, for instance, isn't really designed to be mixed in the same way as electronic dance music. Drum machines, similar tempos and even the beat structure of dance music lends itself to beatmatching, but live drummers, vastly different tempos and sudden starts all mean that some other genres are a lot trickier, and you're best approaching their transitions in different ways.

The wedding/party/rock/pop mix

In many ways, the transition between tunes is a lot harder for the wedding/party/rock/pop DJ. A beatmatching DJ has the safety net of simply matching the beats and then fading between tunes, with no fade out, no sudden start, no change in tempo and no drastic genre change. The wedding/party DJ needs to work with all these issues.

The most important part of this mix is where in the new tune you start. Tunes like 'Brown Eyed Girl' by Van Morrison (a wedding favourite) that have a powerful, recognisable, instant start are great to work with.

You still need to think about beat structure when choosing when to start a tune like 'Brown Eyed Girl'. Starting it randomly won't sound good. As Tune A (the one you're mixing out of) fades out, or as you begin to fade it out, wait until the end of a bar (hopefully at the end of a phrase) and start 'Brown Eyed Girl' when Tune A plays beat one of a new bar, but fade it out completely before it does so.

If you want to mix a house tune with pounding bass beats into a track you can't beatmatch out of (still 'Brown Eyed Girl', for instance), the technique is the same. However, because house tracks tend to have long, beat-only intros, you may want to start them later, when the main tune kicks in.

Looking in more depth at the technique, you have to work out how much you need to fade out a tune before starting the next one, and when to start the next tune. Some tunes sound fine when you start them at the beginning of the outgoing tune's bar; some sound better on the third or fourth beat of the bar. Practice and experience listening to and playing your tunes lets you develop the skill and an instinct for how best to mix your tunes.

Of course, not all records have a powerful point in the tune that you'd like to start from. For instance, maybe you want to play a slow track so people can smooch and dance closer (and you can run to the bathroom or the bar). The mix out of the last track is the same as with mixing in 'Brown Eyed Girl', but instead of an immediate, full-volume start on the new track, it may sound better if you take a full bar (four beats) to go from quiet to full volume, and create a smooth, swelling fade-up of 'Wonderful Tonight', for example.

Another option is to talk during the mix. You can use tales of the buffet, drink promos and good-looking rock chicks and comments about the mother-of-the bride's inappropriate dancing to cover a mix.

The trick is to control the volume of the music as you speak into the microphone: keep the music low enough so that you can be heard, but loud enough so that it doesn't sound like your giving a monologue. Listen to how radio DJs talk over the beginning of songs that they play. They know when the tune changes from intro to the main song and time their chatter to coincide; get to know your tunes so you can do the same thing. Perform a simple cross-fade between the two tunes, speaking over the mix to hide the transition, and stop waffling just as the main tune starts.

The R&B mix

R&B doesn't tend to have the long, luxurious intros that house and trance music have, but the tunes often have a very good opening bar that you can use to mix over the last tune much like the party DJ mix. In addition, R&B tunes often kill bass beats for the last bar of a phrase, making this point perfect for mixing in the new tune because otherwise the complicated, bass-heavy drums could fight with each other.

R&B does have scope for beatmatching if you have tunes with similar beat patterns, but R&B works best when the beatmatch mix is as short as possible. Using the new tune, a short baby scratch (see Chapter 17) in time with the beats on the outgoing tune and then starting the new tune playing from a powerful point is an excellent way to mix when you can't match beats.

Drum and bass, and breakbeat

Drum and bass, and breakbeat are both genres that tend to follow the four-beats-to-a-bar structure that house/trance follows, so you're normally able to follow the basic principles of placement I mention in the earlier section 'Perfecting Placement'. However, the beats in the bars are a lot more complicated, so if you're struggling to beatmatch breakbeat or drum and bass, first see Chapter 14 for more information about beatmatching and then, instead of focusing on bass sounds, focus on the clearer snare sounds.

A huge phenomenon in drum and bass circles over the past few years has been the *double drop*, an extension of breakdown mixing. All genres can benefit from this technique. Beatmatch and start a mix so that two tunes are about to hit a breakdown (also called a *drop*) at the same time – the drop on either tune may be the main breakdown, or a shorter one earlier or later in the tune. The key is to mix the tunes together so they both come out of their drops at the same time, after which you keep both tunes audible, playing through the speakers. So if you're mixing an 8-bar drop into a 16-bar drop, be sure to start the 8-bar drop halfway through the longer one.

Tune selection is vital for creating a good sounding double drop. Don't perform it with just any two tunes – they need to have a complementary rhythm and key, and you need to pay special attention to volume and EQ control on both tunes to avoid a messy sound. Experiment with the tunes and the drops you use in the double drop. Performed well, this live re-mix of playing two tunes over each other sounds really powerful.

Beatmatching tunes with vastly different tempos

Beatmatching tunes with different tempos works across all genres – dance, rock, R&B and many more – but works best with tunes that have a strong but not overly complicated outro and intro. If you're DJing with rock, indie, party/wedding music and even drum and bass or jungle, mixing tunes of different tempos is a quirky way to mix between tunes that can be effective at various points in the night (as long as you don't overdo it).

When DJing in house/trance clubs, you want to keep the tempo high to keep the energy going when people are dancing, so a huge change in BPM might not go down well with the customers. However, if a tune actually slows right down during its outro, it's a good way to get back up to a faster tempo again, or it can be a creative way to change genres of music. This is a once-a-night mix for many house/trance sets rather than a technique you pepper throughout the night.

Beatmatching tunes with different tempos usually takes special equipment to perform well:

- A deck with Master Tempo control on it, which keeps the pitch of the tune the same no matter how fast the playing speed
- A large pitch range (you need a range of around +/–20 per cent at least)
- In this case, a beat counter *does* help you get it right

If you have one rock tune that's banging out a good powerful outro at 125 BPM, and you want to mix in a tune at 100 BPM, spend two or four bars to reduce the pitch control right down so that it now plays at 100 BPM. When you're at the end of these bars, start the next tune and fade out the outgoing tune (refer to all the earlier sections in this chapter for guidance on EQ control).

How long you spend slowing down the tune is up to you – it'll most likely be dictated by the tunes you're trying to mix together. Think about times when you might want to do it the other way too – to add excitement and energy to your mix. It's certainly a technique that works best when slowing down a tune to match the new one, but with the right pair of songs it can work well the other way too, especially if you turn off Master Tempo to let the pitch go up as well as the speed.

Chapter 17

Scratching Lyrical

. . . .

In This Chapter

▶ Ensuring your gear is up to scratch

▶ Marking your records properly

▶ Scratching on vinyl, CD, MP3 and computer

▶ Lending you a helping hand with basic scratching

. . . .

Scratching is a specialised skill that takes a lot of practice and patience to master. When you've taken the time to develop the skill, half the people you know will drop their jaws in amazement at what you're doing, while the other half will open their mouths just as wide – and yawn.

Whether you go on to develop the crab, the flare or the twiddle is up to you, but if you can master the baby scratch, the forward scratch and the cut, even if you consider yourself only a beatmatching, mixing DJ, you'll be adding another weapon to your arsenal of knowledge.

Scratching skills help you develop a smooth, fast technique when using your equipment – especially vinyl. When you've grasped the basics, you develop a feel for how much pressure you need to apply (very little) to hold a record still while the deckplatter is turning, you're able to wind the record back and forth without the needle flying off and you develop solid, stable hands when holding the record stopped, ready to start it.

The website that accompanies this book has audio and video clips to support the information contained in this chapter, because most of the techniques are better shown rather than described. Be sure to log on to check that you're happy with what you're doing (see www.recess.co.uk).

Setting Up Equipment the Right Way

Anyone who has used equipment that was poorly configured or wasn't suitable for scratching will show the emotional scars as proof that you can't afford to get the setup wrong.

If you're using CDs to scratch with you don't need to set up much, apart from maybe the resistance of the platter (see Chapter 8) and switching the CD deck to vinyl mode in order to create the right scratch sounds.

For turntable scratch DJs, I mention a few of the basic but vital requirements that your turntables need to be suitable for DJing in Chapter 6. Turntables built for mixing share many of the same qualities as those you use for scratching: powerful, direct-drive motors are essential, and an adjustable tonearm, removable headshells and sturdy design are also crucial.

However, how you set up the needles, the orientation of the turntable and how you plug into your mixer are just as important as the make and model of turntable that you're using.

A big factor for scratch DJs is the positioning of the decks. Instead of setting them up as the manufacturer intended (tonearm and pitch fader on the right-hand side), scratch DJs rotate the entire turntable anticlockwise by 90 degrees, so that the tonearm and pitch control are farthest away from the DJ.

The traditional setup only gives the DJ around 100 degrees of the record's circumference to work with (shown in Figure 17-1, top), so the DJ can only pull the record back so far without hitting the needle out of the groove. Rotating the turntable by 90 degrees gives the DJ a lot more vinyl to work with (shown in Figure 17-1, bottom), making scratching much easier.

Weighing up needles

No matter what you use, how you set up the needle and the counterweight can drastically affect the stability of the needle. You don't want the needle jumping out of the groove when you're performing a tough scratch. Check out Chapter 7 for information on what makes a needle good for scratch use; the Shure M44-7 needle and cartridge (shown in Figure 17-2) has proved the most popular needle for scratching over the years.

The two ways to control the stability of your needle are through the downforce acting on the needle and the angle that it digs into the groove. Simply set the needle so that it angles into the groove by 10 degrees and it'll stick to the groove like glue. The downside, though, is that the needle wears out the groove like a hot knife through butter.

If you're adjusting the downforce on the needle to control stability, don't automatically add the heaviest counterweight available. Try to take the needle manufacturer's guidance first and then add weight gradually. Although you may only end up a couple of milligrams off maximum, those milligrams can add months to the lifespan of your needle and records.

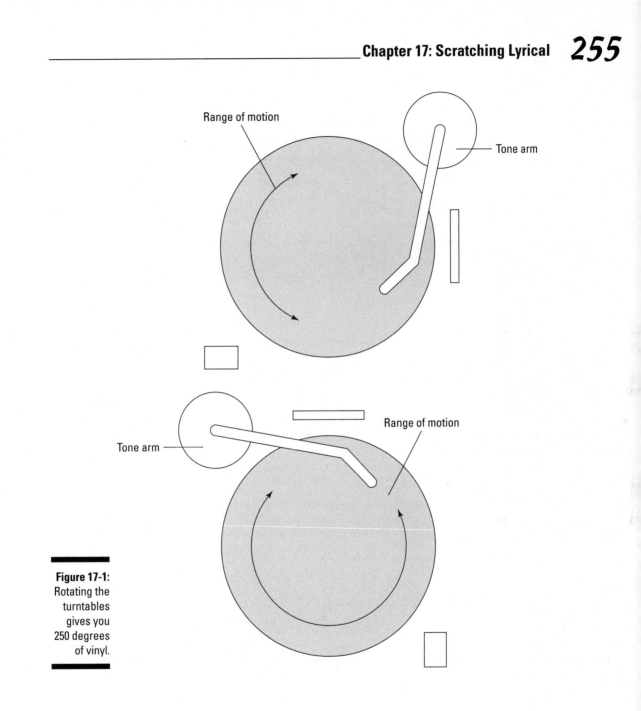

Figure 17-2:
The Shure
M44-7
needle and
cartridge.

If the worst comes to the worst, and the needle still flies when you're trying
to scratch even with the counterweight set to maximum, you can try a couple
of more drastic options:

✔ Put the counterweight on backwards so the black ring (with numbers on
 it) points away from the tonearm. Because the other side of the counterweight isn't tapered, it has more bulk, which adds more weight.

✔ Raise the height of the tonearm so the sharper angle makes the needle
 point down into the groove, creating more downforce. Don't put it too
 high, though, or the front of the cartridge may rub against the record.

✔ The last and most destructive option is to create extra downforce by
 adding a weight, such as a coin or Blutack, stuck onto the headshell.
 Doing this may help keep the needle in the groove, but you'll wear out
 your records and needles quicker than your wallet can buy them!

Wearing out your records

Between the increased downforce into the groove and the repetition of the
needle passing back and forth over the same part of the record when scratching, the record inevitably suffers wear and tear.

However, because audio fidelity isn't essential with scratching, record wear
only becomes a problem if the record is damaged and starts to skip, or if
the sample starts to sound too fuzzy. Keep your needles and records clean
to reduce the possibility of dirt gouging holes in the record or making the
needle less stable, and don't add more counterweight than you need to the
needle, and your vinyl collection will still last a long time.

Giving slipmats the slip

As a vinyl scratch DJ your slipmats should be slippery enough so that they don't resist or drag when you're scratching, yet still have enough grip so they won't skid during a scratch, or when you let go of the record to play it. (Check out Chapter 7 for everything you need to know about slipmats.)

Touching up mixers

Chapter 10 covers the vital functions you need in a scratch mixer, but you can make a couple of further improvements yourself. Firstly, take a look at your cross-fader. Make sure that you keep it lubricated so that it moves smoothly, without unwanted resistance.

Secondly, secure the faders and cross-faders. The parts that you touch to move the faders do have a tendency to fly off if you're a bit rough with them. Pull the knob off and put a piece of paper over the metal protrusion that sticks out, making it thicker, and then put the knob back on. The knob is now wedged and harder to knock off, solving any flying knob problems!

Making the mixer a hamster

Many scratch DJs find it a lot more comfortable to scratch if they reverse the normal function of the cross-fader. This means that instead of moving the cross-fader to the left to hear Channel 1 and the right to hear Channel 2, you move to the right to hear Channel 1 and the left to hear Channel 2.

You can do this either with a hamster switch on certain mixers, or by connecting the turntables the wrong way round; you plug in the left deck, which you'd normally connect to Channel 1, into Channel 2, and the right deck connects to Channel 1 instead of Channel 2.

This is useful from a body mechanics point of view. You can perform some of the scratch moves (such as the crab and the twiddle that I describe later in this chapter) faster if you 'bounce' the cross-fader off the thumb (which is a quarter of the way along the cross-fader slot) and the end of the cross-fader slot to cut the music in and out very quickly. Some moves are quite uncomfortable for a lot of DJs because the standard mixer setup means twisting their wrists to do this, so the hamster switch sets the mixer to make these moves a lot easier and more comfortable to perform.

In case you're wondering, it's not called a hamster switch because a hamster chewed through the cables to reverse the control (which crossed my mind). It's named after The Bullet Proof Scratch Hamsters who used to connect the decks up to the mixer the wrong way round in order to reverse the normal channel and cross-fader setup.

Preparing for the Big Push

You can't scratch if you don't have anything to scratch with. You need to find a section of a tune (called a *sample*) that you'll use when scratching. For most scratches, this sample isn't very long – a few seconds at most – and often only about a second in duration. No rule dictates what to use as your sample, but vocal samples, drums, beeps and brass stabs can all sound great in the right hands.

There's no restriction on what record you can use to take your sample from either. Although you can use 7-inch singles and 12-inch LPs for scratching, they have grooves that are a bit too compact to scratch with properly, making it easier for the needle to jump out the groove, harder to mark the start of a sample and a lot harder to find a sample in a rush. This means DJs more commonly use 12-inch singles, but if you find a sample on an LP or 7-inch, can mark the record correctly and have the technique to scratch well with it, don't let anyone tell you that you're wrong.

You don't even need to pick dance records. Classical tunes, spoken word records, rock, folk and country – they all have the potential to have a sample that sounds great as a scratch. I had a 'Teach Yourself Spanish' record that I used a couple of times because of its strange vocal sounds.

The ultimate records for scratching, though, are specifically designed battle breaks with scratch-friendly samples. Although these records may only have ten short samples on an entire side, each sample repeats at the same point on the circumference of the vinyl. This design means that if the needle skips out of the groove into the groove next to it, you'll still be at the exact same point in the sample, and no one knows any different (unless the needle flies out of the groove by an inch into one of the other samples).

Marking samples

Scratch DJs need to locate the sample on a tune quickly, and be able to return to it accurately over and over again. CD scratch DJs can use cue points to instantly return to the start of a sample (see Chapter 8), but it's a little trickier for vinyl DJs. However, with a combination of markers on the vinyl locating the exact groove where the sample starts, and marks on the label to easily return to the beginning of that sample, it's made a little easier on vinyl.

The first thing you need to do is locate the specific point in a specific groove on a record that contains the sample you're going to scratch and mark it so you can return to it quickly.

One of the most popular ways to mark the start of the sample is to use a small sticker on the vinyl. I use numbered stickers that you used to get with video tapes, because they're small and the numbers help me remember what sample to use next (check out Figure 17-3). Every DJ has a different kind of sticker they like using, so find one that you like and . . . stick with it.

Figure 17-3:
A record with various numbered stickers marking samples.

Mark the groove to the left of the sample so that it's not in the way when you're performing the scratch. Here's how:

1. **Find the sample on the record and press Stop on the turntable with the needle at the very beginning of the sample.**

2. **Place a sticker very lightly (so it's not stuck) directly in front of the needle. Then slowly turn the record with your hand so it plays in the forwards direction.**

Turning the record pushes the sticker out of the way, into the groove to the left of the sample (if it goes to the right instead, try again, but when you place the sticker in front of the needle, offset it to the left slightly).

3. **Check that you're in the right place by gently rocking the record back and forth, and if you got it right, press down on the sticker to make it stick to the groove next to the start of the sample.**

The drawback to marking the record in this manner is that if you want to play the entire track, a great big sticker is in the way!

If you think that you'll want to play the record in full, try using a chinagraph pencil (a white, wax-based pencil) to lightly draw a line (or an arrow, whatever you want) directly onto the vinyl. Be sure not to press down too heavily, or the wax from the pencil gets in the grooves and is just as troublesome as the sticker. Marks made with ultraviolet pens (you need to remember a UV light so you can see them) are good alternatives, as are silver pens (but you still need to watch that the ink doesn't fill up the groove). Eventually, the pen marks do wear off, but as long as you catch the wear in time and reapply your marker, you shouldn't need to worry.

Following a line-up

Marking the start of a sample is a great way to find it initially, but a small pen mark is hard to return to when you're in the middle of a mad scratch move. To help you find the start of a sample quickly, draw a big fat line on the label of the record (see Figure 17-4).

Think of the record as a clock face. The idea is to draw a line on the label so that when it's pointing in a particular direction (12 o'clock and 9 o'clock are best) you know that you're at the beginning of the sample. Here's how:

1. **Find the very beginning of the sample and stop the record.**

2. **Without moving the record (steady hands) use a CD case (or anything small and straight) to draw a line from the centre spindle to the outer edge of the record pointing to whatever clock number you'd like. (I strongly suggest 12 o'clock; straight up.)**

3. **Take the record off the deck to make the line more noticeable by using a thick marker.**

Instead of drawing a line, you could stick a long, straight sticker on the record instead. If the sample is far enough into the record, add the sticker to the outer edge, pointing into the record. Or add the sticker on the inner part of the record so it protrudes over the blank grooves at the smooth, silent part, next to the label.

Fixing the hole in the middle

It's easy to blame a jumping needle on having too little counterweight, but sometimes the jump is due to the record having too large a hole in the middle. A wide hole can be so loose that the centre spindle bangs off the edges of the hole and bounces the needle out of the groove. The easiest way to fix this problem is to pass a 1-inch-long (2.5 centimetre) piece of tape through the hole, sticking equal halves of it to either side of the label. When you've stuck enough pieces of tape at different positions through the hole, the diameter reduces, solving the problem.

Sometimes the hole is too small so that the record won't fit over the centre spindle properly (either not at all, or it's way too tight, causing the turntable to slow down when you try to hold the record still). A simple fix is to get a small piece of sandpaper, roll it up into a cylinder, put it through the hole in the record and then, holding the sandpaper, spin the record round it. Do this action a couple of times and the hole opens up a bit.

If you spin the record too long, you may make the hole too big and have to tape it up. Or, if you're really unlucky and are a bit heavy-handed, you may cause small cracks in the record.

Scratching on CD, MP3 and Computer

CD decks which have large jog wheels (like the Pioneer CDJ1000) or decks which have motorised deckplatters (found on the Denon DNS3500), can let scratch DJs perform just as well (sometimes better) as they can with turntables. (See Chapter 8 for a more detailed description of jog wheels and deckplatters.)

Along with accurately emulating the sound of a record scratching, these decks have other attributes that allow them to compete with vinyl. Memory banks to store multiple cue points (start points – in this case, of samples), built-in effects, instant reverse play and more all make CD decks incredibly versatile for scratching compared to the more traditional vinyl.

These effects and controls have removed some of the art and skill from scratching that you associate with vinyl, but they've evolved the creative process of scratching to a completely new, technology driven level. Even though the fundamental basics of scratching are the same on a vinyl turntable or a CD deck, the skills are slightly different for either format (you can be rougher on CD decks for a start, because you don't need to worry about a needle jumping out of the groove), making direct comparison and competition between the two less and less relevant.

Marking CDs

Because you can't mark the CD itself, displays on the jog dial or a separate display on scratch CD decks have markers that you use to point to the start of the sample. It seems as if they've thought of everything . . .

Scratching on PC

Software like Serato Scratch Live and Traktor Scratch Pro have created the best of both worlds between CD and vinyl scratching. By still allowing DJs to use their turntables, the performance and skill of scratching remains, but with software adding creativity, stability and speed to the game, scratching has moved on to a new level.

Waveform displays on the computer monitor can reduce the need for sticky labels and marker pens. There's also a setting which makes any sample play as though it were on a battle breaks record (see the earlier section 'Preparing for the Big Push'). Computer scratching also avoids skipping problems, and effects, loops and multiple cue points explode the options for creating new sounds when scratching. Add to this the ability to quickly access a huge library of samples quicker than a traditional scratch DJ can change records, and it's no wonder that scratch DJs are falling in love with this way of scratching.

See Chapter 9 for more information about digital DJ setups: how turntables play music on a computer and how waveform displays let DJs see the music they're playing, and help scratch DJs always find the start of a sample.

Mastering the Technique

Technique is everything when scratching vinyl. If you can develop a smooth, flowing, yet still ultra-fast action, you're more likely to keep the needle glued into the groove. With CD decks, you still need a fluid motion to create a great scratch, but you don't need to worry about popping the needle out of the groove.

Practise with both hands. If you spend the time to develop the dexterity and the co-ordination needed to scratch with either hand on either of your decks and move the cross-fader independently, you're well on your way to becoming a world-class scratch DJ.

Getting hands on

Vinyl is really sensitive, and even with the extra counterweight pressure, the new needles, the proper hole size and the slippy mats, if you have a hand like a baby elephant, you're going to make that needle fly!

You need to develop the correct hand technique. Things to bear in mind are that although you're dealing with a lot of quick direction changes, try to be smooth; don't jerk the record back and forth. When performed in succession, too many rough jerky movements will pop the needle out the groove.

When you scratch the record, try to move it back and forth following the curve of the record. If you try to pull the record back and forth in a straight line, you're adding a lot of sideways pulling and pushing pressure, which when combined may be enough to jump the needle out of the groove.

Changing sample sounds

As you start to scratch you need to develop the knowledge of what changes the sound of the sample you're scratching. The five key ways to make a sample sound different when scratching are:

- **Location:** You may have found a nice sample on a record, but you still have full control over what part of the sample you play. Just because the sample has someone saying *scratch*, doesn't mean that you have to play that full word. You may choose only to scratch with the *sc* part of the word, or maybe trying a scribble scratch on the *tch* part sounds unique and matches what you want to do perfectly.

  Changing where in the sample you scratch by just a couple of millimetres (or a tenth of a second) can make the difference between a good sound and a great sound.

- **Direction:** Nearly all samples sound incredibly different when you play them backwards as opposed to forwards, and if you're not too sure about the sound of your scratch, you may find that scratching the record in the other direction improves the sound immensely.

- **Speed:** The speed at which any sample moves can alter your scratch from a low, rumbling, guttural sound to a high-pitched, shrill, chirpy sound. So don't fall into the trap of scratching at the same speed all the time. Change up mid-scratch from a fast-forward motion to a slow backwards move, mix up the speed during a move (see 'The tear' scratch section, later in this chapter) and listen out for how the speed at which you scratch the record can alter the power and sound of the scratch.

- **Audibility:** How loud you hear the sample playing, or whether you can hear it at all, is very important. Although the cross-fader is the main control for whether you can hear the sample or not, don't forget about the channel-fader.

  You can scratch using the channel-fader instead of the cross-fader, and you can use the channel-fader to set how loud you hear the scratch, which adds an extra dimension to the scratch. Gradually fading out the scratch using only the cross-fader is difficult, but when you use it on its own or in conjunction with the cross-fader, the channel-fader can give you an extra level of audio control.

- **EQ:** Using the EQ (equaliser) to adjust the amount of bass, mid or treble present can change a shrill sounding scratch into a muddy, dark sounding one; in the middle of a scratch if you like.

  Unless you have four hands, scratching using the cross-fader, the channel-fader and the EQ control all at the same time is hard, but with practice and patience you'll be amazed at how fast you can move from control to control.

Effects processors can also lend a hand. Effects like filters, flanger, distortion, echo, reverb and delay can all change the sound of the sample you're scratching. As with everything in DJing, experimentation is key. Consider the scratch technique you're performing and whether an effect will help it, hinder it or end up redundant. Give it a try, and weigh up whether the effect made the scratch better or worse.

Starting from Scratch and Back Again

All of the following scratch techniques work with any format, whether you're scratching on vinyl, CD or in software. Try the following scratches on their own first, without playing anything on the other deck. Then when you're happy choose a tune with a slow beat to play on the other deck, and scratch in time with that beat. You don't have to use a beat-only tune, but scratching over melodies and vocals may sound messy and confusing at first.

Check my website at www.recess.co.uk for audio files and movie clips of the scratch if you're unsure of what it should sound or look like. Or search the Internet for video tutorials, such as DJ QBert's.

For all these scratches I give guidance on what direction you should scratch in, and what cross-fader action you may need, but as you get used to each scratch adjust how quickly you do the scratch, what part of the sample you're scratching from and how much of it you play.

Scratching without the cross-fader

The three scratches I discuss in this section help you develop the hand control to work with the vinyl (or CD deckplatter or jog wheel) properly. Plus they're the building blocks of all the scratches that follow in the section 'Introducing cross-fader fever'. Even though they're simple moves, mastering them is very important. You don't need to use the cross-fader for these three scratches, so leave it in the middle position, with the channel-fader at full.

The baby scratch

The *baby scratch* is the first scratch for you to try, and it is by far the simplest, easiest scratch to attempt. This one is for anyone who comes to your house and asks, 'Can I have a go?' It may also be how you broke the needle on your dad's turntable when you were 9 years old . . .

The baby scratch is just a forward movement followed by a backward movement. Both directions are audible throughout the scratch (which is why you don't need to touch the cross-fader on this scratch). If the sample you're using is someone singing 'Hey!', then the sound would be like:

Hey (forwards) – yeH (backwards) – Hey . . . yeH . . . Hey . . . yeH . . .

When you're happy, and want to start scratching to the beat of a tune playing on your other deck, perform the forward motion on the first beat of the bar and the backward motion on the second beat:

Beats:	1	2	3	4	1	2	3	4
Scratch:	Hey	yeH	Hey	yeH	Hey	yeH	Hey	yeH

When you're comfortable matching the 1, 2, 3, 4 beats of the bar with 'Hey, yeH, Hey, yeH', (two full baby scratches), speed up the scratch so that you're going forwards and backwards on each beat (which makes four full baby scratches):

Beats:
1   2   3   4   1   2   3   4

Scratch:
Hey-yeH Hey-yeH Hey-yeH Hey-yeH Hey-yeH Hey-yeH Hey-yeH Hey-yeH

The scribble scratch

The *scribble scratch* is similar to the baby scratch, except the amount that the record moves backwards and forwards is tiny (just the 'H' of hey, if that!), and you get a lot more scratches to the beat, let alone the bar!

By tensing the wrist and forearm while pressing down on the record with one finger, the muscles leading to your finger vibrate, causing the record to move backwards and forwards really quickly. If you think that you can generate enough speed without needing to tense your muscles, just move the record back and forth as fast as you can.

No matter what your technique is, you want to make the amount of vinyl passing under the needle as small as possible (less than 1 centimetre is best).

The tear

The *tear* is similar to the baby scratch, except that instead of two sounds, the scratch splits into three. You leave the cross-fader open (you can hear the sound) for the duration of the scratch, but introduce a change in the backward speed that creates the third part of the scratch.

The forward stroke (move) is the same as the baby scratch, but the first half of the backstroke is fast and the second half of the stroke is half that pace.

Practise changing the speed of just the backstroke first to help you get used to the change in tempo. When you're happy doing that, try adding in the forward stroke to the two-part backward stroke you've just mastered.

Introducing cross-fader fever

The scratches that I describe in this section involve using the cross-fader. Before you go any further, find out where the cut-in point on the cross-fader is. The *cut-in point* is where you have to move the cross-fader to in order to hear the appropriate channel. Depending on the cross-fader curve, this point can be a few millimetres of movement, or you may need to get the cross-fader into the middle before hearing the scratch at full volume. (Chapter 10 has more information on cross-fader curves and cut-in points.)

The forward scratch

The *forward scratch* gives you the perfect start to practising use of the cross-fader. Using exactly the same movement as in the baby scratch, start with the cross-fader past the cut-in point, so that you can hear the forward movement, and then before you move the record back close the cross-fader so that you can't hear the back stroke.

When you're happy cutting off the back stroke of the baby scratch, start to scratch to the beat. With the 'Hey!' example, you match the 1, 2, 3, 4 beat of the bar with *Hey, Hey, Hey, Hey*:

Beats:	1	2	3	4	1	2	3	4
Scratch:	Hey	Hey	Hey	Hey	Hey	Hey	Hey	Hey

If that's a little too fast for you at first, give yourself more time by slowing down the scratch so you only hear 'Hey' on odd beats:

Beats:	1	2	3	4	1	2	3	4
Scratch:	Hey		Hey		Hey		Hey	

The backward scratch

As you may have guessed, the *backward scratch* is exactly the same as the forward scratch, except that this time you hear only the back stroke of the baby scratch. So, you hear 'yeH, yeH, yeH, yeH' as you scratch to the four beats of the bar:

Beats:	1	2	3	4	1	2	3	4
Scratch:	yeH	yeH	yeH	yeH	yeH	yeH	yeH	yeH

You may find it easier at first to use the backward scratch in the off-beat, which is where it would be naturally if you were performing a baby scratch:

Beats:	1		2		3		4		1		2		3		4
Scratch:		yeH		yeH		yeH		yeH		yeH		yeH		yeH	

The cut

The *cut* is when you play the sample at normal speed and direction, but only play parts of it. I used to love doing this scratch with the James Brown 'All Aboard' sample at the beginning of Kadoc's 'Nightrain'. It could sound something like 'All (pause) All All A All-Aboard':

Beats:	1	2	3	4	1	2		3	4
Scratch:	All	(rest)	All	All	A	All Aboard		(rest)	(rest)

After I'd scratched with it for a while over another tune, I'd just let the sample play, the tune would kick in and the mix was done, which shows that scratching and mixing aren't mutually exclusive; they can work together.

To perform this scratch, position the sample so that it's right behind the needle. On a particular point in the other tune (at the start of a bar in my Kadoc example), move the cross-fader in and let the record run. When you want the sample to stop, close the cross-fader, wind the record back to the beginning of the sample and let it run again.

The trick is to make sure that you wind the sample back to the correct place in time. This is the perfect time to mark a line on the record label, so that when the line is pointing at 12 o'clock you know that you're at the start of the sample (see the earlier section 'Marking samples').

The chop

The *chop* is very similar to the cut, except that instead of playing the record at normal pace, you control how fast the sample plays. By varying how fast you play parts of the sample, you can create some strange melodies to accompany what you're scratching over.

And of course, the *reverse chop* (and *reverse cut*) is when the fader is open for the back stroke rather than the forward stroke.

The chirp

The *chirp* is where hand co-ordination starts to become essential. Start the sample with the cross-fader open, but just as you hear the sample play, smoothly (though quickly) close off the cross-fader. For the back stroke, do the exact opposite; as you move the record backwards, open the cross-fader. It'll be easier to play the sample at normal speed at first, but you'll most likely find better results when you scratch the sample quickly back and forth.

With the right sample, speed of scratch and movement of the cross-fader, this technique creates a bird-like whistling, or chirp noise.

The transformer

The *transformer* is another simple scratch that helps with the timing of your cross-fader moves, and also develops co-ordination between your hands.

To get used to the transformer, play the sample forwards so that it lasts one bar's length (probably a couple of seconds, which means playing it very slowly) and then backwards for one bar. You can play for longer or shorter if you wish, but keeping the move to one bar gives you boundaries to work with for now that you can expand on when you get good at the transformer.

As you play the sample, open and close the cross-fader on each of the beats of the bar. As you do so, you hear the sample split into four parts playing forwards, and four parts of the sample playing backwards. When you're happy, double the speed that you cut the music in and out with. Then if you think that you can move the cross-fader fast enough, double it again, so that you're opening and closing the cross-fader 16 times for a bar.

Your thumb isn't only for hitch-hiking

Opening and closing the cross-fader becomes more difficult the faster you try to move it. When you feel limited, use your thumb as a spring to return the cross-fader to the closed position.

If you have a small distance to travel to the cut-in point on the cross-fader, rest your thumb at that point, but angle your thumb so that it leans toward the closed position. Using your middle (or ring) finger, tap the cross-fader so it bounces off your thumb and returns to the closed position, which is a lot quicker. This is easier to do if your mixer is set up hamster style (see the section 'Making the mixer a hamster').

Flares

The *flare scratch* takes the sample and cuts it into two by quickly closing and re-opening the cross-fader. The scratch starts with the cross-fader open, which closes halfway through the sample and then opens again. If the sample you're scratching is just someone saying the word *scratch*, then the flare means you'd hear *scr tch*.

DJ SPEAK

When you close the cross-fader off quickly, it makes a clicking sound. In the preceding *scr tch* example, chopping the sample into two takes one movement, one click, and is called a *one click forward flare*.

Crab scratch

To get used to the cross-fader action for a *crab scratch*, click your fingers. Now instead of just your middle finger clicking off your thumb, click all four of your fingers across your thumb, starting off with the pinkie. This is the crab action: just place a cross-fader knob between your fingers and thumb.

Place your thumb as a spring to the cross-fader in the same way that you use it for the transformer scratch. As your fingers bounce the cross-fader off your thumb, you cut the sample into four, really quickly.

This is another scratch that can be easier to do if you set your mixer up in a hamster style, because you can bounce the fader off the side of the fader slot and your thumb.

Twiddle scratch

The *twiddle scratch* is the precursor to the crab scratch. Instead of using all four fingers to perform the crab scratch, you use only two to twiddle the cross-fader, which produces a slightly more constant rhythm to the scratch than the crab.

Combining scratches

When you're familiar with these fundamentals, start combining them to create strings of different scratches over the beat. Start off simply, by switching from one scratch to another, like changing a baby scratch to a forward scratch, or a forward scratch to a reverse scratch.

Here are a few more ideas:

- ✔ **Transforming with transformers:** Adding transforms to any of your scratches is a great way to change up the sound of some of the basic moves. Add a transform to a forward scratch so that you transform the forward movement but still don't hear any of the back stroke. Or add a transform to a tear to really test your co-ordination!

✔ **Adding flare:** Add a flare or a crab to my 'All Aboard' cut scratch example, which adds a stutter effect to part of it.

✔ **Add a speed bump:** When scratching the record backwards, lightly tap the vinyl with your other hand, adding a 'hiccup' to the sound. Go even further by performing the *hydroplane*, where instead of tapping the record with your other hand you lightly rest your finger on the vinyl. The light touch should mean that friction caused when touching the record will lightly bounce/vibrate your finger when moving the record back, adding a rumble stutter to the scratch but without cutting it in and out.

✔ **Try *drop-ons* to make your own tune:** This is where you hold the needle and quickly touch the record with the needle at different parts of the tune. Each time you touch the record, you hear a musical note. String these all together to make a tune (like, bizarrely, the 'Star Wars Death March', which I've just watched on YouTube . . .)

The fundamentals that I mention here are just building blocks to get you on your way towards a vast array of different scratches. Many combinations exist for how to move the record, how to move the cross-fader and the speed at which to do it all. Check out my website (www.recess.co.uk) and www.youtube.co.uk for a few more ideas on how to mix up the fundamentals.

Juggling the Beats

Beatjuggling is a great skill and one that, when mastered, earns you a lot of respect from your peers. Using two records (they don't have to be identical, but it helps at first) with just a drum beat, you create a new drum beat using a combination of all the scratch fundamentals.

Precision when returning the record (or CD) to the beginning of the sample is paramount, and a real test of your skills. Although the following guide explains the mechanics of how to do this with two records, you may find it a lot easier to do on CD or with software that has cue points saved to a memory that you can access instantly at the push of a button.

Properly marking your records is incredibly important here, because you won't have the time to listen in headphones to how you're cueing up the tune to start it again. You need to rely on spotting the marker line you may have set at 12 o'clock, and have faith that you're at the start of the sample.

Much as you would if you were juggling with balls, start off simply:

1. **With two identical records, cue them so that they'll both play from the exact same point. Then start only one of them playing.**

2. **Play one bar of the drum beat on that record, and then start the other tune while moving the cross-fader over, to play another bar of beats.**

3. **While that second bar is playing, wind the first record back to the start of the bar. When the second record has finished its first bar, start the first record while moving the cross-fader over so you can hear it.**

This method means that you play the same bar of drums over and over again, which may sound easy, but believe me, it isn't! You can get easily flustered, get the timing wrong for the start of the bar and make a pig's ear of something that sounds so simple. Or you might be a natural and get it first time! If you're finding it tricky at first, instead of repeating one bar, try four bars to give you lots more time to return the other tune to the beginning. Then, when you've got that, try three, then two and then one. Start easy and then make it harder and harder. Practise enough and you'll crack it.

If you're trying this on CD or DJing software, instead of winding back the sample to the beginning each time, just hit the Cue button to return to the beginning of the sample and hit Play again at the start of the bar. Your CD decks may differ as to how they return to the cue point and what you press to start the tune again, but as long as you can get back there in time to restart the tune, and start it at the right time, that's all that counts.

When you're happy repeating the whole bar, halve the time that one record plays before switching over (now two beats instead of four). Then when you're really confident, play the first beat from the first record and the second beat from the second record, and keep winding back the beats so you only hear the first two beats of the bar play over and over again.

Offsetting

By the time you can swap from beat to beat comfortably, you'll want to create more complicated drum beats. Offsetting one of the records is a great and simple way to start. Begin by starting one of the tunes half a beat later, so instead of a simple *Bass Snare Bass Snare* for the four beats of the bar, you hear *BassBass SnareSnare BassBass SnareSnare* in the exact same amount of time. The first bass is from the first tune, and the second one is from the second tune.

Leaving the cross-fader in the middle creates that run of beats, but closing the cross-fader off to some of the beats starts to chop it up a lot more.

Beats:	1		2	3	4	1	2	3	4
Sounds:	B1 B2		S1	B1	S1 S2	B2	S1 S2	B1 B2	S1

(Where the B is Bass, S is Snare and the 1 or 2 means from Deck 1 or 2.)

If you have the *Hot Cue* function on your CD decks or software, you'll be in beatjuggling heaven because you can save individual beats to a Hot Cue trigger button. If using Pioneer CDJ1000s, instead of frantically spinning records back and forth you can save the bass drum from one tune to Hot Cue A on one deck, and the snare drum of another tune to Hot Cue A on the other deck. Leaving the cross-fader in the middle, just hit them in time to create your own new drum beat. And with three Hot Cues on each deck, you can save a selection of drum sounds for incredible creativity. You don't even need two decks! Just store the bass drum into Hot Cue A and the snare drum into Hot Cue B on the same CD deck, and create your own drum beat on one CD deck. For more on Hot Cues, see Chapter 8.

It's essential to have a great sense of rhythm if you're creating a full drum beat out of single beats. If you're not sure about creating drum beats, start off by checking out *Drums For Dummies* by Jeff Strong (Wiley).

These methods are only the tip of the iceberg for cutting up and creating drum beats. The faster you cut between tracks, how much you offset the beats and using beats from two different tunes can all come together to make a really complicated beat. And that's without even considering adding cymbals, hi-hats and drum rolls!

Practice, dedication and patience

Practice, dedication and patience should make up your personal mantra for beatjuggling (and scratching as a whole). Record knowledge and manual dexterity are extremely important, but you need to be fluent and tight with the beats. You need to keep your scratch moves fluid and in keeping with the rhythm of what you're scratching over, and if you're beatjuggling, the beat you make needs to flow as though a drummer were playing it – that way, you'll earn respect for your skills.

It's always good to take inspiration from others and set yourself a goal. Check out Kid Koala scratching 'Moon River' (on www.recess.co.uk) – when you can juggle and scratch like that, you'll be among the best.

Part IV
Getting Noticed and Playing Live

MIXING THE FIRST "RUDE AUDIENCE" CD

© RICHTENNANT

"I laid down a general shuffling sound, over dubbed with periodic coughing, some muted talking files, and an awesome ringing mobile phone loop."

In this part . . .

One morning you'll wake up and realise that you're meant for more in this world than DJing in front of your cat (and annoying the neighbours). You may sound great when played through a home stereo or iPod, but the time when you play to a packed hall or a club filled with like-minded people is when you really spread your wings as a DJ.

This part of the book leads you through making the perfect demo mix, trying to secure work, and then what to do when you're standing in the DJ booth with a thousand people in front of you who want you to give them the best night of their lives.

This is DJing.

Chapter 18

Building a Foolproof Set

A fter you've taken a look at the different ways you can mix your tunes together (refer to Chapters 14, 16 and 17), you need to start examining the tunes you're using in the mix.

As well as looking a bit closer at why a tune can mix well with one tune but not another, this chapter covers developing your own style when DJing, rather than simply replicating all those who've come before you. No one's saying that following the same fundamentals as other DJs is wrong, but if you can think about what you're trying to do with the order of the tunes in your mix, you'll be a lot better DJ than the one who mixes Tune A with Tune B just because they sound good together.

Choosing Tunes to Mix Together

The tunes you select and the order in which you play them are just as important as the method you use to get from tune to tune. The best technical mix in the world can sound terrible if the tunes don't play well together, and boredom can set in if you stick to the same sound, genre and energy level (pace and the power of the music) all night.

In order to get a feel for what kind of tunes mix well with each other, you need to consider the core differences that make tunes different from one another (other than the melody, the vocals, the instruments used and so on). The main differences are the driving rhythm, the key in which the tunes are recorded and the tempo at which a tune was originally recorded.

Beatmatching – the next generation

Matching the pounding bass beats of your tunes is one thing, and after you get the knack, playing bass drums together is relatively simple and sounds good. However, the core *driving rhythm* is another rhythm that you need to consider and listen out for in the tunes, and it isn't just attached to dance music. All music is made up of combinations of core driving rhythms.

A track is made up of the *backing track* (the drums, bass line and any rhythmic, electronic sounds), and the main melody and/or vocals. The backing track is the driving force to the tune, and within it is a rhythm of its own that is separate, but works in harmony with, the pounding bass beats. A great example of this is the '*duggadugga duggadugga duggadugga duggadugga*' driving rhythm in Donna Summer's 'I Feel Love'.

If what follows sounds a little childish, that's because it is. I remember it from school, so thanks to Mr Galbraith for making this concept stick!

When beatmatching bass drum beats you only have to consider the solid *thump thump thump* of the beats playing over each other. Now you need to start listening out for one of the four driving rhythms too: *ta*, *ta-te*, *ta-te-ta* and *ta-fe-te-te*. Most popular music has four beats to a bar, and each of the driving rhythm fundamentals occur on the beat so you get four of each to a bar:

Ta is just a single sound on each beat of the bar (sounds like *baa* from the nursery rhyme 'Baa, Baa, Black Sheep'):

Beat	*1*	*2*	*3*	*4*	*1*	*2*	*3*	*4*
Rhythm	Ta	Ta	Ta	Ta	Ta	Ta	Ta	Ta
Word	Baa	Baa	Baa	Baa	Baa	Baa	Baa	Baa

Ta-te are two sounds of equal length on each beat, though often one's emphasised, making it more powerful than the other (sounds like *Have you* in the line 'Have you any wool' from 'Baa, Baa, Black Sheep'):

Beat	*1*	*2*	*3*	*4*	*1*	*2*	*3*	*4*
Rhythm	Ta-te	Ta-te	Ta-te	Ta-te	Ta-te	Ta-te	Ta-te	Ta-te
Word	Have you	Have you	Have you	Have you	Have you	Have you	Have you	Have you

Sometimes you don't hear the *ta* (*Have*) part of the rhythm, and just hear the second, *te* (*you*) part; known as an *offbeat*. This simple offbeat is a favourite rhythm for producers who want a powerful, stripped-down sound to a tune.

Ta-te ta is like saying *lemonade* on each beat. It's very similar to *ta-te*, except that instead of two equal sounds you get two quick sounds (which take up the same time as *ta* in the *ta-te* rhythm) followed by one sound that lasts as

long as the *te* half of *ta-te*. Splitting the *ta-te ta* rhythm into two, the halves
are *ta-te* and *ta* (*Lemon* and *ade*). You say *lemon* very quickly, and it lasts the
same duration as *ade*:

Beat	1	2	3	4	1	2	3	4
Rhythm	Ta-te ta	Ta-te ta	Ta-te ta	Ta-te ta	Ta-te ta	Ta-te ta	Ta-te ta	Ta-te ta
Word	Lemonade	Lemonade	Lemonade	Lemonade	Lemonade	Lemonade	Lemonade	Lemonade

Ta-fe-te-te is like saying *Mississippi* on each beat of the bar; four equal sounds
to each beat give a powerful, hypnotic rhythm to the tune. This sound is the
duggadugga rhythm I mention earlier for 'I Feel Love'. It adds a lot of energy
to a bass melody, and if you add a filter or a flanger effect to this rhythm (see
Chapter 10), it leaves the dance floor in a trance.

Beat	1	2	3	4	1	2	3	4
Rhythm	Ta-fe-te-te	Ta-fe-te-te	Ta-fe-te-te	Ta-fe-te-te	Ta-fe-te-te	Ta-fe-te-te	Ta-fe-te-te	Ta-fe-te-te
Word	Mississippi	Mississippi	Mississippi	Mississippi	Mississippi	Mississippi	Mississippi	Mississippi

Producers combine these base-driving rhythm fundamentals with each
other to make more complicated rhythms when writing tunes. For instance,
they might use three *ta-te ta*'s followed by a *ta-fe-te-te* to make up one bar or
get even more complicated and create bars with *ta*, *ta-te*, *ta*, *ta-te-ta* driving
rhythms. The options are endless, but when considering what tunes to use in
the mix, listen to how well these driving rhythms play over another.

Check out my website, www.recess.co.uk, where you can find various
video and audio clips demonstrating different driving rhythms in tunes.

Mixing with care

Mixing between similar driving rhythms can be a bit tricky. In the right
hands, *ta-fe-te-te* mixes in beautifully to another *ta-fe-te-te* and it's often this
constant driving rhythm that adds a feeling of power and energy to the
mix. But if you don't precisely beatmatch the tunes, the four sounds fall in
between each other, giving eight very messy sounds. The same goes for *ta-te
ta*: you need good beatmatching skills to mix two of these sounds together
(or to mix *ta-te ta* into *ta-fe-te-te*).

Mixing simpler *ta* or *ta-te* rhythms (including the offbeat part of *ta-te*, where
you only hear the second *te* sound) with each other, or into either of the
more complicated rhythms (*ta-te ta* and *ta-fe-te-te*) is a solution to this problem. However, this method will eventually stifle your creativity (and often the

energy of the mix). If you need to go from a complicated driving rhythm to a simple one and then back again to a complicated one in order to progress through a mix, you'll break up the flow of the set. That's why spending time to refine your beatmatching skills is important, so that you're happy mixing complicated driving rhythms.

Although *ta* and *ta-te* are simpler and easier to beatmatch, they tend to be strong bass lines, and because they're so strong they don't always mix well. If the rhythm of one tune is *ta*, and the other is the offbeat *te*, (you don't hear the *ta* from *ta-te*) unless the *ta* note from one tune and the offbeat *te* from the other tune are very similar, the mix can sound strange and out of tune. (See 'Getting in tune with harmonic mixing', later in this chapter, for some tips.)

The same driving rhythm principles apply to the hi-hat pattern (the *tchsss-*sounding cymbals). Though most tunes tend to use an open hi-hat sound played in between each bass drum beat (the same as the offbeat *te*), be careful when the patterns get more complicated. If you try to mix two *ta-fe-te-te* hi-hat patterns together, and get the beatmatching wrong, it'll sound dreadful.

Changing gear

Mixing from one driving rhythm to another is extremely important to the power of the set. Going from a *ta* rhythm to *ta-te ta* can make the mix sound faster and more intense, even if the beats per minute (BPMs) are still the same. Changing from *ta-fe-te-te* to the offbeat version of *ta-te* (only the *te* part) is an incredibly effective way of making the mix sound darker by simplifying and concentrating the sound from a frantic, four-sound rhythm to a single-sounding, simple, basic rhythm. When coupled with a key change (see 'Changing the key', later in this chapter), the effect can lift the roof off!

Getting in tune with harmonic mixing

Your beatmatching may be perfect (see Chapter 14), your volume control may be spot on (see Chapter 16) and you've chosen two tunes with complementary driving rhythms, but sometimes two tunes sound out of tune with each other. *Harmonic mixing* comes in at this point, and is the final step for creating truly seamless mixes. Harmonic mixing isn't an essential step of the mixing ladder by any means, and it may be something party and rock DJs never consider, but as an electronic dance music DJ, if you want to create long, flowing, seamless mixes, harmonic mixing certainly plays a very important part.

Every song with a melody has a musical key, and instruments and vocals play and sing their notes based around this musical key (that's why you may have heard people say 'I'll sing this in C Minor', for example). This kind of key may not unlock any real doors, but it does unlock vast chasms of creativity for you. DJs like Sasha, Oakenfold, John Digweed and many others have all harnessed harmonic mixing to create smooth, controlled mixes that add an extra level of depth and skill to their styles.

Most DJs first approach harmonic mixing by accident, and then try to improve through trial and error. Trial and error is extremely important. Blindly following the rules that follow in this section of what key mixes into what is a bad idea. Knowing how the key affects how well tunes mix together is important, but more important is developing an ear for what sounds good when mixed together, rather than referring to a piece of paper or rule that you read in an incredibly informative book.

However, you need somewhere to start and somewhere to turn to if you're unsure what to do next, which is where the principle of key notations comes in, and you have the choice of two systems to help you understand.

Brace yourself here. The terminology surrounding key notations may seem like a foreign language, but don't worry – it's not something to be too scared of.

Traditional key notation

In the Western world music has 24 different keys – 12 major and 12 minor. This is known as the *traditional key notation* system. Whether a key is major or minor depends on the notes you used to create that key. Each key mixes perfectly with four keys, and mixes to an acceptable level with two other keys, as shown in Table 18-1. Don't worry if Table 18-1 looks like nonsense; there's an explanation of what it means at the end of it!

Table 18-1		Harmonic Song Key Combinations		
Key of Song Playing	**Tonic**	**Perfect Fourth (Sub-Dominant)**	**Perfect Fifth (Dominant)**	**Relative Minor**
C Major	C Major	F Major	G Major	A Minor
Db Major	Db Major	Gb Major	Ab Major	Bb Minor
D Major	D Major	G Major	A Major	B Minor
Eb Major	Eb Major	Ab Major	Bb Major	C Minor
E Major	E Major	A Major	B Major	Db Minor
F Major	F Major	Bb Major	C Major	D Minor

(continued)

Table 18-1 (continued)

Key of Song Playing	Tonic	Perfect Fourth (Sub-Dominant)	Perfect Fifth (Dominant)	Relative Minor
Gb Major	Gb Major	B Major	Db Major	Eb Minor
G Major	G Major	C Major	D Major	E Minor
Ab Major	Ab Major	Db Major	Eb Major	F Minor
A Major	A Major	D Major	E Major	Gb Minor
Bb Major	Bb Major	Eb Major	F Major	G Minor
B Major	B Major	E Major	Gb Major	Ab Minor
C Minor	C Minor	F Minor	G Minor	Eb Major
Db Minor	Db Minor	Gb Minor	Ab Minor	E Major
D Minor	D Minor	G Minor	A Minor	F Major
Eb Minor	Eb Minor	Ab Minor	Bb Minor	Gb Major
E Minor	E Minor	A Minor	B Minor	G Major
F Minor	F Minor	Bb Minor	C Minor	Ab Major
Gb Minor	Gb Minor	B Minor	Db Minor	A Major
G Minor	G Minor	C Minor	D Minor	Bb Major
Ab Minor	Ab Minor	Db Minor	Eb Minor	B Major
A Minor	A Minor	D Minor	E Minor	C Major
Bb Minor	Bb Minor	Eb Minor	F Minor	Db Major
B Minor	B Minor	E Minor	Gb Minor	D Major

It's okay; no need to start worrying: calculating which keys combine best with each other is actually very simple. In Table 18-1, look at C Major and then look at the keys written next to it. It obviously mixes with a tune with the same key as its own (known as the *tonic*), but it also mixes beautifully with the three keys next to it: F Major, G Major and A Minor. However, because C Major works really well with A Minor, you can also incorporate the keys that A Minor works well with. These key combinations from A Minor are acceptable rather than perfect. You have to judge for yourself whether they match well enough for what you're trying to do (which is why it's important to use your ears).

This chart is kind of mind blowing though, and isn't easy to read. The minor/major thing is a bit confusing if you don't have any musical experience, and working out what mixes into what can take a while. Fortunately, Mark Davis at www.harmonic-mixing.com developed the Camelot Sound Easymix System, which takes the confusion out of working out what key mixes with what.

The Camelot Sound Easymix System

The *Camelot Sound Easymix System* is an alternative approach that addresses the confusing layout and label names of the traditional key notation system (see Table 18-1). With the Camelot system each key has a *keycode*: a number from 1 to 12 and a letter (A for Minor and B for Major). Then all the keys are arranged as a tidy clock face, as shown in Figure 18-1.

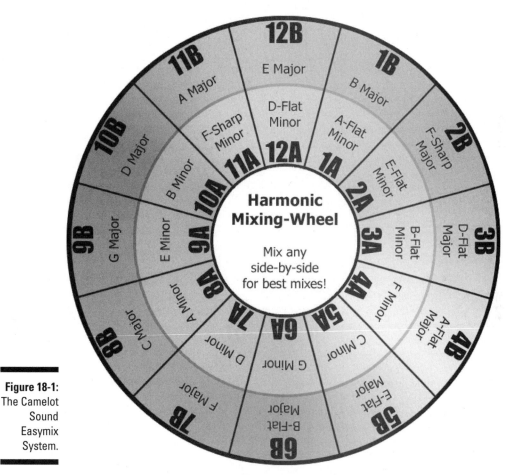

Figure 18-1:
The Camelot Sound Easymix System.

(Copyright 2001, Camelot Sound/DJ Pulse, used with permission)

The keys that mix harmonically are identical to the traditional notation, but rather than looking at a confusing table you only need to look at the keycode for the key of the tune that you're playing, and then look to the left and right and directly above or below, depending on whether the key you're referring to is on the inner or outer ring of the diagram.

So if your tune is 12B (E Major), you can mix it with a tune with the same key, with 11B, 1B from the same major family, but you can also mix it perfectly with 12A from the minor ring and you can get a nice result mixing into 11A and 1A tunes.

This works perfectly if you calculate each of your tune's keys and play them all at zero pitch, never changing their speed. But when beatmatching, you need to alter the speed of your tunes, and on normal CD decks and turntables the pitch of the tune changes as you change the speed, and the original key starts to change into a new one. Therefore, when using the Camelot Sound Easymix System, for every 6 per cent you change the pitch, you need to change the keycode by 7 numbers according to their system.

For example, if you have a 3B tune and pitch it up to 6 per cent, it's no longer a 3B tune but is now a 10B tune. Or if you pitch down by 6 per cent, it becomes an 8B tune. Move round the circle by 7 segments to see for yourself. A 6 per cent pitch change means that the 3B tune is no longer suited to 4B, 2B, 3A, 4A and 2A. For a good harmonic mix, you need to choose tunes which, when you adjust their pitch so you can beatmatch them, play with a keycode of 11B, 9B, 10A, 11A or 9A.

If DJing with turntables this 6 per cent keycode adjustment can depend entirely on how accurate your turntables are. Use the calibration dots on the side of the turntable to see whether it truly is running at 6 per cent. (Refer to Chapter 6.)

Some CD decks, turntables and software titles have Master Tempo controls that keep the pitch of the music the same no matter how you change the speed at which it plays, or a separate control that lets you alter the pitch without changing the speed. This can help greatly when trying to match the keys of your tunes, but because not all decks and DJ booths have this function, don't grow to rely on it.

Harmonic mixing is a vast concept that you can bend, twist, break or ignore at will, and the extreme concepts could take up ten of these books. If you want to delve deeper into the theory of harmonic mixing, visit DJ Prince's website, which is dedicated to harmonic mixing. Visit www.djprince.no when the mood strikes, and say hi from me.

Keying tunes

Both the traditional and Camelot notation systems may sound helpful, and believe it or not they're very simple and easy to understand, but one thing is still missing: how do you determine the key of the tune you're currently playing?

The three different ways to work out the key of a tune are

✔ **Review online databases:** DJ forums and websites across the Internet offer huge databases of song keys. The people who created the Camelot Sound Easymix System have a subscription-based database at www. harmonic-mixing.com, and forums like www.tranceaddict.com/forums have huge posts dedicated to the keys of tunes, old and new.

✔ **Use your ears:** Figuring out the key by ear is by far the hardest amount of work, taking patience, a good ear for music and a fair bit of musical theory knowledge.

   1. Play the tune at zero pitch on the turntable/CD player.

   2. Use a piano/keyboard or a computer-generated tone to go through all 12 notes on the scale, as shown in Figure 18-2.

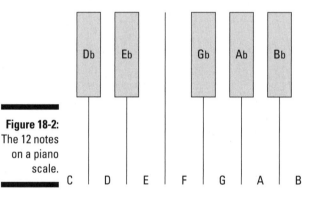

Figure 18-2:
The 12 notes on a piano scale.

   3. The note that sounds the best and melts into the music is the *root key* (the C in C Major, and so on).

Finding whether the key is minor or major takes the whole thing to another level of complication, and if you want to go into that in detail you need to start looking at musical theory books. Check out books like *Guitar For Dummies*, 2nd Edition, by Mark Phillips and John Chappell, and *Piano For Dummies* by Blake Neely (both published by Wiley), because they explain this theory in a way that's easy to understand.

I'm a drummer at heart and have zero musical theory knowledge so the way I was taught how to gauge minor/major by ear is that if the music sounds striking, bold and solid, it's likely to be a major key. If the music evokes emotion and tugs at your heart strings, it's likely (though not guaranteed) to be in a minor key.

If you don't want to delve too deeply into musical theory, you can work out the root of the key and be happy with that knowledge, and then simply use trial and error to find the best tunes to mix in. This isn't much better than trial and error *without* knowledge of the theory, but it's a step closer to harmonic mixing – and sometimes a step is all it takes.

Though it's hard work and takes a lot of musical knowledge, working out the key (or just the root key) yourself is useful because as you listen to the tunes and find out the key, you develop an appreciation for what to listen to and will eventually develop an ear to judge which tunes match together without the need to refer to a list of suitable tunes or a notation like the Camelot Easymix Sound System.

✔ **Software:** Computer programs are available that work out the key for you. One of these programs, Mixed in Key, analyses each of your wave and MP3 files and calculates what key they're recorded in according to the Camelot system (see the earlier section 'The Camelot Sound Easymix System'). The program is surprisingly accurate, extremely effective and available from www.MixedInKey.com.

When you've worked out what key your tune is in, write a little note on the record sleeve or next to the track name on the CD case or digital library.

Knowing how much to pitch

Your decks may offer you an 8 per cent pitch range, or may let you go faster or slower by 100 per cent, but unless you have a special use for going really fast or slow, if you go much over 5 per cent pitch then the majority of music may start to sound strange to the ears of the people on the dance floor. If you have a Master Tempo control on your decks, you can play the music as fast or slow as you like and the pitch won't change, just the speed, but I don't suggest going much past the 10 per cent mark unless you're trying to be creative.

The brain can account for around 5 per cent pitch difference to the original and still consider the music as normal. But as you get farther past that guide number, you risk the listener thinking that something's not right.

How far you can push the pitch of a tune (without Master Tempo) depends entirely on the tune itself, and the genre of music you're playing. When playing rock sets it's rare that I go more than 3 per cent slower or faster – but I've got loads of instrumental house tunes that I happily pitch up to 12 per cent and no one notices. However, I'd never go past 5 per cent with most vocal tracks.

You can transform many genres into something new by cranking up the pitch. A DJ I know used to play a 33 RPM house record at 45 RPM because it changed it into a great sounding drum and bass tune (though I don't think that track had any vocals).

Like everything else in DJing no hard and fast rule exists, but if you find yourself straying too far past 5 per cent it's important to ask yourself whether the tune still sounds okay. The reason you need to increase (or decrease) the pitch by so much may be because you're crossing genres – trying to mix a smooth house track into a trance track, for example. Although the structure, the key, the driving rhythm and the pitch of the tune may all sound fine, from a genre point of view you need to decide whether these tunes really play well next to each other. Like the bully and the weird kid at school, just because two tunes fit together like jigsaw pieces in many ways, it doesn't mean that they're meant to stick together. They may be from different jigsaw puzzles!

Developing a Style

The tunes you pick to play and the way you mix them come together to define your DJ style. Your style can and should be pliable, depending on what club you're playing in and what kind of music is expected of you.

If, like me, you came to DJing because you were inspired by another DJ or a music genre as a whole, you'll already have a basic style before you even start to think about one. However, try not to simply be a copycat of your favourite DJ. Listen to as many DJs as you can for inspiration, then put everything you've picked up into a big pot, give it a stir, add in your own creative ideas that have grown from listening to these DJs and hopefully you have that little twist to your style that makes you different from other DJs.

Your style may also change from what you play in the bedroom and hand out on CD to what you play in a club. You may be a trance fiend in the bedroom, but the club you work at demands commercial dance music, so you have to tone down the music you play. This fact doesn't pigeonhole you as a commercial dance DJ; it's quite the opposite. You're actually a well-rounded DJ: you can play top trance in the biggest clubs in the land, or play commercial tunes and tailor your set list to a mainstream crowd.

The genre of music you play doesn't define how you put it together, though. Between key changes, tempo changes, energy and genre changes, you can put together your own unique style, but also one that's still aimed at the people you're playing for – the crowd in front of you.

Easing up on the energy

Whether it's rock music or dance music, if all you do is play music at full pace, full power all the time, the only thing you can do is slow down or reduce the energy. But if you're almost at full energy, waiting to give more when the time's right, you'll be a DJ in control of the crowd or listener.

If you're at 100 per cent where do you go?

I always think back to a guy called Martin Woods, my old squash coach. One thing I learnt from him was that if I hit everything as hard as possible all the time, I'd never have a way to change my game apart from slowing it down, which would make me predictable and boring. So he advised me to hit the ball at about 90 per cent of power for most of the rallies, so I could inject pace and energy when I knew it was time to add pressure, or slow it down and change my game to keep my opponent guessing. And this translates perfectly into power and tempo when DJing.

When playing live, try to take the crowd through different levels of emotions. Take them from cheering and smiling to a little more intense, eyes closed and hands in the air, and then back to cheering and bouncing up and down on the dance floor. If you can put together a musical experience instead of choosing 20 tunes just because they mix well with each other, you'll be more creative, be able to work the crowd and hopefully be regarded as a great DJ.

If you're DJing at parties or at rock nights, power and tempo can often come second fiddle to how well known a tune is. Consider the big tunes you play at parties – the energetic ones that get the most people onto the dance floor. If you play one after the other for two hours, everyone will be exhausted! In this instance, it's good to think about using slower tracks to give people a breather (and others the chance to fall in love).

You'll want to be at 100 per cent power often through your set, but don't stagnate at that level and become stale. At least look to undulate the power of your tunes from start to finish, if not the tempo. Changing the driving rhythm (see the section 'Beatmatching – the next generation', earlier in the chapter) is a great way to alter the power.

Changing the key

Harmonic mixing (see 'Getting in tune with harmonic mixing', earlier in this chapter) isn't just a way to let you mix in the next tune seamlessly – you can use key changes to step up the power of the night, or take the set into a more intense, dramatic level.

If you're trying to get a bit more moody and serious with the mix, lowering the key of the mix using a simple offbeat bass melody, or a rugged sounding *ta-fe-te-te* driving rhythm (see the earlier section 'Beatmatching – the next generation' for an explanation) can really take the mix into a deep, intense place that's like saying to the crowd, 'Come with me . . . I'm going to take you somewhere for the next 20 minutes.'

When you want to come up for air from a deep place, I find that changing up in key so that the notes are slightly higher in pitch makes the mix sound brighter, happier and full of renewed energy. If you've spent a long time in the set playing dark, complicated trance or hard house tunes, a simple offbeat driving rhythm that changes the mix up in key can be like a strong espresso in the morning – it gives the mix and the crowd a burst of energy, and leads you into a new part of your mix.

Increasing the tempo

For dance DJs, if the first tune you used in a mix was set to play at 130 BPM (beats per minute) and you beatmatched all the tunes that followed precisely, the entire set would play at 130 BPM and bore the pants off the dance floor.

The normal progression of a set is to have an upward trend in BPM from start to finish, with little speed bumps to slow the pace down by one or two BPM for a couple of tunes but then rev it all up again, which can work really well. Slowing down the set slightly can add energy, rather than kill it.

If you have a BPM counter on your mixer (refer to Chapter 10), play a pre-mixed CD by one of your favourite DJs through it, and watch the counter gradually move up through the set, and look for these tempo speed bumps.

Getting a backhanded compliment

I once lost out on getting the big, main-set, Saturday night slot in a club because the owner said, 'You'd only try to take the crowd somewhere special. We just want a DJ who plays random tunes and lets the crowd decide how happy they are.' At the time I was annoyed to be missing out on the bigger slot, but looking back it was one hell of a compliment. It meant the club was noticing everything I was striving to do; even if they did lack the sense to act on it.

The easiest way to increase the pace is to gradually increase the pitch fader through a series of tunes. If you have the patience (and length of tune to allow it), at the end of every two bars move the pitch fader by a small amount (about 2 or 3 millimetres). Spread out through enough tunes, you can get to the perfect BPM at which you want to play with no one noticing.

Be careful when moving the pitch control because if you do it too quickly, the people on the floor will hear the music get higher in pitch (remember, it's not just a speed control – it also changes the pitch of the music). If you have equipment with Master Tempo activated, which keeps the pitch the same no matter what speed you set it to play at, you can be a bit faster about this tempo change (about 15 seconds per BPM).

Jumps

If you don't have the patience to stand over the tune and move the pitch control in small amounts, you can use the breakdowns and other changes in the tune to boost, or *jump*, the pitch by around half a per cent. Use the first beat of the bar on the new phrase to jump up the pitch control. How much you can increase it, and whether you can spread this move over a couple of bars rather than the entire track, depends on the tune you're playing.

Or if you're planning to instantly jump the pitch as the tune hits the breakdown, do it between the last beat of the phrase and the first beat of the breakdown. You're best doing this with tunes that don't have a strong melody to the breakdown, and it takes practice and experimentation to get it right.

Genre changes

Switching from house to R&B or from trance to breakbeat (and eventually back again) can be an extremely effective and unnoticeable way of speeding up the mix because the change in beat structure can hide the tempo changes.

Using your brain

A few years ago I heard a great breakbeat tune called 'Symmetry C' by Brainchild that Oakenfold used as a way to step up energy, if not tempo. So I wondered how well it would work as a tempo change tool too. One night I'd increased the BPM to about 133 by the gradual method, at which point the floor was packed and happy because I'd been playing lots of music they knew and liked. But I wanted to take the mix up a gear.

Instead of playing faster and heavier music from the same genre, which would eventually lead to boredom, I used 'Symmetry C' as a bridge. As it had a swelling, beatless intro, I didn't even need to beatmatch it in; I just faded up over the outro of the last tune. I didn't play it for long, but it meant that I was able to jump from 133 to about 138 in one step. Over the course of the next two or three tunes, everyone went nuts without knowing why!

Avoiding stagnation

When you think enough about the music you play and the order and style you play it in, you start to fall in love with a few mixes. I've fallen into this trap a few times, repeating the same series of mixes week after week, or night after night. (This is especially common in warm-up sets, when you can wrongly assume that people don't care about what or how you mix.)

The downsides to repeating mixes are:

- ✔ A mix that works in one club to one set of people won't automatically work the next night to a different set of people.
- ✔ Regulars to the club recognise the mix, and you appear uncreative.
- ✔ You're going through the motions; the fun and excitement has gone.

Because of the amount of time you've spent practising, you should have a sixth sense about the options that are available to you when mixing in and out of tunes. For the sake of your development, the people on the dance floor and the tunes in your box that never get to see the light of day, don't stick to the same transitions.

Respecting the crowd

Developing your own style is extremely important, but you still need to respect the crowd you're playing to, especially when trying to get work. It's one of those catch-22 situations that you can't avoid: how do you get experience if you need experience to get a job that gives you the experience? If you're a famous DJ, your style can be anything you want. Almost like the emperor's new clothes, some folks will love what you're doing no matter what you do or what you play.

But when you're trying to build up your reputation or just starting off, you need to be careful about pushing the crowd past their comfort level. If you're playing in a rock club where they're used to loads of scratching, samples dropped in all the time and some pretty freaky choices of tunes, then you're okay, the crowd will like what you're doing and if you're any good someone will notice you and you'll get on the next rung of the ladder.

If you're working in a more commercial club, though, and you try to do exactly the same strange, odd-sounding moves from the DJ booth, you may look up and find 200 people staring blankly at you, only to pause to let the tumble-weed roll past them. In this instance, tone your style down to what the audience probably expects: some solid, rocking tunes with a smooth, constant beat for them to dance to, with not many challenging tunes or mix techniques.

This reaction may sound like selling out, but ask yourself whether you'd rather be a poor artist or a paid DJ who can afford the time and money to develop in the right places at the right time, and has the ambition to do so!

Demonstrating your style

When you make a demo mix CD to show off your skills, your style is entirely up to you (head to Chapter 19 to find out more about making a demo). Your demo is a reflection of who you are and what you want to do. Let it rip, show off how good you are at scratching, use your six turntables past their potential and create the most awe-inspiring mix anyone's ever heard.

Have a game plan when you show off this taster as your DJ style. If you're sending it to clubs and the feedback you get it that it's too full on, send another one back to them that you've toned down a bit. But carry on handing out demos to your friends that are mixed in the way *you* want to mix them. Adapt to get work, and then start to drip feed your own style into your sets if you get the chance, but never give up on what truly inspires you and makes you want to DJ in your own time. If you compromise too far in one direction, you may never come back!

Chapter 19

Creating a Great Demo

• •

In This Chapter

▶ Putting together a list of tunes to be proud of

▶ Making sure that the mix has a point

▶ Setting the levels and EQs for perfect sound

▶ Staying focused and being a perfectionist

▶ Recording to computer and burning CDs

▶ Getting noticed

• •

*Y*ou've spent a long time developing your skills as a DJ. Now you have to let people out there know how good you are by making a demo of your best mix.

Your demo reflects you in every way. You won't have the benefit of standing next to the club owner to explain that at 15 minutes and 20 seconds into your mix the cat jumped onto the decks, which caused the needle to jump and threw your concentration, and that's why the mix sounds awful.

You can't send in a sloppy looking (and sounding) CD and expect a club owner to think that you're professional. You must let this taster be your best work. Your demo marks you as a good DJ or a bad DJ, so make it sound great.

Preparing to Record the Demo

The most important aspects of your demo are that the sound is well recorded, the music is mixed well and it doesn't seem as if you've just thrown together 20 tunes with no real thought. Your demo must show that you have a vision of how to entertain and progress a mix from start to finish.

You'll probably make your first demo in your bedroom, but in time you can become comfortable enough with your skills as a DJ to record a live set, and hand that out to people.

Programming your set

Which tunes to put on a demo and how to progress from start to finish is up to you and your DJing style. Some DJs like to make their demos emulate the pro-mixed CDs that they own; start off with a sample from a movie or some ambient sound effects, mix into the first tune that also has a quiet introduction and then build up the mix for the next 90 minutes. Others prefer just to put on the first tune with a pounding beat, hit Start and take it from there; no need for a gentle introduction for these DJs!

Progressive and trance DJs are more likely to be the ones who use the gradual introduction into a mix because it sets a mood for what's to come. House DJs are about the rhythm and the musicality of what they play, so starting off with the bass beat and bass melody or a strong vocal with the beats coming in 16 bars later (see Chapter 15) is a really powerful way to start for this style of DJ.

The quality and style of your demo is a reflection of you as a DJ. If you simply recreate a Zane Lowe set list from start to finish, what are you going to be like when you first stand in the DJ booth and have to create something from scratch? The club will soon realise that you can't mix without the benefit of plagiarism after the fifth week in a row of playing the same set!

The last thing to think about before rifling through your library of tunes is showing what sort of music you can play. If you plan to send in a demo to a rock club, adding some epic trance to the mix isn't very relevant. And if you want to send a mix to a house or commercial club with a view to being the DJ from start to finish, you'll probably want to create your set so that you start off with some relaxed house music, move up in tempo and energy, and finish off with tunes that you know will make the crowd go wild on the dance floor.

Picking and arranging the tunes

In the months (or weeks if you're a natural) you've spent getting to grips with DJing, you should have developed a few mixes from tune to tune that give you goose bumps when you perform them. (There's no shame in taking pride in what you do. If you do a mix that makes you smile, there's a fair chance everyone else will smile too!) If you have six or seven of these individual mixes between two tunes, that gives you 12 to 14 tunes to work with for your demo. Assuming that each track lasts about four minutes, you have just under an hour's worth of music to play.

Depending on the range of music in your DJ box, no doubt some of these tracks differ slightly in style, and won't mix into any of the others. However, you still have a library brimming with tunes that you love to play, so consider some of these as the glue tunes that hold your mix together.

From the 14 tunes you know you want to use in your demo, you can create a map of the mix by arranging them in order. If, for example, your current playlist contains two gentle house tracks, two light, chart dance tracks, four vocal house tracks, two uplifting American house tracks and four trance tracks, you may want to play them in the following order:

- ✔ Gentle house

- ✔ Vocal house

- ✔ Uplifting American house

- ✔ Chart (popular, mainstream) club tunes

- ✔ Trance

The order gives the mix a progression of power from beginning to end. This playlist is very simple and basic in structure, and certainly isn't right for a lot of music styles, DJs and clubs you may apply for, but the idea of progressing through a mix, rather than throwing songs into the mix because you think that they may mix well, is crucial to showing your overall DJ skills, rather than just your mixing and beatmatching skills.

Chapter 18 has more information on creating an undulating set list, so before you make your first demo, try to develop a solid understanding of progressing the mix – then you can start experimenting with the order in which you play your tunes, varying the amount of energy in the mix just like a roller-coaster going up and down.

Bridging the gaps

Take a look through your library of music and hunt for the glue tunes that'll help you progress from one level of energy or genre to the next. Sometimes you find a glue tune that mixes perfectly, is the perfect genre and perfectly increases the energy enough to be a great transition into next track. Sometimes the two tunes you're trying to bridge between don't work because they have such a large divide in pace and style between them that you'd be unwise to keep forcing that mix (what I call *crowbarring in a tune*).

Don't simply include tunes to bridge the gap between your original tracks because they're musical glue. You want to use them because you really like playing them, and really want to include these tunes in the mix. Don't ever add a tune into the mix only with the purpose of bridging from one tune to another. Whether it's a vocal sample, a movie clip or just another tune from the box, you need to be happy that this tune reflects on you as a DJ – because you chose it and you put it in the mix.

Be careful if you plan to use mix techniques like spinbacks, dead stops or even fade outs (refer to Chapter 16) to get around any problems of tunes mixing together. You can use them incredibly effectively and can add a level of excitement (and energy) to the mix, but if performed poorly or at the wrong time (or too many times), they can sound as if you've used them because you couldn't mix from one tune to the other. Your skills as a DJ are on show in your demo, so these techniques may actually work against you.

These bridging tunes, when added to the ones you originally picked out, hopefully end up lasting no more than the 74 minutes you can fit on a CD (assuming that's what you're planning to send out). If the mix lasts more than 74 minutes, take another look at your tracklist and take out some of the weaker tunes.

Practising your set

After you've chosen all your tunes, and you've decided on the order in which you think they play best, the time has come for you to practise your set in stages before trying to perform it all in one go.

Record your practice sessions so you can listen back to them. It's funny how mixes can sound good when you do them, but when you listen back they sound really rushed and amateurish. Alternatively, they may even sound better than you thought.

Feel free to experiment at this stage with how you mix your tunes together. If you think that a mix between two particular tunes can be slightly better, trust your instincts and look at ways to improve what you're currently trying to do.

Ask yourself the following questions about your mix:

- ✔ If you change the mix transition between tunes by 4, 8 or 16 bars, does that make a difference?
- ✔ If you start the new tune 16 bars later, does everything fall into place?
- ✔ Are you using the EQ (equaliser) controls and faders with enough subtlety to create the seamless mix you're looking for?
- ✔ One last time, are you sure that your tunes are in the best order?

Address each possibility and create a mix that's the best you can do.

Practise makes more than perfect

If you take a long time to put together and play the mix in full, don't fret. When you started putting the mix together, you were unlikely to be able to play it perfectly in front of an audience. Therefore, a perfect mix probably wasn't an accurate reflection of your abilities at that point, and practising your set does have several major benefits:

- ✔ When you practise your set to perfection, you put out your best work for people to listen to.

- ✔ Playing the set over and over again and analysing how to make it better is the best way to develop the skills you need to spot a bad mix, and know how to improve or fix it. This skill carries over to all your future mixes.

- ✔ Each time you practise the set, any beatmatching skills and knowledge of beat structure through repetition increase incredibly.

- ✔ Creating a set you're excited about, that has a purpose other than general practice and that uses tunes you love listening to removes any boredom factor, and your skills develop without you realising it!

Practise your set until you're completely comfortable playing it. Reaching the stage where you know the mix points and starting cue points like the back of your hand is important, as is being happy with all the EQ settings and strange volume anomalies that may occur (see the later section 'Looking After Sound Processing').

Setting up to record

Before you can start to record your demo, you need to set up your equipment to ensure the best possible sound quality. Two factors can affect your sound quality:

- ✔ You need a good quality recorder that you know how to work, which can faithfully record your mix without failing on you, crashing or cutting out halfway through.

- ✔ You need to be familiar with your mixer and know how to control the sound output on it.

Avoiding poor-quality recordings

The only thing less appealing than a demo with train wreck mixing and a poor choice of music is one that's badly recorded. Always keep in mind that no matter who you send your demo to – whether it's your best friend, your mother or Paul Oakenfold – this mix demonstrates your skills as a DJ. If it's badly recorded, you instantly lose points and you'll be dubbed as unprofessional!

Tape versus CD for demos

From purely a functional point of view, these days you should really make a demo CD of your mix rather than a tape. Apart from the fact that tape is almost obsolete, the sound quality is far better on CD and the ability to skip tracks to the next mix instantly on CD, rather than messing around with the fast-forward button on a tape deck, makes CD the preferred format.

If you have the time (and the money for the increased cost), make both. It may be a waste of time making a tape, but why reduce the options of how someone can listen to your mix? When you send both formats, you show consideration and thought toward those you're trying to get work from, because they may not have a tape player or CD player where they'll be listening to the demo (a car, for instance).

If you're going to record to tape, it's vital that you record properly. Different makes of tapes have different tolerances to the amount of signal they can handle (how loud you play the music from the mixer to the tape recorder). The packaging on the tape tells you the perfect range (in decibels). If you play too loud, the sound distorts; too quiet a signal and you get a lot of tape hiss, which loses the clarity and brightness of the sound of the music.

Although a CD plays at a quiet volume on a stereo if under-recorded, you shouldn't have any problems with sound quality from low level recordings. Set the recording levels on the CD (or computer) too loud, though, and you'll suffer terribly from digital clipping, with the music cutting and popping in and out – a frankly hideous noise to avoid at all costs.

Don't hand out demo mixes you know are bad

When I first started DJing I had a stereo that would temporarily drop the high frequencies from the music when recording. I was so excited at being a DJ and I really wanted to make sure that all my friends had tapes of me DJing. Everybody would politely take these tapes from me, but one day I went to a friend's house and saw my 'Recession' mix tape sitting next to the stereo with tape over the record-prevent tabs. When I asked him about it, he said that although he liked the mix, after listening to it once he'd got fed up with the sound problems and figured that he'd rather have a recording of Pete Tong from the radio instead. That really hurt, but it taught me a valuable lesson.

Mastering MiniDisc and DAT for demos

You may have a MiniDisc recorder or a professional DAT (digital audio tape) recorder at home, and may be tempted to send out demos in these formats. However, bear in mind that very few people have equipment to play these formats back.

Your best option if you really want to use these for recording is to use them as a 'Master' of your mix, then use this master DAT or MiniDisc to make all the CD and tape copies you're planning to send out.

Correcting recording levels

In order to make sure that the mixes you record hit the balance between enough volume to prevent tape hiss with no risk of CD sound distortion, your recorder needs to have some kind of record level indicator.

This indicator is usually very similar to the output VU meter on your mixer; a set of two lines of LEDs that are different colours (green, yellow and then red) depending on how strong the signal is. The meter should be laid out so that any music you play over a certain level (sometimes when it hits +3 decibels) makes the red LEDs start to flash.

If your recorder can accept up to +8 decibels as an input strength before distortion occurs, and you set the record level to a normal maximum of +3 decibels, if the music spikes by 2 decibels because of an unexpected loud part of the tune, you're still within the recording limits of your equipment (because the signal is only +5 decibels, which is still 3 decibels under the recording limits). If you set the record level so that it's almost hitting the +8 decibel mark for the normal playback of your records, when this 2 decibel musical spike occurs, the level is now +10 decibels, and you'll distort the recording.

Limiters

You use *limiters* to clamp down on any peaks in level, helping to prevent distortion. If you do have a limiter on your home recorder, it will probably have a very harsh attack, so if the music does peak, the limiter immediately reduces the overall level of the music by 2 or 3 decibels. This dip can be very noticeable on the recording, and sounds as though you've crashed down on the output level on the mixer by accident.

Some professional limiters are really good, and you can use them as a great safety net for unexpected peaks in the music signal. But I still recommend that you concentrate on setting the record levels correctly in the first place, so you don't lose some quality and clarity when the limiter kicks in.

Matching the levels

The best way to control the audio levels being recorded is to make sure that when the music is playing at its loudest point, you set the mixer's output level meter to display the same as the recorder's input level meter. This way, you can look at the output LEDs on the mixer showing +3 decibels and be happy that the recorder is recording the music at +3 decibels too.

Lining up your equipment

Setting your equipment so that everything you look at shows the same value is known as *lining up* your equipment. You make this alignment by playing a reference tone through the mixer. A common reference tone is a constant sine wave playing at 1 kilohertz.

A constant tone is preferable because you can be sure you're measuring the precise signal level. When you play music as a line up, the LEDs are erratic and flash up and down to show the different changes in the signal level. A constant tone is just that; constant. The level (and the LEDs) change only if you move the faders on the mixer or the input control on the recorder.

The process of lining up equipment using tone is as follows:

1. **If you haven't got your own reference tone, download one from www.recess.co.uk and transfer it to CD or MP3.**

   Even if you use turntables it's okay; find a CD or MP3 player to plug into your mixer and play this tone into one of the channels.

2. **If you need to press a switch or button to see the input level coming into the mixer, do so now (see Chapter 10 for information on input level controls).**

3. **Adjust the gain on the mixer (using the gain controls) so that the mixer's input level LEDs show +3 decibels.**

   This adjustment may mean increasing or reducing the gain control. If you're playing the reference tone out of the headphones of an MP3 player, the signal may be weaker than normal; if so, turn the volume up on the MP3 player as well as the gain control to make sure that the input level is at +3 decibels.

4. **Set the channel-fader for this channel to the maximum position you'd set it at when playing a tune normally.**

   For scratch DJs this is normally right up to the top. For beat-mixing DJs, party and rock DJs I always recommend setting your maximum point to three-quarters of the way up (the section 'Keeping an even volume', later in this chapter, explains why).

5. **If you need to switch the display LEDs back to display the Master Output level, do so now.**

6. **Use the Master Level control-fader to make the LEDs for the output of the mixer display +3 decibels.**

   After you've made this adjustment, any changes you make to the gain control on the input channel are mirrored by the readout of the mixer. If you reduce the gain on the reference tone to only zero decibels, you notice that the Master Level output LEDs also drop down to zero decibels.

   (If you've just tried setting the gain to zero decibels, return the gain, and therefore the Master Level, to +3 decibels before proceeding.)

7. **Set the recording level on the tape recorder.**

   Setting this level is simply a case of increasing (or decreasing) the input control so the LEDs display +3 decibels on the recorder.

You use the +3 decibel level only to line up your equipment and make the LED displays show the same thing. If you want a +6 decibel output to the recording device, increase the gain control on the channel input to +6 decibels, and you'll see the Master Level Output display and the display on the recording equipment both now show +6 decibels.

Unfortunately, this precise guide on how to line up your equipment only works properly if your recording equipment has a record level control. If you send the music into a home-style hi-fi with a preset record level, you may have to spend a lot of time trying to find the proper output level from your mixer through trial and error in order to create good quality recordings.

Looking After Sound Processing

When you come to look after the sound of your mix, you have two major considerations: keeping an even volume between tunes, and the EQs.

Keeping an even volume

Keeping a smooth volume to your mix is almost as important as keeping the bass beats in time or a smooth fade between tunes. Quieter parts of tunes can still be quieter, but the aim is to keep the overall volume of the mix (when the tunes are at their loudest) the same. If you line up the equipment (see the preceding section) properly, volume control is a simple process.

You need to use the gain controls and the input level meters on your mixer to match the input levels of your tunes.

If you don't have input level meters on your mixer, you'll find keeping the volume of your tunes in the mix the same is a lot harder. What you can do is put both ears of the headphones on and quickly switch from hearing each tune through them. If you hear a drop in volume from one tune to the next, use the gain controls to increase or decrease the level of the incoming tune (the tune you're about to mix in) until they both sound about the same.

If you don't have gain controls on your mixer, I recommend saving up to buy a new one, quickly! In Chapter 16, and the previous section, I mention the importance of setting the channel-faders to three-quarters of the way up rather than all the way up. This is of extreme benefit to the people without gain controls, because if a tune you've just mixed in doesn't sound as loud as the one you're mixing out of, you still have some headroom (the other quarter of the way up on the channel-fader) to increase how loud the new tune plays. With practice and patience, you'll eventually develop the knack to catch these changes before anyone else can hear them.

Digital DJs win out again here, because software titles often have an auto-gain setting, matching the input level of the tunes in the mix automatically.

Assuming that you don't have the luxury of auto-gain, but you do have a mixer with gain controls and input level meters, making sure that all your tunes play out at a similar volume through the duration of the mix is very simple. Here's how:

1. **Before you press record, with the EQs for bass, mid and high frequencies set to the position for perfect sound to come out from the mixer (see the next section 'Setting your EQs'), start a tune and look at the input level LED display on the mixer (you may need to press a button or switch to do this).**

2. **Use the gain control to set the input level to your preferred point.**

   I usually suggest that the meter should light up the first red LEDs (sometimes at the +3 decibel point), and maybe make the next set light up from time to time, but not constantly. Your settings depend entirely on the mixer you use and what you're recording to, though.

3. **Pick out the next tune and play it through the headphones with the EQs set to the optimum play-out position.**

4. **Use the gain control to set the input level LEDs on the new tune so that they're as close as possible to the input level setting you made on the current tune playing through the speakers (see Step 2).**

When you set both the channel-faders to the same level, both tunes should play out of the mixer at the same volume. Unless:

✔ **You forget to set the EQs to the optimum play-out level before check-ing the input level LEDs, which gives an artificial reading.** If you killed the bass (when mixing out of the last tune, for instance) and you don't reset it to neutral (which is hopefully zero), when you check the new tune's input level, the reduced bass will cause it to have a lot less signal strength than it should. So if, for example, you'd set the gain control to make the input LEDs match the +3 decibels of the other tune, when you finally realise you've cut the bass, and put it back in, the tune may now play with a +8 decibel signal strength. Get into the routine of resetting the EQs after every mix so you don't fall into this trap.

✔ **Your tunes have a bass beat and rhythm that, although sounding fine, over-powers the rest of the tune, showing a false 'high' reading.** So although the LEDs show an input strength of +3 decibels, the tune actu-ally sounds weak (reduced volume and power) compared to the other tunes in the mix.

The only way to get around this problem is to get to know your tunes. If this problem happens once in practice, take a note (or make a note on the record sleeve) to remind you to kill the bass level slightly to allow you to increase the gain to match the volume with the rest of the mix.

Cross-fader curves also have a part to play in the volume of a mix. Check out Chapter 10 for information about how the cross-fader curve affects the volume during a mix between two tunes, but if the curve allows both tunes to play at full volume at the same time, the overall output level increases and may cause the sound to distort (see Figure 19-1).

Figure 19-1:
Two tunes
playing at a
similar level
combine to
make the
output from
the mixer a
lot louder.

Resulting volume

Tune 1

Tune 2

The two ways around this problem are to use a cross-fader curve that has a slight dip in the middle to compensate for the boost of two tunes playing together at full volume (see Figures 10-2 and 10-3 in Chapter 10 for more about cross-fader curves), or use the channel-faders to dip a tune's level through the mix and then return it to full when the mix is almost over. Chapter 16 has more information on using channel-faders to enhance the mix.

Setting your EQs

The best way of making sure that you select the best EQ settings for your recording is to start off with a blank sheet. The first thing to do is set all the EQs on the mixer to their neutral point. This point is normally marked with a zero, or is the halfway point on the control (for rotary knobs, this means setting the EQ so that it's pointing to the 12 o'clock position on a clock face.) In this way, the EQ controls aren't affecting the music that you're sending out of the mixer.

However, different mixers process sound slightly differently. With some cheap mixers you need to increase the bass and high frequencies slightly and reduce the mid-range in order to make the tune sound right. If you have a good pair of headphones, use them to gauge the audio quality from the mixer and use the EQs to set the sound of the music so it sounds good to you.

Obviously, different tunes need you to tweak their EQs in separate ways in order to make the bass or high frequencies stand out a little more in the mix. Different tunes also have different sounding bass drums, and you may want to use the mid and bass EQs to try to match the strength of the bass beat as you go through the mix.

Testing, testing

When recording to CD (or to a computer), perform a test recording to make sure no boost or cut in the amount of bass, mid-range or high frequencies occurs in the recording. This is more common when recording to tape, but some computer soundcards and CD recorders can be troublesome.

As well as any problems caused by your recording equipment, you also have to consider how you set up the EQs on your amplifier. If you have the bass set very high on your amp (or stereo), you probably have the bass EQs on the mixer set lower than normal. With this setting, the recordings you make sound a bit thin (a description of a sound that's lacking in bass).

Listen to the recording on equipment other than the one you've used to record it with. I find that car stereos play music back very faithfully. If the music sounds fine in the car (especially when compared to pre-recorded CDs that you normally play in the car) then you can be 95 per cent sure that you've set up the EQs and levels on your mixer (and recorder) to allow the mix to record properly.

If the recording doesn't sound right and you need to add a little more bass, look to the recording unit first before adjusting the mixer. If your recorder has EQs that you can adjust, increase the bass slightly and do another test recording. If your recorder doesn't have EQ controls, you need to adjust the EQs on the mixer in order to make the music sound as good as possible.

The reason you change the EQs on the recorder first is because as a DJ you use the EQs more as a mixing tool than as a sound processing tool. See Chapter 16 for more information on how to use the EQs to enhance your mixes, but the key here is that if you have to boost the bass by 6 decibels (most controls go to about 12 decibels) in order to make the music sound good when recorded, when you mix in another tune with elevated bass frequencies you risk the danger of your mixer not being able to process that combined, high-bass signal well enough, and the sound quality of your mix suffers.

Sound engineers take the time to EQ instruments and vocals precisely, but hardly move the EQs away from those settings after they set them. As a DJ you'll be constantly changing the EQs as you mix, so knowing that you just need to return each control to zero to make the tune sound normal greatly benefits the sound processing and speed of your mixes.

Setting EQs on the recorder or the mixer may take a little time to get right, but helps you record the best sounding mix possible.

Adjusting the amplifier

You change the EQ settings on your amplifier depending on your circumstances. You may be recording the music through your home hi-fi, which also acts as your amplifier, so the EQ settings you make to improve the recording also affect the sound from the hi-fi (amplifier).

If you're using a separate recorder from the amplifier, though, concentrating on the sound that goes from the mixer into the recorder is more important than adjusting the amp. After you've set up the sound to make the perfect recording, you can then go to your amplifier and tweak the frequencies to give you the best sound you'd like to hear from the speakers.

If you set the EQs for the amp first and then find that you have to increase the bass EQ on the mixer to get a perfect recording, the bass through the amp is now going to be too high and you have to re-adjust it, and probably the mid and high frequencies, too. You may also feel reluctant to alter the beautiful sound you've created through the amplifier and sacrifice the sound quality of your recording.

Only you know how you like to hear the music through the amp, but the basic guideline is for the sound to have a clear, solid bass beat (but not so much that the bass frequencies take over the rest of the tune, which may make it sound muddy), and the mid range shouldn't be so high that it dominates the bass frequencies. To still give crisp vocals, guitars and melodies, the high frequencies should be set so that you can hear the hi-hat cymbals playing crisply over the bass and mid frequencies.

Performing the Demo

You've chosen a good order for your tunes that make up the demo, you've set all the recording controls to get the best sound possible and you've practised the set so that you actually dream about how the tunes are put together. Now take the final step and record your demo.

Press the record button on the CD/tape/MiniDisc/DAT/computer (let tapes run for about five seconds to make sure that you're past the blank leader tape at the very beginning) and then take a deep breath – it's for real this time – and start the mix. An hour or so later you'll either have gold dust or fertiliser sitting in the recording device.

If it's the latter, get a glass of water (or similar), compose yourself and do it again, and again, and again – until you get it right. You don't need to get too annoyed with yourself if you mess the demo up (though admittedly messing up right at the end of your mix *is* especially frustrating). Remember that the professional DJs who actually mix on their CD releases (rather than using computer software to do it for them) have been doing this DJing lark a lot longer than you have, and are (for the time being) just plain better than you.

The pros also have the option to stop when they make an error and then start again from where they left off, and piece everything together in the recording studio. If you record directly to CD, you need to perform the entire set from start to finish without getting anything wrong. If you record your mix to a computer first, you can edit out the bad parts and repair your errors by stopping and starting.

When you're starting to learn how to DJ, you're cheating yourself out of an invaluable process of improving your DJing if you use a computer to tidy up your mixes. Each time you go through your set, whether you complete it or not, you're expanding your skills and getting one step closer to being as good as your idols. If you just stop and restart the mix between two tunes after an error when recording to computer, it amounts to nothing more than shortcutting.

But if you do like taking the easy route and cheating with shortcuts, head to the section 'Making a Demo CD on Computer', later in this chapter, to find out more about editing your mix on computer.

Staying focused

If you have to run through your set three or four times (or more) before you create a recording that you're happy with, maintain your composure, stay focused on what you're trying to do and try not to get frustrated and angry by any mistakes you make.

You can do a few simple things to help keep your head in the game:

- ✔ Arrange your tunes in the order you plan to play them in, so you don't have to hunt through a record box, CD wallet or digital library to find the next tune, run out of time and mess up the mix.

- ✔ Wipe off any dust from the records, check for any build-up of grime or fluff-balls on the needles, clean CDs and reboot your computer before you start the mix.

- ✔ Have something to eat before you start recording. Low blood sugar is the number one cause of snapped records in my DJ room. I get grumpy and frustrated when I'm hungry, and (reluctantly) admit to throwing one or two records into a wall after a bad mix on an empty stomach.

- ✔ Keep some water on hand. Hunger can sometimes be thirst in disguise. Keep yourself hydrated so you don't start to feel tired and worn out.

- ✔ If you mess up a mix after getting one hour through it and feel frustration brewing, take a ten-minute break, go for a walk, clear your head and come back to the mix ready to have another go. This break not only takes out any boredom factor that may lead to impatience, but also gives your ears a rest from the music playing out from the amp.

- ✔ Go to the toilet before you start. Needing to pee during a set not only makes you rush a mix so you can run off to the smallest room, but you may be in there a while and miss the next mix. Be sensible and go before you start the mix. Just remember to wash your hands, please.

DJing made me put on weight

I thought I'd be smart about not getting hungry when I recorded mixes. I used to keep a bag of Jelly Babies with me when DJing at home or in clubs, just in case I got a drop in my sugar levels and needed a quick jolt. A bag of Jelly Babies per night makes your waistline grow incredibly fast. Couple that with more time spent DJing than on the squash court and it's no wonder my waistline grew!

Becoming a perfectionist

No matter how long you take to get the mix right, get the mix right. Keep in mind that your demo can be passed to anybody. You never know who may hear your work and have an influence on your career.

The demo has got to be perfect in your eyes. Never, ever utter the words 'That'll do'. If you want to be a bedroom DJ for the rest of your life, then fine, it probably will do. But if you've even a pinch of ambition in you, start again. Even if you miss out one beat, or have a picky problem with the levels, re-do the mix. To make an error is acceptable; not to improve because of your errors, or fix them, is completely unacceptable. Get to a stage that when you hear demos by DJs who don't care as much as you do, you can take pride in being more of a professional than them.

If the demo is for submission to a competition or a job, remember that you're up against thousands of other budding DJs; your perfectionism may be the reason you're hired instead of someone else.

Listening with an open mind

When you listen back to your mix to gauge how your performance sounds, judge it with an open mind. Things to listen out for are:

- Noticeable drops in volume through the tune transitions
- Distortion on the tape
- Galloping horse bass drum beats when beatmatching dance music
- Noticeable pitch bends when you temporarily speed up (or slow down) a tune to get it back in time
- Poor EQ control
- Choosing the wrong time to mix from one tune to another

However, knowing exactly when a mix happens and exactly what to listen to can make you snow blind to the overall sound of the mix, and because you hear the transition you automatically assume that it's a bad mix. I actively encourage you to listen to the mix with a critic's ear, but also listen to it with a passive listener's ear.

If you performed the mix well and it sounds great, is it really bad or have you just fallen into a trap of over-criticism because you know the mix so well? Come back to that same mix in a couple of months' time, when you don't have every second of it fresh in your mind, and I'm sure that you'll like it more than you do now.

Don't use the chance that your opinion may change with the passage of time as an excuse to let poorly beatmatched or poorly conceived mixes stay in your demo. Be 100 per cent happy with your finished product.

Making a Demo CD on Computer

Recording to computer can make your demo a lot more versatile. You can add CD track markers precisely where you'd like them to be before burning to disc, and (although not encouraged) you can edit out your fluffs (mistakes) when recording to a computer first.

After you successfully connect your mixer to the computer (refer to Chapter 13) and set up the software to process the incoming music at the correct recording level (refer to the manual that comes with your software), you need to set the quality of your recording.

CD quality sound is 44.1 kilohertz (or 44,100 hertz), 16 bit (binary notation), stereo (multiple sound), and you should change the audio recording quality to this setting using your recording software (even when using the basic Windows Sound Recorder system). This recording setting takes up about 100 megabytes for every ten minutes you record, so make sure that your hard-drive has at least twice the space you require. Some software records to a virtual cache first, taking up space on the hard-drive, but you need the same amount of space again to save the file.

With the record levels set correctly (see the manual for your software) and sample rates all set, all you need to do is press Record on the software, start your mix, press Stop when you've finished it and save it to the hard-drive.

Editing your mix

To edit your mix you need software that's a bit more sophisticated than the Windows Sound Recorder. For PC, I use Adobe Audition, NGWave or Pro

Tools. On the Mac, I use Apple Soundtrack, Pro Tools and Audacity to edit, effect and save the mixes to different formats. Hundreds of different software audio editors are available. You may even have one installed with your CD burner software. Have a look through your program folder on your PC/Mac before spending any money on some expensive software.

Here's how to fix a mix if you make errors while performing it:

1. **When you record your mix to computer and make an error, press Stop on the software and save the file.**

2. **Call this file something recognisable like 'Mix Part 1' and save it to a new folder, keeping your work organised and tidy.**

3. **If it was a beatmatching error, work out whether this happened because you set the pitch of the incoming tune incorrectly, and if so, adjust the pitch on that tune.**

   Only change the pitch on the incoming tune. If you change the pitch on the tune you were mixing out of, the beats (and pitch of the tune) won't match the saved file where you left off.

4. **Move the needle or skip the CD about 30 seconds before you're due to start the mix. Press Record on the PC, press Start on the CD/turntable and continue with the mix as though you'd never stopped.**

If you make any more errors, save the file each time you stop as a sequential number (Mix Part 2, Mix Part 3 and so on). After you've completed the mix, albeit split into three or four different files, you need to start putting the mix back together again.

The software or even computer you use may be different from what I'm about to describe, but the principle remains the same:

1. **Open up the Mix Part 1 file (the first file) and play it.**

   A visual representation of the music (a symmetrical group of peaks and troughs called the waveform – see Figure 19-2) appears on screen to help you navigate the file. Usually, there's a time indicator bar that moves along the waveform as the music plays to let you see what part of the music is currently playing.

2. **Find an appropriate point on Mix Part 1 to stop.**

   This point is probably before you started mixing into the next tune and it's best to stop playback at the beginning of a phrase (see Chapter 15 if you're unsure what a phrase is). Zoom in to the waveform close enough to see the different peaks as each bass beat hits. When you've zoomed in close enough, you should easily be able to position the time indicator at the exact point the first bass beat of the first bar of a phrase hits.

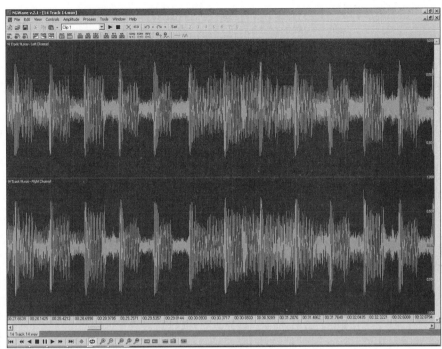

Figure 19-2:
The
waveform
displayed on
NGWave.

3. **Open up the Mix Part 2 file in another window.**

4. **Find an appropriate point on Mix Part 2 to stop.**

   Because you've started Mix Part 2 before the error in Mix Part 1, this
   overlap means you can find the identical point in Mix Part 2 at which
   you stopped Mix Part 1. If you know the tunes well, and stopped Mix
   Part 1 at the beginning of a phrase, this operation doesn't take too long.
   You need to zoom in to the waveform on Mix Part 2 to be able to get the
   time indicator to exactly the same position in the music that Mix Part 1
   has been left at.

5. **Select Mix Part 2's waveform from where you set the time indictor to
   the end of the waveform.**

   (In Adobe Audition, you just click and drag from the indicator all the
   way to the right-hand side of the waveform.)

6. **Copy this selection of the waveform to the clipboard.**

   You normally just press Ctrl+C (or CMD+C on a Mac) or choose Edit
   then Copy from the menu bar.

7. **Change the window back to the Mix Part 1 waveform and write down the time that the time indicator is currently sitting at, so you can easily check your edit point.**

8. **Without moving the time indicator on Mix Part 1, paste the file from the clipboard onto the waveform.**

   Choose Edit then Paste, or press Ctrl+V (or CMD+V for Mac users).

   This stage may vary according to the software you're using, but the essence is that you're pasting Mix Part 2 over Mix Part 1 from the point where you left the time indicator, so you shouldn't have any noticeable repetition, or cut in music, and the music should continue as though nothing's happened.

9. **Set the time indicator to the time you wrote down, and listen to the join between the two parts of the mix.**

   The join should sound completely normal. If it doesn't, undo the paste of Mix Part 2 (Ctrl Z, CMD+Z or Edit, Undo), check where you set your time indicators and have another go.

10. **Repeat this process for all the mix parts you had to make in order to get the end of the mix without any errors, and save this file as Master Mix.**

    You now have one file made up of all your changes that sounds as though you've never done anything wrong.

When saving the file, save it as a Wave file (WAV) (or as an AIFF for Mac) and be sure to check that the save settings are the same as the record settings (44.1 kilohertz, 16 bit, stereo). You may also want to save the file as an MP3 or any other audio format you'd like. MP3s are perfect for uploading to the Internet for others to listen to. I prefer making MP3's at a date rate of 320 Kbps (kilobits per second) but 192 Kbps still sounds fantastic at a massively reduced file size compared to the CD quality WAV or AIFF files.

Burning a CD

After you save your final mix as a WAV or AIFF file, you can burn the mix to CD. Depending on your operating system, you can probably just insert a blank CD into your CD recorder, drag the WAV or AIFF file onto the CD icon on your computer and follow the prompts to burn an audio CD (rather than a data CD, which won't play in a normal CD player).

Or if you have designated software to control your CD burner (like Toast for a Mac or Nero for a PC) you can customise the information that's burnt with the CD. This includes being able to split the one large music file up so that instead of one long track burnt to CD you have a different track on the CD for each tune you used in your mix, without any audio gaps between them.

Creating a track-split CD

Not only does this method make your mix seem a lot more professional, but a demo that you split up into its component mixes means that the people you send the CD out to can easily scan through the CD to listen to just the transitions between tunes, rather than listening to the entire CD or trying to scan through one long, 74-minute track to find your mix points. This does mean they might skip through any mix trickery like scratching or effects you were doing during individual tunes, but unfortunately, some people don't have time to listen to the entire mix at first listen and just care about transitions. Don't worry – if they like what they hear, they'll listen to the whole thing.

You can split a CD in two ways:

✔ **The hardest way:** You can create a CD with multiple tracks by using your audio editing software (see the section 'Editing your mix'). The software gives you a time code for the music, and this code is essential to doing this method properly. The time code is a precise measurement for working out where you are in the tune. The measurement is normally shown as hours, minutes, seconds and thousands of a second (HH:MM:SS:DDD). Here's how to do it the hard way:

1. If your first tune starts at 0:00:00:000 and you want the second track on the CD to start at 0:04:15:150, then save the mix from 00:00:00:000 to 00:04:15:150 as an individual file.

2. If track two ends at 0:09:35:223, save the mix from 0:04:15:151 (notice that it's one thousandth of a second ahead of the last cut point) to 0:09:35:223 as another separate file.

3. Go through this process for the whole mix so that you now have individual WAV files for each tune that makes up your mix. Give the files numbers when saving them, not titles, which makes life easier when you come to keeping them in the correct order.

4. With each file saved in sequence (1, 2, 3, 4, 5, 6, 7, 8, 9 and so on) use your CD burning software to add each of the files to the list of files to be burnt to the CD (in numerical order).

5. Set the gap between each track to zero seconds. You may have to refer to the manual for how to make this setting. If you don't set the gap to zero seconds, you may get a gap of silence between each of your tracks, which won't sound like a proper DJ mix and the club will no doubt file your demo – in the trash can!

6. After you've added all the tracks and set the gap between tracks to zero seconds, burn the disc to CD and play it back to make sure that you've split all the individual tracks up properly, with no blips in sound caused by getting the split time codes wrong.

✔ **The simplest way:** Create a track split CD by using the built-in track splitting functions on software such as Nero Burning Rom or Sonic Foundry. Each piece of software has a way of marking where you'd like to add track split points, without having to split up the wave file itself.

The process is almost the same as splitting the file into separate files. The software normally shows a waveform of the music (see Figure 19-2), which you play through from start to finish, adding markers to the waveform as you review it. You don't need to play the track in real time from start to finish; you can skip ahead, back, play slowly and so on, all in aid of finding the exact point you'd like to add the track split marker.

As long as you remember to set the gap between each of the tracks to zero seconds, the finished CD is neatly split into your chosen tracks, with no danger of blips in the sound from the previous method.

Check the manual that came with your software for more detailed instructions on how to make CDs with individual split tracks.

 Mix CDs you find in shops tend to put track splits at the end or halfway through a mix, but this way if the club owner hits Next on the CD player, he'll skip past your DJing skills. So for a demo, you may want to split the CD before each of the mixes start, so that the club owner can just skip forward to hear how you perform each of the transitions.

Sending Off the Mix

After you've created your demo, the final stage is to create a package that sells you properly and to make sure that whoever receives it knows where it came from, even if the demo gets separated from the rest of the items you send. (See Chapter 20 for more info on where to send your demo.)

To create a selling package you may wish to include a brief CV along with the demo, covering your experience as a DJ, the styles of music you mix, whether you drive, how old you are, where you live, whether you DJ with vinyl, CD or MP3s on a laptop and whether you're comfortable speaking through a microphone. Include a quick paragraph explaining why you've applied to the club for work, and why it would be mutually beneficial for you to be their DJ.

If you think you look good, popping a photograph into the package is a good idea too. If you can show how presentable you are, the club may be more likely to consider you, and if you're good looking, they may not even listen to the mix but just hire you based on how the ladies or guys will fawn over you!

Decide whether you want to send in multiple formats of the mix. Obviously, a tape, a CD and an iPod with just your mix on it covers most bases, but this can get costly when you're sending out loads of demos. If you can, send a CD and a tape. If not, just send a CD. (Sending an iPod counts as bribery . . .)

Include a track list of your mix, and indicate key moments in the demo if you haven't split it into separate tracks.

I can't stress enough the importance of following this piece of advice: clearly write your name, your phone number and your email address on every piece of paper or plastic – every cover, CD, tape, photograph and inlay sleeve – and the covering letter that you send out with your demo.

If you can print a label on your CD, make it a nice design, but make sure your details show up clearly. Add stickers to tapes, type up your CV and keep everything clear and neat.

And remember, the devil's in the detail; get your phone number and email address right!

Chapter 20

Getting Busy With It: Working as a DJ

. . . .

In This Chapter

▶ Marketing yourself the smart way

▶ Dealing with DJ agencies

▶ Schmoozing your way into the DJ booth

. . . .

When you start off as a DJ, the hardest thing you do is master how to beatmatch. Now that you're a great DJ, the next hurdle to overcome is getting yourself that first DJing job.

You've put together a great demo; you love it, your cat loves it, your mum loves it, it's huge on the Internet and even your best friend can't pick any holes in it. So now's the time to put it to good use – selling yourself as a DJ.

This chapter provides you with advice and guidance on how to approach bars and clubs for work and gives you a pep talk about persistence. Though I can't guarantee that you'll get any work, this chapter should fill you up with ideas and enthusiasm for the task at hand.

You have three main ways to get ahead, and get work:

✔ Market yourself

✔ Join an agency

✔ Network

Marketing Yourself

Self-promotion is the key to success. No one else does the work for you. Sure, when you make it as a big DJ, you can farm the hassle onto other people, but when you're starting off you need to promote yourself diligently and single-mindedly. The same unfaltering perseverance and determination that kept you going through any difficulties you had when developing your DJing skills are exactly what you need to effectively sell yourself.

Flooding the world with your demo

You should have a pile of CDs that are properly labelled with your name on them and a tracklist together with an accompanying CV (and photo) packaged up ready to deliver to the clubs and pubs you want to work at. If you've not got that far yet, check out Chapter 19 for advice on making a good demo.

Knowing where to send your demo

Do some research in the areas you're going to spread around your demo so you know all the best places to send it to. Don't just stick to the places you go to on a Friday night; have a look at the area in which you're looking for work and make a list of all the appropriate pubs and clubs that may be interested in your skills.

If you're in a vibrant city with a large variety of bars, no doubt they'll demand the same qualities in a DJ as a club would. But this is great news for you, because by now you're a professional sounding, club-ready DJ.

Include a covering note in each of your demo packages that's specifically tailored to the bar or club you're trying to get work from. Do your research; if it's a club that plays different genres of music each night, mention which night you think you'd be best for. Show them that you know their establishment and tell them what you can add to their success if they hire you, promoting the fact that you're a focused, professional DJ with a goal of working at their club.

If your taste and music collection are suitable for a range of their nights, let the club owners know that you're a versatile DJ who can play anything from dance, to rock or indie, R&B or bhangra. Be as specific as you can; nothing's worse than being on the receiving end of a vague letter that simply says 'I want to be DJ; here's my CD'.

If you don't play a wide variety of musical genres, it may be an idea to only consider establishments that play the music you want to play. This reduces your chances of getting work, but sending in a demo filled with the latest rock tunes to an R&B club is probably a waste of a CD, your time and the club's time.

Offering owners what they want to hear

If you've been to a club your applying to, for research or a night out, you should already have an idea of what rocks the night, and what kills the night.

In your cover letter that accompanies your demo, mention all the things that make the club strong, and give an indication of what you can do to make it even better. Stop short of criticising the club and telling them what they're bad at, though! Use positive language and make the club feel that choosing you is a good thing.

And tell them you'll make them lots of money. Club owners like that . . .

Handing over your demo

By far the best approach when submitting your demo is to hand it in personally. Bars are easy because they're open for most of the day and night, so ask to speak to the manager or bar manager and hand over your demo. Ask the manager if she'd mind listening to your demo, and tell her you'll be back in a few days to see whether she likes it. Be polite and friendly when speaking with the manager, no matter how long the conversation lasts and whether or not she's polite and friendly in return.

If no management is available, don't be tempted to just leave your demo with the bar staff; come back another day when you may have a chance of meeting someone who can help.

Getting hold of someone of responsibility in a club, however, can be a little harder. When the club is open, these people are dealing with all the nuances of running the club and it'll be hard to get them to stop and spend time talking to you. Even if you have to return to the club a few times, strike up conversations with the bar staff or stewards to find the best time to come back with your demo. As long as you're polite and don't take up too much of the staff's time, your demo shouldn't end up in the bin.

If you live in a small town with no bars or clubs that play your kind of music, you need to develop some wanderlust. Look to the city or large town nearest to where you live for clubs that play the music you want to play. Don't try to force your music on people who don't want to listen. But at the same time, don't give up. Don't feel that a brick wall is in front of you and you can't get around. You just need to go to neighbouring towns and cities and dedicate yourself to spending a lot of time there instead.

Geography of a club: How far is too far?

You may want to try for global or national domination, but if you can't get to the club, what's the point? If you live 500 miles from a club to which you're sending your demo, have a think about how you're going to get there and whether it's financially viable to travel that distance. If you're only going to get £100 for a night's work, consider how much you're willing to pay to play by catching a train/plane to get there and then staying overnight in a hotel if you can't get back the same night.

Maybe you've booked a two-week holiday to Ibiza in the hope that you can get a spot in a pub or club out there for one or two nights. Send out a whole load of demos to places you think might let you play a few weeks (or months) before you travel, and keep in contact with them via email. Then, when you leave, take some tunes with you and follow up your submission personally. If you're spending the money to go there anyway, why not give it a bash?

At this early stage in your career, the problem of getting a gig 500 miles away is unlikely to occur, but try to think about every eventuality now so that you're not surprised when it happens.

Following up

When you're sure that the bars and clubs have your demo, follow up with a phone call a few days after you sent it. If someone is kind enough to take your call, ask politely what she thought of it, and hang on every word she says as she criticises your performance. Thank her for her time and honesty, and if she doesn't want to hire you, ask whether you can send in another demo that reflects her comments.

If the club hasn't received your demo, send in another one by the next post (or drop one off personally). Amend your cover letter to include the name of the person you spoke to, and include a line about chatting to her on the phone.

If you suffer from phone phobia, get over it. Don't be scared of phoning clubs and bars. You've nothing to lose in a phone call, and everything to gain.

Handling rejection

You can't afford to have a fear of rejection. You need to put yourself out there, and hope people like you. Different club owners and promoters may respond in different ways: some take time to say no; some just don't get back in touch. The best ones say yes!

If clubs don't respond, keep sending demos until they do get back in touch – remember, persistence is key. If a club owner does respond, but doesn't want to hire you, then hopefully she told you the reason why she didn't like the demo. If she comments on something you didn't realise, and you agree with it, fix the problem and send off a new demo. She may say 'I was actually just being polite before', but perhaps the time you've taken to make another demo reflecting her comments may show her how serious you are about working for her.

The knack is to keep trying until the club owner either takes you on or tells you to stop sending in demos because she doesn't like you! You have to be very strong minded because the rejection letters can come flooding in, and a lot of them won't be polite, but if you have the skills you'll find someone, somewhere, sometime who'll give you a chance and hire you.

Every time you start to wonder if this way truly is an effective form of selling yourself, think of John Digweed. He got his big break when he sent a demo to Renaissance, and he's now one of the most well-known DJs in the world.

Playing for free

Play for free are three little words that can get you very far. Ask yourself this question: would you rather play for free, or not play at all? As you try to get work, getting your foot in the door can be more important than getting paid.

If you think a club or pub might be interested in using you, but the owner sounds a bit unsure, offer to play one or two free nights (most likely as the warm-up DJ) so she can hear how good you are in the club's environment. This 'taster set' is a great way to land your first job; the club will hear firsthand if you're a good DJ in a live situation who can play music suitable for a warm-up or main set. Chapter 21 has tips on choosing music for warm-up or main sets.

Joining an Agency

Joining a DJ agency can be a good way of spreading the word about your skills. What role they play depends largely on how good and how famous a DJ you are.

You have your choice of several different types of agencies:

- ✔ **Artist management:** Catering for famous, established, pro DJs who are in high demand rather than newbies trying to get a break or regular DJs at a small club. These agencies are less about hand-holding and advice, and are more about making sure nights go smoothly, clubs pay money on time and that the high profile DJs on their books are well publicised and booked solidly. As managers, these agencies deal with the publicity, bookings, travel, accommodation and so on, meaning the only thing that the DJ needs to worry about is the music.

  Any booking fees payable to the DJ are paid to the management, who take a percentage cut (usually between 10 and 15 per cent) before passing the rest onto the DJ. The less bookings the DJ has, the less money the agency makes, so making sure that the DJs on their roster are reliable, booked solidly and getting paid is in the agency's best interest.

✔ **Local agencies:** Large towns and cities have DJ agencies that cater for the clubs, bars, function rooms, wedding parties and any reason someone may want a DJ. Although fame won't be as large an issue, a strong track record of playing a lot of gigs is a necessity for these agencies to sign you up.

Local agencies take a similar percentage cut of the booking fee as the artist management agencies. Because the pool of available DJs on their books don't have fame to sell themselves, these agencies work hard for their cut.

✔ **Internet agencies:** Internet DJ agencies help you with promoting yourself, rather than finding work for you. In most instances, they don't actively seek out work on your behalf, but clubs and bars come to them requesting a DJ and the agency passes on your details to the club. Reputable Internet agencies have a large dossier of clubs who request DJs on their roster, and are able to prove a large hit-rate for their DJs working at clubs.

In many cases, you pay a yearly subscription to the Internet agency, rather than handing over a percentage of what you earn. This is an extremely controversial concept, and opinions are very strong on both sides as to whether you should pay upfront to try to find work.

Paying upfront: For and against

Whether you should pay upfront before an agency gets you work is cause for a lot of heated discussion. One side of the argument is that you should only need to pay if the agency gets you work, and the agency should take a cut from the booking. Most bricks and mortar agencies, which have a staff of representatives visiting clubs, use the percentage cut approach. The club promoter pays the agency directly, who then pass the money (minus a cut) onto you.

Because most Internet agencies are actually just middlemen that let you promote yourself to their contacts, they have no way of telling whether you've been hired or paid. Relying on you to declare all the nights you've worked through agency contacts becomes an unworkable proposition; hence the request to pay for their services upfront.

The obvious risk with paying upfront is that you pay the money to the agency but they don't get you any work. Until Internet agencies get a stronger track record, my suggestion is to exhaust every possibility under the sun to get work under your own steam before approaching an Internet agency. If you're still finding it hard to get work, and you're sure it's not your skills that are letting you down, do a *lot* of background research into various Internet agencies and what they offer, and tread very carefully before choosing one and parting with any money.

Researching an agency

Before joining any agency (Internet, or otherwise), take a look at any testimonials that may be on their website, and if you get the chance, get in touch with the DJs and clubs to check that the agency is genuine. Some unscrupulous people out there do make up information to try to seem more professional, so do as much research as you can and post some questions on DJ *forums* (communities where DJs go to chat about their work – Chapter 22 has a list of some forums).

Alarm bells should ring if the agency's website has no recent testimonials from DJs, if DJs mentioned don't respond to your emails, if the agency forces you into a contract longer than a year or if you discover any hidden charges.

Contact the people in charge of running the agency. Even though they may sound fierce in their literature when they mention trying to contact them, they have to show you due care and attention. You need to be sure that you'll get a service for the money that you're looking to invest in their help. If they aren't polite, helpful and professional at the beginning of your relationship, run like the wind!

If the agency you're considering takes a cut of your booking fee, remember that the amount may vary between agencies. If the cut is larger than 10–15 per cent, find out whether you get better services for that extra money. If you don't, think hard about whether you want to hand over money for nothing.

Finally, when you're happy to sign on the dotted line with an agency, show the contract to a lawyer first, just in case you missed something.

Meeting the criteria to join

Pro-agencies for the famous DJ tend to headhunt acts. When someone gains a reputation for drawing a crowd, and has become a well-known DJ, these agencies swoop in and offer to add the DJ to their roster.

But local DJ agencies have a reputation to uphold, and as such, they do have some strict criteria that you must meet before they sign you up. Many agencies won't add you to their DJ roster based purely on a demo CD. They can't take the risk that the DJ may have taken months to perfect that one mix, or that the DJ used a computer program to touch up a sloppy performance. But more importantly, the difference between playing in the bedroom without any pressure and playing in a club in front of a thousand clubbers in a room with a bad sound system is huge. Nerves and comfort aren't an issue in the bedroom, but the first time you play live in a club you'll be nervous and in alien surroundings as a DJ. If you make a mistake because you're wet behind the ears, it won't reflect well on you or the agency promoting you.

Agencies may have a list of restrictions, like age limits and where you live, but the one constant you find is that you need to have had experience before these agencies will take you onto their books. If you've gained experience under your own steam, made your own contacts and developed them to gain you work as a DJ, then you show the talent needed to secure work and the determination and mindset needed to be a professional in the DJing business.

Keeping agencies in your musical loop

The music you play as a DJ may change the kind of agencies that you approach. Some agencies only work with wedding/party DJs, and others only represent club DJs and won't accept a wedding DJ onto their books.

When you approach an agency that represents a vast range of DJ styles, let them know at the outset what kind of music you play best. Even if you have a wide range from R&B to hard house, you need to let the agency know whether you have the music (or desire) to spend an evening playing Frank Sinatra and Neil Diamond tracks at a retirement party.

If you do have the patience to be a workhorse DJ who plays anything just to get ahead, let the agency know that you'll play anything, anywhere; and in time, hope that you've earned their trust so they start putting you in clubs where you can play the music you really want to play. The downside to the workhorse approach is the amount of bowling alleys in which you may have to play Britney Spears' tunes.

Cutting your losses

It's hard work trying to get on an agency's roster. Be persistent, but also be aware of when you're making the wrong move. I spent a long time trying to get involved with an agency in my area. When I finally tracked down the guy who ran it, we just didn't click, and when he found out that I already had work and I wasn't willing to drop it to join his agency, it ended as a very short phone call.

Depending on the contacts you build up through networking (see the next section), and the kind of places and size of clubs in which you want to play, you may never need the services of an agency. I've never been on an agency roster. That's not because I don't want to (or from a lack of trying); it's simply because the contacts I've made through networking have been helpful in getting me work.

Networking Your Way to Success

Get used to the phrase 'It's not what you know, it's who you know'. Everyone you talk to about your quest to find work eventually says this.

Networking can range from a simple meet and greet with a club or bar owner when you hand over your demo, to meeting people who introduce you to more people, and eventually getting work from those connections.

Selling yourself

Attitude and presentation can go a long way in this industry. If you can convince a club or bar owner that you'd actually be good to have around, either because you seem like a reliable kind of person or because you're well dressed and attractive enough to be eye candy for the public, then you've already given yourself a step up the ladder. Some genres of music promote and thrive on the aloof 'too cool for you' style of DJ, but it's not something I'd recommend myself.

Making friends

Going straight to a club owner and asking for work is a ballsy move. If the owner says no, you may have blown your chances of working for the club. However, if you befriend the bar staff and the DJ, who may then recommend you for a small DJing spot, you might get a lot more luck.

How you develop your relationship with people is down to your personality. If you think you're the type who can strike up a friendship with a DJ in a pub, and use that friendship to get somewhere, by all means go for it. Just realise that the DJ will peg you for a DJ wannabe from the moment you even glance around his or her DJ booth. Don't pretend that's not why you're there, but unless you think it's worthwhile pushing it, play it cool and hold off the hard sell for a while.

Getting to know bar staff, particularly senior bar staff, can be another good avenue to get into the club, even as a warm-up DJ. Again, you need to take some time, become a regular, get to know the staff and the club well, and when you're happy that you can start to push your luck, hand over a demo and see what becomes of it.

Beginning my journey

My journey began when I was a barman in a pub in Glasgow called Café Cini. Before the DJs arrived, a tape would play at low level through the sound system. After a couple of months of working behind the bar, I slipped one of my tapes into the machine. Luckily Pauline, the manageress, liked the tape and asked who'd made the switch. When she found out it was me, she offered me a one-hour warm up before the DJ arrived (paid in Irn Bru). This spot led to an hour during the main part of the night (more Irn Bru) and then became a night of my own for money (which I spent on Irn Bru), and expanded on from there (as did my waistline due to all that Irn Bru!).

One of the other DJs who'd just opened up his own club offered me a warm-up spot, giving me my first piece of club experience. From there, I met another DJ who was giving up his Friday night residency at a club and suggested, with his recommendation, that I should get in touch with the owners to take over.

So from a basic bar job, my DJ career began. It can be that easy for you too.

Going undercover

Getting a foot in the door when you're already inside is easy! Insider knowledge is the best advantage you can have. A bar job in a club or pub you want to work in is an excellent way of selling yourself surreptitiously. You can subtly spread word of your skills and repeatedly let people hear your demo until they realise that they like you and want to put you in the booth. By the time they grasp your true agenda, it's too late: they're already happy to have hired you as the DJ!

Marketing Yourself on the Internet

Creating the best website in the world won't get you any work on its own, but a website that backs you up as a professional DJ goes a long way to impressing those who choose to check it out.

As well as hosting your latest mix and a DJ CV for future employers, your site can also promote the nights you work to other people. If you establish a good following that you can keep up to date through your website, and almost guarantee a club that a certain number of people will turn up, your case for working at the club is sweetened by the guaranteed door money they'll receive.

With the creation of social networking sites like Twitter and Facebook, you don't even need to have your own website any more, and can instantly get in touch with all your 'friends' to let them know where and when you're playing next.

Websites like MySpace and Bebo let you create a more tailored page for your visitors to see, and you don't need any web-design knowledge. WYSIWYG (*what you see is what you get*) layout editors let you create vibrant, well-laid-out profiles that sell you just as well as a personal website.

The only downside to using these kinds of sites compared to your own website is simply the professionalism of the web URL. I think that as a web URL www.recess.co.uk looks more professional than www.myspace.com/dj_recess.

For a more dedicated DJ approach to the websites your profile is viewed on, check out sites like www.djpassion.co.uk, www.djpromoter.com and www.mydjspace.net.

Some DJ profile sites link to venues that use the DJs who submit profiles. Others on the Internet are enhanced forums and Internet radio stations. But as long as they're free, sign up and promote yourself as much as you can through all possible avenues.

Internet forums are a great way to promote yourself and find out what's going on in the music world. Chapter 22 has a list of the best forums on the Internet. And the discussion forum for this book is located at www.djrecess.co.uk/php.

Chapter 21

Facing the Music: Playing Live

· ·

· ·

*Y*ou're ready. You've practised for months, your friends know how good you are, you've sent your demo to bars and clubs to let them know how good you are, and now's your chance to show hundreds of people on the dance floor just how good you are. Stepping out of the bedroom and into a club's DJ booth is a big leap, so you have a few things to consider.

I've always said that this leap is like driving a car. You spend ages with a driving instructor who teaches you how to pass your test, and then only when you're on your own in the real world, making decisions for yourself, do you really learn how to drive. As a new DJ you spend a year or more in your bedroom perfecting your technique and building knowledge about your music, and only when you get out into the real world and find work do you develop the skills to become a true DJ.

The difference between DJing in the bedroom and in a club is crowd control, knowing what people want to hear and being able to adapt to how they're reacting to the music you're playing. Knowing when to move up from one genre to another or when to increase the energy of the mix is something that comes with experience and practice, but the most important skill you develop is the ability to lose yourself and love what you're doing while simultaneously reading the crowd's reaction to the music you're playing.

Investigating the Venue

Nothing's scarier than the unknown. Investigate the club or hall you're booked to play well in advance. If you're putting on your own night in a club, you only have to worry about getting people to turn up. If you've been asked to play a party or wedding in the local town hall, you need to find out what you're expected to play and what equipment you need to take, and start memorising the bride and groom's names!

Scoping out a club

No matter whether this is your first ever set in a club, or if you're an established DJ, do your homework. Set up a meeting with the club owner, manager or promoter to discuss a few things. If you can't set up a meeting, try to go to the club on a similar night to the one you've been booked for (the same night a week before is perfect), listen to the music the DJ's playing and watch the crowd's reaction (see 'Reading a crowd', later in the chapter).

When you're doing some investigation at the club, try to strike up a conversation with the bar staff and the toilet attendants (if the club has them). Because they hear everything that's said and everything that's played through a night, staff can sometimes be a better font of knowledge than the club promoter for the music that works best, the kind of people who go there and the general mood and patterns of the people who frequent the club.

When you're the warm-up DJ

If you've been asked to do the warm-up set before the main DJ comes on, ask the promoter/manager if he has any limitations to what kind of music you can play. Whether it's a house/trance club or a rock/indie club, the promoter may want you to play lighter, well-known, musical tunes to help warm up the crowd, so the main DJ can take the mix from soft tunes to harder ones when he takes over the main set of the night.

The warm-up set is extremely important to the club, and your career. If you treat this gig as a throwaway hour and a half where what you mix doesn't matter, the customers at the club won't get warmed up, and the club won't ask you to return. Although the music may be softer than you normally play at home, suppress your musical snobbery and realise that playing whatever the club asks you to play is really important, so you can keep your foot in the door and hope that they'll eventually let you play the main set where you can show them what you're capable of.

When you're playing the main set

As the main set DJ you have fewer constraints, but you still need to find out whether the club has a music policy. They may have a limit as to how fast a tempo you can play and limit you to playing certain genres (perhaps they'd rather you didn't play hardcore stuff in trance clubs, or death metal in rock clubs).

You may think that you're there to play the latest, greatest underground tunes, but maybe the guy you've been hired to replace just played hard, loud music all the time and the club's looking for a change. So if you've been brought into a club that used to play hard dance music and they're now trying to move away from that, you may find that they'll ask you to throw in some lighter, commercial, popular, maybe even older tunes in the main part of the set.

Every set may be your big break. So swallow your pride and realise that for every five commercial tunes you play, you may be able to play one or two that people haven't heard yet but that you know will be massive. But don't push your luck! Research the music scene, read magazines, listen to other DJ mixes and listen to suitable radio shows, and you'll develop an ear to pick tunes that eventually become popular. You won't have to gamble with what you play; you'll know that you're playing the next big thing.

Provided this doesn't annoy the management, when you pick the right tunes that launch from underground to mainstream, the club owner and promoter will recognise that you know your stuff and will hopefully start to respect your musical knowledge and give you a little more musical wriggle room.

When you're replacing a DJ

If you're replacing a DJ, finding out whether and why the club asked him to leave is important, because you don't want to end up making the same kind of mistakes as the last guy. Ask the promoter what led to the DJ's dismissal and if he was doing something wrong.

I was lucky enough to be invited to watch a DJ that I was replacing play the week before he finished up, so I could hear for myself what was going wrong. I had to tell the promoter what I thought he was doing wrong, though, and how I'd do it better as a test of my DJ skills, but fortunately, I passed his test!

You may find that the DJ has been doing everything perfectly, but that a personality clash has led to his dismissal or resignation, in which case put on a smile and remember what the DJ was doing that worked.

A little reconnaissance

If you've managed to secure a meeting with the manager when the club is closed, try to get a sneaky peak inside the DJ booth and take a note of its equipment and where everything is located. The main things to check are:

✔ Which mixer, turntables and CD decks they use

✔ Whether a booth monitor is provided

✔ Where you put your records/CDs

✔ Where the amplifiers are

✔ Whether they have a digital DJ installation

If the club doesn't supply a monitor, you can ask about getting one, but unless you're a famous DJ that'll make the club loads of money, they probably won't agree to your request. If you don't have a monitor, you need to work out the best way to get around the audio delay. (See Chapter 14 for different headphone monitoring options that'll help you.)

If you're unsure of how to use any of the controls in the club's DJ booth, do some research before you turn up on the night for your set. If the mixer has functions that you'd like to use, but don't know how, finding out how is very important. The first time I used a DJM-500 mixer I had no idea how to work the effects on it, and was banging the yellow button with no result. I didn't find out how to use the mixer properly until I got home and read about it. Most house/trance clubs still cater for vinyl DJs and tend to use the industry standard Technics 1210s, but if they're innovative and use turntables with extra features like the Vestax, Gemini and Numark range, a quick read over an online manual gives you all the knowledge you need to properly use them. If you're an indie/rock DJ who uses vinyl you might not be as lucky, because not as many of these clubs continue to provide for vinyl DJs. This makes it especially important to check out the DJ booth before you play.

If you use bottom-of-the-range twin CD decks at home, and you're faced with top-of-the-range single CD decks at the club, check online or ask someone who has those decks, to make sure that you're happy using them on the night.

As much as all DJs would love to use their own turntables, mixers and CD decks, not many clubs let you take your own kit. If you're lucky, in the right club, with a friendly manager, you may be able to take along your own mixer if you're working the entire night, but CD decks and turntables are normally off-limits to change.

Blowing speakers by proxy

I know from experience that you need to be very careful when swapping over equipment. I used to take my own mixer to a club because theirs was quite basic. Unfortunately, the cables weren't marked well, and when I plugged them back into their mixer at the end of the night I didn't do it right. The next night the unknowing DJ turned on all the amps and almost blew out most of the speakers due to the electrical *pop* my incorrect connections created.

Digital DJs enter a new realm of caution in the DJ booth. Not only do you need to make sure you can fit in your computer (which is a lot easier if you use a laptop style PC or Mac) but you also need to wrestle with how to connect to the club's sound system.

Chapter 9 has more information about different ways to connect a digital DJ setup to a DJ booth, but they're split into two different camps:

 ✔ All mixing is performed in software on the laptop (sometimes with an external controller), with the mix output sent to an input on the mixer in the DJ booth, and played through the club's amplifiers and speakers.

 ✔ Outputs of the turntables and/or CD decks in the DJ booth are redirected to an *audio in/out interface* (a specially designed external soundcard) to control music playing in software on a computer. This music is then sent back to individual channels on the DJ mixer to be mixed like a normal CD/record and played through the club's sound system.

The first option is easier. It usually means connecting an audio output of the computer to a spare input on the mixer using a pair of phono (also known as RCA) cables and setting the controls on the mixer for that channel so the music plays out loud and clear (normally the channel-fader is between 75 per cent and maximum, and the EQ's at centre position, but this varies depending on the club's sound system setup).

The second option can be a lot more difficult. If a club isn't prepared for a digital DJ, it can mean unplugging CD decks and turntables from the mixer in order to reconnect them to the audio in/out interface. If you're DJing for the entire night you can do this when you arrive at the club and then disconnect at the end of the night, but if the club's brought you in to do just two hours in the middle of an eight-hour night, it'll be a *lot* harder to get in and out of the back of the mixer while someone's still using it!

As more DJs go digital, clubs buy audio in/out interfaces to permanently install into their DJ booth, taking care of all the connections themselves so all the DJ has to do is plug the computer into this hardware box with a USB cable. Check, however, that the software that a club's audio interface works with is the one you use. If a club has a Serato Scratch audio interface installed and you use Traktor then you still have some rewiring to do, because Traktor software and control records/CDs don't work with Serato Scratch hardware.

Money matters

The last thing to discuss with management before you come to play your set is money. Different clubs, nights and locations change how much you can charge. When you get your first gigs, you're DJing for the love of music and the opportunity, not the financial gain, but it doesn't hurt to get something in writing that states how much you'll get, and when the club's going to pay you!

Gearing up to party

Houses and town halls aren't designed to be makeshift clubs, so you need to do a little more investigation to make sure that you're well prepared for playing at these venues.

If you decide to have a party in your house so that you can impress your friends with your skills, the only things you have to worry about are the neighbours, keeping enough ice in the fridge and where to set up. But if you hire a hall to play at, you need to think about suitable amplification (refer to Chapter 12), lights and something to set up on that's more substantial than the kitchen table. If you've invited 200 people along, think about security; you may need a few big fellas there, just in case things get out of hand.

Whether the party you're running is at your house or in a hired hall, music policy isn't an issue because you decide what to play. You do need to react to how people at the party respond to what you're playing, though. Don't be bullheaded: don't persevere with music people aren't enjoying just because you want to play it.

If you're booked to play at someone else's party – be it a birthday party, leaving night or wedding – the client can give you an indication of what he expects you to play beforehand. If it's someone who knows that you're a DJ, but doesn't know that you specialise in drum and bass, you may want to let him know, so he doesn't expect Britney Spears and Beyoncé but actually get old Roni Size and Goldie tracks instead.

Unless you're told otherwise, don't expect the client to provide any equipment. You'll be lucky if you find a table for your equipment setup. So arranging suitable amplification and lighting is down to you, and you'll need to use your own DJ setup. Visit the venue you've been booked to play at well in advance. Someone who works there should be able to tell you the most popular place to set up your makeshift DJ booth, and when you see the hall you can work out how much amplification you need.

Preparing to Perform

Baden Powell wasn't wrong about the value of preparation. When your set looms only hours away, try to think of everything before you play so you're not faced with any big surprises.

Selecting the set

From your music policy discussions with the club owner or organiser of the party, you should know what music you're able to play during your set. With this in mind, you can flick through your collection or library and pick out the tunes you're most likely to play that night.

Now go back into your collection and pick out the same amount again. There's nothing wrong with taking loads of music with you. If you have the space, use it. Longing for a tune that you haven't put in your selection is a bad thing, but reaching for that tune – the one that you'd otherwise have left at home – and using it to win over a tough crowd can only be a good thing.

Predetermined set lists

Trying to work out the entire set from start to finish before you get to a club isn't a good idea. Even if the club owner has given you a music policy to stay within, you still need to tailor the music for the people on the dance floor.

If you decide before your set to play light house music for the first two hours but the club is packed after an hour, demanding more energetic music, you have the choice of playing the other hour of house music (which may bore the people out of the club) or skipping directly to the music that they want to hear – only to worry about the extra hour of music you have to fill at the end of the night.

You might want to put a lot of thought into your opening tunes if you're taking over from another DJ, though. Don't get tunnel vision and think of only one or two openers. Have enough tunes with you to cover many eventualities; one tune if it's a bit low key, another if the dance floor is going wild and another if it's in-between, in a bizarre transitional phase.

Checkpoint tunes

If you don't like the idea of a completely off-the-cuff set but don't want to create a start-to-finish set list, use key tunes for your set, like checkpoints that you pass as you increase the energy and the tempo of the night. If the checkpoints are tunes that people love to hear, you can use them as markers to help you map out your set from start to finish.

Provided you practise enough with your collection, you should be able to choose from a lot of tunes that you can mix in and out of the checkpoint tunes, all of which in turn mix into another large number of good tunes. Keep your eye on the dance floor, and try to estimate when you think you're going to change the pace or energy again, and work towards putting in the next key tune to move the mix to another level.

But remember, on every journey you sometimes need to take a detour. Even with a skeleton framework of tunes to link your mix, you still need to be flexible and react to the crowd (see the section 'Reading the crowd', later in this chapter).

Organising your box

You don't have to organise your tunes alphabetically or by genre if you don't want to, but by having an order to the chaos of your record box or CD wallet, you make it much easier to find that elusive track when you need it most. You have a couple of organisational options:

- ✔ **By genre:** If you're doing a set that requires you to play multiple genres, or multiple subgenres of music, grouping each genre together in the record box or CD wallet makes good sense. Especially because most of these genres relate to a specific point in the night (for instance R&B at the beginning, then vocal house, then commercial dance, then trance and then progressive house), grouping these genres together makes navigating your way through the set more manageable.

- ✔ **Multiple boxes/bags:** If you have a few boxes and bags that you take with you, have one for each genre or power level in the night, splitting your boxes so that all the beginning-of-the-night tunes are in one box, and all the main-set tunes are in another box. This way, you won't have to wade through two boxes crammed with 120 records (or CD wallets with thousands of tunes) to find a specific track.

Laziness has its value . . . at last!

I'm quite lazy as a DJ when it comes to arranging tunes. I pick them out from anywhere, but always replace them at the front of the box. But this method means that the tunes I play most often are always at the front of the box. Before I set off for a night, though, when I look through the tunes that I think I might play I put the ones

I'm 90 per cent sure to include at the front of the box, the ones I'll play only if I think the crowd's the type to respond are next and then ones I'll only play in an emergency, or if the night's going *so* well that I can play anything, go right at the back.

DJ software (or even your iPod if you use that for DJing) takes a lot of effort out of organising your tunes. Not only do most software titles include a handy search box, so you can instantly call up a tune you want to play, but you can quickly and easily sort the library of tunes by artist, genre, BPM (beats per minute) or any other definition you may have given them.

I like giving power ratings to each of the tunes in my digital library. So, for example, I can find progressive house tunes that I think will hit the dance floor at full-power, or try to find a good trance tune that has a lesser effect on the dance floor for use as a 'breather' in the set.

Knowing What to Expect at the Club

Getting to a club early lets you plan your evening properly and gives you time to get used to the equipment, chat to the bar staff and promoter about what kind of night they think it's going to be and steady any nerves that may have snuck up on you.

Dealing with nerves

Unless you're a rock, you'll feel nervous on the first night you play. If you're lucky, your nerves will subside with time, to be replaced by magical, nervous excitement. I believe that the moment you stop getting that excited feeling in your stomach before playing a set, you should take stock and ask yourself whether you still love what you're doing or are just going through the motions.

You may be tempted, but try not to turn to alcohol as a way to get over your nerves, even if it's free. You want to be as clear-headed as possible when you're playing. Dutch courage isn't courage, it's a mask. Your nervousness reduces after a few good mixes anyway, but you should leave yourself aware of this feeling and use it as a reminder that what you're doing is important, and your fear of messing up is born of your desire to be a great DJ.

Getting used to your tools

Take the opportunity of turning up at the club early and throwing on a couple of tunes to get used to the equipment. You should already have investigated the club's setup (see the earlier section 'Scoping out a club'), but if you've

338 **Part IV: Getting Noticed and Playing Live** _____

only read how to use something in the booth you've not encountered before in a manual, this time is great for working through anything you're unsure of.

Setting the levels and EQ

As well as getting used to the equipment, you can figure out how the sound comes across in the club and hopefully change it to your liking. There's a long night ahead of you. If you don't like the sound, it'll be even longer!

Put on a tune you know really well, with all the EQs set to 12 o'clock (this is the *flat* position on your mixer, where you haven't added or cut any frequency by any amount). Turn the music up loud and stand at various parts of the dance floor. Don't only stand in front of the massive bass speakers, where you'll be shaken to pieces by the vibrations; move around, from the outskirts of the dance floor to the centre and in front of the booth.

During your journey around the dance floor, listen to the sound in each position. If the different areas of the club are covered by multiple amps and EQs, ask whether you can change them to suit the sound that you prefer. If only one amp and EQ is available for the entire dance floor, stand in the middle and set the best sound for that position.

Unfortunately, it's likely the club won't let you adjust the sound system, so you'll need to use the EQs on the mixer instead. This isn't the best option, but is still better than the music sounding shrill, with no bass in it. The tune that you use to check the sound should be a benchmark. Use this tune to set the EQs, and then match everything that follows to this benchmark.

Don't forget that people suck up sound vibrations. Clothes, skin and big gangly bones all absorb sound frequencies as the club gets busier and busier. This fact means you have to set the mixer to play louder as the club gets busier and you'll also find a lot of the bass frequencies disappear into the crowd's greedy bellies.

Every once in a while (probably when you need a pee), jump onto the dance floor and have a quick listen to how the music sounds. If you can hear too much conversation rather than music, of if your ears start shimmering with the amount of mid range, cross your legs and adjust the EQs or output level so the music sounds better – then go to the bathroom during the next track.

Setting the monitor

If you have a monitor in the DJ booth, take time to adjust it to create a virtual stereo image between the music in your headphones and the music playing from the monitor. (If you have no idea what I'm on about, see Chapter 14.)

Pop in an ear plug (honestly, I strongly recommend that you use an ear plug in your *live* ear – refer to Chapter 11) and set the level so that you can hear everything clearly but the music isn't so loud that you're eardrums are quivering. I've heard people talk about *tiring* the ear – which, to me, means if you play music too loud, for too long, you find that concentrating on the music blaring out at you is hard and you'll run the risk of ending up with permanent hearing damage.

If the club doesn't have a monitor, I hope you found that out when you went for a visit to the club and have either spent time learning how to mix with a split cue function (if the club's mixer has it; see Chapter 14) or you've been practising mixing with both tunes playing in both ears of the headphones.

Working in a loud environment

This job may be the first time that you play in a volume level louder than your home stereo, so use the opportunity of turning up early to get used to all the differences that a club's volume may throw at you.

Nothing prepares you for the feeling of the beat thumping through your body when DJing. When you're in a club as a customer on the dance floor, it's a cool feeling, but as a DJ if the beat is slightly delayed to what you're hearing through the monitor or the headphones, you can find the timing a little disconcerting at first.

It's not all bad live, though. A club's sound system can be very forgiving for small beatmatching errors. The heavy sub bass can be so thick sounding that a slight *l'Boom* or *B'loom* (see Chapter 14 if you've no idea what I mean) is easily hidden. With good headphones you can hear this small timing error before anyone can hear it on the dance floor.

The music sounds different too. The sound system in a club doesn't have the full fidelity of your headphones, with the sub-bass sometimes overpowering the bass and mid-range melodies, so you find that some mixes that don't work quite as well on CD work fine played live with the right EQ controls or by minimising any key or melody mismatches – see Chapter 16 for some examples.

Playing Your Music

You've investigated, discovered and prepared until you're blue in the face. You've been a polite DJ and turned up as early as possible (even if it is just to give you the chance to sit in the bathroom). Your night's about to begin.

Reading a crowd

If this night is your first time playing to a crowd of people you don't know, the main difference you notice is how much thought you need to put into your tunes in order to keep people on the dance floor.

In time, you'll become a body language expert, looking at the reactions of the people on the floor as they throw their hands in the air and dance like there's no tomorrow, or throw their hands up in the air in disgust . . .

First, think about how *you* react when you're at a club. When you're enjoying yourself, what do you do? If you're the type who grins from ear to ear and throws your hands in the air to dance music, or headbangs to rock music, and you're playing the kind of music that makes you want to do that, look for this kind of response from the people on the dance floor. When you're bored and listless, how do you react? Look into people's eyes. If they're staring into the distance or at the floor, or if they're dancing with no real thought or energy, they've gone to a happy place in their heads, waiting for something to change. It's up to you to make that change.

Don't base your readings on just the people in front of you. Look through the crowd. If you get a chance to go for a wander, walk around and look at how people are responding to the music. A glum face isn't a good thing to see. Fifteen glum faces are a kick up the backside that should make you play something better.

Just ask . . . if you dare

The relationship you've developed with the toilet attendant and bar staff can really help you out. They're a great source of information on how well you're doing, and how the night is going.

In one club that I worked at, the toilet attendant knew everything that was going on. If the people who came in to use the facilities were having a good night, he'd be quick to feed that info back to me, and if he heard tales that something wasn't quite right with the music, I'd know before it was too late. Never before or since has a visit to the bathroom been so enlightening.

If you want, you can just ask people how they're enjoying their night, either personally or collectively, over the microphone. If you get a collective groan, or even worse, silence, change the music quickly. If you get cheers, whoops and hands in the air, keep it going; you're doing well.

Progress the set

If DJs played the same style of music all night, things would get very dull. Dance DJs may start off with house music and end up playing pacey, chunky trance by the end of the night; rock DJs may start off with a mixture of older tunes and lighter rock to break people into the night and end up playing harder, newer music from heavier sounding groups.

DJing isn't a race. You won't win anything for playing all the newest, best and biggest tunes in the first 30 minutes; you'll lose everyone on the floor. You'll wear them out, they'll become bored with the same sound and because you won't have any big tunes left the people on the floor will get bored with the rest of the set. If you resort to repeating tunes, they've already heard them so they aren't as excited. Your light shone brightly, but not for long enough.

Use the checkpoint tunes (see the earlier section 'Checkpoint tunes') as a way to pepper the set with good tunes and to move the set on in energy and tempo. But don't just arbitrarily decide to change things. Always keep an eye on how the people on the dance floor are reacting to what you're playing. If the dance floor isn't busy enough, or if the alcohol level hasn't kicked in yet, playing slightly heavier music may empty the dance floor. Or maybe it's getting busy and you've played the same style for a while; if you don't change the pace soon, your set could start to sound dull and monotonous and people will start to haemorrhage off the dance floor.

Test the waters. If you can't tell what people want by the reaction on the dance floor, take things a little harder or faster, bit by bit, to see what the response is. Or maybe lessen the pace from time to time or throw in an older track to see what kind of stuff people are responding to, and then stick with that level until your crowd reading skills reveal that the time has come to move up (or down) a gear.

Handling requests

I deal with requests with the following considerations:

- ✔ Was I going to play the tune they've asked for anyway? If so, I'm happy to say yes when someone asks, and say when it'll be on.

- ✔ How polite was the person about the request? Manners go a long way. I'm not saying I'd play *anything* if someone was polite enough, but bad manners make me less likely to play something. *Please* and *thank you* don't take much time or effort to say, and they can get you so far in this world.

No matter what you consider when someone asks for a tune (this includes how good looking the person is), remember that he's paid money to get into the club and is expecting to be entertained, so at least let him down gently.

If you don't want to play the tune someone's asked for, either because you don't have it or it's not the right time to play that tune, say the following, depending on how hopeful you want to leave the person:

> ✔ 'I've left it at home . . . sorry.'
>
> ✔ 'I'll take a look, but I *think* I've left it at home . . . sorry.'

Requests as a warm-up DJ

The warm-up set can be difficult for requests. The owner/promoter's told you to play lighter tunes that everyone knows, not too hard and not the latest, biggest tracks. Halfway through the set a couple of people ask you to play the big tunes of the moment, or as someone once 'asked' me, 'Play some heavy stuff I can dance to – this stuff sucks.'

Herein lies a couple of problems. The place isn't near full and the promoter has strongly said no to playing those tunes, but this is the customer and he has paid to be entertained. This situation is why I stress the importance of talking to the owner/promoter when you get offered the job, to iron out these possible problems (see the earlier section 'When you're the warm-up DJ'). Maybe this is exactly why the club has a music policy; to weed out the kind of people who just want to dance or mosh at full speed on an empty dance floor.

Requests as the main DJ

Playing the main set in a club removes a lot of restrictions to what you can play. Requests become problems when someone asks for a tune that you don't like or don't have, or that isn't appropriate for that point in the night.

This situation can arise if someone doesn't realise the kind of club they've gone to. The amount of times I've been asked to play an R&B track in a trance club amazes me, but usually this request is prefaced by, 'I was dragged here by my friends and don't like this music, so . . . '

Friendly lighting jocks and bouncers can sometimes step in and take the role of a mediator in passing on requests. This option saves you from entering into a three-minute argument with someone over a tune that you're not willing to play and then end up missing the next mix.

Requests as a party DJ

As a club DJ you have some licence to say no to people when they ask for tunes – you got the job because you should have a superior knowledge about the music. But as a party DJ you have to appear at the mercy of the people you're playing for, whether you follow through with their requests or not.

However, a few occasions can crop up when you'd say no to a request, if you don't have that particular song or if it wouldn't go down well at all.

If you're working at a wedding, and the dance floor has all the grandparents on it, dropping the latest gangsta rap or nu metal tune may be a bit of a mistake. Or if you're a rock DJ and everyone's going nuts for the 1980s Bon Jovi/Van Halen set you're currently playing, agreeing to play one request for White Zombie may not prove to be the best decision you make all night.

Don't beat yourself up

You're in control of everybody's night as the DJ, and with that comes quite a lot of pressure. This pressure can make you flustered, and can lead to panic if things start to go wrong. In the bedroom if you make a mistake it doesn't matter, because you can start the mix again and no one will know any different. In a club if you make a mistake it means a lot more.

If your last mix was a disaster, be hard on yourself by all means because you're a perfectionist and should have done better, but don't let one mistake spoil the rest of your set. Not everyone hears errors, no matter how bad they are. A lot of people aren't as tuned in to the music as you are, or they're having too good a time to care. Watch for reactions: if the people on the floor start chanting 'Sack the DJ', you know that you've made a boo-boo, but if they're still smiling and dancing, don't beat yourself up over something that didn't matter in the end.

Taking over from someone else

The warm-up DJs have a hard life; they turn up, play for an hour and a half to get the crowd in the mood and then the next DJs push them out of the way and finish the job they started. When you're the person doing the pushing, pause and pay attention to what was happening before you entered the DJ booth.

Aim to get into the club at least 15 minutes before you start so that you can listen to the end of the warm-up DJs set. This time gives you a chance to gauge how the crowd is responding to the music, and also avoids you repeating a tune that's only just played. Ask the warm-up DJ questions about the crowd's reaction to the music already played and how he feels the night is going to continue based on his experience so far.

Checking the setup

Checking the setup is extremely important. Look at what the DJ is using. If he's only using CDs and you're about to use the turntables, quickly check the turntables and the settings on the mixer to make sure that the previous DJ hasn't disconnected, broken or switched off something that will end up causing you problems.

Look at how the DJ is mixing too. If he's only using the channel-faders, look at the cross-fader. If the mixer has assignable switches, the DJ may have switched off the cross-fader so it has no control over the mix.

A cacophony of sound

The very first time I played live, the warm-up guy before me had turned off the cross-fader and used the channel-faders on their own. The problem was, I forgot to turn the cross-fader back on, and as I needed to mix with the head-phones on both ears because the DJ booth didn't have a monitor, it ended in disaster. I put on the headphones, set the input level for both channels, pressed the cue switches so both tunes played in my headphones and then raised the channel-fader to full and slowly moved the cross-fader from left to right.

Because the headphones were over both ears, I didn't hear that when I raised the channel-fader

the new tune crashed in at full volume over the other tune, and when I moved the cross-fader from left to right nothing happened; both tunes continued to play over each other at full volume.

I took my headphones off and only after a brief moment of panic at the terrible noise coming from the speakers was it obvious what had happened. I slammed the channel-fader on the out-going tune to zero and hung my head in shame. But the lesson here is that no one else noticed! I couldn't believe it.

Gauging the mood

Use your body language skills to judge what mood the crowd is in before deciding how to start your set. If the club is busy, with pent-up energy, and the warm-up DJ has been getting loads of requests for more upbeat tunes, use that to your advantage by instantly changing up from light, warm-up music to something a lot newer, faster and harder. That change gives an instant boost to the crowd. Bear in mind, though, not to blow your entire set trying to take the crowd even higher, only to run out of tunes to play.

If the people are still tentatively moving onto the dance floor, be a bit more gradual about the change in music. Do start to move on from what the previous DJ played, to add a feeling of impending energy and excitement, but do it gradually to keep the people on the dance floor.

Playing with momentum

If you're taking over from someone who's already playing fast, powerful tunes, you have a choice: you can mix out of the DJ's last tune in a smooth, seamless, unnoticeable mix, announce your arrival with a change in tempo/genre/key/volume or try something like a dead stop, spinback or power off if you really want to let people know that you're taking over. (Check out Chapters 16 and 17 for more on these techniques.)

DJ DANGER

Playing too much, too soon

Although not always a mistake, slamming in a really heavy tune when only 20 people are on the dance floor is a dangerous gamble. I heard a DJ make a terrible mistake when the warm-up was still playing light vocal house as the dance floor was only just beginning to fill up. Instead of gently coaxing more people onto the floor with a steady increase in pace and energy, the new DJ tried an instant, dramatic change using an older, classic tune: 'Born Slippy' by Underworld. It's a great tune at the right time, but straight on the back of light, musical house music, the change was way too much, and the 20 people who *had* made it to the dance floor quickly left, leaving an empty, desolate dance floor for the DJ to panic about.

My preference is to use a basic, simple sounding tune. Something that's just drums and a powerful, offbeat bass melody coming out of a quite frantic tune is a good way to change the power without changing the tempo (described in Chapter 16 as an offbeat only *ta-te* into a *ta fe te te*). I can then build the set back up to a fuller feel in my own time, rather than carrying on with the same sound as the other DJ, which the crowd will soon tire of.

TIP

You can also be a bit cheeky, and gradually for the last couple of minutes of the warm-up DJ's last track lower the volume it's playing out a little. Then when you play your powerful starter tune at the same volume the warm up *was* playing at, it'll actually sound like you've really cranked up the sound-system at the start of your set.

Changing the music

One of the most interesting things I've ever had to do was take over from a heavy metal DJ. Changing from Iron Maiden to David Morales isn't a natural thing to do! I used a simple fade out with an instant start of the next tune, which isn't a particularly hard mix, but choosing the right tune to start with is important. The tune I used, 'Needin' U' by David Morales, was a simple, recognisable tune with the offbeat simple bass line I mention in the previous section, and it worked very well.

Finishing the night

After a successful night in the DJ booth, putting on the last tune and letting it run out can be hard – you just want to keep playing all night long. Have a think about how you want to finish your set about an hour before you finish.

How busy the club is determines how you end the set. If the club is still packed, keep playing great tunes until the end, and then try to finish with the best tune you can think of. I used to love finishing with BT's 'Believer' because it's an energetic, musical track that finishes with a repeating vocal line 'I'm a believer . . .' echoing into silence. This is so much better than just fading out drums, or a tune that whimpers off into silence.

Some clubs request that you tone down the energy and pace of the music towards the end of the night or when the dance floor starts to get quieter, so people aren't hyperactive as they leave the club. I think that sells the club and the customers short a bit – you need to play the most suitable music for the people who are there from start to finish.

Respect the licensing laws for the club you're playing in; you don't want them to lose their licence just because you wanted to squeeze in one more track. Even if people are screaming for another, don't take the law into your own hands and play another tune. That's a sure route to the club not asking you back next week! The owner/promoter will probably hang over you towards the end of the night to make sure that you stop anyway, so don't push your luck.

The last things to do as you finish your night are to pack up all your tunes (and any equipment you brought), disconnect anything you've used to record your set, put it all in a safe place and then find the person who has your money!

If you're working through an agency, your payment gets sorted through them, so you only need to say your goodbyes and leave with the knowledge that you've had another successful night. Otherwise, you have to play what I call *hunt the money-man*. You may have to look in some strange places, but you'll eventually find the person who pays you. Unless you've something better to do, don't leave their sight until you get paid. In full.

While you're still in the club, have a last word with the bar staff and the toilet attendant to find out how they felt the night went. Always listen to feedback. If they say something you don't agree with, that's fine, but remember it and look out for it next time, in the unlikely event that they know better than you.

Part V
The Part of Tens

The 5th Wave   By Rich Tennant

"Pull the Tchaikovsky out of your mix, dude. Too many people are breaking into 'Swan Lake'."

In this part . . .

The Part of Tens is a regular feature in all *For Dummies* books. Short and snappy, these chapters are the really fun ones!

From how to go to the toilet in the middle of a DJ set, to where to go to find out more information on DJing, the nuggets of information in the final chapters of this book aren't as much the icing on the cake – more the knife to cut the cake!

Chapter 22

Ten Resources for Expanding Your Skills and Fan Base

*T*he skills you're developing are the strong foundations that lead you to become a good DJ. Unfortunately, you can't rest on your laurels. Your skills and reputation need constant bolstering, and the following ten resources keep you ahead of the scene and boost your reputation so that people know who you are when you're playing, and will seek you out.

Your thirst for knowledge should never end. The moment you think that you know it all, you start going backwards. Keep up with new equipment and technology, keep an eye on the scene so you can start to read drifting music tastes, and share as much information as you can with other DJs.

Staying Current with Media

TV, radio, DVD, magazines and the Internet are all incredible resources for your development as a DJ.

Magazines (and their supporting websites) dedicated to DJ culture, equipment and music always keep you up to date. Music reviews and DJ charts in magazines can be invaluable as long as you trust the DJ or reviewer's opinions and they keep you ahead of DJs who think that going to a club once a month is enough.

I'm on the mailing list for a magazine that's dedicated to news about new clubs opening, new sound installations and all the juicy information that you usually only hear about a couple of months later. If you can find out about a new club development in your area before the other DJs, you can get a head start and send off a demo to the developers before the other DJs know about it.

Radio shows are great ways of hearing new music. Most of them announce what tracks they're playing regularly (or have a website that updates with a track list). BBC Radio 1 is an unbelievable resource for new music. If you're outside the UK, check out (www.bbc.co.uk/radio1) – most evenings they play the best new music from various different genres.

TV programmes that interview DJs who play music you love, have features on equipment and culture, and reviews about the clubs that play your style of music can give you insight into how you need to develop in order to progress in an ultra-competitive market.

DVDs and videos that show you how to DJ can be a great help. Sometimes you need to see a technique to fully understand it (which is why my website, www.recess.co.uk, has video clips of most techniques). Inspirational footage or video clips of your favourite DJ hosted online (do a search through www.youtube.com) can light a fire under you to make you more determined to become a DJ as well as show you a whole host of new skills.

Visiting DJ Advice Websites

Ten years ago, the Internet had a dearth of information about DJing, with only a couple of websites trying to shed light on *how* to be a DJ.

Since then, many sites have sprung up with different ways of explaining how to DJ. Apart from my own website (www.recess.co.uk), the best websites on the Internet for club mixing are www.djmandrick.com (a great site about how to beatmatch), www.djprince.no for incredibly detailed information about harmonic mixing and www.i-dj.co.uk, the website for *International DJ* magazine, which keeps you up to date on the music scene and new equipment.

Getting Answers through DJ Forums

DJ forums are a great place to post any questions that are troubling you, and are also a fantastic way to get involved with a good community that listens to your mixes and gives you brutally honest feedback to help you with your development. Create a screen name (go for an anonymous one, so that you can post those embarrassing questions without fear of personal ridicule), and visit forums like:

- ✔ www.djforums.com/forums A huge community with advice on technique, a classified section, mix submissions, advice for mobile DJs and a lot more.

- ✔ www.i-dj.co.uk/discussion This is the forum for *I-DJ* magazine, which has loads of subsections and a lot of members on hand to help you out. Nearly all magazines have their own forum, so check out the homepage of your favourite magazine to see whether it has a community you'd like to join.

- ✔ www.tranceaddict.com/forums A friendly, fun community, not just for trance fans, with a great thread for DJs to post pictures of their own DJ equipment setup. Humour, advice and guidance are all on hand here.

- ✔ www.djchat.com/boards The previous forums are primarily for the club/electronic dance music DJ. DJChat.com has tens of thousands of members, but more importantly, deals with all different types of DJing, from country to Christian to karaoke to Latin music.

Most users on forums are polite and helpful, but to minimise any *flaming* (abuse), try to post into the correct section, check your spelling and be polite – also, do a quick search to check that someone hasn't already posted your question.

You'll find me on any of the preceding forums as Recess or DJ Recess or on the forum on my own website (www.djrecess.co.uk/php).

Reading Other Books

I'm hurt that you'd think of reading another DJing book after this one.

On a serious note, of the other books out there on the market on DJing, by far the best one to buy, in my opinion, is *How to Be a DJ* by Chuck Fresh (Premier Press). The book covers every aspect of becoming a DJ, and is aimed at every kind of DJ, from wedding to radio to club DJing. But the best thing is how it's written: Chuck's very friendly, he doesn't patronise you and he doesn't spend the whole time swearing and trying to be cool.

Beware of some of the e-books and guides available in the back of DJ magazines or online. Although many of them are genuine and very helpful, others are a complete waste of time and money or, as I've found, are rip-offs of my website! Post a request on a DJ forum (see the previous section for ideas on where to go) for a review of a particular guide, just to be sure.

Getting Hands-On Advice

If you have the money and want hands-on advice on all aspects of DJing, then academies like DJ Academy (`www.djacademy.org.uk`), SubBass DJ Academy (`www.subbassdj.com`) and Point Blank Music College (`www.pointblanklondon.com`) in the UK, or Norcal DJMPA (`www.norcaldjmpa.com`) and Scratch DJ (`www.scratch.com`) in the US are the most popular. Because courses cost money (out of your own pocket), do some research into a course before signing up for it, to ensure that any money you spend will be money well spent, rather than thrown away.

Universities and colleges have also realised that there's an avenue for teaching DJs, with the formation in the UK of the *National Certificate in Music Technology, DJ & Mixing* course. Covering beatmatching, scratching, studio production, computer technology, sound creation and more, these courses, like the private DJ academies, can teach you a lot about DJing and related industries, but have the added advantage of keeping your mum off your back because you can tell her you're at college, learning a skill.

The benefit of formal training is that you have the continuity of someone who's there to correct you when you're doing something wrong, who makes you practise (rather than you drifting off to play your Xbox) and, most importantly, someone who you can ask questions when you're unsure what to do.

Check locally in your area too. A local experienced DJ may like to share knowledge with other people. This is something I like to do on occasion, because it's always great to meet and help new DJs.

Courses can show you the mechanics of how to mix, and they provide information on the other aspects of DJing (sound production, accountancy, promotion and so on) but what they *can't* teach you is how to be a DJ in a more esoteric sense. What do I mean by *esoteric*? That partly you develop and absorb DJing into your knowledge not by the process of someone telling you what to do, but through spending time practising; through experience, confidence, failure, trial and error; and simply by listening to your tunes. If you do a course, you still need the same amount of time practising and developing to grow into your talent and truly become a great DJ.

Listening to Other People's Mixes

When you listen to different genres and different DJs on the radio, the Internet or in a club, you open your eyes to different techniques. No matter how good or bad the performance, you always gain something from listening to any kind of mix, including music you haven't heard before.

Listening to a bad mix is just as helpful as hearing a good one. If you can recognise what makes a bad mix bad, you can listen out for those same things in your own mixes (such as bad tune selection, poor beat-matching and sloppy volume or EQ (equaliser) control) and keep those problems out of your mixes.

Participating in Competitions

You can hand out as many demos as you like, but sometimes you need a few more strings to your bow so that you can spread the word about your DJ prowess. Take a look at magazines, the Internet and what's on in your local area to see whether any DJ *battles* or competitions are on the horizon that provide the perfect opportunity for you to show off your skills.

Due to its very nature, club DJing is quite hard to put into a proper competition format without becoming a competition for how many tunes you can play in your 15-minute slot. However, *Bedroom DJ* competitions invite unknown DJs to send in a full-length mix and are a strong avenue to propel DJs' careers.

For scratch DJs, you don't get a better opportunity than the DMC Scratching Championships to show off your *mad skillz*. You'll be up against really tough competition, but hopefully the experience and the chance to meet top level DJs will improve your career prospects.

If you can't face any competitions or the rejection of not making the final of a magazine competition, look for clubs and bars that have an *open booth* night, where DJs take half-hour slots to play music and impress the people on the floor. If you're good, you'll be noticed.

Hosting Your Own Night

If you can't find anyone to let you work on a Friday night in their club, the solution's simple. Put on your own night. You may have to settle for a town hall somewhere, or a Tuesday night in a dingy club, but if you can get enough people to turn up to a night you run, if you organise it well and if you make it a complete success (which means loads of people come and no one gets hurt!), word will spread and you may get headhunted (in the good way). Even if the night doesn't generate any direct interest from a club owner or promoter, you'll have a very strong section on your DJing CV to show people you're driven and serious about becoming a DJ.

Promotion is the key. Get as many friends and friends of friends along as you can. If you can run the night with another DJ, all the better; that's two sets of friends you can get into the club. Hand out flyers (without littering or getting arrested), wander around a few pubs to get more people to come along, run an Internet site promoting the event and do everything you can to try to get as many people to come as possible.

Make sure that everyone knows what music to expect, try to get a group of *ringers* (people specifically invited for the task) who'll dance on the floor no matter what you play and don't forget to read the crowd and play music that they want to hear. If you only play *your* set all night, and don't try to entertain the people who've come to see and hear you, you'll find a dramatic drop in numbers the next time you play.

Under-18 discos and running a night in Scout halls and town halls are a good idea, but can be fraught with logistical problems. Most often, the problems involve alcohol and security, so be careful if you're trying to run a night without professional help – be sure that you're on the right side of the law.

Uploading Podcasts or Hosted Mixes

As disc space and bandwidth gets cheaper and cheaper, more websites (such as www.djpassion.co.uk, www.djmixtape.net and www.mydjspace.net to mention only three of the hundreds available) give you the choice to upload and promote your set for anyone across the world to download (and sometimes cast judgement on).

You find many different podcasting directories out there, from iTunes to www.podcast.com. Each one has a slightly different requirement on how to upload and set up the podcast, so I recommend that you visit the website of the directory you wish to use, and follow their tutorials to get your podcast . . . cast.

Immerse Yourself in What You Love

The most obvious resource for your development is visiting the clubs that you love. In the same way that listening to as many mixes as possible can help your development, so can going to as many clubs as possible. Clubs with music other than the genre you play can teach you a lot, but your best development comes from going to clubs that play the music you love.

Split yourself in two. Be the DJ who absorbs what's happening, recognising how the DJ is working (or alienating) the crowd, and take everything you can from a good DJ and absorb the good things into your own skills. But also, spend time on the dance floor as a normal clubber. Dance like a mad person, feel the music, let the bass flood through your body and don't stop smiling the whole time.

This is what you want to make other people do – experience and recognise a good night when you're on the dance floor, and then look for yourself in the crowd next time you play live.

Chapter 23

Ten Answers to DJ Questions You're Too Afraid to Ask

This chapter covers miscellaneous FAQs. The following ten questions are the most popular *sheepish* questions I've been asked over the past decade, and although I answer many questions in this book, these two handfuls don't really fit in anywhere else, and are perfect as a Part of Tens chapter.

What kind of DJ you are, and where you're playing at, can generate a different answer to a lot of the following questions. Where applicable, I split the answer into club DJ and party DJ (which covers weddings, parties, bowling alleys, anywhere that's all about fun and entertainment).

Do I Need to Talk?

Whether you need to address your audience when you're DJing is a really good question. A lot of people become DJs because they love the music and love mixing it together, but many of them don't figure that they'll ever have to use a microphone and speak to the audience. In short, yes, you need to talk.

The mechanics of using a microphone are simple enough. Put the microphone very close to your mouth, and as you speak reduce the channel-fader of the music that's currently playing, so you can be heard over it. When you're not talking, move the microphone away from your mouth (so the audience doesn't hear you breathing at 100 decibels) and raise the channel-fader back to normal. You could be raising and lowering the fader many times in one sentence, but as long as you do it quickly, and with confidence, it's okay.

You may have a *talk-over* button on your mixer that does the same thing. The drop in volume of the music can be a bit sudden though, so if the sound isn't right, forget about it and use the channel-faders instead.

If you want to run a party or wedding night well, you need to get used to talking to people on the dance floor. You may be asked to introduce the bride and groom or announce that the buffet is open, so you need to be comfortable, clear and confident when you speak through the microphone. If you're a shy type, just become an actor and put on your DJ voice. If you think that your voice is a bit dull, add a little *radio DJ* inflection to your voice while you're talking to the partygoers. This may sound a bit forced to you, but they won't know any better (and, let's be honest, probably won't be listening). No one wants to hear you announce the buffet with nerves in your voice; they may wonder what you did to the potato salad!

What Should I Wear?

If you're a club DJ, the question of what to wear is easily answered by taking your lead from the dress code of the club you're playing and picking a comfortable version of that. I tend to wear a black T-shirt, fawn coloured jeans and Timberlands when I'm DJing. The T-shirt keeps me cool and comfortable in a hot DJ booth, and the colour of the jeans tends to fit in with most clubs' dress code. If you're doing the whole set on your feet for six hours, choose comfortable shoes.

Famous DJs can wear what they want. As they become icons though, their fashion sense can be held to scrutiny, so expect their black T-shirts to be made by a top fashion label.

If you're a wedding DJ, remember that everyone else at the wedding has made an effort. I'm not saying to turn up in a frock, tux or kilt (though it *would* probably be appreciated), but turn up smart, with a pressed shirt and trousers.

You're probably charging a lot of money for your service, and the reason you can charge this amount is because you're a professional DJ. Be professional and turn up smart and smiling.

How Do I Go to the Toilet?

Quickly.

If you can, try to *go* before you go. If you're nervous, you may be hopping on and off of the lavatory anyway, but try to make sure that any visits to the toilet are quick, and won't involve a long time sitting down (if you get what I mean).

If you're a club DJ and have an urge to purge, put on a long record, ask a *trusted* friend or a bouncer to stand by the decks, then get in and out as fast as you can. By trusted, I mean someone who won't think that he or she can take over while you're gone.

As a wedding DJ, however, you may be on your own. If the pressure mounts so to speak, first try to hold it in until the buffet break (if you get one). If you can't, quickly make friends with a waiter or girl/guy who you think that you can trust to look after your decks, or just make a break for it – and get back as quick as you can.

Just remember, you always have enough time to wash your hands!

No matter what type of DJ you are, the tune you put on to cover your comfort break is quite important. It has to be long enough to cover your absence, have little chance of skipping or jumping while you're gone and not be too repetitive (so the crowd doesn't get bored with it).

Worst case scenario for blokes involves peeing into a beer bottle. Not nice.

Can 1 Invite My Friends into the DJ Booth?

Whether you invite your friends into the DJ booth very much depends on what kind of place you're working at. If you take your girlfriend/boyfriend with you to a party as your DJ assistant to make your life easier by getting drinks and taking requests, it's probably welcomed. If you're in a club and your other half sits grumpily behind you in the DJ booth, takes up space and gets in everybody's way, the club manager may eventually ask her or him to leave the booth.

Your friends will just want to have a laugh in the DJ booth and will probably end up ripping the needle off the record, or pressing Stop on the CD decks for a lark. If you got your friends into the club for free, make them pay their way by spending most of their time on the dance floor, having the time of their lives, keeping the night looking like a huge success.

How Do 1 Remove the Beat, or Vocals?

How you go about completely removing the beat or vocals from a track is a tricky one. For an entire tune, currently, you can't. Sometimes, you can remove enough of the frequencies from a *sample* (a small section) of music so that it sounds clean enough for you to play over something else.

A friend of mine, in a band called Pacifica, did this with the 'Ooo ooo – aa aa' vocal hook from Blondie's 'Heart of Glass'. Unfortunately, even the cleanest sounding part of 'Heart of Glass' still has drums and a bass melody over it. Eventually, with patience and a good engineer using compressors, expanders, filters, EQs (equalisers) and a little voodoo magic, my friend cleaned up the sample for use in the song.

Another method is to use computer software to embrace the stereo properties of music to isolate the vocals, and only then remove unnecessary frequencies to 'tidy up' the sound. It's not a perfect science yet, but it's getting better.

When you record music, the standard procedure is that the instruments are *panned* left and right into a stereo signal, but the vocals remain centered in the middle. Computer software works out what's what and can remove everything that's in the centre pan (the vocals), leaving only the stereo music information, or vice-versa.

Some tunes work better than others with this method, and like everything else in DJing, it takes a lot of time and practice to get right.

The danger with both of these methods is that stereo and mono sounds and audio frequencies are mixed together through all parts of the tune. For example, some of the frequencies that make up the drum sounds and music also make up the vocal sample. So when you cut the high frequencies to remove the high-hats cymbals, you also remove all the *sibilance* (the *sssss* sounds) from the vocal. The same applies to the bass and mid frequencies, with the end result sounding poor.

Also, the stereo image is never as clean cut as 'all music left and right – vocals in the middle'. Although the vocal will predominantly be centred, sound engineers cleverly mix the vocal into the stereo field to create better soundscapes, meaning you'll still be able to hear some of the vocal playing even after removing the centred sound.

If you do ever hear a clean vocal-only version of a tune, it's probably an *a capella* (vocals with no accompanying music) released by the artist, or maybe someone has recorded a very good imitation of the vocals and used that, hoping no one could tell the difference.

How Do I Choose My DJ Name?

You may decide that your own name isn't powerful enough to be displayed on a billboard (here's hoping), or perhaps you're looking for anonymity and crave a DJ name. In which case you can create a full name pseudonym (such as Bob Sinclar – real name Christophe LeFriant) or come up with a DJ name, in DJ 'Something' format, or just one name. That's why I came up with Recess, because John Steventon wouldn't look that good on the back of a bus.

When trying to pick a name think of what you do, who you are, what you play, how you play, what your other interests are, what your real name is – and see how you can mutate that to a good DJ name.

Or, if you're lazy or looking for inspiration, check out the website called Quiz Meme (www.quizmeme.com) where you type your name and it spits out a DJ name for you. I typed in John Steventon, and got DJ Flowing Cranny. I typed in Recess – and got DJ Vinyl Artist; so it must be right!

Another way to come up with a name is to mutate words. Think of ten words that you'd use to describe yourself or your music, and consider whether they (or any derivations of them) would be good. For example, if you're a deep house DJ who likes to fish you might come up with DJ Deep Lure, which you could then mutate into DJ D'Allure. Or not . . .

However, how you're commonly known is still one of the most personal ways to create your DJ name. Nicknames are a great start, but if, like in my case, you were called something stupid like 'Butter' at school, you may want to explore other avenues. Alexander Coe had the easiest name change in the world, and is now one of the most famous DJs on the planet – he could've chosen Xander, Zander, Alex Coe or anything else as his DJ name, but instead he chose Sasha (which is the Russian derivation of the similar Aleksandr), and that worked out very well for him!

In my case, Recess is bit of both. My initials are J.R.C.S. and I dropped the J to leave RCS, which mutated to Recess. (JRCS reads too much like jerks . . .)

Do I Get Free Drinks? (And How Do I Get Drinks from the Bar?)

If you're a club DJ, try to negotiate whether you get free drinks when you first speak to the owner/promoter about working at the club. The worst the promoter can say is no, and it saves any future embarrassment.

If you're well enough known as a DJ, you can submit a *rider* (a condition of the job) before you get to the club, demanding a case of Bud, a bottle of Jack and a bag of green Jelly Babies to be in the booth for when you start. But for local clubs and lesser known DJs, you probably find that you only get a free drink when the bar manager comes into the booth for a chat.

If you're a party DJ and you're lucky, the father of the bride, or birthday girl or boy, may offer you drinks through the night when they're having a really good time and at their happiest point – but don't count on it.

At clubs, leaving the DJ booth to head to the bar for a drink is usually a big no-no. If you don't get free drinks at a club, and no one's available to go to the bar for you, you'll probably have to go thirsty until a glass collector or a member of bar staff comes along and you can ask him or her to get a drink for you. But take a bottle of water (or whatever you think is better for you) just in case no one's kind enough to offer.

At pubs, parties and weddings, popping to the bar to buy a drink is normally okay, and if the staff know that you're the DJ (believe me, some don't) you'll probably get served really quickly.

Who Does the Lighting for the Night?

Regarding the question of who does the lighting for the night, wedding and party DJs tend to bring their own lights, as well as amps and DJing equipment, and they control the lights. When choosing lights, you may want to go for ones that have sensors in them to make them move and flash based on the sound of music (no, not the film starring Julie Andrews and some mountains). With these, all you need to do is set everything up and the lights take care of themselves. The other option is to get a compact control unit with different preset patterns to make the lights move and flash in different orders (though usually still in time with the music).

As far as clubs are concerned, I've worked in a few that had a similar pre-set lighting arrangement, except that they tend to have more lights than the wedding or party setup. However, most of the places I've worked in (and been to as a clubber) had a separate lighting jock to control the lights.

The difference that a good or bad lighting jock can make is almost as important as the music you play. Creative use of strobe lights, *gobos* (the rotating flashing lights) and intricate laser shows along with *VJs* (video jockeys), who use machines like the Pioneer DVJ-1000 to create incredible displays with video images, can really enhance the clubbing experience for the crowd.

If you strike up a good relationship with the lighting jock, and explain anything peculiar about the tunes you're playing that may help him or her work in harmony with your mix, the two of you can eventually build an incredible show together that feels like an orchestrated event. Or you can just ask him or her to get your drinks for you . . . it's your choice.

Should I Reset the Pitch to Zero After Beatmatching?

Do you reset the pitch to 0 after beatmatching one tune with another? No.

The two main reasons why you beatmatch tunes when mixing are:

- ✔ To keep a constant, pounding bass beat for the clubbers to dance to
- ✔ To play the music at a pace that matches the speed of the clubbers' beating hearts

If you decide that 135 BPM (beats per minute) is the perfect pace at which to play your music, and you put on a tune that plays at 130 BPM when set at 0 pitch, you need to raise the pitch control to about 4 per cent in order to get it to play at 135 BPM, and then leave it there to keep the music at 135 BPM.

Setting the pitch control back to 0 after you've beatmatched and mixed the two tunes together sounds terrible as the pitch of the music lowers (unless you're using decks with *master tempo*, which keeps the pitch the same no matter how fast you play the tune). And now the tune's playing at a speed that's way below the pace of the clubbers' heartbeats, so they have to dance slower and you kill the energy of the night.

The result is even worse the other way round. Imagine that you've had to reduce the tempo of a 140 BPM tune to –4 per cent. When you speed the track up by resetting the pitch to 0, you tire everyone out by the end of the tune because it's now playing at 140 BPM to a dance floor that's used to grooving at only 135 BPM!

Fluctuations in BPM as you progress through a two-hour set can be useful (refer to Chapter 18), but when you're beatmatching, you'll find you'll rarely play any of your tunes at 0 pitch.

What Do I Do If the Record or CD Skips or the Software Crashes?

You're a professional DJ. Be professional about getting around what to do if the record or CD skips or jumps. A jump on a record isn't too bad, as at least it's just a repeat of one or two seconds of music that plays through the PA, but if a CD skips it's a nasty sound, and you need to do something, instantly.

If you can't just skip to the next track on the CD, hit the Search button on the CD deck to advance five or ten seconds past the part that's skipping (lower the channel-fader at the same time to hide what you're doing).

With a record, the best thing to do is quickly lower the channel-fader to about 25 per cent of normal playout volume and knock the needle forward through the record by half a centimetre or so. Yes, this method won't sound too good, and yes, you may damage your record, but your record's already damaged if it's skipping, and it already doesn't sound good because it's repeating itself!

Prevent this sort of occurrence happening by cleaning your records or CDs before playing them (head to Chapters 4 and 7 for more on caring for your music collection).

I like to cue up the next track almost instantly after mixing into a track for this very reason, because then I have the next tune sitting there, ready to mix in quickly if something goes wrong. Sure, an emergency mix won't sound great, but how does that compare to how the music currently sounds?

If you're a digital DJ and the software crashes, it may feel as though your whole world has collapsed around you. In many cases, if you don't have any other CDs, or the CD/turntables aren't able to play without the software, the only thing you can do is reboot – quickly – and get back into the mix.

If you do have access to a CD and a CD deck that plays without needing to be fed through the computer, quickly put in the CD and press Play. You may even want to keep a CD deck with a 'safety CD' inside it, or an iPod/MP3 player hooked up to your mixer for this kind of occasion, just to give you time to reboot your system and get back up and running again.

Succeeding in anything you do, DJing or otherwise, involves skill and knowledge, but also how you cope under pressure. If you can fix a catastrophe like a skipping, damaged CD with composure and professionalism, you show all those around you that you're in control and meant to be where you are – in the DJ booth as a professional DJ.

Chapter 24

Ten Great Influences on Me

*Y*our influences are very personal: look at the music you listen to, the people you meet and the places you go as key points in your career. With these influences, you should be able to make a map of how you developed as a DJ. This chapter describes my journey.

Renaissance: Disc 1

Renaissance – Disc 1 was my first introduction to real dance music. Until I heard this mix by Sasha and Digweed, I thought that dance music was the acid scene and pop acts such as Snap releasing repetitive, obvious music. Up until I heard this disc, all I listened to were rock bands like Van Halen and Mr Big.

Individually, the tunes on the mix are powerful, well-made pieces of work, but the way Sasha and Digweed mixed them to create a 74-minute journey has always affected me. I think that the skill it involves is the reason I've always strived to create a seamless mix that has a start, a middle and an end – rather than just 20 tunes thrown together because they sound nice.

I've always had a copy of this mix to hand since the day I first heard it. I had it on tape on my Walkman while mowing lawns, on a CD in the car when driving to college, on a MiniDisc in my pocket looking for a job and now on an iPod strapped to my arm as I go to the gym before work.

Tonsillitis

An odd choice as an influence, I agree, but as I lay in bed, ill, for a week, falling in and out of consciousness, with only Radio 1 to keep me from a fevered delirium, I was able to hear music that I'd never heard.

I'd never heard of a guy called Pete Tong, and at six o'clock on a Friday night his show started, and my eyes were opened to so many different genres of dance music. From trance to drum and bass, to American house, I lay in bed, struggling to stay awake. I'd never listened to Radio 1 during weekends, so the Essential Selection, Trevor Nelson, Dave Pearce and the Essential Mix all opened my eyes to more than just the same Renaissance CD I'd been listening to over and over again.

What started off as an accident because I was too ill to stand up and change the station (or turn on the TV) ended up as a Friday night ritual; me, Pete Tong, a piece of paper and a tape recorder to take note of the best tunes.

La Luna: 'To the Beat of the Drum'

I couldn't dance, I had long hair and I wasn't dressed very well. I spent most of the night a bit lost, standing on the stairs while everyone had fun, but what I do remember is that the very first piece of music I heard as I walked into my first dance club was La Luna's 'To the Beat of the Drum'.

The piece of music was really simple, but seeing the reaction of the people in the club, feeling the bass drum vibrating through my body and hearing dance music at this volume, in this atmosphere, for the first time unlocked something in me that left the Van Halen and Mr Big CDs unplayed for the next seven or eight years!

(A haircut and better clothes followed almost immediately.)

Ibiza 1996, Radio 1 Weekend

BBC Radio 1 has developed a tradition of broadcasting from Ibiza since 1995. This event became a solid part of Radio 1's programming, but for me, they've never done better than the 2 to 4 a.m. slot at Amnesia in July 1996. I can honestly say that the reason I became a DJ was because of the 90 minutes I could fit on tape of Sasha in the mix. So if you want anyone to blame, give him a call!

As far as a DJ set is concerned, Sasha's set was a step forward from the Renaissance mix I'd heard over and over again. Because it was in a live situation, there was an obvious gearing of the set list to working the crowd rather than appealing to a home listener on CD, and it showed me the magic of DJing – that DJing was about more than just playing other people's records.

What sold this mix to me, and still gives me goose bumps when I listen to it (which I am right now in case you're wondering) was at around the halfway point – after playing some really strong, energetic, pounding tunes, he played 'Inner City Life' by Goldie. While still keeping the energy and the tempo of the mix at a similar level, Sasha was able to completely change the dynamic of the mix with just this one tune. It was like having a rest – without having a rest!

Bringing the power back into the mix using the snare beats of a tune called 'Yummy' by Agh was the turning point for the real power of the mix. The crowd went wild, and I can't say I've heard a mix since that's affected me as much.

The Tunnel Club, Glasgow

The Tunnel Club in Glasgow was like my home for six or seven years. It still exists now, in a slightly tamer version of its past, but it still holds incredible memories for me.

The three things I'll take away from that club are the smell of dry ice and Red Bull that blasted into your face as you entered the club, the constant quality level of DJs and music that they played every weekend, but most importantly, that I met my wife Julie there – dancing with friends on the other side of the floor.

Julie's support, advice and ability to smile politely when I'm boring her with new music and new ways to mix from tune to tune has kept me striving to improve myself since the mid '90s. Because it was due to the Tunnel that we met, I can hold the club responsible for my current happiness, and position to write this book.

Jamiroquai: 'Space Cowboy'

Jamiroquai's 'Space Cowboy' was the first time I'd ever heard an original tune remixed to be something better in my eyes than the original.

I didn't know much about Jamiroquai, but did know 'Space Cowboy' when they released it as a single. I thought it was okay, but nothing special. Then David Morales gave the tune an overhaul. His remix of 'Space Cowboy' is always in my record box (mostly unplayed, unfortunately), and is always in my top ten favourite tune list.

Listening to this track was the first time I'd been able to compare the original to a remix and understand the elements needed to change a song from a good original recording to a dance remix, and have the structure and sounds that work perfectly on the dance floor.

Digital DJing

After CD DJing really took hold of the DJ market, like thousands of other DJs I moved toward this format and started leaving the dust covers on the turntables more and more often. For me, this was always with a sad reluctance. I loved what CD decks could do, and I loved the fact that it was so easy to find and remix new music and burn it to CD ready to play that night, but not using turntables to play the music left a real hole in my heart.

This all changed when I first used my turntables to control DJ software. Now I had the best of both worlds: the flexibility of any music available at the click of a mouse, but the tactile sense and the showmanship of using turntables to control the music instead of button clicks and CD trays.

I felt like a real DJ again. Each time I stepped into a DJ booth, instead of feeling apologetic for using CDs, I felt empowered and at one with the music I was playing. The combination of the strong historical foundation of turntables alongside the versatility, stability and creativity of using DJ software made me feel like I was coming home – no matter where the DJ booth was.

Alice Deejay: 'Better Off Alone'

Not all my influences have been positive ones.

I found this tune when it was just an instrumental by DJ Jurgen. It has a lovely little hook in it, and sounds great. I played it a lot, and got a good response in the pubs and clubs whenever I played it.

The problem was, someone got hold of the tune and put a vocal over it, changing the dynamic sound of the track from something that was an interesting musical piece to commercial cheese. Because I preferred the original tune I automatically disliked this vocal version, because it managed to turn a good track that I liked to play into a bad track I hated playing.

Unfortunately, everyone else loved it, so I still had to play it. The places I worked at demanded a high amount of commercial tracks on the playlist to offset any unknown, more underground sounding tracks (ironically, the track was classed as underground before getting the vocal).

This track, and several others to come, taught me that sometimes you have to play what the club and the clubbers want. Until you become a DJ with the renown and power of Tiesto, Sasha or Oakenfold, you have to follow the club's guidelines. At the beginning, DJing is all about keeping people happy, and making enough money to eat. If I'd refused to play that track, I wouldn't have been asked to return as the DJ, and I knew that the right thing to do was just keep playing the tune until the appeal wore off.

Delirium: 'Silence'

In Chapter 4, I write about falling in love with the tune 'Silence' by Delirium, playing it as often as I could, and how it still means a lot to me to listen to. But I see this tune as a double-edged sword. I see this tune as the turning point in my DJing career, when it went a bit sour. This tune wasn't directly responsible, but after 'Silence' was such a success, the market was flooded with records that were very simple, obvious, bland melodies with some woman singing over them.

Obviously, people had released records of this sort for years before 'Silence', but the success of 'Silence' opened the gates for money-grabbers who figured they could release a weak record with vocals and make some money. Which they did. Not all of them were bad; some really good vocal tracks came out of this wave. But many producers missed the point that 'Silence' was such a big success because the music was really good and stood well on its own, but more importantly, Sarah McLachlan's voice was haunting, unique and perfectly matched to the music and a club atmosphere.

Ultimately, this crossover commercialisation of the dance scene drove the good music away. The people who were buying these records started to go to the clubs that would normally play less commercial music, and they started to demand to hear what they knew. Club owners, reacting to a new voice, seeing the rise in profits with the new batch of clubbers, happily agreed. This move drove the music I loved playing deeper and deeper underground to a point that it was hard to get work playing it.

The problem with commercial trends is that by their very nature they move from fad to fad. Eventually, as each new track sounded more like the old one, the novelty of this music wore off and the clubbers moved away to R&B and nu metal. This meant that the clubs that had abandoned their old music policy needed to readjust.

Some clubs started to play heavier and heavier music, to let people into the clubs that they wouldn't have in the past or to change their music scene completely. This left music (and the club scene as a whole as I saw it) in a state of flux, leaving me a bit concerned for my future as a DJ and for the music I loved to play.

Sasha and Digweed, Miami 2002

My last key influential music moment in this chapter is the Radio 1 Essential Mix that Sasha and Digweed did in April 2002 at the Winter Music Conference in Miami, USA.

By the time I heard this mix in late 2003, I was spending more time teaching DJing than performing, because I wasn't as in love with the music as I used to be. But I did still have a soft spot in my heart for Sasha and Digweed – I still thanked them for the reason I'd started to listen to dance music in the first place. A friend had this mix on his iPod, and I asked if I could have a copy, just to hear what was going on.

Two hours later, I realised that my assumptions and prejudices about music and how the dance scene had ended up after its hyper-commercialisation were wrong in a more global view. I felt as if I was being musically reborn.

The mix was incredibly well thought out and some of the tunes were amazing (the mix from Adam Dived 'Headfirst' to Solid Session 'Janeiro' almost blew the speakers in my car I played it so loud!). This mix was the key that marked my return to this music, and to DJing – and is the reason why I'm here, writing this book.

Chapter 25

Ten DJing Mistakes to Avoid

In This Chapter

▶ Avoiding mistakes that make you look and sound unprofessional

▶ Leaving for the night with all your equipment and tunes, and all your money received

*T*he ten common mistakes I describe in this chapter are exactly that: common. A couple of them may never happen to you, but, unfortunately, some may happen too often. I haven't made all the mistakes in this chapter. Most of them, yes. But not all.

What's important about the mistakes you make (in DJing or just life in general) is that you learn from them. Make sure that you don't do them again, or at the very least, make sure that you know how to cope with the consequences . . . such as the sound of silence in a club.

Forgetting Slipmats/Headphones

Forgetting your slipmats (which is an easy thing to do) isn't too much of a big deal because most clubs have their own set, but if you fail to bring your headphones, the club is unlikely to have a spare pair of quality headphones lying around for forgetful DJs to use.

Check out Chapter 26 for a checklist of ten things that you need to take with you when DJing.

Taking the Needle off the Wrong Record

Taking the needle off the wrong record is exactly the same as pressing Stop or Eject on the wrong CD player. I guarantee that at some stage in your DJ career, you'll make this mistake. Hopefully, you'll be in the sanctuary of your own bedroom, where only the cat can judge you on your error.

If you're unfortunate enough to make this mistake when DJing live in a club, put the needle back on (carefully, don't throw it back on the record in a mad panic), or quickly press Play on the CD deck. If you ejected the CD, press Play on the other deck and quickly move the cross-fader over to that channel.

Next, deflect blame like a true pro. It's probably easier to blame the sound system. You never know, someone in the crowd may be gullible enough to believe you! Then squat down to hide in the DJ booth for a couple of minutes and wait for the abuse to die down.

Banishing Mixer Setting Problems

Mixers are now available with an increasing number of functions, which unfortunately means that the chance of you forgetting to change these settings increases too.

Leaving assign controls set to the wrong channel is easily done, so when you move the cross-fader, you're fading into silence (or the wrong tune). Or you may unwittingly leave bass kills on during a mix, and it only dawns on you halfway through the tune that the bass is missing. And you can easily leave on effects like flanger or echo because you're focusing your attention on the next tune (or the girl/bloke on the dance floor). A lapse of concentration is all it takes to ruin a good mix (and sometimes your night) – so concentrate!

Getting Drunk when Playing

You need to be fully in control of your equipment but you won't be able to do that if you've had too many beers or Jack's back there in the DJ booth. Having a couple of alcoholic drinks for Dutch courage is all very well, but no one's going to think you're professional if you're so plied with booze that you can't even see the mixer in front of you and can't mix properly.

I've heard tales of DJs guzzling a case of Bud before going behind the decks, but unless you have a liver the size of a small house, if you must drink just make it a couple and then stick to water.

Surfing while Mixing

A new mistake for the digital DJ: you have a computer in front of you and you're connected to the club's wi-fi – surely it can't hurt to check a couple of emails, or update your Facebook status? Take it from me, you'll spend too long away from the mix, and either have to rush the next transition or miss the next mix altogether, leaving silence and tumbleweed on the dance floor.

Copy-cat rip

I saw a great photo in *DJ* magazine a few years ago of Sasha leaning across the decks so that someone from the dance floor could light his cigarette. (I actually have it as a poster above my home setup). Back in the days when I did smoke (it's not big, it's not clever and it *will* kill you) I thought this look was so cool, I'd try to do the same.

Not only did I receive some friendly abuse from the lighting guy while I waited for someone to oblige with a match, but when I did lean over the decks my T-shirt got caught on the needle on the record, ripping it right off. (The needle, that is, not the T-shirt.) Fortunately, it was the cued record rather than the one playing to the dance floor, but it was further compounded by me dropping the lit cigarette onto the turntable because I was so flustered by what I'd just done.

Leaning Over the Decks

As the DJ, you're the *host* of the evening, and you're allowed to show or receive some appreciation (handshakes and kisses on the cheeks being the best way). Just make sure you're appreciated a little to the left of the decks so that you don't bump into them or hit something on the mixer.

Avoiding Wardrobe Malfunctions

Avoiding a wardrobe malfunction is harder than you think. From jeans that are cut too low (so when you bend over to pick up a record, everyone can see your butt-cleavage) to ladies wearing a white bra under a black top so the UV lights show off their glowing chests, you'd be surprised what can go wrong.

Hats, scarves, ponchos and false beards will all eventually get tangled up in your equipment, or fall onto the decks. Wearing costumes (think Elvis costumes, gorilla outfits or Tarzan wraps) seem like a good idea in principle, but try to have a quick practice wearing them before you start mixing; your furry paws or rhinestone cuffs may turn your mixing into a nightmare.

Spending Too Long Talking to Someone

Stay professional: don't spend so long talking to a friend, potential employer or member of the opposite sex that you don't have enough time to properly cue up and mix in the next track. Even if you do have enough time to cue up the tune, don't rush the mix just so that you can go back to talking to them. And whatever you do, don't spend so long talking to someone that the record runs out completely; unless of course you want to get fired.

Leaving Your Last Tune Behind

If you're just doing part of the night and someone's taking over from you, chances are you finished your set on a really good tune, so you don't want to leave it behind. Wait until the next DJ has mixed out of your last tune, then pick up your record/CD, pack your bags and leave the booth. If you're pulled away by someone, ask the DJ to put your tune to one side and say that you'll pick it up later – at least that way he or she won't walk off with it by accident.

And digital DJs – remember to leave with your laptop . . .

Not Getting Paid Before You Leave

After a night rocking the crowd, don't leave the club before you've been paid in full. Don't fall for excuses such as 'I don't have my cheque book' or 'I don't have it all here; can I give you half now and the rest next time?'. I've fallen for this in the past (both times with club promoters whom I thought I could trust; the irony of being stung like this in a club called Pravda – Russian for *truth* – is still very much with me).

Every case is different, and you should know how much you can push and stand your ground with the club promoter or owner or bride and groom to demand payment. The safest thing to do is to agree on an amount before you set foot in the DJ booth (preferably on paper, signed by both you and the client). That way, you can be very persistent about making sure that you get all the money you're due.

If you don't agree on an amount before playing, though, good luck with that . . .

Chapter 26

Ten Items to Take with You When DJing

· ·

In This Chapter

▶ Tooling up for a night of DJing

▶ Remembering things to keep you going through the night

▶ Getting home with your head out of the clouds

· ·

*F*rom the obvious items like your CDs, records and headphones, to the less obvious matter of taking a drink and something you can use to record your mix, the ten items I describe in this chapter are everything you need for a successful night on the decks.

Keep this list taped to the back of your door, or next to your car keys, so that you can check it over before you leave the house. (And take the list with you, so you know to bring everything back with you!)

All the Right Tunes

You may have thousands of records or CDs in your collection. Make sure that you're taking the right ones with you. Checking for one last time that you've picked up the right box or CD wallet won't hurt! Also take a carbon brush to clean your records, and a soft cloth for CDs.

If you're a digital DJ you need your computer (normally a laptop), or an external drive that contains all your music if you're using a club's installation (remember to check that they use the same software as you, though!).

If you're taking your laptop, boot it up before you leave and make sure it still works and that all the music is stored on it (not left on an external drive). Remember power cables, audio interfaces and controllers/control vinyl if you use them too.

Making It Personal with Headphones and Slipmats

Have a last check to make sure that your headphones still work and that you take any adaptors you need to make them work. If you use headphones that you can repair with spare parts (like the Sennheiser HD25s), take your bag of tools and spares.

Put your slipmats between some records in the record box so they stay flat and undamaged. Just remember to take them back at the end of the night!

Using your own slipmats prevents any problems with fluffy, thick, dirty slipmats that a club may use. You'll have become accustomed to how slippy your own slipmats are on a set of Technics 1210s. Basic slipmats on a club's set of decks may create a lot of drag, and even worse, may damage your records due to dirt and crusted beer spillages.

You're a Star! Taking a Digital Recorder/Blank CD

Make the most of every opportunity by recording yourself in the mix, which is especially helpful at the start of your career. You'll benefit dramatically because you can study your performance and improve on it. If a club doesn't have any means to record the mix (check beforehand), take along something you can use to record your mix so you can take away evidence that you rocked the crowd!

Packing Your Tools and Saving the Day

Any homeowner knows that the only tools you need are WD-40 and duct tape. But if you want to get fancy, throw some differing sized and shaped screwdrivers into a bag too, because you never know when you may need a Phillips-head screwdriver to save the day.

Always Being Prepared: Pen and Paper

Not just for taking phone numbers of good-looking clientele, you need a pen and paper for taking requests, sending drinks orders to the bar and swapping phone numbers with people who want to book you.

Keeping Fuelled with Food and Drink

Unfortunately, you're not there to have a picnic; you've got a job to do. But take some sustenance to keep you going in case your body needs fuel.

Contrary to popular belief, you don't have to put vodka into your Red Bull or Irn-Bru 32. Keep one or two cans of your chosen energy drink with you, and if you start to flag halfway through the night, drink one for the caffeine fix.

Be warned, though, that some people don't react well to the sudden hit of caffeine. So trying an energy drink in the middle of a set in front of 1,000 people isn't the best time to find out whether your body likes caffeine and guarana!

In addition to an energy drink, you also need to take something to eat in case you get hungry. Hunger leads to bad moods, which can make you lose your concentration, and you won't be as attentive to the crowd's needs. Wine gums and jelly babies give you a quick sugar fix, and they contain almost no fat. Eating an energy bar gives you a better range of nutrients and fills you up for longer, but it has a larger fat content and does run the risk of tasting like cardboard.

Spreading the Music with Demos

Nothing beats someone asking for a copy of your work after hearing you play in a club. Nothing's worse than not having one with you. Take a few CDs of your most recent mix (check out Chapter 19 for tips on how to create the best-sounding and best-looking CD) and hand them out with a big smile on your face.

A few examples of your best work are also really handy if someone wants to book you for a night somewhere. If you give people a great mix to take away, they won't forget about you – just remember to include your phone number!

Keeping Moving with Car Keys

You're not going to get far without your car keys. I've spent many an evening standing at the boot of the car, head in hands in disbelief that I left my keys behind again! Okay if you're just leaving your house, but not okay if they're in your jacket pocket, in the locked-up club in which you've just played.

Have Wallet, Will Travel

You never know when you'll need a little cash, either for taxis home (because you left your car keys behind) or just to go grab some chow after your set.

If you have a few business cards, keep them in your wallet or purse, on hand to give out when you need to do some self-promotion.

Just Chilling: Chill Mix for the Ride Home

Sometimes, I finish my set at four o'clock in the morning, and am in no mood to keep the buzz going by listening to more pumping tunes on the way home. So I keep a copy of the soundtrack to the film *The Big Blue* in my car for such occasions. It contains some of the most fantastic pieces of music I've heard in a long time. My wife Julie worries about the music sending me to sleep on the drive home, but all it does is take the edge off the natural high I've got from an evening of energy and musical rapture (but it doesn't do much about the caffeine rush I have due to one too many of those energy drinks!).

I recommend the film too . . .

Index

• C •

FOR DUMMIES®

Making Everything Easier! ™

UK editions

BUSINESS

978-0-470-74490-1

978-0-470-74381-2

978-0-470-71382-2

Anger Management For Dummies
978-0-470-68216-6

Boosting Self-Esteem For Dummies
978-0-470-74193-1

British Sign Language
For Dummies
978-0-470-69477-0

Business NLP For Dummies
978-0-470-69757-3

Cognitive Behavioural Therapy
For Dummies
978-0-470-01838-5

Cricket For Dummies
978-0-470-03454-5

CVs For Dummies, 2nd Edition
978-0-470-74491-8

Divorce For Dummies, 2nd Edition
978-0-470-74128-3

eBay.co.uk Business All-in-One
For Dummies
978-0-470-72125-4

Emotional Freedom Technique
For Dummies
978-0-470-75876-2

English Grammar For Dummies
978-0-470-05752-0

Flirting For Dummies
978-0-470-74259-4

Green Living For Dummies
978-0-470-06038-4

IBS For Dummies
978-0-470-51737-6

Lean Six Sigma For Dummies
978-0-470-75626-3

REFERENCE

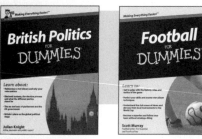

978-0-470-68637-9

978-0-470-68837-3

978-0-470-74535-9

HOBBIES

978-0-470-69960-7

978-0-470-68641-6

978-0-470-68178-7

**Available wherever books are sold. For more information or to order direct go to www.wiley.com
or call +44 (0) 1243 843291**

FOR DUMMIES®

A world of resources to help you grow

UK editions

SELF-HELP

978-0-470-74830-5   978-0-470-74764-3   978-0-470-68472-6

STUDENTS

978-0-470-74747-6   978-0-470-74711-7   978-0-470-74290-7

HISTORY

978-0-470-99468-9   978-0-470-51015-5   978-0-470-98787-2

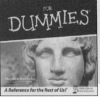

Neuro-linguistic Programming
For Dummies
978-0-7645-7028-5

Origami Kit For Dummies
978-0-470-75857-1

Overcoming Depression For Dummies
978-0-470-69430-5

Positive Psychology For Dummies
978-0-470-72136-0

PRINCE2 For Dummies, 2009 Edition
978-0-470-71025-8

Psychometric Tests For Dummies
978-0-470-75366-8

Raising Happy Children
For Dummies
978-0-470-05978-4

Reading the Financial Pages
For Dummies
978-0-470-71432-4

Sage 50 Accounts For Dummies
978-0-470-71558-1

Starting a Business For Dummies,
2nd Edition
978-0-470-51806-9

Study Skills For Dummies
978-0-470-74047-7

Teaching English as a Foreign
Language For Dummies
978-0-470-74576-2

Teaching Skills For Dummies
978-0-470-74084-2

Time Management For Dummies
978-0-470-77765-7

Work-Life Balance For Dummies
978-0-470-71380-8

13061 p2

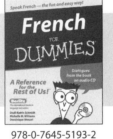

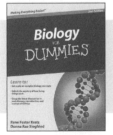
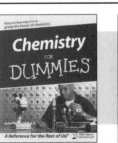

FOR DUMMIES®

Helping you expand your horizons and achieve your potential

COMPUTER BASICS

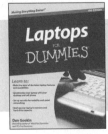

978-0-470-57829-2

978-0-470-46542-4

978-0-470-49743-2

DIGITAL PHOTOGRAPHY

978-0-470-25074-7

978-0-470-46606-3

978-0-470-45772-6

MAC BASICS

978-0-470-27817-8

978-0-470-46661-2

978-0-470-43543-4

Notes

Notes

Notes

Notes

Notes

Notes

Notes

Notes